ON THE WIRE

Dave Peel

authorHOUSE®

AuthorHouse™ UK Ltd.
500 Avebury Boulevard
Central Milton Keynes, MK9 2BE
www.authorhouse.co.uk
Phone: 08001974150

Front cover photograph by Capt. John Bell (CG Flt)
Back cover photograph by Mick Rowsell (CG Flt)

First published by AuthorHouse   05/17/2011

ISBN: 978-1-4567-7805-7 (sc)
ISBN: 978-1-4567-7806-4 (hc)

CONTENTS

ACKNOWLEDGEMENTS

I would like to thank all who have been mentioned and those who have helped me to complete this memoir, many with only one aim which is to help others. I would particularly like to thank Kate Mattinson, the wife of one of our pilots, for the time she spent helping to make sense of my original draft some years ago. Kate achieved this without altering anything I wished to portray and it was that help and advice that gave me the confidence to continue with the project.

I clearly owe my skills for the role I do to the training received during my time in the Royal Navy, a period that I was to make many friends for life and would mould the career that I have enjoyed so much.

As this is a memoir about my life as an Aircrewman I would like to mention the Aircrewman's Association (ACA). I have used the association logo as chapter markers within this book because of the pride in both earning those wings and of being a member of the association since its formation and will add an appendage in relation to the ACA at the end.

Our current Patron, Captain Andy Barnwell RD, RNR, whose Royal Naval Career, both Regular and Reserve, spanned over 30 years is also an experienced commercial pilot with 21 years of service with British Airways flying the Boeing 747, 757, 767 aircraft and Concorde. He continues to maintain close links with and is totally committed to promoting the Royal Navy and the Fleet Air Arm in particular. His unstinting enthusiasm, dedication and loyalty to the ACA, as our Patron, is very much welcomed and respected by all of the members. I feel honoured that he has agreed to write the Foreword for this memoir.

FOREWORD

Captain Andy Barnwell RD, Royal Naval Reserve
Patron Aircrewman's Association

I am delighted and feel most privileged to have been asked to write the foreword to this most fascinating and informative book, which pays a very personal tribute to the aircrewman's role in Search and Rescue from the perspective of a man who spent the best part of 40 years on the 'front-line'.

Having served for over 30 years in the Royal Navy, Fleet Air Arm, both regular and reserve, I have personally encountered similar situations, but by no means quite so many or so hazardous to those mentioned by the author. As a result, I can empathise with the sadness, self-doubt, and at times helplessness the author faced but also with his euphoria, pride and joy in the role.

I am now honoured to be the Patron of the Aircrewman's Association and it was in this capacity that I first met the author. He, along with so many of his fellow members, forms one of the most courageous and highly decorated body of men I have ever met. Whilst they may have been involved in some of the most dramatic and heroic rescues, by helicopter, the United Kingdom's waters have ever witnessed, most would selflessly reflect on their part as being "all in a days/nights work"! Dave Peel, the author, is no exception to that rule. This book tells his story, on a very intimate level through the experiences he shares with the reader, during his career covering nearly 4 decades at the sharp end of the UK's Search and Rescue Organisation as a Search and Rescue Diver and Aircrewman.

From the outset it becomes very clear that the personal qualities and sacrifices required, or rather demanded, of those wishing to become a Search and Rescue Diver are not found in us all. The foolhardiness of youth meant that, in the early days, courage and commitment could, at times, be substituted with the cavalier and obstinate. Very quickly the romance of the role is replaced with heartfelt emotions such as self-doubt, stoked by sheer fear, forever playing on one's subconscious, with the deep soul searching enquiring if this chosen profession really was the right career move? And this was just the beginning at the selection and initial training stage.

Any reader will be captured and enthralled, feeling as if they are a part of every rescue the author describes: some may well have been in similar predicaments and will be able to relate, on a personal level, whether victim or rescuer. The author's journey takes one through almost 40 years of his life, which has been spent on the front-line of Search and Rescue in the UK. He has dedicated those years to saving the lives of others, with little thought for his own personal safety. The book reflects on his career with openness, honesty and humility always as part of the team who do their best even when the odds are so heavily stacked against them. The highs and lows, the joy and sadness, the fear and reality just some of the emotions that partner the author on his journey.

The future structure of the UK's Search and Rescue Organisation is still to be decided but one thing can be assured and will never change and that is the unswerving dedication of those men and woman who will be part of it. So sit back and relax whilst the author takes you on a very special journey "On the Wire".

INTRODUCTION

This record of my time in helicopter Search and Rescue was originally started as a record for my family. Once I had started I soon realised very little had been written about the aircrewman's role in Search and Rescue, especially from an aircrewman's perspective and felt perhaps that should be addressed.

I had commenced the role as a Search and Rescue diver in the early days of coordinated Search and Rescue, when all the United Kingdom's SAR helicopters were military aircraft controlled by two military rescue coordination centres, with the Coastguards having access to those facilities.

Close to 40 years later, I am still at the sharp end of the role and have witnessed quite a few changes over that time. Including the introduction of civilian Search and Rescue helicopters contracted to the Coastguard.

The most difficult thing with trying to put something like this together is actually writing about incidents and explaining how I really felt during certain rescues.

Occasionally a winchman, who has just successfully completed quite a difficult rescue in which he and the crew have taken risks achieving that rescue, may on return to base find a barrage of media asking questions about the difficulties experienced. The reply will invariably be along the lines of "it was no problem; that is what we as a crew are trained for." They may drag some of the feelings out of the winchman before he can gather his thoughts, but all the thoughts and feelings that winchman had at the time of the rescue will rarely be released except, occasionally, in the crew room away from the media.

For the majority of jobs we carry out, that description of "no problem; that is what we as a crew are trained for," will fit perfectly well. Nevertheless, almost all Search and Rescue crews (and I guess all the emergency services) occasionally face situations that could in all honesty not be described as straightforward situations that require the winchman to make true fight or flight decisions to achieve the rescue.

In the main, I would say the selection, training and pure job satisfaction for those who qualify to carry out this role help to produce those who can break through those awkward situations and with the help of the team, remain calm enough to find the best way to achieve a particularly difficult task that may be facing them. I have tried to be honest with my feelings and can certainly remember the incidents that have forced me to face my fears over the years as though they happened yesterday. I also recognise I have done some daft things along the way, but please read through those incidents as well. I do grow up through the experiences and Search and Rescue develops along the way, as better aircraft and improved technology force a more professional approach to the role.

Talking honestly to the aircrewmen I work with, they will also admit, away from the media, that they have their own collection of incidents not far from the back of their minds. Mainly the awkward ones, perhaps on a cold dark and stormy night, forcing them to fight the doubts they had felt on leaving the door on the end of the wire. This does not apply just to the winchman: the winch operator and the pilots have the responsibility literally in their hands, of getting that winchman safely to the point of rescue.

Dave Peel

Part 1
Training & Gaining Experience

Transfer to Aircrew

I joined the Royal Navy as a boy sailor at the age of 15 and having served ten years, I could reflect back to the good times travelling around the world. I had spent two years in the Far East visiting many major ports in Asia and Australia, a year in the Middle East and several shorter trips to Scandinavia, the Mediterranean, South Africa and South America. At the age of 24 with just over two years left of my contract with the Royal Navy, I had the naivety to think I had seen, done, tried and had it all. I was now a married man with two young children and had decided it was time to settle down; I would leave the Navy and attempt to find a new career closer to home.

At this time I was a Leading Seaman waiting for advancement to Petty Officer. I had qualified for the promotion a couple of years earlier and there was quite a waiting list before I would actually pick up the rate. This in itself was a sore point with me because some branches could pass for advancement and receive promotion almost immediately. Unfortunately, my branch had one of the longer waiting lists; this led to a certain amount of discontentment and was one of the reasons I had decided I would leave the Navy.

I had always been a little dissatisfied with my career in the Seaman branch, which was separated into three separate trades: Anti-Submarine (SONAR); Gunnery and Radar Plotters. I joined as a Radar Plotter. This meant my main duties at sea were spent in the darkened Operations Room.

Although an extremely interesting job, especially during exercises when every member of the operations room had an important role, I had always

1

felt happier doing the more seaman like duties - operating the ships boats, splicing rope and wire and carrying out the various evolutions required for transfers at sea, etc. The gunnery and Sonar ratings carried out the majority of these tasks, so I always felt I had joined the wrong branch.

The road to my career change commenced in my early 20's while on one of my shore time periods when I was stationed at HMS Raleigh a training establishment at Torpoint in Cornwall. I had a job I enjoyed very much working with a Chief Petty Officer (CPO) Clearance Diver, carrying out familiarisation diving courses for new recruits.

I was a qualified ship's diver, which was an additional qualification that anyone could apply to do. Every ship required a ship's diving team consisting of approximately eight divers, trained to work in a team to carry out searches for mines on the ship's bottom and to carry out underwater repairs as required.

I had been fortunate and managed to get on one of these courses as soon as I was old enough to do so, which at the time was seventeen and a half. This course had quite a high failure rate, mainly because it was quite a physical course including mud runs and circuits. About 50% of the dives were carried out in nil visibility.

Because of this high failure rate, ratings could do a familiarisation in the ship's diver course as one of their leisure activities during their initial training. This in turn would give them some idea of what to expect should they wish to qualify sometime in the future.

The familiarisation was a relaxed approach to diving and the main drills were carried out in the swimming pool. To make it clear it was not all fun and games, the candidates would have to carry out a few short mud runs (a requisite of all naval diving courses) and a couple of dives from a pier in poor visibility. Those who were still happy eventually had a weekend away camping and diving at one of the enjoyable diving sites off the coast of Cornwall.

One of the other tasks we had was to go to establishments that did not have their own ship's diving sections, to carry out aptitude tests for those that had requested to become ship's divers. Again, this was to wheedle out those unlikely to pass the course. The aptitude test would always include some form of physical activity such as mud runs, followed by controlled dives in nil visibility, underwater mask clearance and a jump wearing a dry suit and fins from between 15 and 20 feet.

It was on one of these trips that I became acquainted with the Search and Rescue role and immediately knew I would enjoy that job. We had arrived at the Royal Naval Air Station Brawdy in Wales, which, like most of the Naval Air Stations, had a very good sub-aqua section operated purely as a sporting activity. This section, because of its compressed air facility, was set up next to the Search and Rescue (SAR) Flight.

The SAR Flight looked after us for our short stay, during which I managed to arrange a couple of flights with the SAR helicopter. The helicopter was a Whirlwind Mk 7, a single piston-engine helicopter. The crew consisted of a Pilot, Winch Operator and SAR diver.

The SAR diver was a specialisation I knew very little about, as there were very few of them; approximately 27 in total in the Navy at the time. The original concept of the SAR diver came to fruition after several accidents on aircraft carriers while launching fixed wing aircraft. Occasionally aircraft taking off from the carrier were unable to get airborne successfully, forcing a ditching into the sea. The pilot invariably went down with the aircraft because they did not have time to get out before the aircraft sank.

On one particular occasion in 1958, a Scimitar from HMS Victorious went over the side. The Scimitar remained floating on the surface long enough for a Whirlwind helicopter to arrive on scene and lower a winchman to the aircraft. The pilot was conscious but having trouble releasing his leg restraint straps and the canopy was still in position; the only tool the winchman had to break into the canopy was an axe. Before a rescue could be achieved the aircraft sank below the surface and the pilot was seen to give a shrug of resignation, as if to acknowledge his fate as the aircraft slipped below the surface.

This incident played on many people's minds, the result of which was to look at a way of speeding up that initial rescue attempt. An idea was conceived to have a dedicated helicopter with a diver on board hovering alongside the aircraft carrier's port bow during fixed wing take off and landings. The close immediate response capability of the helicopter and diver would give pilots a chance of rescue should they ditch. The admiralty thought it to be a good idea and the concept of the Search and Rescue diver was born.

The SAR diver would be trained to effect a rescue: learning how to jettison the canopy (which would be designed for underwater release internally and externally); how to make the ejection seat safe and how to release the pilots harness, etc. The rescue attempt would be continued if necessary as the aircraft sank, until either the diver rescued the pilot or ran out of air. If he ran out of air, he would carry out a free ascent back to the surface.

3

The SAR diving qualification first introduced in 1961 would, in time, lead to all Royal Naval SAR helicopters carrying a SAR trained diver, both ashore and at sea.

I knew after that first flight that this is what I would like to do; in all honesty, I was green with envy of the SAR diver's role. I felt at the time it was the most exciting job imaginable and wanted to be a part of that. I also knew it was very unlikely that I could transfer since the SAR divers were recruited from volunteer ships' divers within the Fleet Air Arm, although occasionally, when they had a shortage of volunteers from the Fleet Air Arm, they would recruit from the General Service branch.

As soon as we returned to HMS Raleigh after that course at Brawdy I requested to carry out a SAR diver's course. My divisional officer informed me that this would not be possible: I was doing well in my present branch and that is where my future remained. However, not being satisfied with this, I periodically pestered my divisional officer on this point. Eventually my chief, CPO Gibson, managed to convince him that I should at least be given the chance to take the aptitude test and if successful, let it go through the normal channels.

Being a Clearance Diver (CD-the fulltime diving branch in the Navy), CPO Gibson was able to arrange an aptitude test for me very quickly. I found the majority of the aptitude test relatively easy, as it mainly involved tests I had been putting other people through. However, one of the main requirements for the SAR diver was to jump from heights wearing a diving set.

The final part of the aptitude test was to carry out two jumps from above 40ft wearing just a dry suit and fins (to wear a diving set as well would have been extremely dangerous without considerable training building up to jumping from those heights). On this occasion, I had to jump from the flight deck of an aircraft carrier berthed in Plymouth Harbour.

The jump was about 50ft, considerably higher than any jump I had done before. The dry suits we wore had a metal collar which formed a yoke that connected the neck seal to the main suit. I had to hold this yoke with one hand otherwise it was likely to do quite nasty damage to my chin as I hit the water. I also had to remember to keep my fins pointing down; if I entered flat-footed, the fins would either come off or force my legs up with the possibility of dislocating limb joints.

That moment standing on the flight deck I suddenly knew fear; a feeling I had not expected, but a feeling I was to get used to over the years to follow. All I could think of was the fuss I had created to get this opportunity and now I was faced with the possibility of having to return having failed at the first hurdle. In that moment I knew I had to jump. I closed my eyes and stepped over the edge.

I can remember every second of that jump: my arms and legs going everywhere and the sudden realisation that I was falling backwards and did not have hold of the metal collar round my neck. I knew I had no chance of hitting the water straight, let alone worrying about my fins being pointed. At the last second I managed to hold the collar but hit the water like a bag of spuds and was left feeling like a mangled sack of washing. The fins had whipped off my feet. One was lost completely but, fortunately, no damage was caused

I felt sure that was the end of my aptitude test. At least I had tried, but there was no way I was going to jump again. The CD conducting my test gave me untold stick for the faults with my jump and for losing a fin. I found all my courage returning to show this bastard that I could do the jump correctly – which I guess was his intention as he would have wanted me to pass; he was a friend of my chief who had gone to a lot of trouble to get me here in the first place. I had also breezed through the early part of the aptitude test.

Once again, I found myself on that flight deck preparing to jump; this time I managed to compose myself enabling me to pull off an half decent jump, even managing to keep both fins on.

The next day I was back at HMS Raleigh feeling really pleased with myself and knowing that I was over my first hurdle to getting the course I wanted. However, it soon became apparent that the transfer was not possible. My divisional officer, after he had tried to process my request through the normal channels, informed me that transfers out of my branch only happened in very special circumstances and this was not considered one of those special circumstances.

From that day on I decided I would make the best of things as they were until my 27th birthday (my required minimum length of service) and then leave the Navy. However, I continued to pester my various divisional officers just on the off chance one of them may manage to arrange a transfer for me.

It was at this point, with a little over two years to go before leaving the Navy that my divisional officer called me into his office for a standard career progression interview. I had informed him that I would be leaving the Navy.

He said that he would be sorry to see me leave, but could see from my records that I had applied on several occasions for the SAR diver's course. If the course meant that much to me, he would make every effort to arrange this.

A few weeks later he informed me that a transfer would be possible and explained that there would be a requirement to do quite an extensive aircrew course as well as the SAR diver course. This would mean signing on for extra years so that the Navy would get a return of service for the training. Although feeling a little bitter that I was unable to do the course earlier, I knew this is what I wanted so agreed straight away.

SAR Diver Course

Within days, I found myself drafted to HMS Daedalus at 'Lee-on-Solent' in Hampshire. This was a Fleet Air Arm base and its main role was as a training base for naval aircraft engineers. I had suddenly entered the Fleet Air Arm, excited about the possibility of my new job and feeling very lucky to be getting this opportunity.

While waiting for the course I joined a team of divers who worked in the Helicopter Underwater Escape Tank (Dunker) at HMS Vernon in Portsmouth. The role was to teach aircrew how to escape from helicopters underwater, should they be that unfortunate to ditch in the sea.

I had to get used to several differences between General Service and the Fleet Air Arm. The first was that you no longer called your divisional officer 'Sir'; you called him 'Boss'. The Boss in this instance was a lieutenant called Andrew George Linsley and what a character he was. He always looked after his lads and, if we were not instructing, we could do pretty well as we liked, much to the envy of other departments. We invariably finished dunking (term used for each cycle of underwater escape training) early afternoon in time to make it to what became our second home, the Crofton Pub in Stubbington.

Quite often, Andrew George and his wife would join us; somehow, he had managed to convince his superiors that keeping a happy team was good leadership. Looking back, I guess spending as much time in the pub as we did may not have been the best thing. However, the system did work as everyone enjoyed the job, even though the work side of it meant spending many hours in cold water, continuously being turned upside down in this cramped mock-up of a helicopter.

One of the other things that amused me, in these early days with the Fleet Air Arm, was that I often used to hear arguments amongst 'Wafu's' (the nick name for Fleet Air Arm personnel). The arguments were along the lines that one person had a draft to sea after only five years ashore, while the other one had perhaps been ashore for six years and felt he should have gone to sea first.

In the General Service, the argument was always the opposite because you spent very little time on shore, so normally wanted more time with your family. The maximum time on shore would be 18 months for a Seaman. In this new world of the Fleet Air Arm, I was meeting people who had not been to sea for eight or more years.

The underwater escape team consisted of the Boss, a Chief Petty Officer and Petty Officer (who were both qualified SAR divers) and four ship's divers like me. The two SAR divers were Terry Scott & Terry Short who took me under their wing, preparing me for what to expect on my SAR diver's course.

There were two of us waiting to go on the course: a Leading Chef called Jim Brodie and me. Jim like me had become dissatisfied with his previous trade and due to leave the Navy in a couple of years. He was a very keen ship's diver and had badgered away at his divisional officer until he managed to get a course, under the same arrangement as me.

We soon became run ashore oppo's (more naval slang for best pals) and were quick to find our feet in this rather strange world, to the amusement of the Wafu's. As we were both 'Fish Heads' (the Naval term for general service personnel) the guys in the camp mixed 'Wafu' and 'Fish Head' together and called us the pair of 'Wafheads'.

After just a few months in the underwater escape trainer, Jim and I found ourselves at Bincleaves, a Naval underwater trials unit in Portland harbour to commence our SAR diver course. Our instructor was a Chief CD1 (Clearance Diver) called Cliff Clifford and the course officer a lieutenant observer called Pat Dalton. Cliff would be our main instructor and he had a leading clearance diver to assist him. Cliff would prove to be tough but fair.

There were eight of us on course all quite experienced ship's divers a pre-requisite for the course. We knew at the time only a few of us would complete the course. Jim and I had convinced each other that we would be amongst those that did pass.

We spent the first day continuously jumping about 20ft from a concrete building wearing the BASAR (Breathing Apparatus Search and Rescue), a self-contained compressed air breathing set with enough air to spend approximately thirty minutes underwater at a depth of 30ft.

We soon got used to the jumping, but the climb up the vertical ladder after each jump was extremely strenuous. The last few jumps of the day were from a forty-seven foot board (this time without the BASAR), but even so I felt the fear I had felt on the flight deck during my aptitude test – only this time I had Jim to give me encouragement. That first day we lost two from the course. One had frozen on the higher board and the other lost the energy to keep climbing the vertical ladders laden with diving set and weights.

Tuesday was spent doing the same thing; in addition, we carried out endurance dives along a sea wall. This was the first time any of us had dived on our own. Under normal ship's diving rules, we would dive with a 'dive buddy', connected to each other with a line or, if diving on our own, secured to a lifeline controlled by someone on the surface.

For SAR purposes, jumping from a helicopter, we are on our own from the moment we leave the aircraft. To prepare us for this lonely environment, we spent considerable time on the course carrying out endurance dives, concentrating on controlling our breathing to get the maximum time out of our sets, at the same time allowing us to get used to diving without a 'dive buddy'. We lost another course member on the second day when he found he could not get used to diving without the security of a 'dive buddy'.

On the next day, they seemed to hit us with everything, including fast dressing drills, which meant getting into the diving dry suits as fast as possible. This required dressing in pairs, as the suits are impossible to get into on your own. Then put our BASAR on, carry out our safety checks, climb up the ladder and jump. We had to achieve this in less than four minutes. If we did not make it, we had to swim across the bay and back or carry out some equally difficult task. The worst part for me was stripping off to carry out the swim; being of thin build I found skinny-dipping in winter quite cold.

Every so often, quite unexpectedly, Cliff would send us off on a run round the dockyard, followed by an endurance dive and more jumps. By the end of the third day, we were down to four; the number they had expected to remain after the first week.

Thursday arrived with some trepidation for the four of us, as we knew that some time during the day we would have to jump from the 47ft board, only this time we would be wearing our breathing apparatus weights and fins.

It was bad enough without the BASAR because the board was set in a corner of the building, the jump being down the side of the building. Each time we jumped without the BASAR we felt we would fall backwards on the way down and glance off the side of the building.

We had now convinced ourselves this was even more likely to happen with the weight of our breathing apparatus on our back. It was difficult to jump out to clear the building as it made it awkward regaining balance on the way down. Bearing in mind we still had to enter the water with fins pointed, one hand holding our facemask and now wearing the breathing apparatus, the other hand still had to hold the yoke attaching our neck seal and our forearm had to secure the weighted quick-release pouch strapped across the chest. The weights were required to assist us to descend once in the water.

Most of the day was spent jumping from the lower level, but by this stage each time we entered the water we had to head for the seabed (about 30ft below), pick up some mud from the seabed and then return to the surface. If we did not manage to return with some mud in our hands, our instructor knew we had not entered the water correctly.

If we did not keep our fins straight one or both would come off, normally wrapping around our ankles. This meant we could not fin to the seabed and would float to the surface. The other problem was of not holding our weights down properly. If we failed to they would fall out of the quick release pouch and again we would float to the surface.

When this happened we knew we were in for a lot of abuse. So much so, we started cheating by wearing extra weights, so that we would sink to the bottom even if our fins came off. We then only had to concentrate on keeping the weights in the pouch and our facemask on, if our fins came off the extra weights would allow us to sink to the seabed giving us time to replace our fins before returning to the surface.

The risk of making ourselves negative buoyant when jumping from the board was really quite foolhardy. There was always a possibility of being knocked unconscious on the jump, especially from the 47ft board and, if that happened, we would simply sink to the seabed. Nevertheless, at the time the risk seemed to be worth taking to avoid the hassle when we got things wrong.

When the time came to jump from the higher board, Jim and I, still working as a team, climbed up. Jim climbed over the guardrail first, said goodbye as though he was convinced it was goodbye, screamed Geronimo, replaced his mouthpiece and stepped off. When he surfaced he was so excited he took his mouthpiece out and started yelling for me to go for it.

I closed my eyes and stepped off, also screaming Geronimo. Except I was screaming it all the way down, which meant I had not replaced my mouthpiece. The result of that was that I came screaming back towards the surface trying to work out why I could not breathe. Just before I got to the surface I realised what had happened, replaced my mouthpiece, blew out the excess water and proceeded to the bottom to pick up my handful of mud.

When I returned to the surface, Jim was waiting for me; we congratulated each other for getting past another psychological barrier and climbed out of the water ready to provide encouragement for the other pair to jump. They in turn went through much the same procedure as Jim and I. We went on to do several more jumps from that board before finishing for the day.

Friday was our first day of jumping from a helicopter. We were quite excited about this, especially Jim and me as we had little experience of them. From now on operating with helicopters would be a regular occurrence. We spent the morning carrying out endurance dives and further jumps from both boards. Early in the afternoon, we were taken in the Gemini (a small inflatable craft with an outboard engine) to the centre of Portland harbour and then left in the water to wait for the helicopter. The sound of the helicopter was deafening and none of us prepared for the downdraught that seemed to hit us like a hailstorm. Yet another experience we would have to learn to tolerate.

The helicopter had us winched up very quickly. The crew lined us up ready to jump out again. The winch operator would decide when it was safe to jump. He would look for a 'thumbs-up' signal from the diver to let him know the diver has completed his pre-jump checks. Then, when the aircraft was at the required height and the winch operator was sure there was nothing directly under the aircraft, he would give the diver two sharp taps on the shoulder.

It had been impressed on us that we had to jump as soon as we received that second tap; there was no time for delay as the aircraft would still be moving and any delay would mean us jumping at the wrong spot or from the wrong height. We carried out the first session of jumps from about 20-25ft to allow us to get used to the procedures. We soon got used to stepping out the instant that second tap on the shoulder came. The next session was much the same but from 30-40ft. At the end of this week, we felt quite exhilarated, having reached this landmark.

We arrived back first thing Monday morning to an onslaught of everything we had done so far. This time during our session with the helicopter, we were introduced to plane guard procedures, which was the method used to recover pilots who had ditched during take-off. This was the primary role for the SAR diver back then; the helicopter would sit in the hover off the port bow of the aircraft carrier at approximately 100ft, with the diver sitting in the doorway ready to jump. The helicopter would be at that state of readiness throughout all fixed wing launchings and landings from aircraft carriers.

If an aircraft ditched or the pilot bailed out, the helicopter would swoop down aiming to flare out at a height of approximately 30ft at the scene of the incident. Just at this crucial point, the winch operator would give the diver the two taps, the aim being that the diver would end up in the water alongside the casualty. This required perfect timing, especially for the pilot who had to judge his flare just right, otherwise there would be too much forward movement when the diver was despatched. The winch operator had to make sure the crucial taps on the shoulder were given at the right time.

To practice this procedure we worked in pairs. The first diver would jump from the helicopter, dive to the seabed and stay there. The helicopter would circuit then swoop down on the bubbles of the first diver and despatch the second diver who would then follow the bubbles down and recover the first diver.

The early jumps using this technique were quite hair-raising, we never really knew what height we were jumping from and often we left the aircraft with too much forward speed on. The main reason for so many inaccuracies in these early jumps was that the training was also for the pilots and the winch operator's benefit and, as they were not an operational aircraft carrier SAR flight, some of them were quite rusty in this technique.

We took quite a lot of injuries this week and once again started questioning the reasons for wanting to continue. No longer could we manage to stumble down the pub for a couple of pints and try to relax in the evening as we had in the first week. We just made it back to our digs, had a meal and crashed out; praying our aches and pains would disappear by the morning. Before the end of the second week one more candidate had decided enough was enough, leaving just the three of us.

At this stage I wanted to call it a day myself; I had an aching back, both knees had been wrenched and my right ankle felt as though it was broken. Jim, who was in a similar condition convinced me we should crack on. That night we did make it to the pub and, with a few pints in us, convinced each other we were invincible and rolled up the next morning with renewed enthusiasm.

Cliff seemed to take it easy on us this day as if he knew we had all come close to giving up the previous day. Most of the day we spent doing endurance dives, jumps from the lower board and only one session of jumps from the helicopter.

At the start of the third week, it was just Jim and I; the other remaining diver had pulled out over the weekend. There was some discussion about continuing the course with just the two of us remaining. Jim and I would have hated to be required to endure those first two weeks again when they arranged the next course. Fortunately, the decision went our way and they continued with the course.

Throughout the rest of the course, we went through many difficulties; one day I would be providing the encouragement, the next Jim would. We had to carry out many other drills including parachute disentanglement i.e. freeing someone tangled in a parachute. This meant coming up underneath the survivor and cutting the parachute cords free. The survivor role was played by our course officer, Pat Dalton.

Pat was very good at his job as an Observer and SAR Diving Officer and the fact that he was one of only a few officers who had completed this course made him a person looked up to by the qualified SAR Divers.

We had been pre-warned by Terry Short (one of the SAR divers we had worked with in the underwater escape tank), that Pat would make things extremely difficult for us if we did not take charge; he would rip our facemask off and pull our mouthpiece out the first opportunity he got. In fact, Terry had advised us that when this happened we should grab his wedding tackle and apply pressure until he lost any desire to act the fool!

Jim was first to go and duly applied pressure when required. It worked, but for a moment we thought Jim was going to be thrown off the course. However, Pat eventually saw the funny side and later admitted this technique had completely taken away any thought of being awkward.

It was my turn next and I was warned that I was not going to get away with Terry's Technique. I was hoping I would be able to get a firm grip of him from behind. However, everything went to rats as soon as I left the aircraft and the downdraught lifted the parachute canopy. Not knowing this I had managed to come up behind Pat and had the firm grip I wanted. The next thing I was aware of was the sensation of movement through the water at some considerable speed.

The downdraught had lifted the canopy allowing the wind to take charge. I was all right as I had my mouthpiece in and could breath but Pat was not so fortunate. Both of us were dragged quite some distance before the Gemini caught up with us and Pat's head had been underwater for a lot of this time. By the time we stopped, Pat was in no fit state to create a problem and I guess was just happy to be free from the parachute.

Another skill we had to learn was free ascents to the surface. It was in our brief as a SAR diver that when attempting to save life we would follow a sinking aircraft until we ran out of air. With controlled breathing, it was hoped to get up to thirty minutes of air out of the set at 30ft, but at 120ft, we only had a few minutes of air. This was because of the greater volumes of air required to counteract the hydrostatic pressure of the water squeezing the body and lungs. From this rather basic description, you can see that it would not take long to run out of air completely, whilst following an aircraft as it sank below the surface.

The problem with the free ascent situation is that, having ditched the breathing apparatus, it is necessary to breathe out on the way to the surface at a steady rate. The volume of air in the lungs would increase all the way to the surface as the hydrostatic pressure on the body decreases. If not controlled, the excess air could damage our lungs causing a life-threatening embolism.

We carried out the training for free ascents in a controlled environment, in the submarine escape tank at HMS Dolphin in Gosport. This was a 100ft tank provided to teach submarine crews the same technique. After this we would do further training at the helicopter escape tank at HMS Vernon before practising for real in the sea.

The training to release someone from a sinking cockpit was carried out in the helicopter escape tank, with Andrew George strapped into a mock up of a buccaneer jet cockpit, complete with full harnesses and oxygen connection, exactly as the real thing. His brief for this exercise was to make things a little difficult for us.

He was strapped in the cockpit then lowered into the water by crane at approximately the same rate an aircraft would sink. We had to jump from the rafters of the building and follow the aircraft down, release the canopy, simulate making the ejection seat safe, remove the harness and finally his oxygen supply. The intention was to release Andrew George before the aircraft had sunk to 57ft, which was the depth of this tank.

We then had to carry out a controlled ascent, keeping our eye on the survivor's mouth ensuring that he was breathing out. If not we had to give him an occasional punch in the stomach, to force him to breath out. Invariably Andrew George (being the nice fellow he was) would throw a little panic scene and remove our facemask, which meant continuing the rescue by feel.

On completion of the course Jim and I went back to work at the underwater escape tank while we waited for the Aircrewman's course.

This was another period with plenty of socialising and letting off steam. I guess as the two 'wafheads' we were trying to make a reputation for ourselves (a macho thing I am afraid); having just completed the SAR diver's course, we felt we had something to live up to.

We did not know when we would get on the aircrew course since the next two courses were full. After about six weeks, Andrew George decided to get our aircrew medicals completed so we would be ready to join a course at short notice if a place became available.

The aircrew medical would be quite stringent; this had not really worried us, as we thought it would not be any different to the diving medical. Jim came out of that medical as white as a sheet. I immediately knew something terrible was wrong; he had failed his medical. Apparently, he had a hearing problem in the higher frequency range, which put his hearing outside the range required for aircrew.

By this time, Jim had become very popular and the air selection board were keen for him to continue. They made every effort to get him through this test without actually fudging it. He had to spend a week isolated from diving and any loud noise sources, but when he took the test again the result was the same.

He came back from the second medical crying like a baby; the macho image we had been trying to put across completely blown. I fully understood this and knew I would have done the same; this course and our ultimate aim had come to mean so much to both of us.

I felt devastated as well; we had become such good mates. All I could think about was the course we had gone through. I knew without any doubt that I would not have passed without Jim's encouragement.

Jim wished me the best of luck when Andrew George managed to get me on a course starting the following Monday. He had also managed to persuade the drafting board that Jim should stay on at the underwater escape trainer, for a normal shore time tour and even arranged that he should keep his SAR diver's pay while he worked in the dunker.

Aircrewman Training

The aircrew course took place at HMS Osprey at Portland, Dorset. It was a nine-week course and proved to be quite difficult, especially for me as there was a lot of classroom work, something I had not done for years.

I had never been very academic; my parents had sent me to a boarding school in Suffolk (Royal Hospital School), because I had failed my 11 plus exams and it was hoped the school would improve my education. Unfortunately, the school had very good sporting facilities, so for me sport took preference to school work.

Many years later I was to find I was seriously dyslexic, which was quite possibly the reason I shied away from classroom work. I joined the Navy at fifteen with no qualifications at all. I studied and took the necessary exams to gain the qualifications required for advancement and fortunately, as a seaman, the majority of the qualifications were practical based. However, I had not realised that I had joined this course with less than the minimum academic requirements.

The selection board had not picked up the fact that I did not have the correct grades for the course until a few days before I was due to start. Andrew George had managed to convince the board I would be up to it. So, yet again I found I had something to prove and realised how much Andrew had done to help me get this far. I was informed I would be required to gain the qualifications if I passed the course, but was never actually called on to do so.

The other course members had been together for a few weeks. They had undergone a pre-selection course, which had been quite tough. This had included various mental aptitude tests, plus seven nights' survival in the New Forest. The survival commenced with a night spent in a leaking life raft in the middle of a quarry, followed by an escape and evasion exercise leading on to the survival exercise itself. The only aid was a parachute to make shelter with and the cords of the parachute to fish with or to make traps.

On the penultimate day, each of the teams were given a live rabbit to kill, skin and eat. To make matters worse for the squeamish, the rabbit was a white one. However, some of the candidates had been unsuccessful with their traps or fishing and had not eaten anything for the whole week, so any thoughts of letting the rabbit go had completely disappeared.

I had to do the survival course later as it was considered an essential part of the qualifying process for aircrew; nevertheless, I had escaped the other tests they had been given. I felt initially that I was at a disadvantage as they had gone through quite a lot together and had already bonded as a team. The course members I had joined with had started out as a larger group but one or two had fallen by the wayside.

I was never sure why I had managed to jump the queue but failures on that pre-selection course created the place that I took. I can only guess they considered that having already qualified as a SAR diver was enough.

Our Instructors were a Chief Petty Officer called Mick Cromby and a Petty Officer called Carl Fairbrother. Our course officer was a lieutenant called Graham (Jan) Greener who, like Andrew George, really made every effort to look after his lads. Carl Fairbrother was a SAR diver and made it quite clear I would have to work hard and not let his side down.

The aircrew branch at the time had no real structure. Everyone was a volunteer and once we changed to aircrew, under normal circumstances, we would stay aircrew for the rest of our naval career. However, for advancement purposes we remained in our parent branch, in my case as a seaman.

We had to be a leading rate to be aircrew but, for many of the course members, to get any further advancement they would have to return to their parent branch at some time in the future. This was a ridiculous situation and Jan Greener our course boss managed, a few years later, to help champion the case for all aircrewmen, convincing the Ministry of Defence to form the Aircrewman's branch with its own promotional structure.

At the time this was not a problem for me as, although I was still a Leading Seaman, I had already qualified for Petty Officer so my rate would come through in time. Advancement to Chief Petty Officer was on merit so I had no further exams to take for that.

The branch as it stood at the time was split into five specialisations.

1. Anti Submarine: the aircrewman's role was to operate sophisticated equipment to search for and monitor submarine activity, while the helicopter sat in the hover with a sonar buoy dangling in the water beneath them.

2. Commando Aircrewman: Responsible for the control of the aircraft cabin, controlling many different types of troop manoeuvres and insertions, loading of the troops and their equipment, security of under slung loads, map reading and navigation. This would mainly be in support of Royal Marines.

3. Missile Aimer: Normally attached to a small ship's flight, he would control one of the aircraft's weapon systems. At the time, the missiles were wire guided, so the crewman would require special skills to achieve hitting a designated target, they were selected for those skills at the aptitude stage.

4. Search and Rescue Aircrewman: Responsible for navigation, map reading, communication between the Coastguard and the aircraft, operating the winch and would generally control most of the Search and Rescue sorties.

5. Search and Rescue Diver: Assist the SAR aircrewman, as required, recover any casualties to the aircraft operating as a diver, free swimmer or as a winchman lowered on the wire to the casualty. Both the SAR aircrewman and SAR diver were also trained in advanced first aid.

All these specialisations had to learn various SAR procedures including winch operations as the winch operator and the winchman. All Royal Navy helicopters had a winch and the crews were expected to carry out rescues if the situation arose.

We also had to learn navigation, map reading, radio procedures, airmanship, meteorological forecasting and rules of the air.

The Basic Aircrew course was to teach these standardised subjects, so that all aircrew whatever specification, would use the same basic procedures. On completion of the course, we would go our separate ways to specialise in our chosen sub branch.

Again, I learned how lucky I was. A few others on the course wanted to be Search and Rescue, but the normal procedure was to train aircrewman for SAR after they had completed at least one full front line tour in one of the other specialisations. I had escaped this because there was such a shortage of SAR divers at the time. Only one other course member John (Speedy) Ball, would be going on to specialise in Search and Rescue on completion of this course.

In no time, Speedy and I had teamed up and I soon felt part of the course. Once again, I had another run ashore oppo to make our impression, this time on Portland.

For the course it was compulsory that we lived on the base and were all accommodated in the same block. The course was designed to make us work in the evenings as well, keeping the pressure on all the time and encouraging us to work as a team. We would take our notes back at night, work on them until about 9:30 then relax with a couple of pints in the NAAFI bar. One night a week, we would go ashore as a group and blow off steam. Eventually these runs ashore became more frequent, but that is another story.

The course was a good mixture of practical and theory; the helicopters used for our training were Wessex Mk1's, single turbine engine utility helicopters that had fourteen seats in the back. The majority of our flying training was carried out using two helicopters; we were split into two groups, one instructor with each group.

The aircraft did not have any navigational aids. All the navigation was carried out by dead reckoning, which required very accurate plotting and a considerable amount of calculations using a Dalton computer. The Dalton computer was a circular slide ruler, used to compute a true course by setting the wind direction and speed against the track required. Then a few adjustments were required to take account of the magnetic variation. Finally, we needed to find the true speed against the recorded airspeed to find out how many minutes were required on each leg – the aircraft is directly affected by the wind. For example, if we are flying at 90 mph directly into a 30 mph head wind, the aircraft speed over the ground will be 60 mph. The Dalton computer was required to work out this speed when the wind force was affecting the aircraft from other directions.

For training purposes, we had many plotting exercises in the classroom; the practical training being carried out by flying in the channel out of sight of land. We would take it in turn to navigate a series of legs until the instructor gave a point on the land to head back for. In the early days we could only guarantee if we simply headed north we would eventually hit England. I am not so sure we could even have guaranteed that, if it was not for the fact Portland was in the middle of the south coast.

Eventually we did improve but, in all honesty, the method could never be completely accurate because the system required accurate winds and we often only guessed at the wind by observing the sea. It also required the pilot to fly an accurate course and speed and there was considerable scope for plotting errors. Occasionally we received Radar fixes that we used to find a more accurate wind.

The standard eventually achieved would be to return within half a mile of a given point, after an hour out of sight of land, having already altered course on ten or more legs.

The winch training was carried out on a satellite airfield called Little Bredy. The training, although potentially dangerous, was extremely comical. Fortunately, the instructors stepped in to prevent any serious accidents.

The pilot cannot see what is happening underneath the aircraft so he takes his instruction from the winch operator who uses verbal commands to control the pilot's speed, height and direction. A set SAR winching pattern called a winch circuit is used, ensuring the aircraft always approaches the casualty flying into wind. Once the pilot loses sight of the casualty, the winch operator provides verbal directions (con) to the 'on top' position.

For training purposes, one of the course members would be on the ground as the survivor, another in a double lift harness attached to the winch wire and one on the winch switch with the instructor looking over his shoulder. Unfortunately, in the early stages when in the role of winch operator, we found ourselves focusing so much on the survivor and trying so hard to use the correct patter to control the aircraft, the poor fellow on the end of the wire was completely forgotten about.

On a regular basis the winch operator would be concentrating so hard on the approach that he would forget he was also winching out; the result would be that the winchman could find himself being dragged along the ground. If the speed was too fast, the winchman was at risk of injury. If that looked likely the instructor would take over. However, some of the instructors had a sadistic streak and we would all experience being dragged along under the aircraft. I tried running but I could not keep up. Once dragged, the lesson was learnt.

I adapted quickly to the practical aspects of the course but did struggle with some of the theory. Fortunately, my mate Speedy (being considerably academically brighter than me) would help me with some extra study and I was able to talk him through some despondent times on the practical side. Rather like Jim and I on the SAR diver's course, we were able to help and encourage each other.

Pete Jays, Slim Freelove, John Sheldon, Jeff Coward, John (Speedy) Ball and I completed the course and celebrated with a memorable course thrash before proceeding in different directions to our various specialisations.

Our paths would cross on many occasions after the initial training. One of the nice things about the branch was that it was small enough to keep track of each other.

SAR Aircrewman Course

Speedy and I stayed with '771 Squadron' to commence our six week SAR aircrewman's course. We were joined by two other aircrewmen, Bob Hitchman and Jerry Riddel; both were qualified aircrewman who had completed a tour on a commando squadron.

The course specialised in winching techniques, despatching divers, consolidating our navigation, night SAR procedures and refreshing our knowledge on first aid procedures.

Speedy and I thoroughly enjoyed this course, with only four students and two instructors it was considerably lower-key than the course we had just completed. The instructors, Colin Larcombe and Brian Johnstone, treated us as though we had been aircrew for years.

The winch training went a stage further than our basic course and consisted of a lot more winching to different types of vessels under way. When the opportunity presented itself, we would winch to vessels in heavy seas allowing us to get used to the rather daunting task of selecting the right moment, between waves, to put the winchman on the deck. To gain precision skills we would winch each other to small platforms attached to buoys in the middle of the harbour. In this situation, the pilot would not have any visual references, requiring the verbal con and coordination of the winch operator to be extremely precise.

Periodically the instructors would give us an exercise scramble by giving us latitude and longitude positions or a range and bearing from a given point. The object we were searching for would be a marker buoy dropped from a helicopter on an earlier training exercise. This would also involve a search pattern using the original drop point as the Datum. They would also arrange SAR scenarios on exercise boats in the Weymouth area, scrambling us without warning.

We used the Portland SAR flight's divers to carry out the diver despatch training. I had a dual role in this as I was the only SAR diver on course and obviously knew by now the importance of picking the right time to tap the diver on the shoulder. The diver could and did get very angry when you got it wrong, especially when practising the plane guard procedures.

As mentioned earlier, this had the potential of causing serious injury to the diver if despatched at the wrong time.

We had time for socialising on this course and certainly took advantage. Speedy and I no longer had to live onboard; Portland was short of accommodation so we were placed in digs in a house midway between Portland and Weymouth. Most evenings we would meet up with Bob and Jerry in Weymouth and would do the rounds of the popular pubs, invariably ending up back in Portland at the Ship Inn. This was the local pub adopted by the SAR Flight and the Aircrewman's school. I cannot remember if it was for the good ale or the fact it had by far the prettiest barmaids. Whatever the reason, it was like a magnet to us.

On completion of this course, we carried out an advance first aid course at Seafield Park, in Stubbington, Hampshire, which was the home of the Air Medical School. On completion, Speedy and I joined the SAR Flight at Portland, Bob went to Yeovilton SAR and Jerry went to Culdrose SAR. Speedy would also be joining Yeovilton SAR Flight in a couple of months. I would eventually be heading back to Lee-on-Solent, to join a new SAR Flight that was forming at HMS Daedalus.

The flight at Lee-on-Solent was forming to replace the RAF Search and Rescue flight that operated from the RAF airfield at Thorney Island in West Sussex. Thorney Island airfield was in the process of closing down and the RAF Search and Rescue flight was being moved to RNAS Lossiemouth in Scotland, where the RAF was in the process of taking over the Royal Naval Air Station. The RN Search and Rescue flight at Lossiemouth would relocate to HMS Daedalus and take over responsibility for the Solent area. Thus the SAR Flight at HMS Daedalus was formed.

Commencing the Search and Rescue Role

The next few weeks I felt on top of the world. I thoroughly enjoyed my new job where I was in a crew on Portland SAR after only a few days of joining the flight. Obviously I was crewed with an experienced winch operator, an aircrewman called Tony Gardner who I got on with straight away. Tony went out of his way to show me the ropes. He was a SAR aircrewman also qualified as a ship's diver and waiting for his SAR Diver's course, so was a little annoyed I had managed to get mine before even qualifying as aircrew: he would moan about it but still helped me every way he could.

I spent six months on the Portland flight before going off to Lee and during this time, the scrambles were not too difficult. I had experienced the rush of adrenalin that always added additional drive to the crew and had experienced the apprehension felt regarding the situation we would be heading towards, when the scramble siren was activated.

The majority of scrambles had been to escort aircraft returning to the airfield with some form of emergency. The other common occurrences were scrambles for casualty evacuation from ships and these were normally straightforward transfers of naval personnel taken ill or had suffered an injury. The casualty had normally been stabilised by medics on the ships, so they would only require transfer to hospital.

The squadron at Portland had a secondary task which was to take the Flag Officer Sea Training, (F. O. S. T) staff out to ships on exercise in the Portland exercise areas. Portland was the main operational exercise area; all the ships would carry out many forms of training, preparing the crews in the operation of the ships' weapon and defence systems and teaching the crews to work as teams during many differing evolutions. This would involve exercises between ships of different nationalities.

To achieve all this involved the transfer of training staff to and from shore and between ships. A considerable amount of winching was required so extremely valuable for me, helping me to gain more confidence in my new role.

Unfortunately, my change of career was having its effect on my marriage. I found myself going home to Plymouth less frequently than the weekends I had available and when I did go home, I felt like a stranger in my own home. It was something I could never quite put my finger on. My wife had become independent, bringing up the children, mainly on her own while I was away from home.

In our seven years of marriage, I had lived at home for less than three years. Now the prospect was for many more years living apart from each other as my wife did not want to move to Lee-on-Solent and there was no possibility of getting a posting to Plymouth.

Even before I had accepted the aircrew course, my wife had made it clear on many occasions that she felt we had married too young and often felt she had missed out on normal life. I had never felt quite that way but then I had been travelling around the world and perhaps enjoying myself more than I should. Eventually we grew apart and my trips home would be just to see the boys, until we both found separate partners and divorced.

Lee-on-Solent SAR Flight

I joined the newly formed Search and Rescue flight at HMS Daedalus in May 1973. We operated with three 'Whirlwind Mk 9' helicopters. The Whirlwind was considerably smaller than the 'Wessex Mk1's' used at Portland. The 'Whirlwind Mk 9' was a 3 bladed helicopter powered by a single Rolls Royce Gnome gas turbine engine and was more reliable than its predecessor the 'Whirlwind Mk 7' that I had first flown in at RNAS Brawdy which was powered by a piston engine.

This flight, unlike Portland, was to be a dedicated SAR flight under direct control of the Coastguards and partially funded by the Department of Trade and Industry. This meant that the Coastguards could scramble us without having to go through the military controlled Rescue Coordination Centres. A Coastguard officer was attached to the unit to coordinate the operations between the Coastguard and ourselves. Mick Mickleborough was the first Coastguard officer appointed as the liaison officer. He worked a normal working week but lived very close to the base and would invariably come in from home to operate the radios when the aircraft was scrambled out of normal working hours.

During these early days, the aircraft was not equipped with radios to communicate directly with the Coastguards so everything had to be relayed through Mick who would pass the information to us by UHF Radio on our military aviation frequency. Mick had many other tasks to carry out while we were airborne; assessing the type of searches required based on the information received, arranging hospital landing-sites and fuel at other airfields if required.

It was soon apparent that at least 98% of our tasking was for civilian incidents and, without Mick coordinating these incidents they could get extremely difficult. Occasionally we would have to carry out the whole task on information received before takeoff. We were unable to have messages relayed through the military control tower out of working hours, as they did not operate early evenings and weekends.

Mick was completely dedicated to his job, making every effort to return to the flight whenever the aircraft was scrambled; however, it did mean he spent many hours at the flight, far in excess of anyone else. Eventually it was decided that a second Coastguard officer would be attached to the flight, but that was to be several months later.

The whole set up at Daedalus was wonderful; the flight was stationed well away from the main camp so we escaped most of the usual hassles attached to military life. The building, although adequate, was being modernised to meet all the needs of a SAR Flight and was paid for by the Department of Trade. They were even going to treat the divers as human beings by providing us with proper showers and drying rooms to clean off after diver training or jobs. At Portland and virtually everywhere else, we used a cold-water hose outside.

Most of the SAR crew had been working together for a while, the flight being the operational one that had moved down from RNAS Lossiemouth when the RAF took it over. The only crewmember I knew was Terry Short who had joined from the underwater escape trainer. I had one day to settle in, the next I joined my crew.

The flight operated a three-crew system covering daylight hours only. We worked three mornings in a row, from thirty minutes before sunrise until midday; a day off; four days from midday until thirty minutes after sunset, followed by two days off after the first full cycle of duties and four days after the second cycle of duties. The four days off were always over a weekend, so we were assured one complete weekend off every three weeks. The routine worked very well, the hours were long in the summer but we certainly made up for it in the winter.

We also had stand-by duties that required the off-watch crew to be at one hour's notice. If we wanted to go out, we could, but had to contact the flight and let them know our intentions.

For the first month, I crewed up with a pilot called Bill Fewtrell and an aircrewman called George Cottrell. I was to spend the first month with the same pilot and aircrewman to form some sort of continuity which gave George a month to knock some of the newness out of me.

One of the first jobs I had with this crew was to an injured angler on a small fishing vessel south of Littlehampton. I was quite excited at the prospect of this job. It had sounded quite straightforward; we knew the angler had an injured wrist but it did not sound to be too serious. My thoughts were simply that I would get to use some of my newly learnt first aid skills.

En-route, Mick had relayed via Shoreham Air Traffic that the boat crew were having difficulty stemming the casualty's bleeding. This started to put some apprehension in my mind but had not prepared me for what to expect when we arrived. They had quite a difficult job getting me on board as there was no wind and the vessel was being blown all over the place by the downdraught from the blades.

Once on board I found the casualty semi-conscious with his arm over a bucket half-full of what I had thought was all blood. I later realised this was a bucket of water that the blood had been dripping in to. His mate had tried to stem the bleeding with rags and by applying pressure.

I suddenly felt very queasy myself but knew I had a job to do, although for a moment I was not sure what to do. In those days there was a lot of controversy about applying a tourniquet as it had a risk of causing tissue damage. In addition, I was not experienced enough to weigh up the balance of loss of blood and possible tissue damage.

Initially I decided to work on direct pressure, using the man's thick leather trouser belt to strap around his arm over the existing cloth that was acting as a wound dressing. Being able to tighten the strap, I managed to stem the flow long enough to get us both winched into the aircraft.

It was not long before considerable bleeding commenced again. This time George decided we had no choice and would have to apply a tourniquet, which proved effective. I worried all the way to the hospital landing-site, convinced I was going to be responsible for him losing his arm, but knew the tourniquet was now a possible life-saving measure. We landed very shortly after this and, with some relief, handed the casualty over to a doctor and ambulance waiting at the helicopter landing-site.

The next day we heard from the hospital that the man required surgery but expected to regain full use of his arm. George and I contacted the Air Medical Board to clarify the use of tourniquets and we were assured that we had done the right thing; the timing involved would not have caused any serious complications. Later we had further guidance; we could use a tourniquet when direct pressure failed, providing we released the pressure occasionally to allow normal circulation. Views on the use of tourniquets would be reviewed several times during my career, as greater knowledge on haemorrhage control in triage was understood.

This rescue proved to be extremely useful to me, as it taught me that I had to put any feeling of inadequacies behind me, accept the situation as it was and respond as best I could, using the equipment available. In these situations, there would be no one to turn to for advice.

That first month we rescued seven people cut off by the tide, a woman from a capsized dinghy, two children from an inflatable blown out to sea, searched for a boy missing in a dinghy off Bournemouth and rescued a

Coastguard who was firmly stuck in the mud, after he himself had rescued someone else.

For the next couple of months I swapped around with different crews. Apart from Bill the pilots were John Dransfield (the commanding officer of the flight), George Bedford, Roger Asbey and Dave Johnson. The aircrewmen: Fred Queen (who was the chief aircrewman), Sam Lawson, Lou Armstrong, Denis Kermode, Rod Caunter, Charlie Charlton, Terry Short (diver), Derek Oakes (diver), Blackie Blackman (diver) and Roger Bigden (diver).

Lou soon became my run ashore oppo along with Denis Kermode. Terry Short lived locally so was not allowed out to play as often as the rest of us. The majority of the aircrewman lived in the same accommodation block so we had a great social life.

Lou was quite a character. He was a Navy sprinter, a combined services rugby player and had represented the Fleet Air Arm in the field gun crew. All these things had a certain amount of prestige within the Navy, which meant he was extremely well-known and liked by everyone. This also meant he had to live up to that reputation. Because of this, and the fact Lou had a tremendous amount of charisma, virtually every night out would have a tale to tell.

We normally started our run ashore in the Crofton at Stubbington. The Crofton was the pub used by the underwater escape team and in turn adopted by the SAR Flight. In fact, we used the Crofton so regularly that it went in the phone book as the SAR annexe! Because of our shift system, you could almost guarantee that there would be someone from the flight in there during most of its opening hours.

This would make it sound as though we did not do anything other than drink when off duty and looking back now makes me wonder if that statement was not true. We certainly did waste a lot of time in the pubs and, on sunny days when the Crofton closed in the afternoon, we would hit the beach with a carry-out until the pub opened again.

The reason we chose the Crofton as the flight's local was because, like 'The Ship' in Portland, it had the prettiest barmaids and the tenants Dave and Janet would put up with our antics. The beer was probably quite reasonable as well.

This time when I came back after my time at Portland, a new barmaid called Margaret had started working there. I was immediately attracted to her. Lou had already checked her out and it seem she was dating a local fire fighter; however, after only a moment of fleeting eye contact, I felt sure that one day we would get together.

As a married man, although now separated and quite sure my marriage was over, I did not feel I had any right to try to interfere with Margaret's situation; if indeed there was any possibility that I could. I obviously had my own problems to sort out.

Around this time, I was really quite confused as to what my future held, or even what I wanted out of life. I knew I could not be happier career wise; however, as for my private life, I did not have a clue, so simply made the most of the situation as it was and enjoyed myself to the full. Fortunately, I was with a group of mates who were mostly in the same frame of mind.

Lou had a tremendous line of chat. His opening line when chatting up the girls went along the line of "Hello my name's Lou Armstrong perhaps you have heard of me? Navy sprinter, Navy rugby player, leading force in winning last year's field gun tournament and all round good egg." Although you could not get much cornier than that, it always got a response.

Occasionally he would say it in earshot of other people that knew him and had heard the line so often that they would back him up in unison, which often had an even greater effect. I was really quite introverted compared with Lou, which I expect helped these first impression situations. I feel sure if we had both been so flamboyant, the talent would have run a mile.

Over the next few months, our scrambles had been for varying types of incidents; capsized dinghies, injured crewmembers from yachts, more people stuck in the mud, missing sub aqua divers and cliff rescues. Most of these rescues had been reasonably straightforward and in good weather conditions.

The only ones that had presented any problem were the cliff rescues; we had quite a few of these, the majority at Culver Cliff on the Isle of Wight. The main cause of this was the easy access around the headland from Bembridge when the tide was out. When the tide came in there was no way back. The sensible ones would attract the attention of a passing boat who would normally alert the Coastguards and either the helicopter or a lifeboat would recover them.

Occasionally the odd one would decide to try to climb out, possibly trying to get help for the others still at the bottom of the cliff; it looked feasible to attempt this. The cliffs are approximately 250ft high and the first 100ft are easy to scramble up but beyond that, they are positively dangerous even with proper climbing equipment as not only do they get very sheer but also quite crumbly.

Over time the cliffs got so unstable as erosion took place that it became obvious that they were not safe to climb, which resulted in fewer people attempting it; however, back then it looked feasible hence the many jobs Culver cliff would create over the earlier years.

The result was nearly always the same, they would reach a certain point before realising they could go no further then find that it was extremely dangerous trying to climb back down. Fortunately, they would normally be spotted silhouetted against the white cliffs and seen by crews on fishing vessels, or small pleasure craft leaving or returning to Bembridge.

Rescuing them could prove quite hazardous, especially if they had reached the more sheer part of the cliffs. The aircraft only had 67ft of usable cable, so it was always touch-and-go as to how close to the cliff face the aircraft would be able to get, even with all the cable out. The winchman in these situations relied entirely on the skill of the winch operator and the pilot.

The pilot concentrating on the power in hand has to feel his way extremely slowly towards the cliff face whilst making continuous adjustments on the collective lever in his left hand which controls the power and which in turn provides adjustments to the aircraft's height. The cyclic stick in his right hand, in conjunction with the power changes on the collective, allow forward, backward and sideways movements. His feet control the yaw peddles to move the tail of the helicopter to the left or right. In the Whirlwind any movement on one control required a counter-movement on the others, particularly in the slow manoeuvres and the hover.

This was rather like trying to pat your head with one hand, carry out circular movements on your chest with the other while carrying out the Irish jig with your feet. This situation was even more precarious close to cliffs because of the downdraughts, up-draughts and wind circulation caused by the cliffs themselves. In addition to this, the pilot has to rely on the winch operator's verbal con to edge him as close to the cliff as possible.

As the winch operator cons the aircraft towards the cliff, he is keeping a good eye on the tips of the blades, the tail rotor and the winchman who by now may be 67ft below the aircraft. At times, because of the limited length of cable, the winch operator would con the aircraft as close to the cliff as he could possibly go, then try to swing the winchman towards the casualty.

With my second cliff rescue this proved to be the case. The helicopter was as close as it could go but this still left me on the end of the wire approximately 5ft short. The casualty was on a very tiny ledge and the winch operator, Denis Kermode, was able to induce a swing on the wire until I was able to get a foothold on the ledge. In those situations, I had to learn to put my fears behind me. It can feel extremely daunting to look down to see jagged rocks 100ft or so below. Looking up I would focus on the blade tips, often having a better view of these than the winch operator as it can be very deceptive judging the blade tips by looking horizontally from the door.

Watching the blade tips move closer to the cliff, you simply pray that they keep that small gap between safety and potential disaster. Once on the cliff face as with all the rescue situations all the fears seem to disappear and you do what is necessary to conduct the actual rescue. As soon as the casualty is in the strop or stretcher, the helicopter will winch you off then slowly move away from the cliff, descending when safe to do so, aiming to keep the winchman and the casualty at a safe height over the ground or water as the winch operator winches in.

The other problem often faced, particularly in the cliff situation is the wind direction. A helicopter is more stable when pointing into wind, particularly at slower speeds. In simple terms, the wind bears an exact relationship with the aircraft's speed. If a fixed wing aircraft takes off flying directly into a 30 mph wind it will require less distance on the runway to achieve take off flying speed than in a nil wind situation. If that aircraft's normal take off speed was 90 mph it would be capable of taking off at only 60 mph ground speed.

If that same aircraft took off downwind, which of course would be foolhardy, it would now require 120 mph ground speed to take off, requiring a greater take-off distance on the runway. In addition, in the event of an emergency such as an engine failure, the pilot would have less time to react and would soon run out of runway. Hence the reason for all take-offs and landings being carried out to the runway that provides the best headwind.

The fixed wing aircraft has flaps to control the airflow. For example, when landing the aircraft the pilot wants to be descending close to the minimum safe speed required to remain airborne. To achieve this, the power is reduced to the propeller and the flaps lowered to increase drag on the wing and the aircraft descends. When taking off, the power can be increased and the flaps slowly raised, reducing the drag as the aircraft gains speed and climbs.

A helicopter operates under the same principle; however to climb or descend the pilot will increase or decrease the lift generated by altering the pitch of the blades, which in turn requires an increase or decrease in power from the engine. All hovering or slow manoeuvres would normally be carried out into wind since it is a phenomenon of helicopter rotors that a headwind actually decreases the amount of power required for the helicopter to remain in the hover.

The worst situation for us would be nil wind conditions or having to attempt a rescue facing downwind when occasionally, dependant on the weight of the aircraft at the time; we would not have enough power to stay in the hover. In these situations all we could do to lighten the load was to land on and remove equipment since we did not have a fuel jettison facility in the Whirlwind.

The problem in the rescue situation is that we can't always guarantee the luxury of being able to hover into wind. The pilot and the winching position were on the right hand side, meaning we always had to approach with the right side of the aircraft facing the cliff.

Fortunately, the prevailing wind in the south of England is south-westerly, which often gave us a favourable wind for the cliff jobs and allowed us to approach with the helicopter roughly into wind. On the odd occasion, the wind would be from a north or north-easterly direction; this would prove to be nothing short of a nightmare. In these situations, we would land on the top of the cliff and empty the heavier items of equipment such as life raft and diving equipment before moving in to attempt the rescue.

On another cliff winching occasion, Bill Fewtrell was the pilot and Denis Kermode the winch operator. I was in my usual position, looking up at the aircraft blades from the end of the wire. We were in a down-wind situation and had already off loaded equipment to try to gain enough power for the rescue. This time it was taking a considerable amount of time to edge in towards the cliff, which again was extremely disconcerting dangling on the end of the wire above the rocks.

As the blades were getting closer to the cliffs, I felt the aircraft descending and my heart was in my throat. If it was likely the aircraft was going to ditch the winch operator and pilot both had a button they could press that would fire a bolt through the cable to jettison the winchman.

That is not so bad over the water but, from this height over rocks, I would not have stood a chance. I just prayed they would not touch that button until the last minute because I was convinced we were ditching.

As it happened, Bill had completely run out of power and was not able to remain in the hover; he had been using all his well-practiced skills attempting to get close to the cliff when suddenly the aircraft started to sink through lack of power. He was obviously aware of my situation on the end of the wire and had dropped away as gently as he could in the circumstances, diving away from the cliff at the same time as turning into wind, until he gained the wind-assisted lift. Bill was in full control and confident he could fly out of the situation while keeping me clear of the ground, but obviously had to react quicker than he could explain to Denis.

Denis in the meantime had also thought we were ditching and had seriously considered pressing the button. He would have tried to wait until the last moment to give me a fighting-chance; at least a better chance than the aircraft landing on top of me. Fortunately, everything was back in control before he had been able to react to that decision.

This time we landed back on the cliff top, emptied everything out of the back, burnt off a little more fuel (as we were already down to what we considered our minimum) and managed successfully to lift the casualty.

That evening Denis and I had a few extra beers and even Bill joined us for a couple before going home. We were completely subdued as, for the first time I reflected on how many variants there were in conducting a rescue. Until now, I had not really thought too much about the pilot's role and the problems he faced. To be honest I had not fully understood the power problem at all. Bill had certainly used all his skills to recover from that situation, while maintaining enough height to keep me from coming into contact with the ground.

Crew Photograph

Dave Peel,   Denis Kermode,   Bill Fewtrell

Winch Transfer 'Whirlwind Mk 9' (Photo - Mick Rowsell)

Diver drop from Whirlwind

Lou Armstrong leaning through the window giving the pilot the instructions required to remain in stable hover and height while engineers sort a problem on the undercarriage.

Crew Green Endorsement given for one of the early cliff rescues (1973)
Lieutenant W. J. T. FEWTRELL

LREM D. J. KERMODE D066751P
A/Petty Officer D. R. PEEL D065673T
SAR Flight HMS Daedalus

On 24th August 1973, information was received from Bembridge Coastguard that a boy was stranded on Culver Cliff, Isle of Wight.

The SAR helicopter from Daedalus was scrambled and the casualty was located uninjured but in a dangerous position on a ledge under an overhang. As it appeared that other assistance would not be available for some time the decision was made to attempt the rescue by helicopter.

All excess SAR equipment was off-loaded on the cliff top and a downwind hover, dictated by the circumstances, established adjacent to the boy. LREM KERMODE then lowered Petty Officer PEEL to the full length of the cable whilst conning Lt FEWTRELL towards the cliff face. The length of cable wire was just sufficient to enable the rotors to clear the overhang giving enough tip clearance from the cliff face to allow PO PEEL to place a strop around the boy. A successful double lift was then completed.

This operation demonstrated the highest standards of crew co-operation and individual skills.

Cliff Rescue Culver Cliff Isle of Wight

**Recovering 2 young men from small ledge 100 ft above cliff bottom
(Photo Mick Rowsell)**

Safely on top (Photo Mick Rowsell)

Pre-Flight Brief

Dave Peel   Clary Gear   Geoff Sutcliffe   Bill Fewtrell

'Whirlwind' with Selsey Lifeboat
(Photo © Motor Boat & Yachting / IPC+ Syndication)

Diver Drop session from the 'Wessex Mk 1' at Portland

taking advantage of the rough seas in the Portland races

In June of that year, my Petty Officer's rate came through quite unexpectedly; I was not expecting it for another six months or more. This brought quite a change in lifestyle with many extra privileges and a considerable increase in pay. In addition, it meant a change of uniform from the square rig with its bell-bottom trousers to a uniformed suit. I also had to move accommodation to the Petty Officers' mess, which was more plush than my previous accommodation.

I had quite a time adjusting to this because there was no one on the flight in the PO's mess so I had no friends to mix with. The senior rates' messes had their own bar facilities and had extremely good socials. Unfortunately, my best friends were not allowed into these functions. In one swoop I was supposed to be isolated from Lou and the other aircrewmen; they were allowed to invite me into the NAAFI, but this was frowned upon if done too often.

One of the benefits of our job was we never had to wear uniform; therefore, it was quite a while before anyone in the junior rates' mess realised I had been promoted, so I got away with joining the rest of the team there. Eventually someone did complain and the president of the Petty Officers' mess gave me a warning; if I did not want to be a Senior Rate, he could arrange that.

After that, I would meet up with Lou ashore. I never managed to settle in that mess as our shift routine was so different to everyone else; it was actually quite difficult mixing with anyone other than people from the flight. The situation was quite strange: when I was a seaman I had looked forward to picking up my PO's rate and the privileges that would come with it. Now it seemed less important as I was enjoying my job too much and that was as far ahead as I could see at the time.

I still had this attraction to Margaret in the Crofton; I now knew she was divorced with a three-year-old daughter and living with her father in Stubbington. She had taken this job to meet people her own age as she had spent the previous 18 months feeling isolated after her marriage break up and her move to Stubbington to live with her father. She had met her boyfriend through the job and seemed quite content with life. I still felt I had no right to attempt to interfere in this situation but still had an attraction towards her.

I had a few dates over the coming months, but strangely enough, I rarely took these dates to the Crofton. On the odd occasions when I did turn up with a date and, if Margaret was in the bar, I would have one drink and move elsewhere. Obviously, my date would never know why but, such was my attraction for Margaret, I felt I was two-timing her even though we were not an item.

I apologise for the next account, very irresponsible for someone in my role and I was extremely lucky to get away with it. I still recall it as though it happened yesterday and an important lesson in responsibility, something I had a complete lack of that night.

In the August of 1973, Lou Armstrong was due to join a commando squadron at Yeovilton. The day he was due to leave we decided to have a few drinks in the Crofton before he travelled down to Yeovil. This turned into a session that nearly got us both into serious trouble.

We started the session after coming off watch at midday. We had a few pints in the Crofton, remaining there until closing time. Lou then decided he would leave in the morning about 6 am to get him to Yeovilton for 8 am when he was due to be there. We moved on to a restaurant that had a side bar and used to allow us to have a few drinks out of hours. We were meant to have a meal, but they were quite happy to serve us drinks providing we had a sandwich.

After that, we decided we would make a night of it and go to a social in the Chief Petty Officers' mess. The social was in aid of St Dunstan's week.

St Dunstan's week was when the Fleet Air Arm field gun crew entertained ex-serviceman who had become blind or had severely impaired sight due to either injury or illness. At that time many of them had been blinded in the Second World War.

The event took place annually after the Earls Court field gun tournament; the field gunners put a lot of time and effort into providing a week of entertainment for the St Dunstaners. It always took place during the camp's leave period so that they could be accommodated on site; the St Dunstaners lived in the Petty Officers' mess with a volunteer field gunner attached to small groups of them to act as full-time guides.

Throughout the week, many activities were arranged: sporting events; sailing; flights in gliders and helicopters; trips to sea in auxiliary boats plus plenty of drinking. Lou, being an ex field gunner, had acted as one of the guides the previous year and had volunteered our help this year, which we had been doing throughout that week in between duties. The social in the Chiefs' mess was for the St Dunstaners and the field gun helpers. This particular night we thought we had a head start on them as we had been drinking most of the afternoon.

Not a chance! This group seemed to be well ahead of us, having themselves had a long session in the bar that afternoon, because heavy rain had curtailed their activities. They would take pride in drinking us under the table. Throughout the evening small challenges had been going on between the St Dunstaners and the guides until we were all well-oiled and not too sure what was happening.

Around midnight, Lou and I had a minor disagreement over who could run the faster. Lou was a sprinter and at that time I had been doing quite a lot of long distance running and felt sure I could beat him on a run around the airfield, just under three miles. Egged on by the St Dunstaners, off we went – the last back would buy the drinks for our group.

Once we got outside, we found the airfield was in thick fog. We did not take any notice of this and set off, Lou at a great speed until I lost sight of him in the fog. About a mile further on I caught sight of him again and caught up. We ran side by side for a while but Lou, who had more competitive spirit than anyone I had ever known, eventually sprinted off again. I kept at my pace, convinced he would soon burn himself out and that I would catch him up again.

I did not see him again until I got to the finish. I had followed the grass verge, which, although I had not realised it at the time, took me down the disused runway knocking a couple of hundred yards of the perimeter track, so found I was first back. I thought I must have passed Lou in the fog so was feeling pleased with myself as I waited for Lou to come running out of the mist.

Lou had stuck to the perimeter track, although I am not sure how in the fog that night but it was clear he had, Lou considered I had cheated, accusing me of such and we had a flaming row that ended in us having a punch up on the perimeter track; no one else around just the two of us. Fortunately, as I do not know what we would have done to each other and I am quite sure I would have come off worst, the Naval Patrol doing their security rounds broke us up. They had come across us fighting; in fact, they nearly ran us over as they were late seeing us in the fog and, at that time of night, they would not have expected anyone to be on the airfield.

This was to be our first piece of fortune that night as, under normal circumstances, a patrol would have taken us straight back to the main gate and charged us.

As we were both to blame I am convinced we would have both lost our rates. Instead, the patrol, realising the implications of the situation if they reported us, accepted that we would sort it out sensibly between us and they dropped us back at the Chiefs' mess, much to the amusement of the St Dunstaners who calmed us down and made us settle on being quits.

However, we were still sizzling inside and started arguing again, leading to another set-to in the mess. The mess president was threatening to call the patrol back; the group of St Dunstaners talked him out of it by expressing that they had egged us on in the first place. (That was our second piece of fortune for the night).

Lou and I decided enough was enough and we drove back to the flight in Lou's beaten up old Austin 1800. We drove in a straight line back to the flight, straight across the centre of the airfield, in thick fog.

The following day we realised the white marks on the newly dented Austin's door had come from a football post in the middle of the airfield which we must have bounced off; the post was broken and had collapsed. Our third piece of fortune that night was that, not only did we escape any injury when we hit the post but the authorities never found out who did it, probably because Lou had left the camp before anyone realised the football post had been knocked down.

I feel sure the patrol that had been on duty that night would have had their suspicions, but could not say anything because they had not reported the previous incident involving the pair of us. At the time, we thought this drive across the airfield in the fog was great fun. I can think back now to what sort of havoc we could have created had we gone out on to the open road, not very clever at all.

I was duty diver in the morning, so had less than three hours sleep ahead of me before first light and turned in immediately. I was going to wake Lou about 5:30 so that he could leave for Yeovil.

Again, looking back, it was ridiculous drinking so close to going on duty and would be completely frowned upon these days and quite rightly so. Lou and I had already demonstrated the effects of booze more than once that night.

The arrangement for commencing duty was that, if you lived at home, you had to be back at the flight thirty minutes before sunrise. If you slept at the flight, either the aircrewman or diver was to be up at first light to sign on with the Coastguards and operate the radios.

The duty pilot, Bill Fewtrell, who had come in from home, tried to shake me to operate the radios, as was the arrangement and it was my turn.

Only, in my mind, I was sure I had developed some contagious disease and assured him he had to keep away from me. Bill persisted in trying to wake me out of whatever fixation I had in my head when I suddenly sat bolt upright asking him to return my head, which I was now convinced had fallen off as I could see it on the floor! Bill was not quite sure what to do in the situation and went through the motions of picking up my head and replacing it on my shoulders.

I settled down again and went back to sleep. Bill in the meantime decided he would leave me in bed for a while longer and shook Denis Kermode who stood in and manned the radios. Bill thought that, if the worst came to the worst, he could wake Lou to stand in for me, he did not realise Lou was nearly as bad as me.

About two hours later Bill thought he had better check if I was all right and, of course, whether I was capable of carrying out my duty. At this stage, he must have been considerably concerned as to whether he should have had me relieved immediately, but now it was rather late, as questions may have been asked as to why he had not reported me initially.

He brought me a cup of coffee, hoping that would wake me. Unfortunately, I was on a second bunk and, although I accepted the coffee, I dropped it on the engineer who was in the bunk below. He leapt out of bed screaming abuse at me, which I sorted out with one punch and immediately went right back to sleep. Poor old Bill had a real problem on his hands: he now had an engineer who wanted me reported.

Lou, who had woken up in the kafuffle, had talked the engineer out of reporting me; Lou would normally get his way. (This was my fourth piece of fortune that night). Bill then decided that they would attempt to shock me into a state of alertness. He informed the others there would be a practice scramble and set off the alarm. The next thing I knew I had leapt out of bed, rushed out to the aircraft wearing only my underpants, finding myself sitting on the step of the aircraft attempting to put my fins on. I quickly sobered up after that.

Later Bill took me aside and explained the position I had put him in. It was only because he felt I had previously shown above-average dedication to the job and that he was sure this situation was a one-off that he did not take it further. Knowing the consequences if he had reported me made him take the decision not to. If he had, once again, I would have certainly been busted and it could even have been the end of my career.

On top of this, for the rest of the watch I was in complete agony. Not just from the hangover but the sole of my right foot was one complete blister; the run in the early hours of the morning had been carried out in my bare feet as I found the shoes I was wearing too uncomfortable to run in.

I learned an awful lot from that completely irresponsible episode and certainly realised how Bill and others had put their heads on the line. I knew I would never allow myself to get in that position again prior to a duty.

I had a few other apologies to make: one to the president of the Chiefs mess who banned me from functions for six months, one to the president of my mess for letting the side down (my second to him in the short period I had been in the mess) and finally to the engineer I had thumped. I could not believe I had done that, so felt extremely fortunate that he accepted the apology. After that, I knew I had to settle down.

Lou, who should have joined Yeovilton at eight-o-clock that morning, rang Yeovilton explaining that he would not be arriving until the afternoon, saying he had been required to stand in for someone taken ill. He could only hope that they would accept this situation without checking up and fortunately they did.

We both knew how lucky we had been and parted best of pals. The next time we met up, a few years later, we had both remarried and were considerably more sensible; however, I hope not to the point of being boring.

The rescues carried out over the next few months were all reasonably straightforward. The silly season between April and August, when we had the majority of jobs, was over. The rescues over the winter months would normally involve larger vessels getting into difficulty in the rougher seas, the smaller vessels being laid up for the winter. We did several medical evacuations from cross channel ferries and larger yachts and several searches for vessels overdue, which were usually found safe and sound.

Things were rather quiet since Lou left, until one night when I spent most of the evening at the Crofton with Denis Kermode and another aircrewman called 'Willy' Lines. Margaret was working behind the bar and had made a comment that things were not quite right between her and her boyfriend. I had not picked up on that comment straight away, but it obviously niggled away in the back of my mind. We went from the Crofton to have a quick pint back at the base before the NAAFI bar shut, which was half an hour after the pubs ashore.

I was sitting enjoying this last pint when I suddenly realised that, if I really wanted a date with Margaret, I should have made it clear that night. I just got up, leaving the rest of my pint and told Denis "I have something to do." Denis said "She will have already gone home Dave."

I was a little taken back as to how he had guessed what was on my mind, as it hadn't been a topic of conversation that night, although he had known for a long time that I had a crush on Margaret. I simply said, "We'll see," gave them a grin and disappeared. I arrived at the Crofton just as Margaret was pulling out of the car park with Ena, another barmaid, who was giving Margaret a lift home.

Ena had worked at the Crofton all the time I had been going there and was a favourite with the flight. She also knew I had a crush on Margaret and had decided we were right for each other. Ena, on seeing my car pull in stopped and (before Margaret realised what was going on) had coaxed her out of the car and started to drive away.

Margaret, a little dumbfounded, walked across to my car and got in. I apologised for my cheek and asked which restaurant she would like to go to. She thought Ena had planned this with me and was quite angry with her. I did not care what she thought at the time, she was now in the car and it was obvious we were going to discuss the situation over a meal. We ended up talking most the night.

The following night she went out with her boyfriend as she had told me she would and that she was not going to start two timing him. I was not sure what the result was going to be but, when I rang the following night, I was expecting Margaret to say that she would not be coming out with me. This was not the case; she had explained the situation to her boyfriend and had finished with him. We had become an item.

Margaret had even explained the situation to her father because she did not want any messing around pretending one thing and doing something else. I picked Margaret up from home that night and met her father and Kerry (her daughter) straight away. Over the next few months, we spent all our spare time together. All Ena could say was "why didn't this happen months ago?"

Shortly after Margaret and I had become an item, I received a draft to '848 squadron' at Yeovilton. It was to be as a SAR diver attached to the squadron, but I had to go to Yeovilton after Christmas to carry out the Commando Aircrewman's course.

I was not very happy about this at all; I had expected to stay at Lee-on-Solent for about two years, which was rather naïve of me as I had been lucky to go straight to an SAR Flight in the first place. I would be joining '707 Squadron' in January for a commando conversion course, then back to Lee SAR for a few months before joining '848 Squadron' in June.

That Christmas Margaret, Kerry and I stayed with friends in Plymouth so that I could spend some time with my children David and Matthew. This was the first opportunity for Margaret to meet my boys and was quite a difficult time with many emotions passing between us all.

The situation was obviously difficult for the children. David was seven years old and Matthew was five. They enjoyed the outings and Kerry loved having them around but there was a considerable element of confusion as to what was really happening.

Margaret, on meeting my children, felt a tremendous amount of guilt as she thought that, if she was to finish with me, I might be able to reconcile with my wife. She was willing and even tried to end our relationship for the sake of the children but I knew without a shadow of doubt that my marriage was over. It was a terrible time with awful guilt over what was happening, but the one thing clear in my mind was my marriage was over and, whether I was with Margaret or anyone else, it would not change that fact. Eventually Margaret came to understand that and we did manage to sort out the problems.

Part 2

Operational Roles

The Commando Aircrewman Course

I commenced my course at Yeovilton on the 7th January. My instructors were Bob Niblock and Tony Gerrard. There were five course members including Carl Fairbrother who was one of my instructors in basic training.

The main elements of this course were many hours spent honing map reading skills, load lifting, controlling the aircraft into confined areas and on to rough or sloping ground, mountain flying and the control of troops entering and leaving the aircraft in varying roles.

Tasking in the commando role would be to insert troops at a given reference point often flying as low and fast as possible then, once at your destination, despatch or pick up the troops as quickly as possible. The map reading was extremely difficult as you had to carry this out looking through the door facing backwards. The helicopters we used were the Wessex Mk 5, which was the same airframe as the aircraft used for my basic training, only it had the luxury of two engines.

The Aircrewman could not look forward as the cockpit area was raised above the cabin of the aircraft. Under normal operations it was single pilot and the pilot needed to keep his wits about him, concentrating on what was ahead, especially when low level looking out for wires and other hazards. He really could not spend too much time looking at maps.

We achieved the map reading by the aircrewman following a line on a map and verbally transferring what the pilot should be seeing in front of him. For example, "You have a village coming up two miles ahead with a road passing north to south through the centre of the village and a church with a steeple to the southeast of the village. To the southwest of the village there is a disused railway leading into a valley. We will be following the disused railway into the valley for two miles until we sight a forest on the ridgeline. Our pick up point will be the north-westerly point of this forest." The pilot will be confirming that he can see whatever the aircrewman is describing.

Often the picture the aircrewman was painting simply did not match up with what the pilot could see. We would very quickly get hopelessly lost and would have to fly around until we found some prominent feature and start again. Not very clever being low-level and lost as we were then completely unaware of where the wires and pylons were.

Fortunately, during the early part of training, we had an instructor in the back. Many of the flights would also have a trainee pilot who also had a flying instructor with him. Even with the backup, we occasionally got lost and it was clear to see why a considerable amount of practice was required in low flying techniques to make it safe.

We carried out the confined areas training in a specially-prepared cut-out area in a group of trees at Merryfield, a disused airfield close to Yeovilton. This was just big enough for the aircraft to land in and required a lot of juggling of the aircraft with movements left and right and pivoting the tail to port or starboard as we conned the pilot down. The pilot had to carry out the manoeuvres precisely as we stated as he could only see ahead and to the right.

Quite a few aircraft over the years suffered blade strikes in this clearing, a few suffering serious damage. Fortunately, the Wessex had blade tips designed to break off if they skimmed anything. Although this would put the aircraft considerably out of balance, you could at least land safely without too much damage to the aircraft. The noise created when flying with the tips missing was something else and could be heard from miles away; assuring a welcoming committee of people that knew another crew had messed up.

We operated from RAF Valley for our mountain flying training. The training, which was carried out in the Snowdonia mountains, involved making approaches and landings (when possible) on ridges, tops of mountains, in bowls and in valleys. All these situations had their own problems because of the varying wind forces found in mountainous terrain. As aircrewmen, we had an important input to the final stages of a landing.

The mountain training was even more important for the trainee pilots, who had to learn to respect this environment and to learn how to assess the wind forces and approaches; there really was no room for error, if they got it wrong it could easily be their last mistake.

Time was also spent on firing ranges in South Wales, the pilots firing their two-inch rockets against tanks and the aircrewman firing the general-purpose machine gun at targets from the back of the aircraft. Quite good fun but there were not too many hits on target. However, I feel sure it would have forced the enemy to keep their heads down as bullets went everywhere.

Load lifting was carried out mainly at Merryfield; under slung loads such as Land Rovers, field guns and netted supplies were picked up then a circuit was flown and the load positioned as close as possible to a given point.

The verbal con for this was much the same as for winching except the load could not be winched to the ground. The aircraft had to be conned down verbally by the aircrewman very slowly until the load touched the deck. The load was attached to a strop of varying lengths, depending on the type of load and terrain. The other end of this strop was attached to a cargo hook suspended from four strong points underneath the aircraft.

The cargo hook had a quick release mechanism which was operated by the pilot pressing an electronic release button on instruction from the aircrewman. There was also a manual release system as a backup if that failed. Flying around with a load had the potential to make the helicopter considerably unstable. The aircrewman would keep his eye on the load throughout the flight, very uncomfortable on long flights as it meant lying on the floor with your head and shoulders out of the aircraft door. If there were any signs of the load starting to swing, the aircrewman would instruct the pilot to reduce speed until the load was stable.

Occasionally, the load would become so unstable that it would endanger the helicopter and the only option was to jettison the load. Fortunately, this did not happen too often as continuous calculations were carried out to take account of the aircraft weight including crew, equipment and fuel. The calculations were used to work out the maximum weight of a load to be lifted. Under normal circumstances, the logistic ground crews had the load prepared for maximum stability and at defined weights.

One thing we had to watch out for, not under the training environment but out in the field, was less experienced marines who when ordered to strip down Land Rovers (remove doors, spare wheel and other panels etc.)

to reduce the weight to the maximum we could lift would sometimes put the equipment in the back of the same vehicle!

Five days of the course was spent at the Royal Marines Barracks, Lympstone, instructing the Royal Marines under training in troop drills and fast deployment from helicopters, both on the ground and in areas that the helicopter could not land. If the aircraft could not land, the marines had to practice fast deployment abseiling or sliding down ropes.

We also had to complete a short course under the instruction of the Marines as our future in this role would be to operate with them, often out in the field. This was not too bad; it included lectures on essential equipment for living in the field and survival techniques. The course backed up and built on the lessons taught on aircrew survival courses.

We finished our part of the course by carrying out the infamous endurance and assault course, wearing just standard combat gear, (the Marines have to complete the course wearing backpacks and carrying their rifle). I could clearly see how much more difficult that would be; however, it was still met with some trepidation by some of our chaps, as part of the course meant crawling through a short pipe that was under water.

There were a few longer underground pipes not underwater and I found these to be the most awkward; crawling over mud and loose stones inside these pipes played havoc with our elbows and knees. I feel the Marines must have had some technique for crawling through these as they had to do it so often, but they assured me they did not. My theory is the Marines are not as broad in the shoulder as they always appear; it is simply that this is where they keep their knee and elbow pads until needed for these crawling exercises.

The course terminated with a week's exercise on Dartmoor and Bodmin Moor, living in field conditions on exercise with the Marines. This was tied in with the passing out exercise for one of the marine courses; the exercise would involve all our newly learned skills during day and night field conditions.

The course was really good value and I feel sure, under normal circumstances, had I not been miffed at having to leave the SAR flight, I would have loved every minute of it; however, I did eventually settle down to the course realising this was the very best of flying. The flying proved to be the most exiting possible in a helicopter, with low flying in the varying terrain and the wide variety of tasking we would get. In addition, I was quite sure that, between the commando tours, I would go back to SAR.

On completion of this course, I rejoined Lee SAR for a few months before joining '848 Squadron'. It was great to be back.

Margaret and I were positively committed to each other; the time apart had not altered anything. She knew I would be away again soon, but seemed to accept this. My divorce was well under way but it would not have been practical for Margaret to come to Yeovil with me. I still had considerable financial commitments until my marital situation was finalised, so was not in a position to set up a second home. In addition, I would be away on exercise for the majority of the time I was to be on the squadron.

The rescues during this short stay at Lee had been bread and butter work, searching for missing persons and locating vessels that had put out distress calls or fired flares. Often the searches were because vessels had broken down, not necessarily in immediate danger but if not located quickly the situation could change rapidly, especially if the sea got up and the vessel was not equipped for the open sea. It does not take long to drift from what would seem to be the relative safe Solent area out to unsheltered waters.

In these situations, we would be scrambled on almost any red flare sightings or distress calls over the radio. It would not be known if the casualty was in severe danger or not. Invariably, there would be a search involved in finding the vessel, which we could carry out very much faster than surface vessels. If the casualty was not in immediate danger, we would direct a lifeboat on to the vessel, the lifeboat crew would take the vessel in tow and assess if any further assistance would be required.

One of the exercises carried out on our training flights was to practice auto-rotations. This was the method of landing in the event of an engine failure, which the pilots practised regularly. The whirlwind was a single engine aircraft and as the majority of our flying was carried out low level, it meant that the pilot had to react almost spontaneously to gain control and land safely if that engine failed.

Many people are under the impression that if a helicopter has an engine failure it will simply fall out of the sky, unlike an aeroplane that can glide and, providing a flat clear surface can be found, will land safely.

In a single engine helicopter, if the engine fails the pilot can put the aircraft into auto rotation, rather like the sycamore seed (often termed as the spinning Jenny). The blades continue to turn and the pilot can still control the aircraft, although the control will of course be in the descent with the rate of descent dependent on the wind strength and type of helicopter. The pilot has to assess the situation quickly, while looking for a piece of flat ground clear of obstructions and wires.

He also needs to assess the surface wind, the aim being to land facing into wind, at 0 speed and 0 feet. At the last moment as the aircraft starts to feel its own cushion of air, the pilot flares the aircraft, pulling up on the collective and back on the cyclic, altering the pitch of the blades to catch the maximum air and washing off the forward speed. When the speed is washed off, he pushes the cyclic forward to level the helicopter, letting down reasonably smoothly and sinking through its own ground cushion.

Unfortunately, the Whirlwind did not have a very good record regarding engine failures and quite a few of the members of our team at Lee had been involved in ditching due to engine failure. Terry Short had been involved in two, one on land in which the aircraft turned over leaving the crew badly shaken, and one over water that had required an underwater evacuation.

Terry's first ditching, putting aside the seriousness of the situation, was actually quite comical. He was sitting in the door of his Wessex helicopter (the single engine version), in the plane guard position during a fixed wing launching on an aircraft carrier, when he heard "Mayday, Mayday, Mayday". Terry shouted, "Did you hear that boss? One of the aircraft's ditching!" The last thing Terry heard just prior to swapping his headset for his face mask and preparing himself for a rescue was "Yes you idiot: it's us!" The next thing Terry knew, he had been forced back inside the aircraft by the influx of water, the helicopter was upside down and the underside of an aircraft carrier was skimming alongside. Terry felt he was the lucky one – at least he had a diving set on. Fortunately, the pilot and aircrewman remained calm until the carrier had passed and they all made a successful escape.

Terry had a second incident not long after while carrying out a map reading exercise round Dorset, this time in a Whirlwind helicopter (again a single engine aircraft) when the engine failed. Terry knew where the Mayday had come from this time. They were flying over the famous white horse on the hill at the time which was unfortunate because the aircraft landed on the sloping hillside and rolled–over, beating itself to death but, fortunately, again the crew got out safely without serious injury.

Because of the Whirlwind engines' rather poor reliability record we used to practice the engine off procedures regularly, the aim always being to chose and then arrive at a safe, flat site. Judging the distance, height, rate of descent and speed took some practice. Sometimes the whole sortie was dedicated to auto rotations from different heights and configurations, with quite an emphasis on low-level rejections.

On normal training flights, the aircrewman would initiate a practice engine failure, trying to catch the pilot unaware. Just a verbal instruction and the pilot would lower the collective to simulate the engine failure and search for a convenient spot to land, line the helicopter into wind and pull in the power at a safe height to recover to the hover, at which point we would decide whether we would have been able to land safely or not. If we were over the airfield, and providing he could receive ATC clearance in time, he would pick a spot on the airfield to aim to land on and complete the landing with the engine off rather than coming to the hover. Always the aim was to see how close he could get to the point he had chosen.

The SAR Flight at Lee was to lose two Whirlwind's during the early years. The first ditched in the Solent when a malfunction occurred with the engine whilst it was on the way to a rescue at Culver cliff. The helicopter turned over and sank. The crew, John Dransfield, Sam Lawson and Derek Oakes, had to make an underwater escape. This was a low-level occurrence and justified our practice of low-level engine failures, as the pilot was able to react quickly enough to wash off the speed and turn the situation into a survivable ditching. The helicopter was never recovered.

The second incident involved an engine failure on the approach to Lee airfield. Again, the incident happened while flying low-level and the pilot managed to land on a small piece of grass between the perimeter fence and the main road outside the camp. On this occasion, the tail was ripped off but the crew got out safely.

Occasionally, during training trips, we would take one or two passengers with us on familiarisation flights. They would normally be service personnel who were considering entering the flying world, or Coastguards and lifeboatmen who we could familiarise with the problems from our side. Occasionally we would take W.R.E.N.S., mainly because a member of the crew was trying to impress, and these were also logged as familiarisation flights.

On one of these flights, we had two very attractive WRENS on board, arranged by a pilot who was dating one of the girls. There would usually be a certain element of showing off the aircraft's abilities, the helicopter being thrown around a little more than perhaps was required, and we would always carry out an auto rotation or two as these were impressive to a passenger. We would of course, pre-warn them because the sudden descent in the initial stages came as a shock, forcing your heart into your throat.

Invariably on these flights, because we only had three proper seats, one of the back seat crew would sit on the sill in the doorway, with his feet on the step. When sat in the doorway we had a dispatcher harness attached around our waist with the other end secured to a strong point in the aircraft.

When we landed after this particular flight, one of the Wrens said she thought I was extremely brave, since on this occasion it was I who was sitting in the doorway. She had been worried throughout the trip that I was going to fall out, especially with all the manoeuvres we had been doing. I immediately turned round to demonstrate that the dispatcher harness would prevent me from falling out when I realised it was not there; I had carried out the whole flight without the harness attached. That turned me rather pale; I had forgotten one of the crucial safety checks that by now should be second nature to me. Another valuable lesson learned regarding complacency.

848 Squadron

I joined '848 Squadron' in May 1974 and found the first few months quite hard work. I felt that rather more was expected of me than I was capable of. The problem as I saw it was that because I was a Petty Officer the pilots tended to think I had been aircrew for years. This would have been a normal assumption, except that I had come into flying rather late and promoted as a seaman, not aircrew.

This was one of the problems which resulted from the aircrew branch being a secondary qualification. I was one of the senior aircrewmen, even though I had been flying for a relatively short period. We had twenty aircrewmen on the squadron, sixteen of them junior rates and most of them had been flying longer than I had. Some of them had been flying for over ten years, but had not been able to gain advancement because that would have meant them leaving flying and going back to their initial branch.

The situation was soon to be rectified; Jan Greener (my course officer on basic flying training) and the CO of the aircrewman school Lt Cdr Frazer had both been campaigning on the aircrewmens' behalf for a recognised aircrewman branch. All their hard work on behalf of the crewmen was reaching fruition, resulting in the aircrewman's branch being formed later that year. It would still be a sideways entry branch, which meant selection of recruits from other branches in the Navy but, on qualifying, the aircrewman would automatically become a leading rate and have the chance of future advancement by qualification within the branch.

This meant the possibility of a quick jump up the promotion ladder for many volunteers, providing they passed the course. In my case and a few others in my position, it meant that we would have to carry out another Petty Officer's qualifying course This time the course would be set in advanced aircrewman's studies.

The course would be a pass or fail. If I passed I would keep my rate, but as a Petty Officer Aircrewman not Petty Officer Seaman. If I failed I would have a choice: either I could stay flying by reverting to Leading Aircrewman and then go through the normal promotion procedures, (which would probably take five or more years to get back to being a senior rate) or alternatively, I could remain as a senior rate and leave flying altogether, returning to my previous parent branch.

I enjoyed this way of life far more than that of my parent branch so had decided that even if I failed, I would stay in the aircrew branch. The drop in pay would not be too bad because our additional flying pay and SAR diving pay was greater than the difference between a leading rate and senior rate and I really enjoyed the flying.

With this course in mind, and knowing I would be on one of the first Petty Officer aircrewman's courses, I realised I had to try and pick up enough knowledge as quickly as possible if I was to have a fighting chance of passing. I now realised how lucky I had been to get this draft to '848 Squadron' as, with the role being so varied, it was to help me gain experience in almost all of the aircrewman skills that would be expected of me on the Petty Officers' course.

Fortunately, as was my experience on all the squadrons I was to serve on, everyone seemed to knit together very well. It was never difficult to get help when I was unsure of something, which was quite often. I really was thrown in at the deep end, as were all the new members of the team.

Each morning we were given our training programme, perhaps sent off on a training sortie, possibly with a newly qualified pilot who was as green as I was. Half an hour later we could be flying around Dartmoor trying to reach a number of reference points, often just about muddling through. I felt at times that it was like the blind leading the blind.

I Soon realised that I was not the only one who had gone through this learning curve. Quite often we would head off on formation navigation exercises and take it in turn to be the lead helicopter. On these exercises, it was soon obvious that other crews managed to get lost as well.

During training, the instructors had drummed into us the importance of admitting to being lost as soon as we realised all was not well, then to climb to a safe height and look for a positive feature, recommencing only when sure of our position. This would be extremely embarrassing when you had a formation of helicopters following you.

One of the mistakes I made in the first few weeks was to drag the load-lifting hook along the ground for about a mile, thereby making it unserviceable. The hook, suspended from wire strops attached to four strong points on the underside of the helicopter, would be lowered by a length of rope controlled by the aircrewman from inside the aircraft, allowing the weight of the hook to be taken up by the strops. When the hook was not in use or at the end of a load-lifting sortie, it was the aircrewman's job to recover it to its stowage position flush with the bottom of the helicopter and not dangling below the undercarriage.

I had landed on after a load-lifting sortie without pulling the hook up and we had taxied back to the squadron hanger, dragging the hook all the way. The hook was a very expensive piece of equipment and, unfortunately, several hooks had been damaged in the same way over the past few months. The engineers were getting a little hacked off with this so the senior engineer had decided the next time it happened, the aircrewman responsible would have a lesson in respect of aircraft equipment.

Just my luck, the next time it happened it was to be my fault. I had to follow the hook around for about three days, going through all the procedures involved in assessing whether it would be scrapped or repaired. First, I had to take it to the inspection bay and follow it through all the tests required to see if it was possible to salvage the hook; this one was not. Then I had to run around with a report gaining signatures from different departments – the report was required to declare the hook unserviceable beyond economic repair. Next, I had to follow up the stores procedures to obtain a new one.

Finally, there was the pre use servicing of the new hook before fitting to the helicopter. All the way along I was getting hassle because they had all been pre-warned that I had been the one who had caused the damage. It was all a little bit over the top but I never made that mistake again and neither did anyone else on the squadron.

The full time Search and Rescue flight at Yeovilton had been disbanded a couple of years previously, so the SAR cover for the flying at Yeovilton was covered between '848 Squadron' and '845 Squadron' who would take it in turns to provide a crew and aircraft for the week. We had a pack of rescue equipment kept on a trolley, ready to be loaded in the nearest available helicopter. Being SAR qualified I was invariably nominated as SAR crew when it was our squadron's turn.

As Yeovilton was inland, it was very unlikely the diving capability would be used though the capability still had to be maintained to cover the squadrons when operating from the aircraft carriers. To carry out our allotted requirement of jumps and dives to stay current as SAR divers, we would go down to Portland whenever possible and join the Portland SAR flight's Thursday morning diver drop sessions.

This was invariably difficult to achieve as our squadron had so many commitments, making it awkward to schedule our trips to Portland; nevertheless we would muddle through, but often with a panic at the end of each quarter to arrange diving sessions in order to meet the minimum requirements to remain current.

When the Yeovilton dedicated SAR flight was disbanded, my mate Speedy Ball joined '848 Squadron', along with another mate from basic training, Slim Freelove.

Speedy was now married and living in Yeovil, so was not able to get out very often for a drink but, as we were both SAR trained, we went on quite a few detachments together, so had plenty of time to socialise and get up to our old antics.

Slim Freelove had also been promoted to Petty Officer since leaving basic training and was billeted in the same mess as me, along with the two other divers on the squadron, Tony Duriez and Tab Hunter. We were all in the same position, with a commitment to a partner away from the Yeovil area. This did not mean we had to stay in every night so we often went ashore together, meeting other members from either '848 Squadron' or '845 Squadron' and invariably having a good laugh.

During the rest of that year, we carried out exercises all over Britain, in support of Royal Marines and various Army units. Some of the exercises involved as many as sixteen helicopters; others would be eagle flights with two to four aircraft.

Invariably we would live in the field with the troops, but would have a relatively easy time of it. The troops would do most of the trench digging and security watches. We would carry out a lot of flying on these exercises: as a general rule, if we were not flying, we would be sleeping or trying to sleep. At some stage during these exercises we would expect the camp to come under attack from the opposing forces.

In preparation for this, we had varying degrees of alert states. At the highest state everyone would be involved in one task or another, the majority spread around the perimeter of the camp on lookout in trenches.

During the alert phase of these exercises we had to sleep fully dressed, so that if a high state of alert was called all we had to do was grab our rifle (which we kept by our sleeping bag) and man our allotted position. During one of these exercises I had just turned in, exhausted after a rather gruelling night troop move, and having had only about one hour's sleep in the last twenty-four, when the alert went off.

I woke up still in a daze. I knew I had to grab my rifle and head off to my position, which was a trench quite close to our tent. The next thing I knew, I was lying in the trench with my torch pointing towards the open ground.

In my dozy state, I had picked up my torch instead of my rifle. Although amusing to the guys in my trench, I knew that if I was found to be without my rifle I was in for a serious ear bending.

It was considered a serious offence being without your rifle at any time, let alone during an alert; our rifle had to go everywhere with us and I mean everywhere. In addition, I knew that the internal patrol would be going round the tents, to check that everyone was up and felt sure they would find my rifle. I decided I would crawl back to my tent, which was only fifty yards away, in the hope that I could retrieve my rifle before the internal patrol found it.

At various points around the camp trip wires connected to flares had been set in the areas that would be difficult to guard, and set away from the normal routes used by members of the camp. Unfortunately, I had decided to crawl through one of these areas to get back to my tent. I knew it would be unlikely that anyone would be watching in that direction. I also thought I knew where the trip wires were having set some of them. I had only crawled a few yards when the whole world lit up; I had tripped one of our own wires. All hell broke loose, blanks were being fired from rifles, thunder flashes being thrown – I just threw myself back in my trench hoping I had not been seen.

The alert went on for some hours because it was thought we had infiltrators inside the camp. Someone from another trench, who had started the firing, had reported he had seen two infiltrators run towards the centre of the camp. I was quite happy to let him believe he had seen someone, but all he could possibly have seen was me diving back into my trench.

A thorough search of the camp was carried out by the internal patrol who did not find anyone or notice my rifle still in the tent. We even had a Royal Marine sergeant visit our trench, questioning whether we had heard any movement before the flare went off being the nearest trench to the trip wire. He had not noticed that I did not have my rifle; the other two lads in the trench with me (Tab Hunter and a Royal Marine) covered for me.

At one stage, I was going to come clean about the whole thing, but the marine thought I would be stupid to do so. I would get as much hassle if I owned up as I would if my rifle was found and there was a reasonable chance that they would not find it, especially since the trip wire had gone off and the patrols would now be looking for infiltrators.

Eventually, when we had stood down and I was safely in my tent, I was able to breathe a sigh of relief. The following morning's briefing concentrated on how the enemy had managed to get so close to the camp and how we would have to tighten up the camp's defences.

In this particular case, the SAS were our enemy. The following night they actually got into the camp and removed one of the helicopter's logbooks as proof that they had been there. At the final wash up, they insisted they had only carried out the one raid on our camp but I am sure they did not mind being credited with two!

I managed to see Margaret on those weekends I was not away on detachment and during the leave periods, we would travel to Plymouth to give me a chance to see the boys who had now got used to the situation and Kerry loved having them around.

My ex-wife Mary had met someone she felt she could settle down with and they were going to take over the mortgage, which would free me from that commitment. This of course, when finalised, would make it a little easier for Margaret and I to settle down on our own. At last, we could see some light at the end of the tunnel. We never expected the situation to be settled without any difficulties, nor should they have been and we were prepared to wait as long as it took.

There was no way I could fight for anything other than was offered from my marriage as I felt that would deprive the boys and of course, they were completely innocent in all this. It was just as traumatic for them and was bound to have some effect on their lives. Margaret fully understood this; she had left her marriage with nothing and only received maintenance for Kerry for a very short while, so knew all the difficulties that caused.

59

In the August of 1974 I went with a two aircraft detachment to Prestwick, to cover the SAR for that area for a few weeks. The Search and Rescue for that region was normally carried out by '819 Squadron', an anti submarine squadron that had gone off to carry out a large exercise requiring all their aircraft.

During our spell at Prestwick, we were tasked to pick up an American ambassador who was on holiday in the remote Island of Barra. This was after the American ambassador in Cyprus had been assassinated, creating a volatile situation. The American we had to collect was required in Washington for a briefing on the situation before flying out to Cyprus as the new Ambassador.

There was a fair amount of urgency required and we were tasked to fly out to Barra to pick him up and bring him back to Prestwick where a Navy fixed wing aircraft would be waiting to fly him to London.

At the time, we did not know why we had to carry out the task, only that it was urgent. We had been given a grid reference of a hotel on the island where we had to land in the car park; the car park was being cleared for our arrival.

When we arrived at Barra, which was approximately 130 miles northwest of Prestwick, we found the grid reference we had been given was wrong; it was miles from anywhere and we had no radio contact with anyone. We had hoped to remain in radio contact on HF, the long-range frequency, but that failed us early on.

We decided we would look for any sign of activity, or a telephone and would land to contact the police who we hoped would know where the ambassador was as we did not even have the name of the hotel. Flying around we saw what looked like a small fête taking place in a park, with a clear football field next to all the activity, so we opted for landing there.

When we landed, dozens of excited children surrounded the aircraft; they simply could not believe their eyes, a military helicopter landing beside them, which was not a common sight. I went off with one of the children to use his mother's telephone. In fact, all the children whose parents had a telephone wanted me to use theirs; I had a difficult job finding out whose house was nearest.

Most of the kids followed me and I felt like the Pied Piper of Hamelin. At least it drew them away from the aircraft. We couldn't shut down to make it safe, as it was likely we wouldn't have been able to start again, so before leaving the park I had also commandeered a teacher to make sure no one went near.

Eventually, I managed to get through to the local police officer. It was like speaking in foreign languages, we simply did not understand each other, what with my Lancashire accent and his Western Isle brogue. I was trying to explain that I had landed in a helicopter and was looking for the hotel where the ambassador was staying. He kept saying they were waiting for a helicopter from the mainland and asking what time we would be arriving. When I finally got him to understand that we had arrived on the Island I realised I would never understand his instructions, so asked him to send a police car to where we had landed. When the police car arrived a few minutes later, I asked him to put his blue light on and said that we would follow him to the hotel. We picked up the ambassador and were soon on our way back to Prestwick.

We never did find out why we had been given the wrong grid reference, but I found navigation by following blue lights worked well.

Shortly after the Prestwick trip, I was informed I would be going to RNAS Culdrose in June of the next year (1975) for my Petty Officers Aircrewman's course which meant my tour on '848' was going to be cut short. The reason for this was that the Navy wanted to get all the aircrewmen in my position, i.e. already petty officers, qualified as aircrewman petty officers. I mentioned earlier that this was make-or-break for me as, if I failed, I would have to return to my previous branch as a seaman or revert to a leading aircrewman and wait for another chance in the distant future.

I had six months to prepare myself and, fortunately, one of my mates Tony Duriez was going on the first course. Tony was one of the other SAR divers on the squadron and had been aircrew for quite some years, an excellent aircrewman who was likely to do well. Tony's was to be the first course and all he knew was that it would be for nine weeks and he had only been given a rough syllabus for the course, so wasn't really sure what to expect.

Fortunately for me Tony, would be coming back to the squadron and would at least be able to pass on the course structure before my course. In the mean time, we would be carrying out a few small exercises prior to embarking on to HMS Bulwark for deployment to the Mediterranean to carry out troop moving exercises with the Royal Marines.

During this deployment, Margaret would be joining me for a month in Malta. The crew of HMS Bulwark were arranging a charter flight to coincide with a refit period in Malta. A few of the aircrewmen's wives would also be flying out so this was something to look forward to and for

Margaret and me it would be very special, as we hadn't had any real time together since we met.

Tony Duriez rejoined the squadron just prior to the Mediterranean deployment, having successfully completed his PO's qualifying course and had brought all his notes to help me prepare before my course. Three of the twelve on his course had failed; they were aircrew like me that were already Petty Officers from their previous trade.

As Tony's was the very first PO aircrewman's course and there had been a few anomalies getting the right structure for the course, it would have been unfair to the three that had failed to stick to the decision about losing their rates or returning to their previous branches. So, those that failed were given a second chance: they would keep their rates, go back to their squadrons for a few months and then join my course, which was to be the third one.

The next couple of months were spent carrying out deck landing practices, troop and load lifting drills, exercises inserting troops ashore on various islands in the Mediterranean, finishing with quite a large exercise in Cyprus prior to our refit in Malta.

The families arrived in Malta the day after we arrived. I had rented a small villa in a place called Bujiba. Three of my mates (Scouse Hogan, Sooty Sutcliffe and Jed Clamp), also flew their wives out and had hired a large villa in the same complex. Their wives had met up with Margaret at Gatwick and they had all flown out together.

We did not have leave for the full month that our wives were in Malta since there were still a few exercises to carry out with the Marines; however, we did have most evenings off and had pre-arranged leave for the last fortnight of the month's stay.

The break turned out just right and we all had a great time visiting the entire island, sometimes together as a group. Occasionally, Margaret and I would get off on our own. We felt we needed our own space as we were still quite vulnerable and needed to be sure of each other, as it was on the cards that this relationship had a future. We met up with the others in the evenings for a meal out, having found and virtually taken over a local bar that accepted our antics, and were often joined by other aircrew from the squadron.

As the time drew near for Margaret to fly home, I knew I wanted to spend the rest of my life with her and I proposed. I was not confident that Margaret would agree so soon, as her previous marriage had left her with many doubts and worries. I was also fully aware of my own hang-ups from my previous marriage. We had quite long discussions on our fears but eventually concluded it was right and Margaret accepted. We decided to have a small wedding with no fuss shortly after I returned from this deployment. Margaret would start the arrangements when she returned home.

After Margaret's return, I still had a couple of months to spend in the Med before I would be leaving the squadron to fly home. I would be flying home on the 1st June and our wedding was arranged for the 7th June, prior to me going on the PO's course.

The next two months were taken up with more exercises and troop moves, including visits to Barcelona and Cannes before returning to Malta. This time I would be leaving the ship to fly home via an RAF VC 10. The lads were fed up of me by now as I had spent the last few days walking round singing "I'm Leaving on a Jet Plane."

On the final day, I was packed up and getting ready to fly home. The squadron had been despatched ashore for a large exercise so I had said my goodbyes. I thought that was the last I had seen of the lads for some months; however, they had decided that they would not let me get away with the ribbing I had given about flying home…

Just prior to leaving the ship, I had a message that a Wessex was coming in to pick me up in an hour's time and that I was required for the main troop move. I knew they were short of aircrewmen and had been worried all week that my flight might be delayed until after this exercise was over. I now thought this had happened.

Initially I was furious considering that it was only an exercise and I was finding it difficult to come to terms with the decision. However, there was no argument – I had to go so I unpacked my flying kit and went to the flight deck to meet the helicopter that was arriving to pick me up.

When joining the exercise in the field the lads did their best to sympathise with my situation while listening to my mumblings. When it came time for the big exercise brief, we mustered at the briefing area and had the brief as normal.

I was still muttering to myself, half-heartedly listening to the brief when the flight commander called me forward. He apologised for my rude removal from the ship and presented me with a leaving and wedding present on behalf of the aircrewmen. I had been taken in hook, line and sinker! I still had to do the first part of the troop move, but this was only because it tied in with the arrangements to fly me back to the ship in time to pick up the rest of my kit and make my way to the airport.

I arrived back in the UK at Brize Norton and Margaret was there to meet me. That was a wonderful reunion, as I knew this was the start of a new phase in my life. We had only six days left for the final preparations for our marriage.

Kerry, Margaret's daughter, who was four years old thought she was getting married as well and was often seen swinging on the garden gate telling all the passers-by that we were all getting married. Kerry was very popular with the neighbours and we had plenty of congratulations cards, some from people we did not know.

The marriage was planned to be a quiet Register Office affair with close friends and family and it turned out to be just right for us. Margaret's brother had come down with several bottles of champagne and fresh orange juice so the day commenced with Bucks Fizz in the garden. The marriage ceremony was held late morning and was followed by a small reception in our local hotel, a wonderful day with family and friends.

We were married on the Saturday and I was to join HMS Sea Hawk at Culdrose in Cornwall on the Monday for my Petty Officer's course

Petty Officer Aircrewman Course

The Petty Officers' course, as expected, proved to be extremely difficult. I had put in a considerable amount of preparation for the course but, being relatively new to flying compared to the rest of the lads, I felt a little apprehensive, just hoping I had done enough.

I already knew four of the twelve course members. Derek Oakes and Ray Higginson had been divers on Lee SAR flight and Denis Kermode had been a winch op. I had also worked for a short time at Portland with another course member Dave Groves; we all got on with each other, making the earlier days of the course much easier.

Like the majority of aircrew courses, the whole course soon bonded as a team, helping each other through the ups and downs and I managed to knuckle down in my attempt to keep up with the others, although I felt sure I had blown it very early on.

One of our course instructors was a notorious Chief Aircrewman called Ted Crispin who was nicknamed 'two fingers Ted'. Ted had lost three fingers on one hand after a mid air collision forced a crash in the jungle in Borneo; he was the only survivor and his injuries had initially meant the end of his flying days. That was something Ted would not accept and, after many a battle with the MOD, had managed to get that decision reversed, returning to flying duties after convincing medical boards he could do all that was expected of him.

Ted was definitely of the old school and was incredibly proud of the aircrew branch; he had run many of the basic aircrewmen's courses. If you got on the wrong side of him, or he thought you were not the right material for the branch, he would hound you until you either requested to come off the course or failed. Once on his hit list the only way out was to prove you could hack everything he threw at you.

Fortunately, I stayed clear of Ted's 'hit list' and avoided the somewhat barbaric attention, but one day I came very close to it and still today wonder why I didn't receive the wrath of Ted.

The incident happened during a navigational exercise, similar to the ones carried out on the basic aircrewman's course. We had headed out to sea in our Wessex Mk 1 helicopter, six students and Ted. Each of us had a leg of navigation to carry out using radar fixes and wind-finding techniques, plus problems thrown in like being routed away to a mayday call, all under pressure as Ted made things as difficult as he felt fit. I, as normal, felt particularly under pressure, not helped by having the last leg which required that I make a given landmark and then map-read back to Culdrose.

Making a landmark was often hit-and-miss because of the inherent mistakes made on previous legs while out of sight of the land, so each of us would carry out 'follow navigation' hoping that we had a good idea of the position when it was our time to take over. When I made landfall I had to change from navigation charts to maps, find the exact position we had made landfall, then map-read back to base.

When I first sighted land, it was obvious that it was not the point I was meant to be. Not knowing the area, I had to quickly locate my position from the maps but, when I put my chart down and went to pick up my map it had disappeared and Ted had a huge grin on his face! I was trying so hard to get things right that I lost my senses, convincing myself that Ted had hidden my map to see how I would get out of the situation.

I simply did not know what to do and very nearly burnt my bridges; I was so convinced Ted had hidden the map that I asked him to stop messing around and give it back. He said he did not have it and I could see his grin turning to anger. This got my back up and I started arguing that it was not safe to start messing around like this. The rest of the lads were gesturing behind Ted's back trying to tell me something; they were looking after my welfare and making every effort to calm me down.

I had one more attempt to get the map off Ted when I threw all caution to the wind and grabbed Ted's lapels on his flying suit, telling him I no longer saw the funny side. The look on Ted's face was complete disbelief; he simply said, "Dave your map went out of the door when you opened it on making landfall." The slipstream had whipped it away. The look on the other guys' faces told me straight away this was true – that is what they had been trying to tell me, I felt sure I had blown it.

Ted's face was thunder as I let go and the lads passed me another map to get us back to Culdrose. When we landed on Ted laid in to me verbally in front of everyone and then took me aside for another serious ear-bending. I never did find out why he didn't take it further or why he didn't make life difficult for me after the event, even during the many times we were to meet in future years the incident was never raised. I can only presume he saw the funny side of the situation and perhaps recognised the effort I was putting in to get through the course.

The course continued with us having to learn all the many disciplines required for our various roles including advanced navigation, meteorology, rules of the air and radio procedures. We even had to learn Morse code at eight words a minute. The practical side included confined areas, low-level flying, mountain flying, a considerable number of navigation exercises, winching techniques and a long-range navigation exercise (in our case to Holland) for a weekend land-away.

I guess the course format suited my particular roles having trained for Search & Rescue and being a Commando Aircrewman, I need not have worried about the course as much as I had. I still found the course difficult but the ones who struggled most were the aircrewmen who had specialised as Anti Submarine Aircrewmen and the Missile Aimers: not their fault it was simply a case of them not having as much practice in the disciplines required for this course.

The three that had failed the first course all passed this one, but we did have two failures. One of them decided to remain aircrew and was demoted to Leading Aircrewman; the other decided to keep his rate and returned to his parent branch.

I felt on top of the world on completion of the course: the branch was now recognized, I was in a job I loved, I had no more courses ahead of me and I was heading back to Lee-on-Solent. This would be the start of my new life with Margaret and I would be commencing a full tour back on the Lee-on-Solent SAR Flight, which I considered the best job in the Navy.

Return to Lee-on-Solent SAR Flight

I had a couple of weeks leave before joining the flight but still had no time for a holiday to celebrate our recent marriage, the leave being spent arranging married quarters and settling into our new home.

I joined the Lee SAR Flight for my second tour in August 1975 and straight onto duty. We still operated whirlwind Mk 9's and a few of the crew from my first time at Lee were still there. It immediately felt like I had never been away; even my mate Lou Armstrong had returned after his tour on a junglie squadron. Terry Short had left the flight; following promotion to Chief Petty Officer, he had been appointed as Chief of the Helicopter Underwater Escape Trainer.

It was October before I had my first demanding job. I was crewed with Slim Freelove (one of my mates from the initial aircrew course) and Bruno Brunsden was the pilot.

We had been scrambled to the report of a diver missing from a trawler south of Newhaven. The trawler had snagged its nets on something on the seabed and one of the crew had decided to attempt to free them. He was using diving equipment but the incident was not reported until the diver had been down longer than the endurance of his diving set.

When we arrived on scene, I was lowered to the trawler with my diving gear. After talking to the crew I realised I would almost certainly be looking for a body as the missing crew member's compressed air would not have lasted this long. The aircraft immediately started a search around the datum just in case the missing man had surfaced away from the vessel.

I was in the water within a couple of minutes of getting the details and following the lines down to the snagged nets some 60ft below the surface. At that depth I would only have between 10-15 minutes diving time.

The visibility was nil and the search carried out by feel. I had pulled myself down to the source of the snag to find the net well and truly caught around what felt to be a large propeller and engine cowling. I could only feel around the loose part of the netting in the hope I might find the missing man.

The next few minutes were to be the most frightening of my life as I found myself snagged in the net. My first reaction was to head for the surface but soon realised that was not possible. The fear was indescribable, knowing I had only a few minutes air left. I was unable to control my hyperventilating which I knew if I could not get under control would reduce even further my endurance. I can honestly say I felt absolute fear.

The first thought should have been to use my knife to try to cut myself free, but I was trying to pull myself clear with my hands and making the situation worse. I was also trying, quite unsuccessfully, to control my panic. When I did decide to try to cut my way out and went to get my knife out of the leg pouch, I realised the net was snagged round it; in freeing it I was able to break away.

Unfortunately I had also lost hold of the lines and the visibility was so bad that I was not sure which way was up. I was negatively buoyant at that depth in a wet suit and wearing a buoyancy aid, which in 1975 was the same design as the aircraft's crew lifejackets losing its usefulness below 30 to 40ft even when inflated.

This was yet another scare and one I had not experienced before. Initially I thought I was finning to the surface and found myself hitting the seabed. I ditched my weights, operated the buoyancy aid and pushed myself off the seabed, fortunately finding I now had enough buoyancy to start me heading towards the surface. Once on the surface I clambered back aboard the trawler, still not sure, if the missing diver was down there.

I was finding it very difficult to hold things together as I had scared the living daylights out of myself. I had now run out of air, had no weights and had used my buoyancy aid so could not make a second dive. I requested backup from another diver if possible and more diving equipment and the motions were set in place to scramble another aircraft.

While waiting for the second aircraft I learnt that the missing person had recently been married and expecting his first child. This played on my mind so when the crewmember on the fishing vessel pointed out they had another compressed air set and weights onboard, I felt I had to have another go. A little foolhardy as I knew nothing about the diving set, it did not have a gauge attached so had no idea of its endurance and I had inflated my buoyancy aid so that was now unusable. After my double-scare, the last thing I wanted to do was enter the water again.

I went down the line, very tentatively this time feeling around as best I could until I struggled breathing in the air warning me that the set was running out and letting me know that I had to return to the surface. Being clear of the nets and returning to the surface could only be described as complete relief.

Shortly after this, the second aircraft arrived with John Humphries (one of my diver colleagues) bringing extra diving sets and equipment.

Once I had briefed John, we made a final dive as a pair, considerably safer as we could look after each other. We were not able to clear the net, but between us we felt quite certain that the missing person was not trapped in there and a quick seabed search around the net was to no avail.

Later, during a search by a police diving team it was established that the trawler had caught its nets on a ditched World War II bomber. The body was not located on the site but I believe did turn up some days later on the surface.

This was to be one of the jobs that made me question whether I was right for this role, but I soon understood that the majority of the crewman and divers who had been in the role for a few years had faced their own demons and managed to put them to the back of their mind.

I guess the answer was, if you could tuck your fears away, it was all right to continue in the role; if you could not it was time to leave. I was to learn over the years that the awkward jobs happened infrequently. I did manage to tuck them to the back of my mind, although they would bubble up occasionally – sometimes as a good memory of a job well done, other times more like a nightmare. The secret was to dwell on the awkward jobs that had resulted in a positive outcome; they far outweighed the nasty ones.

I was to gain plenty of experience over the next few months working in various crews. I was happy working with them all and the team spirit was incredible. It really was something special to work in an environment where every person on the unit enjoyed their work; this was something I was to experience for the rest of my career in flying.

Unlike the last time I was on the flight, the majority of the crews had families at Lee (including me) and I was settling down to family life, sure I had done the right thing; we had settled into our house and were very happy. The flight was very social with many nights out and plenty of laughs.

The jobs over the next few months all helped to build up my experience and confidence in the role, even the so-called smaller jobs such as searches locating missing persons safe and well, the recovery of people from capsized dinghies or helping people who had found they were cut of by the tide. Few of the jobs were difficult, simply helping people out of awkward situations but it all helped prepare me for the more serious ones.

One Sunday morning we were sitting in the crew room listening to the start of a major powerboat race off the Isle of Wight and intended to get airborne later to watch the race (one of the benefits of the job was getting a bird's eye view of the many events that took place in the Solent!) However, it was soon clear that something nasty was happening; some sort of collision. We even manned up before being scrambled, as we felt sure the aircraft would be required.

As soon as we got into the aircraft, the Coastguards scrambled us to a capsized powerboat that had gone right through another vessel. There were plenty of safety boats around as it was the start of a major race and people thrown in the water in the accident were being recovered from the water by race safety boats.

We were tasked to a seriously injured casualty, the driver of the powerboat 'Blitz', who had been recovered from the water by a local rescue boat. Mick Rowsell lowered me to the vessel and I knew immediately how serious the injuries were. The rescue boat had a stunt mast on the stern, which precluded getting a stretcher onboard.

I immediately opted to recover the man by a normal winch, protecting his injuries as best I could. I had based this decision on experience and was convinced that if we wasted time trying to find another way of carrying out a transfer, (e.g. taking him ashore to be met by ambulance) it would be too late to help him.

We had the man in the hands of doctors at the Naval Hospital Haslar within ten minutes of arriving on scene. Unfortunately, he died in theatre shortly after arrival.

A few days after this incident, we had a complaint that we may have contributed to his injuries by not using a stretcher, which was not an option under the circumstances. There will always be doubt in situations like this; I had made my decision, as I felt sure the casualty was unlikely to survive a few minutes, let alone a long trip to shore followed by an ambulance trip to hospital.

The Coroner had to investigate the claim so Mick Rowsell (the winch operator) and I found ourselves in the Coroner's court answering some very awkward questions. This was my first experience of this type of complaint and indeed my first time in a Coroner's court.

I found it quite daunting and could only explain my reasoning as to why I had carried out the lift in the way I did. Fortunately, when the doctor who met the aircraft was called, he had nothing but praise at the care and first aid we were carrying out on the casualty. The surgeon confirmed we had given him the only chance he had; his injuries were so severe that they could not support life. In fact, the only chance was in the operating theatre but, even then, it was too late.

We felt especially grateful when his family went out of their way to thank us for giving him the only chance he had.

By coincidence, not many months later we had another seriously injured powerboat driver from a race off Poole. He had been picked up by the same boat only this time the stunt mast had been removed and I was able to carry out a stretcher transfer.

Incidents such as the unfortunate power boat driver have always caused me concern, as we often have to make decisions that we know go against the rules. for example, carrying out an evacuation of an injured casualty from a sheer cliff, when there is often no way of completely stabilising the injury before that evacuation, or moving a badly injured casualty from further danger such as a freezing sea or incoming tide.

We simply have to do the best we can in the situations we are presented with, often coming up with most unusual ways of making the best of a bad situation. On many vessels we winch to (particularly the smaller yachts) it is impossible to get someone onto a stretcher so we have to balance any delays against possible further injury. Over the years, extraction devices such as spinal immobilisation boards, splinting systems and cervical collars would be developed and introduced to help in these situations.

I was to have quite an unusual year in 1976 with several awkward incidents on cliffs and yachts. A few had outcomes I found quite distressing and some left me feeling quite uneasy, with considerable soul-searching as to whether the incident could have been handled differently. I often talked it through with the crew and other crews, usually deciding, although not always, that we had made the right decision. It was a normal and healthy process to question situations and I was soon to realise this was to be essential in our role, occasionally coming up with better ways of doing things and learning from each other.

Another incident that was to have an effect on me (although not to do with our care of the casualty it was a hospital transfer, not a rescue) was after a young courting couple had been involved in a motor boat incident off the Isle of Wight. They had started the engine of the boat and it had exploded causing a flash fire. The youngsters, both badly burnt, had jumped into the water and were rescued by a passing boat. The vessel that had rescued them took them ashore where they were taken to hospital by ambulance.

Later we were tasked to take the couple from the island to a burns unit near Salisbury. When we arrived for the pickup, both the casualties had been stabilised and the young lady, although badly burned, appeared to have escaped burns to her face. She was a very attractive young lady who was showing a tremendous amount of courage and was even smiling. She was excited about having a ride in the helicopter and was trying to sit up in the stretcher to look out of the window, which we could not let her do.

The young man was more subdued but I now understand why; his burns were more superficial, leaving the nerve ends intact and much more painful.

The crew was Bill Fewtrell and Mick Rowsell and we had all remarked on how brave this young lady was. We would ring up Odstock hospital for the next few days to see how the couple were doing, promising them a visit to the flight when they recovered. One morning when we rang, it was very distressing to be told the young lady had died.

Her father, who was a fire fighter, took the time to write to thank us for our thoughts and to explain how excited she had been with the flight in the helicopter. He also said she had remained cheerful, as we had seen her, until the end.

I am not sure why this stands out in my mind as I was to see many a situation like that in future years. We had not actually rescued the couple, but I often find myself thinking of her and can still picture that beautiful, brave face even now many years later.

Towards the end of 1976, we were scrambled to a single-handed yacht to the west of the Needles (IOW) that had put out a mayday in force eight conditions. The crew included Colin Rose (who had taken over as Chief pilot) and Mike Walton (Wally) as the winch operator. As we approached the yacht, the single occupant fired a red flare but unfortunately temporarily blinded himself in doing so, leaving him in charge of a yacht that he was unable to sail or steer. We did not know what his original emergency was.

There was no way we could winch to the yacht as the vessel was moving around ferociously in the rough seas and the casualty was clearly unable to handle the hi-line; we could see that he was in distress, sat in the cockpit covering his eyes.

After watching the yacht for a while, I noticed that the guardrail would get quite close to the sea as the yacht rolled and pitched. I felt that if I could grab the guardrail on one of these rolls, when it rolled the other way I would be able to scramble onboard, we continued to watch for a while to work out the best direction to approach.

When I Jumped in the water the yacht and I seemed to drift together - I hardly had to put any effort into it. I managed to grab the guardrail as I had hoped to do and at the same time the yacht rolled over to the other side and whipped me onboard. The process was far easier than I was expecting – obviously a little luck was involved and I had grabbed hold of the guardrail on just the right wave.

It turned out that the guy who had recently purchased the yacht was not too badly injured and, although I could not be sure what damage he had done to his eyes when he fired the flare, there was no sign of serious burning. He was however, disorientated from lack of sleep, having spent the last couple of days trying to sail the yacht in seas he was not used to and, he knew he would not have the skill to get the yacht through the Needles channel in those conditions. On top of this, he had nearly capsized on several occasions.

I knew it would be extremely difficult getting him off the yacht so opted to stay with him until the Yarmouth lifeboat turned up to transfer him across. I was then able to leap back into the sea for pick-up by the aircraft.

It was too rough for the lifeboat to get a tow onboard safely so once they had the casualty on board they left the yacht to its own devices.

The guy had sunk all his money into the yacht and had not yet insured it; this was a great shame as the yacht eventually drifted ashore, beaching itself in such a safe place that some very astute person had leapt onboard and claimed salvage. We were surprised when we heard this but understand the person who was claiming salvage was successful and the owner lost his yacht.

In February 1977, we were scrambled at changeover time to the report of a landslide at Lulworth Cove in Dorset. It was believed that a class of geology pupils had been caught in a cliff fall.

The morning's crew had scrambled just as the afternoon crew were arriving at work. It was soon apparent that a second aircraft would be required and the engineers pulled out all the stops to get one on line. Within ten minutes, we found ourselves heading towards Lulworth not too far behind the first aircraft.

En-route we were informed that the beach parties and Coastguard teams were digging out casualties from the landslide. When the first aircraft arrived, it was required to pick up the badly injured first.

On scene, the wind was south-westerly gusting 35 knots; the landslide was on the east side of the cove on a southwest facing cliff. The crew found the turbulence at the top of the cliff made it impossible to hover into wind at height above the incident; therefore, they opted to winch from a much lower position closer to the cliff but away from the severe turbulence. This meant they would have to back the aircraft in to the winching position to enable the pilot and winch operator to keep the cliff face and winching area visual, making for a very tricky manoeuvre but the only way to effect the rescue.

The first aircraft was crewed by pilot Graham Dunn, winch-op Geoff Sutcliffe and diver Chris Crossley and managed to winch onboard a stretcher with a critically injured casualty and transfer him to Weymouth Hospital.

We had the advantage of the first crew's assessment of the conditions so did not have to spend too long deciding how we would approach. Using the same technique Bill Fewtrell edged backwards into position by the verbal direction from Mick Rowsell. As Mick lowered me to the base of the landslide, the ground rescue teams had two more casualties waiting for transfer.

I felt I had the easy job sorting out the injuries and preparing the injured casualties for the winch back into the aircraft; the ground teams were trying to dig out casualties knowing that another landslide could bury them.

We transferred our casualties to the hospital landing site, while the first aircraft went back to recover two bodies to the top of the cliff (a teacher and a pupil) before having to refuel at Portland. When we arrived back on scene it was confirmed that everyone was accounted for and the less injured had been taken to hospital by ambulance.

It was clearly a disturbing incident for all involved and attracted considerable media attention. When a tasking catches the media's interest I find myself dwelling more than I should on the incident; you cannot help reading these reports and often get detailed information about the casualties from their family and friends. This would make me reflect quite deeply about the rescue almost as though I knew the casualty or casualties personally.

This was another aspect of the job I had to get used to and learn to put things into perspective. In this particular case, the survivors were in hospital considerably quicker than they would have been by any other means. I would force myself to think of the positive side; the accident did happen but, hopefully, we made a difference to the outcome for the survivors.

Later that day we had a second cliff incident on the Isle of Wight, this time the casualty had been trying to recover his dog that had fallen over the cliff. A Coastguard cliff team had recovered the man but could not reach the dog. We would not normally carry out a job like this but felt it had good training benefit so I was lowered to recover the dog. I was more than happy to do so and it helped to divert my thoughts from the earlier tragic incident.

Receiving FONACS commendation for Lulworth Cove Cliff Rescue

Every Thursday the divers would get together for the diver drop sessions. As mentioned previously this involved jumping from the aircraft wearing a diving set and practicing various rescue techniques on each other. The jumps were carried out from various heights and we would always have to dive to the seabed to pick up a handful of sand to prove we had made it the bottom.

These sessions were often hilarious with each of us trying to out-do each other. The divers on the flight at the time were Clive Taylor, (the chief aircrewman) Ray Higginson, John Humphries, Brian Spendlow and Loz Coleman. Every one of them a character in their own right, I could easily write a chapter on each of them.

For example, Ray holds the 'Queen's Gallantry Medal' awarded for a rescue in which he was scrambled from an aircraft carrier to a ditched civilian aircraft; when the helicopter he had scrambled in crashed on takeoff. Ray climbed out of the wreckage straight into another aircraft and continued on to carry out a successful rescue. The others had all been involved in situations that had taken them beyond the boundaries.

Terry Short, who as part of his duties running the Diving Section and Underwater Escape Trainer, was required to supervise these sessions providing the safety divers and safety boat but he would also join us for actual jumps to keep in practice himself.

Brian Spendlow was one of the natural jumpers who nearly always made the perfect jump whatever height he went out from; however, one day he forgot to take off his dispatcher. The dispatcher is the harness we wear round our waist to stop us falling out of the aircraft when the door is open. Obviously, the harness needs to be removed prior to jumping.

The dispatcher in the Whirlwind was on a rail so that we could move around the aircraft easily. Brian had forgotten to remove the dispatcher before his jump; one end was attached to the after-end of the rail and the other end round his waist. When Brian jumped, it dragged the secure end from the back of the rail to the front. The result of this was the most almighty clunking sound that made the pilot think we had had a catastrophic engine or gearbox failure and he very nearly put the aircraft in the water. I was also convinced the aircraft was ditching.

Brian was left dangling and in a fair amount of pain. We used the winch to get him back into the aircraft with no serious damage to Brian only damage to the aircraft where he had snapped off the UHF aerial while swinging underneath. We could not continue that session, the laughter and diving did not mix!

A few years later Brian, not learning from his mistake, did exactly the same thing again only this time he damaged his back quite badly grounding him for some time.

In the March, we had a tasking at first light. A postman delivering his mail at West Wittering in West Sussex had spotted what he thought was something unusual in the water, possibly a capsized dinghy. He was in two minds whether to report this and decided to do so.

We were scrambled to the reported position to find a man clinging on to a capsized dinghy, it was clear he was in a bad way. I did not have time to gather my thoughts; just jumped straight in the water and supported the casualty until Don Sowden (the winch operator) winched the strop to me.

I put the strop around the survivor but forgot to hook myself on. We could, if a situation dictated, send a casualty up on his own but only when there was time to brief the casualty and we were sure they are in good health. When a casualty is unconscious or close to it, they lose their muscle tone and their arms go floppy, which meant they were likely to fall out of the strop, even with the becket that is designed to hold them in slid down compressing the strop around the casualty's body.

Knowing this casualty could well go unconscious on the wire I just held on to the top of the strop with one hand and closed the two ends with the other. I thought, as I was not attached to the hook I would have to drop back into the water when Don had the casualty by the door.

Don, fortunately, had realised my predicament and managed to pull us both into the aircraft. I mention this not because of my error (mistakes like that we beat ourselves up about, learn from and prevent from happening again) but because discussing the mistake with others may stop them from making it themselves.

The main thing about a job like that is it was a definite 'life saved'. No one else was on the sea front other than the postman; he had the presence of mind to report something he thought was unusual and in this case, the helicopter base was quite close. That combination was to save that man's life – he would have drowned in just a few more minutes. Both Don and I would often reflect on that simple job as a reminder that every tasking could make the difference to someone.

In the April, we changed from the Whirlwind Mk 9 to the Wessex 5. We were the last Royal Naval SAR flight to do so and had waited quite some time for this upgrade; we were looking forward to the aircraft's arrival.

The Wessex 5 was the same aircraft as used on the Commando squadrons, later implemented as the next generation of SAR helicopter and a quantum leap from the Whirlwind. It had nearly twice the cabin capacity, two engines, a lot more power, was more reliable, had considerably increased endurance and would be fitted with a 100ft winch. The Wessex would prove a very successful SAR aircraft for some years to come.

All three Whirlwinds were replaced and it was sad to see them disappear. They had been affectionally called Faith, Hope and Charity and had lived up to those names, having carried out a very successful role over many years both at Lee-on-Solent and, prior to that, at Lossiemouth SAR in Scotland.

We knew it was the end of the day for these aircraft but I felt very fortunate to have flown in them. Many challenges had been faced to overcome the shortfalls: cabin size, power problems, endurance and short winch. Working round these problems, I feel, helped to improve our skills.

A couple of months after our conversion to the new aircraft I had joined the rest of the divers for a diver drop session in the Solent. It was a normal session, several jumps from the aircraft and dives to the sea bed including practice rescues diving on each other's bubbles. On completion of these diver drops, I took over the afternoon watch from the morning crew. During that watch, we had quite a heavy session of general pilot flying practice, involving several practice engine failures and auto rotations back to the airfield.

A few hours after this session I developed a form of vertigo, I could not walk in a straight line, the room was spinning and I started vomiting quite violently. I had to be relieved straight away and taken to the naval hospital where they carried out several tests including an ECG. My eyes were continuously flickering and the horrendous nausea remained. The tests did not show up any abnormalities.

All they could do was to lie me down and monitor my progress. Within 24 hours, it settled down and the hospital released me to the air medical school to investigate further. Clearly I could not go back flying or diving until they could find some answers.

It was an awful week as they tried to diagnose the problem. Several tests were carried out including syringing my ears with cold and warm water which was an objective and quantative test of the balance mechanism. I was also put in the vertigo chair (a system that was used to check that trainee pilots were not susceptible) which really was an awful experience and I had to go through it a few times.

The only explanation given was that the repeated dives to the seabed in the morning, followed by the unusual attitude flying during the general flying practice in the afternoon, had disturbed the balance mechanism in my left ear but they could not recreate this artificially. The Air Medical Board grounded me for six weeks just to check that there was no re-occurrence indicating that there may be some other underlying problem.

I was so fortunate that the medical board made that decision as it allowed me to stay in the job I loved. Many years later, the problem reoccurred but the medical world had moved on and I was treated for the problem: this would not have been the case back then.

Even that grounding was bad enough as it was during the Queen's 25th Jubilee with a fleet review at Spithead, so considerable activity in the Solent. I had to miss a fly-past of over 90 helicopters along the line of the fleet revue in front of the Queen. I watched the fly-past from the beach with the rest of the crowds of spectators knowing I was missing out on being in one of those aircraft in that historic fly-past.

One of the first jobs after I was returned fit to fly was the rescue of two young men who were stuck halfway up Culver cliff on the Isle of Wight. It was the classic situation where they had been cut off by the tide and attempted to climb the cliff, until it was clear they could not go any further and the crumbling screed made it too dangerous to get back down.

They had found themselves stuck in an area of cliffs that I had recovered people from before. I was with Bill Fewtrell and Mick Rowsell, both with experience of this area, indeed Bill had been the pilot on the second job I had done at this point when we had run out of power. We landed on the cliff top to offload some equipment (to reduce weight) then went straight into the job. The wind was more favourable this time so the task was made easier.

Mick Rowsell was a naval photographer before transferring to the aircrew branch; his camera was never far from his side. He was also a very proficient winch operator and I knew he would get me to the spot safely. When I looked up (something I cannot help doing – checking the tips of the blades as they get closer to the cliffs), Mike was standing in the doorway winching me out with one hand, conning the pilot to the point we needed to be at, and taking photographs with the other hand. I felt this was taking PR too far!

Anyway, that was Mike and he would never change. I did have a go at him, not too seriously though, as I knew he would not have done it if he were not sure that all was safe, the pictures did make all the papers.

This seemed to be the year for cliff jobs for me with some awkward situations to sort out and serious injuries to deal with. Although trained in advanced first aid, I would still question if perhaps we should have more enhanced skills.

That was the way of it in those days, even amongst the ambulance crews. It was mainly a case of stem the bleeding, protect airways, immobilise broken limbs, scoop and run. The majority of the time that was the best thing to do but, just occasionally, I felt some extra skills would be useful either at the scene or in transit.

Underwater Escape Trainer

Towards the end 1977, it was time for Terry Short to move on from the Helicopter Underwater Escape Trainer (dunker) as he had been drafted to a commando squadron. Terry was keen that I took over from him but it was a Chief Petty Officer's billet. I felt that I was not ready for that and, anyway, I was not a Chief so thought no more of it.

However, Terry and the dunker officer Jan Greener (who had been my course officer when I qualified as aircrew) had pulled strings with Charlie Wines in drafting and I ended up taking over from Terry. This meant I would be promoted to 'Acting Local Chief Petty Officer' with the salary increase and the benefits this entailed.

This was a double-edged sword for me; I was to be put in quite a responsible job, which could only help my career, but it would also remove me from my flying job for a while.

The dunker was the place I had worked as a safety diver when I was waiting for my SAR divers' course. The role of the dunker team was to train all naval helicopter crew, plus crews from the RAF and Army who were flying regularly over water, in how to escape from a helicopter if they were unfortunate enough to ditch in the sea. The helicopter module could be altered to represent different aircraft types and each candidate had to complete four capsizes from different seats.

Naval aircrew had to repeat this training every two years. We were also starting to train civilians who were flying regularly to oilrigs in the southern sector of the North Sea.

Our secondary duty was to run the diving section at HMS Daedalus, which was responsible for providing diving continuation training for the ship's divers and to run the diver drop sessions on a Thursday morning. This would also allow me to get the odd jump in myself.

I had to go on a diving supervisor's course before taking over the dunker; a course I quite enjoyed and did well on and this helped give me the confidence to take over from Terry.

I soon settled into the role, initially as the Chief under Jan Greener – a great guy to work with. Jan was later relieved by another observer (Ivor Milne) who was also trained as a diving officer and, like Jan Greener, Andrew George Linsley and Pat Dalton, had completed the SAR divers' course. I believe they were the only officers to do so.

Ivor was an extremely good organiser very proactive in everything he did and easy to work with. He had joined with the brief to wind up the diving section at HMS Daedalus and move the helicopter escape team to HMS Vernon where the dunker was based. Unfortunately, that was a General Service camp and the plan was to move us completely to HMS Vernon. Being ex General Service, I knew the problems this would cause.

I would remain in charge without a controlling officer. In other words, he would be removing his own job and eventually the diving section at HMS Daedalus would close. The diver drops would still have to be carried out on a weekly basis, but it was thought the RN Diving School at Portsmouth would be able to look after that.

This was a situation I did not like or agree with; we would be under the control of a General Service camp and I would miss the diving section side we had at Daedalus. Running between the two bases gave us quite a lot of freedom as we would leave and return from both camps at unusual times so were not tied to strict work schedules. Aside from that, I thought it wrong to be shutting down the diving section at HMS Daedalus. Still, we had our orders and we would make it happen.

This did turn out to be a bad move for many reasons. The Commander of the base could not understand the freedom we required to do our job. I needed the divers at unusual times because of our training schedules but he thought we were trying to pull the wool over his eyes so insisted on the start times being the same as the rest of the camp (07:15 for junior rates and 08:00 for senior rates). All but one of the divers were junior rates so had to start at 07:15 even if we did not have a course until 10:00. Seemingly ignoring the fact that my team would often still be working when the rest of the camp finished, in my view the Commander was being very inflexible.

While we were still operating from Daedalus, I had a mate of mine join from the SAR Flight at Portland: Billy Deacon, quite a character and a brilliant diver.

Bill was having a problem on the Portland SAR flight as he had a serious conflict with one of the officers. Bill never suffered fools and the conflict was leading to confrontation. Such was his character, Bill had to let his feelings be known and, obviously, as he was up against an officer, he would not win. He had requested a move before he did something stupid and I was asked if he could work in the dunker.

I jumped at that opportunity, as it would be great working with Bill again. This was shortly before we had moved to HMS Vernon full time. Bill settled in well and moved his family up to the Portsmouth area.

It was great having Bill working here as he helped me sort out all the disruption the move was causing (which was considerable) and he could be relied on to look after things when I was not available. We got on well both at work and socially.

When we operated from HMS Daedalus, we would leave the diving section in time to meet our course at Vernon. The aircrew came from all parts of the country so we had very unusual starting and finishing times. If the course started late and was likely to go on late, we would turn up at the tank from home.

The system worked well and no one ever abused it; however as mentioned previously, the Commander at HMS Vernon could not accept this flexibility so stamped on it a few months after we had made the full-time move.

I still tried to be as flexible as possible, finding ways around the problems we were having, but in the main, we had to start at the times stated so Bill had to be in at 07:15 and I had to be in at 08:00.

One day Bill had problems with his car and rang me up. I did not consider this a problem and said I would pick him up on the way in. I got him into the camp without any difficulty as the main gate accepted a fair amount of flexibility with us, providing the Commander wasn't on the gate watching out for late arrivals.

We were about to enter the lift at the bottom of the tank when the Commander walked around the corner. I was in uniform and therefore saluted him as I was required to do. Bill, who was in civilian clothing, also saluted him. The Commander was shocked at this person in civilian clothing (who he would have thought was one of the civilian workers) saluting him, so wanted to know who he was.

We were not quick enough to come out with a good enough excuse and, realising Bill was a junior rate, he wanted him trooped (put on charge) for not being in at 07:15. I had admitted that he had come in with me so he wanted me trooped as well.

The Master at Arms came up to see me later that morning and informed me that the Commander was after my rate. He thought the only way out of it was for me to troop Billy for being late but I felt this was ridiculous, as the Commander already knew I had brought Bill in with me and I did not believe he would take this in front of the Captain anyway. I expected a good dressing-down and even thought it may give me a chance to air the problems we were having working from HMS Vernon.

If he did take it in front of the Captain I felt the Captain would not take it seriously enough to take my rate from me. After all, no allowance was being made for the lads when we had to work late (as we had the night before) and the problem with the car was genuine and could be proved. I had tried to explain all this to the Commander but he would not listen.

Bill was mortified: there was no way he would want to drop me in it and was angry with himself for saluting. Saluting was not really Bill's scene anyway as he did not have too much respect for officers unless they earned that respect, he always felt a person should be measured by their abilities not their status. Hence the reason he had requested to leave Portland, finding it very difficult to work with a particular officer that he could not respect.

Anyway, it went all the way with both of us on Captain's report; Bill for being late and me for not taking the responsibilities of my rank, I managed to get Ivor from HMS Daedalus to come across to Vernon to defend us both on the day we had to see the Captain.

In the Navy, we had six monthly assessments as part of the advancement strategy; the top assessment was 'VG Exceptional'. While working at the SAR flight and on my first assessment on the dunker I had been given this top assessment, so felt confident it would be difficult for the Captain to take the matter too seriously. Ivor emphasised those points in my defence and did an equally good defence for Bill. I was prepared for a good dressing down (which I got) and was given a warning; Bill had a couple of days leave stopped plus a small fine.

The Commander was seething and made it clear via the Master at Arms that he would make my life difficult, which he did. I knew I could not remain in that situation for too long, operating the dunker with all these restrictions and aware that I was being watched, I decided I should move on so requested a draft.

I was open with my reasons for wanting out and fortunately Terry was available to return. He did not relish the idea of working from HMS Vernon but agreed to take it on so I moved back to flying and was drafted to '846 squadron' at Yeovilton.

I had to lose my 'acting local Chief Petty Officers' rate – although I picked it up again officially a few months later as the time spent as the dunker chief accelerated the normal promotion procedure.

It was quite ironic really, Bill had come to the dunker to escape the situation with an officer at Portland and I was leaving the dunker to escape a similar situation! This was the final straw for Billy and he left the Navy a few months later at a normal break point and went to work for British Airways Helicopters, in a winching role. I would get to work with Bill again many years later.

When Terry took over he also found it difficult working full time from HMS Vernon. The Commander and the rules he had imposed continued to make it difficult for the dunker crew but eventually he moved on and things got a little easier; however, operating from Vernon was not working out for many other reasons so Terry kept the pressure on to go back to the previous system.

In the meantime, things were not working out at HMS Daedalus either; it was causing too many problems trying to operate without a diving section. The main diving school in Portsmouth rarely had time to run the diver drop sessions, meaning it was difficult to keep the SAR divers in date. In addition, it was making it virtually impossible for the once very active sub aqua club to operate; they relied on the diving section for their facilities.

When things got too difficult, the dunker crew went back to the original routine, controlled from HMS Daedalus and the diving section reopened. This episode was to be a reminder of why I was so happy to get away from General Service when I transferred to aircrew.

During the time I had been working at the dunker, Margaret had managed to get a job as a secretary for a solicitor. This helped us to get over the financial restraints of my divorce and we managed to get ourselves back into the housing market, enabling us to leave our married quarters and purchase a new house in Lee-on-Solent. We both felt very secure together, so it was much easier this time when I had to go away. I knew it would not be for too long and was convinced I would bounce back to the Lee SAR Flight within a year to fifteen months.

Part 3

Final Years of Naval Career

846 Squadron

I joined '846 squadron' based at Yeovilton as my previous commando squadron '848' had been disbanded and '846' was doing a similar role supporting marines on exercises mainly in the UK, the Mediterranean and Northern Norway. There were fifteen aircraft on the squadron, but we would normally go on exercise with three or four aircraft, with the odd major exercises when all the squadron would embark on HMS Bulwark for deployment to Northern Norway or the Mediterranean.

We had approximately twenty aircrewmen attached to the squadron and what a great bunch they were. Many of them I already knew from the SAR world – this was becoming the norm, as the majority of commando aircrewman would alternate between SAR and commando. This was probably not fair really, because it made it difficult for the aircrewman in Sonar or the missile aimers to break out from their roles into a role perceived to be more enjoyable. The situation would be addressed in later years with all aircrewmen given more opportunity to change roles.

The Chief Aircrewman was Ian Mitchell (Mitch) who was nicknamed Bald Eagle Leader; he was quite a guy with an unusual way of leadership. He would have the mick taken out of him something chronic and just laugh along with it.

Mitch had the silliest things done to him, like topping his pipe up with match heads so that as he smoked his pipe, the match heads would pop away. He would simply shrug and say things like, "you can't get decent tobacco nowadays." We would be in fits, not over the silly pranks but the way Mitch would shrug them off as though it was normal. Such was his laid back manner and in his own quite extraordinary way he was a brilliant leader who gained respect rather than try to demand it and as such no one ever let him down.

The runs ashore as a squadron were always special and we had a silly chant, always carried out when ashore as a group. One of the lads would start humming, usually bald eagle leader; the hum was picked up by the others until it built up in to a crescendo when everyone would break in to song, singing "just one cornetto; give it to me; delicious ice cream from Italy" etc. from the popular advert that was running at the time. This always had an effect that would often lead to a good night out joined in by the other people in the pub.

One of the other SAR divers on the unit with me was, Pete Gibbs, a diver who mainly operated from the Culdrose SAR flight and a Queens Gallantry Medal holder. He had earned the medal from one of his very first jobs as a SAR diver when involved in the rescue of survivors from a life raft in horrendous seas off Cornwall. Pete was lowered to the life raft, but unfortunately the cable broke leaving Pete in the life raft with the survivors until another aircraft arrived. It was quite a traumatic time for Pete which included one of the survivors dying in his arms.

The rest of the diving team were Scouse Hogan and Tab Hunter who were good pals with me when I was on '848 squadron' and Smiler Grinney, another diver who normally bounced between Culdrose SAR and Commando. It goes without saying that we had many good runs ashore together while on various exercises in the UK and abroad, many with tales to tell that are probably best left untold! Nothing our wives needed to worry about, just silly challenges and things men get up to when they have difficulty coming to terms with the fact they are not teenagers anymore.

In February of 1979, I went off to carry out cold weather training in Northern Norway, to cover aspects of supporting troops in arctic conditions. Specific flying training was required in that environment because of the associated problems regarding icing conditions and snow landings – not straight forward in a helicopter as landing in loose snow would mean flying into your own downwash, creating a white out.

The pilots had to learn special techniques to achieve safe landings in snow and deal with the effects of icing on the aircraft, plus recognising the conditions that would be safe to fly in and, just as importantly those conditions where it was essential to land and wait for heavy snowstorms to clear or icing conditions to abate. We also had to learn how to survive if grounded for a few days; this would require a cold weather survival course prior to the operational training.

All the training took place while supporting Royal Marines on their own cold weather trials and exercises and the six-week period would finish with a major exercise.

The flying in Bardofos, the Norwegian Base we operated from, was out of this world: travelling round the fjords had to be the most incredible flying I was ever to do.

I had gone on this trip as the Senior Crewman of a small detachment of four aircraft and crews. The aircrewmen with me were Lyle Bradbury (Brad), Ian Weston (Aggie) and Graham McRoberts, (Mac 'R' as we called him). They were all aircrewmen I had worked with on Lee SAR and good pals of mine.

The pilots were a mixture of flying instructors and their students who had completed initial flying training but now in the operational training stage. One of the pilot instructors was my old SAR pilot Bruno Brunsden, who had gone on from Lee SAR to become a Qualified Helicopter Instructor, a great guy and a pilot I had enjoyed flying with when he was a SAR pilot.

Brad was another character of the aircrew world, very popular with everyone. He had just received the good news that he was to be a father; a fact that we had celebrated at the first chance that we managed to get a night off. This was to be another night of stupid behaviour which included a competition to see who could eat the most tulips! Why we did daft things like that, I have no idea. The tulips had been on the tables in the bar and it obviously seemed a good idea at the time. Anyway, we well and truly celebrated Brad's good news, all light hearted and egged on by the amused Norwegians.

A few days later, we had an exercise to carry out troop drills with groups of Norwegian troops before moving them to a forward base. Two of the aircraft would leave very early to arrive at the pick-up point at first light and the other two aircraft would be joining the exercise later. Brad and Aggie would go with the first two aircraft.

The pilot in the second aircraft, Sub Lt Clark, had reached his solo stage. He was a nice young guy who I was beginning to get to know and felt would be good to have on the squadron. The training pilots would still fly occasionally with these recently qualified pilots, to check they were coping and keeping up the standards expected of them. Bruno decided that he would join this flight for a check ride and they took off, the two aircraft in formation heading off to the rendezvous point.

Although the Fjords were beautiful to fly around, they had many dangers – the worst being wires strung up all over the place. The first thing we did when joining Bardofos was to update all our maps with all the known wires. Once we had done this, we had to rely on very accurate map reading to avoid these wires.

Unfortunately, the Norwegian logging industry had a habit of stringing up wires to carry logs down hillsides and across ravines etc. The aircraft that had flown out that morning had to fly over a spur as they made the approach to the landing site where the troops were waiting for them to arrive.

Aggie Weston's aircraft ran in and landed. Brad's aircraft must have taken a slightly different profile and the tail wheel caught one of these unmarked logging wires – the wire was never clear enough to see. The aircraft pivoted round the tail wheel that had caught the wire and crashed. The two pilots had almost certainly been killed outright. Brad was found unconscious but still alive amongst the wreckage.

When we received the message back at base, we did not know how serious it was but we took off immediately in another aircraft and headed to the scene. By the time we arrived, Norwegian paramedics had already left with Brad, who they had managed to recover from the helicopter alive. Unfortunately, he did not survive the flight to Tromso hospital. Bruno and Sub Lt Clark were being recovered from the wreckage. They had both died in the accident.

The flying was cancelled that day as we went off to digest the awful incident, a very difficult thing to do. I could not stop thinking of Brad and celebrating his good news only a few days before the accident. I had also had many flights with Bruno in the SAR role and he had been one of my favourite pilots. I knew Brads wife and Bruno's family - the situation was extremely difficult to take in.

I ended up taking an immature way out by disappearing with a bottle of whisky. I needed to be on my own to come to terms with what had happened. Really, I wanted to get home to my family but that was not an option.

We spent the next day flying the accident investigation team around and were kept quite busy on other exercises, something we would clearly rather not be doing, but probably essential to stop us dwelling on the accident.

Mac 'R' was having a particular hard time, being Brad's best friend and close to Brad's wife Leslie. He was flying at the time of the accident and had been practicing approaches to pinnacles in the mountains when he was informed of the accident on the HF radio. The aircraft was recalled to our operating base; he had been told that one of the aircraft had crashed but (at the time) was unaware it was Brad's aircraft.

I tried to arrange for Mac 'R' to be flown back to the UK for the funeral but, unfortunately, it was not the sort of thing the military allowed in those days. I felt that to be a real shame as it would have been the right thing to do in Mac's case. He would have been able to give considerable support to Leslie and might have helped him come to terms with the situation quicker.

Mac was able to join Leslie's family later for a special remembrance gathering in Scotland and even became a godfather to Brad's son Neil when he was born and has been keeping in regular contact ever since.

During the rest of the year we were kept extremely busy, the whole squadron had a few months on HMS Bulwark in support of '45 Commando' on exercises in the Mediterranean. We had other short-term exercises on Salisbury Plain, Bodmin Moor and Dartmoor.

I had another unusual detachment to a place called Kinlochlevan in Scotland. There were just two aircraft in support of a small exercise, the other aircrewmen with me were Pete Mesney and Pete Imrie. This turned out to be a memorable detachment.

The exercise was quite low key. The scenery was wonderful, a time when we feel extremely privileged to be in a position that allowed us to fly around the most beautiful countryside at low-level and be able to land almost anywhere we wanted.

We were billeted in mizzen huts on the edge of the village and on the first night, a few of us were invited to the social club for the evening. Pete Mesney was a natural comedian and started with his repertoire of jokes, so it was not long before we had a crowd of villagers joining our group and plying us with drinks.

One of the officers with us was a good pianist and he soon got a singsong going which made for one of those more memorable evenings. The evening went down so well with the villagers that they invited us back every night and it was as if the whole village turned out for the subsequent nights. I had never experienced hospitality like it.

Another comical moment on the flight was the day that a new Commanding Officer took over the squadron. He wanted to introduce himself to the squadron and clearly hoped to make an impression but his plan very much backfired.

The whole squadron had been assembled in the hangar where a makeshift podium had been set up. It was midday and everyone was in a relaxed mood when suddenly we were called to attention as the new CO walked in, he stepped on the podium and proceeded to make the shortest and most unusual introduction that I had ever heard. It went along the lines of. "I am Lt/Cdr ******* I am married with two children. The Royal marines role is to kill Russians, our role on '846 squadron' is to support the Royal Marines in killing Russians and when we are called upon to carry out this role we will do it well." He then stepped off the podium and marched out.

This was at the time of the Cold War and our primary role on '846 squadron' was to support the Royal Marines on the Russian borders, hence all the cold weather training. It was thought at the time that any advance made by the Russians would be made on the northern borders of Norway, probably during the winter months when the snow and ice would support the tanks and heavy equipment.

I thought after this short speech that the cold war hostilities were taking a step towards reality. We were all quite dumbfounded but it was soon clear this was just his way of making an initial impression. Unfortunately, it backfired within a few hours as all sorts of comical things happened.

Yeovilton was the base for three Commando squadrons: '845 squadron', ourselves ('846 squadron') and '707 squadron' which had the role of training pilots, crewmen and engineers for the commando role.

The training sorties on the commando squadrons were staggered and the crews used to get meals on an opportunity basis. To enable us to do this we had a cafeteria-style dining hall kept open nearly all day, known as the ACRB (Aircrew Restaurant Buffet) and housed in the building that '845 squadron' and '707 squadron' operated from.

When I went over for my meal, just a couple of hours after the introduction by the new CO, posters had appeared all over the passageways and in the ACRB. Some of them were produced quite professionally, even though it was before we had access to computers. They read along the line of, '846 Squadron kills Russians' another would read '845 Squadron are proud to backup 846 Squadron in the role of killing Russians' another '707 squadron train 846 squadron to kill Russians.'

The posters made it well and truly clear that this was not the way to rally the troops. Though it may have worked on the eve of a battle, it certainly did not in peacetime.

Towards the end of the year, I went off with my old mate Mick Rowsell to join HMS Hermes for a tour to the States. This was an unusual trip; we had embarked on the aircraft carrier to support an anti submarine squadron while on NATO anti submarine exercises. For Mick and me it was purely a Search and Rescue role; we would be on stand-by during all the exercise phases. It was quite a relaxed deployment for us and we had a holiday to look forward to when we arrived in America as our wives were flying out to meet us.

During the transit to America we took every opportunity to carry out winching practice, diver drops etc. We had a number of scrambles to shepherd aircraft back to the ship after they had put out pan calls for various reasons. One of the Sea King helicopters actually ditched during an exercise which was taking place off Bermuda. The crew had made a successful escape and been picked up by another Sea King operating on the same exercise. The aircraft was still on the surface, its huge flotation bags keeping it afloat.

The salt water activated buoyancy bags would only keep the aircraft afloat for a short while as they were designed only to give the aircrew time to escape.

We were tasked to pick up a team of ships divers and a Gemini (a small semi rigid inflatable), which we would take out to the scene with a small team of ships divers. In addition, we took buoyancy bags to attach to the Sea King in the hope we could keep the aircraft afloat long enough for the carrier to get alongside and crane the aircraft onboard.

This was a well-practiced routine and a Gemini plus floats was kept fully rigged for such an emergency. The general idea was that the Gemini would be carried as an under slung load and would be dropped in the water alongside the ditched aircraft. I would then jump in alongside it, climb aboard, remove the under-slung attachments, then the rest of the ship's divers would be lowered to the Gemini.

One of the divers had been briefed to go inside the aircraft to recover a top-secret folder. The cold war was still on then and these exercises were always monitored by Russian warships or Russian fishing vessels littered with aerials and listening gear. The folder in question was recovered and I believe one floatation bag attached before the Sea King capsized. It remained afloat upside down but in imminent threat of sinking; it was now too dangerous to try to attach further floats.

The ship's divers were recovered to the aircraft but prior to my recovery; the carrier ordered the aircraft to return immediately. The carrier had lost power while heading towards the incident at max speed trying to get there before the aircraft sank. The carrier's speed must have built up too quickly and the boilers tripped.

In the ensuing panic, they had ordered our aircraft back to the ship; I never did know why because it was a clear day and the helicopter would not have had any difficulty getting out of the way. Unfortunately, the pilot obeyed that order leaving me behind in the water.

That was to be a very strange ten minutes or so; I could not make it to the Gemini that had also been left behind and all around me, items such as seat backs were coming up from the ditched Sea King. Every time something popped up on the surface, I thought it was a shark. I had never given that a thought when I was with the other divers but, on my own, my mind ran riot. I had no idea why the aircraft had suddenly flown away; I thought it must have had some form of emergency and all I could see was it flying off into the horizon.

Mick, in the meantime, was not happy at leaving his diver behind and had quite a row with the pilot for obeying that command to return to the ship before picking me up, but the order had been return immediately. Mick called the carrier, explaining that I was still in the water and the aircraft was despatched back to pick me up. The Sea King did sink completely and in water too deep to attempt salvage.

On completion of the exercise, the carrier berthed in Jacksonville, a large American military port, and we disembarked to an air station called Mayport to act as a helicopter despatch service. Fortunately, they only needed one aircrewman for this so Mike and myself were able to split the time between us when our wives arrived at Jacksonville, including being able to have a fortnights leave.

Margaret and Kerry joined me a few days after we arrived and it was to be a fantastic time. During the two weeks leave we went to Orlando to take in the attractions. I am not sure who enjoyed that the most, Kerry or me! I was like a big kid in Disney World, Water World and all the other attractions Orlando has to offer. I was lucky Kerry was there to give me the excuse to go on all the rides; Margaret was not so adventurous but fortunately, Kerry was.

Once the families had returned home, the ship joined a NATO exercise culminating with the fleet docking in Philadelphia to prepare for another large exercise that would take place on transit back to the UK. We had several days in Philadelphia, which allowed time to do the tourist trips including New York and Manhattan.

We had quite a serious fire on board while in Jacksonville, causing damage to one of the engine rooms. This meant the ship could not take part in the exercise intended for us so, once the emergency repairs had been carried out, we were released early and limped back to the UK for refit.

The time on 846 was particularly good for me as it consolidated all I had learnt to date in quite a relaxed environment with a brilliant crowd of guys, quite possibly the best mix of personalities I ever came across. Fortunately, many of them I got to work with again in the future and most of us would meet at various events over the years.

846 Squadron detachment of aircrewmen onboard HMS Bulwark.
Top Splash Ashdown, knelt at the bottom Ian Mitchell
The rest left to right Pete Mesney, Tab Hunter, Pete Imrie, Aggie Weston,
Dave Peel, Mark Shurmer, Peter Gibbs, Scouse Hogan and Clive Rankin.

846 Squadron GPMG practice from 'Wessex Mk 5' safest place when I was firing was the target

Troop Drills on HMS Bulwark (Photo Mick Rowsell)

Survival Course Bardofos Northern Norway 1979

Back To The Dunker

Shortly after returning to the UK, I was informed that I would be returning to Lee-on-Solent to take over the Dunker from Terry. He was heading off to set up a diving expedition centre for the Army based on an island off Belize. The centre was to be set up as a rest and recreation activity for the troops stationed out there. This was probably Terry's dream draft as he could never keep away from the beach back home and had an addiction to sunbathing!

I was not too bothered about going back to the dunker, the commander who had caused me the problems had left HMS Vernon and the unit was again being run from the diving section at HMS Daedalus. I would rather have gone back to the SAR flight but this was at least getting me back home earlier than I should, so I was not going to argue. With a bit of luck I would go back to the SAR flight on completion of my tour at the dunker.

One of the first tasks when I rejoined the dunker was to carry out an escape trial for the Lynx helicopter. Terry remained for this trial as he had been involved in the first part and it would be a couple of weeks before he headed off to Belize.

The trial was unique. The Lynx aircraft had not long been in service and there was some concern as to the effectiveness of its flotation aids: would it remain on the surface long enough for the crew to escape? To date none had ditched.

One of the research engineers working for the MOD had thought, by his calculations, that the aircraft would not remain afloat long enough for the crews to escape. As the aircraft was already coming into service the trial had been set up quite quickly.

The trial took place in a naval research establishment near Helensburgh in Scotland where they had a huge tank with a wave-making machine. The tank was big enough for a Lynx helicopter to be suspended above it and the whole of one side was a glass wall with an observation room full of electronic monitoring equipment, quite an impressive place. A real Lynx helicopter (one of the initial flying production aircraft) was used for the trial.

The team had to sit inside the Lynx, strapped to the seats using various harnesses in service at the time; the aircraft was suspended above the tank by a crane. (The engineer had made calculations to find the height to suspend the aircraft above the water so that, when released, it would hit the surface at the approximate speed expected of an aircraft landing after an auto rotation.)

Once launched, it was not possible to lift the Lynx out of the water in an emergency as it took a lot of preparation to recover the aircraft after each dunking. Ropes were tethered to the Lynx so that it would not actually rest on the bottom of the tank, possibly crushing someone if they escaped at the wrong time. The ropes would also stop the Lynx from smashing against the huge glass wall.

We did not wear breathing apparatus for the trial because it needed to be as realistic as possible; there were safety divers on standby in case anything did go wrong.

The engineer's calculations proved to be very much as he predicted; the aircraft did not behave as expected from the pre production models. Having landed on the water the Lynx floated on the surface for approximately sixty seconds, providing the flotation bags positioned on either side had operated.

As the aircraft filled with water, it would suddenly tip forward, pivoting around the flotation bags and putting the crew underwater. A short while after that, as the whole aircraft filled with water, it would start to sink and the buoyancy bags would either break away or burst then the aircraft would sink like a brick.

We did dozens of these runs working out the best time to make the escape. Occasionally, we could get out before the first pivot forward, but risked disorientation if it suddenly tipped forward while we were making our escape and were pushed back inside. If we did not get out prior to that, it was important that we waited until it settled a second time, remaining strapped in the seat until the movement stopped.

These drops took place in different sea conditions created by the wave machine and were not without event. On a couple of occasions one or both bags burst as we were making our escape.

One of the escapes Terry made involved waiting until the second stage; he then had to have the presence of mind to escape from the position of a particular seat that was in use with the Dutch Navy Lynx helicopters. The only way out of this seat was to pull a lever which pushed the seat back, pull another leaver, swivel the chair round before releasing the harness and pulling free from the aircraft! I doubt if anyone would have escaped from that seat for real. Terry would admit that it took all his will power to remain calm even in semi-controlled conditions.

The main recommendations of this trial was to make the nose of the Lynx more buoyant, which would give a longer flotation time on the surface before the aircraft pivoted around the sponson buoyancy aids. I expected that would still happen but hopefully, after modifications to the aircraft the crews would have time to make their escape beforehand, If not they would have the knowledge to wait for the second chance before the bags broke off.

Lynx at moment of release

Lynx at the moment the nose tips forward

Ditching Trials Team
Top Row: Dave Peel, Terry Short, John Ascott,
Bottom row: Mark Spode, Neil Downs, Andy Jenrick

Andy has a black eye in the photograph a result of a punch up with his friend Neil. The argument was over a silly challenge that went wrong and to top it all, they were picked up by the patrol. Unfortunately for John, Terry and myself, we had returned from a few quiet pints ashore when we walked straight into the aftermath and had to spend virtually all night persuading the regulating staff not to troop them.

I could not help seeing the funny side, as I knew they would still be the best of friends in the morning. It reminded me of Lou and I after the run round the airfield, so found it difficult to take it seriously – definitely a one off!

My second tour on the dunker was much more relaxed and enjoyable than the first time. We would just get on with our job with no threat of losing the diving centre at HMS Daedalus and no pressures from anyone at HMS Vernon as we were back operating from HMS Daedalus. We would turn up at HMS Vernon when we had a course to train in the tank, the escape training took priority and the diving requirements required for HMS Daedalus were planned around it.

My No 2 was a PO called John Ascott, he was an ex field gunner and keep fit fanatic and his enthusiasm for sport and fitness rubbed off on the rest of the team. We were only a small unit, ten of us in total, but under John's guidance we entered several inter-departmental contests, winning some of them even when competing against sections with a few hundred students in them.

As Daedalus was a training establishment it was felt unfair that a unit not full time at Daedalus was entering these competitions, so I was asked by the PT staff if we could step back from them; however, working with John was to re-new my desire to keep fit, which continued for the rest of my career.

Back to Lee SAR Flight

I had only spent six months on the Dunker when Charlie Wines (our drafting controller) called me asking if I wanted to return to the Lee SAR flight and relieve the current Chief Aircrewman who had to leave the job at short notice. Not only was he asking me to return early to the job that in my view was the best job in the Navy, he was asking me to return as the Chief Aircrewman. I jumped at the chance!

I joined the squadron at the end of 1980 and shortly after we had a new Chief Pilot, Dave George, who was a great guy to work with and one who backed me to the hilt if the crewmen had any problems. Dave worked equally as hard looking after the engineers' welfare. This led to the flight settling down to be a very relaxed squadron with everyone wanting to be there, which made running the aircrewman side of things very easy.

John Spencer, one of the divers not long out of training as a SAR diver, had joined the flight a short while before I took over. John reminded me of myself on my first tour; in particular, his enthusiasm for the job – he had that natural affinity to the role of SAR diver just as I felt and still feel.

One of the first jobs John had was the rescue of a man trapped still alive in a capsized barge. Rescue teams were preparing to drill a hole in the bottom of the vessel, close to where they could hear the man tapping, but it was felt the release of air would probably force the barge to sink.

When John arrived on scene, he knew the only chance was to dive inside and hope he could locate him. It was not going to be an easy task, there was virtually no visibility, the position the sounds were coming from was at the front of the boat and the only entrance was towards the back.

This is the sort of job the SAR diver is trained for; however, there were so many variables to this one, including the fact the vessel could sink to the bottom while he was in there and that there was a limited supply of air in the sets we used. John would have been well within his rights to wait until a backup team of divers arrived, but once he had heard the tapping, he felt he had to get straight in there.

He really did have a task ahead him. At one stage, he went into a compartment, and while feeling his way with his hands, he banged his head. He had actually pulled himself into a toilet compartment, bearing in mind the barge was upside down he ended up with his head firmly in a toilet bowl!

He eventually found the compartment with the air bubble and heard a sobbing sound, so knew immediately he had located the survivor.

John had to tell the guy not to grab for him as he felt he could easily dislodge his equipment. He had to reassure the guy that he would be alright whilst at the same time knowing that there was no way he would be able to lead the survivor out, he would have to try to make his own way out then go back in with another set for the survivor.

John must have known that was a lot to ask, to go back in knowing he would have to try to teach a man who was in a nightmare situation how to use a diving set. He would have to try to show him how to breathe from the set while they were both in the water, in the dark, inside a vessel that could sink at any minute.

John told the guy that now that he had located him he would have to leave and collect the equipment required to get him out, assuring him that he would be back.

When John resurfaced, the aircraft had returned with another SAR diver, Dave Brown (Bomber). Dave had also brought extra diving sets so John changed his set, briefed Bomber and they both went into the upturned barge.

John, knowing the situation and the position of the survivor, led the way to the air lock. Once the casualty was briefed, Bomber positioned himself at the entrance of the compartment ready to grab the survivor's legs when John started to get him out. They still had a passage to pull the survivor along and he was likely to be panicking. I know from my own experience when I was trapped in the fishing net that both John and Bomber would have been fighting their own demons at the time.

As soon as John got the set on the survivor (almost before John could position the mouthpiece) he sank below the surface. The sets we used were not buoyant and, of course, the survivor was not wearing a diving suit, which would have helped counter-balance the weight of the set.

Bomber grabbed his legs and pulled him along the passageway, through the next hatch and up to the surface. In the meantime, as John tried to follow the casualty down, he realised his exit had been blocked, a ladder or something like that had been dragged across the hatch as the casualty went through. John realised he was breathing too heavily in his panic and knew he had very little air left in his set so went back into the air pocket to gather his senses.

He then felt with his feet as he breathed from the air pocket until he was sure where the exit and obstruction were. Once he was able to work out what had happened he was able to replace his mouthpiece and squeeze pass the obstruction.

When he got to the surface he could see the survivor being winched into the disappearing aircraft and could hear the discussion taking place when Bomber and another diver now on scene (Chris Crossley) realised John was still inside. They were on the opposite side of the upturned hull from where John had surfaced and were preparing to go back inside to look for him. They must have been extremely relieved to hear John shouting, letting them know he was out of the barge.

John still does not know if the survivor had managed to breathe from the set or if he had just held his breath. Anyway, a brilliant job by both

John and Bomber. This was one of those rare jobs, which can only be described as exceptional.

John received the Queen's Gallantry Medal for the rescue and Bomber the Queen's Commendation.

During the previous year's Fastnet sailing race '1979', a huge storm developed, wreaking havoc amongst the fleet of yachts of which many capsized or crewmembers were lost overboard. Both RAF & Navy helicopters from a number of units around the coast played a large part in rescuing up to 140 casualties of which 15 died. Some of these were seen to be conscious in the water when aircraft arrived but never survived the rescue, a phenomenon not fully understood at the time but later known as post rescue collapse.

This phenomenon clearly caused concern and was taken up by a naval doctor, Cdr Frank Golden, who was doing a study on cold water immersion and other hypothermic causes. In fact many of his trials were carried out by SAR Divers in cold water tanks and field environments. The divers were all volunteers and would be put under quite gruelling conditions, wired up with thermometers then warmed up again by various methods, all for the sake of helping doc Golden (who was a very likeable character) and the promise of a free tot of navy rum at the end of the trial. Partly as a result of the trials he was adamant that every effort should be made to lift casualties from the water horizontally, especially when in cold water.

His reasoning was backed up by trials he had conducted and information gained from trials carried out by the Germans in World War II, which he was studying. What follows is my basic description of post rescue collapse drawn from the lessons learned. Being very complex, the human body will make every effort to survive in cold conditions by a process of slowly closing down and shunting the blood from the extremities to the inner core to provide oxygen and nutrients to the vital organs; this is a normal reaction as the body becomes hypothermic. When in cold water this is assisted by hydrostatic squeeze which applies pressure to the extremities, assisting with the shunting of blood to the core.

In the rescue situation the normal practice was to arrive on scene and pick the casualty out of the water vertically by a single lift strop. This allowed the blood to suddenly shift back to the extremities as the casualty was lifted clear off the water. The shock of this in some cases was catastrophic.

Here at Lee we were tasked to carry out trials to find ways of achieving a horizontal lift, but the various ideas of lifting contraptions proved too dangerous while hanging on the end of a wire, especially in rough seas. Eventually we got round to the idea of simply using two strops, one placed over the shoulder and one under the knees, allowing the casualty to be recovered in the semi incumbent position which proved to be a perfect position for what we were trying to achieve. The two strop method, known as either the 'Hypothermic or Hydrostatic lift', would eventually become the norm for recovery from the water, especially cold water when it is not known how long the casualty has been in the water.

I have to mention that this is not always achievable because trying to achieve the two strop method in heavy seas and surf is not always possible and in time medical skills and equipment will be carried to hopefully reverse that catastrophic event should we face it. However that discovery would save many casualties' lives in ensuing incidents.

The Solent is, in the main, the ideal place for water activities as there are good harbours, rivers and marinas leading onto the Solent such as Portsmouth, Southampton, Bembridge, Fishbourne, Cowes, Lymington and Yarmouth Harbours. The rivers Hamble, Beaulieu and Medina have marinas and berths all along them. In addition, Cowes is the venue for many of the major sailing events.

One of the advantages of the Solent is that, being between the Isle of Wight and the mainland, it is mainly in the lee of the Island or the mainland depending on the direction of the wind. The land mass either side is not high enough to steal all the wind. This makes a great environment for sailing, with calm areas close to the land-mass for novices and maybe more challenging conditions in the central Solent for the bigger yachts, depending of course, on the strength of the wind.

Occasionally, squalls would funnel through the Solent, the prevailing winds funnelled between the narrow point at the Needles and Hurst Castle. When these squalls were forecasted, the local clubs and the more sensible people with the smaller craft would cancel sailing for that period.

The very worst situation was when the day started with ideal conditions that enticed people out and the weather was expected to stay reasonable or was difficult to forecast, then with very little warning a rogue squall would rip through the Solent.

A series of these happened in the early months of 1981, when the sailing clubs were having their early season races. This was to be one of my busiest shifts to date with smaller dinghies and even some of the larger yachts capsizing in the squalls.

I was in and out of the water like a yo-yo, mainly helping to right capsized boats or transferring survivors from the water to safety vessels, a couple of casualties with head injuries were taken to hospital and we were finally scrambled to a capsized yacht off the Needles where one of the crew unfortunately lost his life. I was amazed that we had not had more fatalities that day. If it had been high season, it would have been a different story.

Another of the divers Loz Coleman, a well-known character in the SAR world, was a law unto himself but a brilliant SAR diver and SAR aircrewman. He was one of those people who would be the centre of any mischief but always come up smelling of roses. Loz helped to provide a lot of the laughter on the flight and everyone had stories to tell about him. I think having guys like him around makes the difference between a good working group and a great one, so I was chuffed he was at Lee.

He had a lucky escape one day when scrambled to the dredger 'Margaret Smith'. The dredger's load of gravel had shifted, making the vessel unstable. The incident happened only fifty metres in front of the Royal Yacht Squadron at Cowes on the Isle of Wight, so quite a number of people had gathered to watch events unfold.

The aircraft was scrambled and when on scene, Loz was lowered to the vessel where the crew onboard were preparing to board a ship's lifeboat. Loz, deciding this to be the quickest way to get them off (especially so close to shore and the lifeboat already prepared) helped the crew into the lifeboat. He had just helped the last man in when the vessel started to capsize with no warning. He tried to jump over the guardrail into the water but was on the opposite side to the direction the vessel was capsizing.

So he simply ran on the by now horizontal surface of the side of the vessel, just trying to make it to the water as the ship continued to capsize. He was in effect running round the rotating hull until he found himself on the keel of the now upside down boat. The helicopter moved in and winched him off. It was all captured on film, featured on the news that night and was quite comical to watch, particularly for those that knew Loz, but the possible consequences did not bear thinking about.

In the December of the same year during a nasty gale, the aircraft was scrambled to the vessel 'Bonito' in difficulty south of Portland Bill with (I believe) twenty plus crew and passengers onboard, including the Captain's wife and child.

I should have been on duty this day but had a family function to go to in Bristol. John Spencer had volunteered to stand in for me by swapping shifts.

The weather turned so bad that I did not make it to the function; we had to turn back half way as the roads were so treacherous. The weather was atrocious; I actually remember thinking that it would not be very nice being scrambled in the conditions.

In accordance with sod's law, as I was making my way back from the abandoned journey the aircraft was battling its way to the stricken craft and John was probably asking himself why he had agreed to the swap! He was crewed with Paul Sparks as the pilot and Roger Brooks was his aircrewman. When they arrived on scene, the vessel was moving so awkwardly they wondered if it would be possible to get John onboard. If they tried, it would clearly be a hazardous situation not only for John, but for the aircraft as well.

They decided, as invariably they would in these situations, that they had to make every effort to get John onboard. Several attempts were carried out, before John was firmly deposited on the deck and immediately the child was placed in his arms. Roger, on seeing that John had a firm grip of the baby, winched him clear of the vessel, recovering them to the aircraft.

After that first lift, which had helped Paul and Roger work out the safest way to carry out the winching, they managed to get John on to the vessel a further three times, allowing the recovery of the lady and two other crewmembers in three separate lifts. One of the crewmembers took quite a knock when John and the casualty hit an obstruction as they were winched clear of the vessel.

After the fourth recovery, Paul had to accept they had no time to attempt any further rescues as they were at minimum on-scene fuel - they only had enough fuel remaining for the return to Portland. That must have been an awful decision but one that had to be taken otherwise they would be facing a ditching, not only putting the crew at risk but also the survivors already rescued. They knew lifeboats were on the way so headed back towards Portland.

Not having the luxury of modern navigation equipment, they relied on navigation by dead reckoning so did not really know how far they had drifted with the vessel. When they hit landfall they were a little further west of the airfield than expected, which meant that being so low on fuel they were virtually flying on fumes: they realised they may well have to land prior to reaching the airfield. Paul decided to continue, being prepared to put down if necessary and, on the final approach to Portland airfield one of the engines flamed out. Fortunately, being in the Wessex 5, they had two engines and the second remained running to allow a safe, controlled landing.

Two Sea King helicopters had been despatched when the seriousness of the situation had been realised. Unfortunately, the Sea Kings were unable to get a winchman onboard the vessel but they did manage to recover one more casualty by winching an empty strop to him.

John was expecting to go out again once the aircraft had refuelled but, while the aircraft was refuelling, the Coastguards informed them that the lifeboat had arrived on scene and was attempting to get alongside the 'Bonito'. This would be an extremely hazardous manoeuvre in itself, but again there was no way the lifeboat crew were going to stand by and watch a disaster happen. Fortunately, the lifeboat did succeed and managed to get all the remaining crew onboard.

John, as could be imagined, was relieved, not only that the crew had been rescued but that they did not have to go back as they would have had to try again. I also know John would have agreed to make further attempts.

John later got the bar to his Queen's Gallantry Medal for that job; he had only been in the role for a couple of years and was now the most decorated SAR diver in the Navy.

I had seen many medals awarded and occasionally thought a few of them were not necessarily deserved; after all, we do a job that we are well trained to do. I did feel both of John's medals were well deserved, I know that he would have drawn on a fair amount of inner courage and would have had to fight back the fears that may well have led to a different decision; however that was John.

Towards the end of the year, during yet another round of defence cuts, the Navy asked for volunteers to take redundancies. They would be from any branch, no matter if the branch happened to be short of people. The redundancies would not take place for another eighteen months or so and only a couple of years before I would be due to leave the Navy.

I felt that if I took up this offer it would increase my chance of starting a second career. I had been thinking about my future on leaving the Navy and was hoping to get into a flying job in the North Sea and if that failed I would try to get into the Fire or Ambulance service.

Another mate of mine, Dave Morris, who was the same age as me had the same choice; our ages meant it would have been silly not to take it. We would still have all our pension rights and a redundancy payment and we would be leaving at the right side of forty.

Leaving the Navy before that magical age of forty was an advantage, as it was not only considered old in the Navy, but was also a landmark for employers outside of the forces, who at the time, would look for employees under the age of forty. My next draft, which would have taken me to the end of my career in the Navy, would almost certainly have been a desk type job or a training role which was not really my scene.

I was convinced this was the way forward, as was Dave, so we both volunteered. It seemed a long way ahead and we would definitely stay at Lee SAR until then. We had volunteered for the last phase of the redundancy programme as requested.

Anyway, quite a lot was to happen between making that decision and leaving the Navy, so it was back to work knowing I would now almost certainly be leaving the Navy from the job I was extremely happy doing and still had eighteen months or so in the role.

Falklands Factor

Early in 1982, problems were starting in the Falkland Islands. Argentina was making threats that they intended to take back the Islands; there had been a long dispute between Britain and Argentina as to the rightful owners of the Islands. This posturing happened every so often, but no one really thought this would turn into anything more than that. On the 2nd of April, the Argentineans invaded the Falkland Islands.

This was the start of a flurry of activity, which was to affect just about everyone in the services. A task force was formed at very short notice, the main body of which was assembled here at Portsmouth. I could not believe the speed this happened. As well as the military warships gathering, many civilian ships were converted into troop and helicopter carriers. Even the cruise liner the 'Queen Elizabeth II' was converted as a troop carrier with helicopter platforms rapidly built on its decks.

HMS Daedalus, where we operated, soon became a place of high activity with helicopters operating from the base helping to speed up the loading of the extra equipment on the vessels gathering in the Solent.

The MOD, recognising that more crews and helicopters would be required, decided that Portland SAR flight would close down so Portland's aircraft and some of the crews found themselves as part of the task force.

Shortly after that decision, they closed down Lee SAR flight and moved us to Portland to cover SAR for both regions from Portland. I believe this was because of the training requirements still needed at Portland (the Navy's main sea training area). The ships destined for the South Atlantic that had not been operationally prepared would still require a work-up at Portland.

The sea training at Portland required helicopters to transfer training staff and crews between ships. More helicopters turned up from storage and aircrews were drafted in from various nooks and crannies to help fulfil this role.

The nucleus of the SAR crews that had moved from Lee would remain dedicated SAR, but we would now have two areas to cover encompassing from Eastbourne in the east to Start Point in the west.

The whole situation was bizarre to me. The task force left with many of my friends on board. Mick Rowsell who had recently left Lee to go back to a commando squadron was heading south on the QEII, Terry Short found himself on HMS Hermes then, during the trip south transferred to HMS Intrepid which was an assault troop ship. The Intrepid and HMS Fearless had won a reprieve from being sold off or scrapped because they would now be required for this campaign.

Most of the lads that I had worked with on '846 squadron' were heading south on various ships and carriers; nevertheless, I still could not come to terms with the thought that they were heading into actual conflict. I thought that the threat of the task force would be enough to end the situation.

Like the majority of the country, we could not miss news items as the task force headed south and, when the conflict actually started, I knew all the aircrewman would be right in the thick of it. They would be carrying out insertions of troops, forward base troop supply; rescue missions, the risks would be endless. I was also quite sure that we the crews left behind would be in the next wave of aircrew required to go down there when the crews needed relieving, as many of us were trained as commando aircrewmen as well.

I had mixed feelings about that, especially after hearing the stories coming back from the Falklands. The reports left us in no doubt that every one of the aircrews would be working almost on autopilot, ignoring the dangers and just getting on with the job. That is the way it was and not just for aircrew but for all the troops. Even the crews on the ships had to live in constant fear of attack after the sinking of the first ship.

Two of the aircrewmen (both Commando aircrewmen) had already lost their lives: Petty Officer Ben Casey, on the way down to the Falklands while carrying out a helicopter replenishment transfer from HMS Hermes, and Corporal Michael 'Doc' Love, the crewman of the Sea King that ditched while transferring troops between HMS Hermes and HMS Intrepid. Twenty-one troops plus 'Doc' lost their lives that night including eighteen SAS troops; the largest loss to the regiment since the Second World War. The accident also killed a member of the Royal Signals and a RAF Flight Lieutenant.

We still had a Search and Rescue role to carry out back home, as people did not stop getting into difficulties and, with a bigger patch to cover, we were kept quite busy, but thoughts of our friends in the Falklands were never far from our minds.

Towards the end of May, Pete Imrie joined the flight; Pete was one of the aircrewmen with me on '846 squadron' and had later qualified as a SAR diver. Pete had been involved in a clandestine military operation in the conflict; it was common knowledge that he was a member of the helicopter crew that had landed in Chile. The incident had quite a lot of media coverage when it happened but why they were there was not disclosed. The Chilean authorities released them quite quickly and they were flown back to the UK.

Pete could not talk about what happened or what the mission was about but we knew it was hazardous. The crew were all volunteers and when they left the ship, they would have known that they would not have enough fuel to get back to that ship or to any other that could help them. However hard we tried it was not possible to get the mission details out of Pete and believe me we tried, even by getting him drunk on several occasions! We did however; get a feel for what was happening down there as obviously there were things Pete could mention.

Pete earned the nickname 'our man in Chile'. His nickname when I was with him on '846 squadron' was 'slingshot' but I will not go into that.

In the middle of June Argentina surrendered. It had been a nasty, dangerous encounter; the whole war took place in just a little over ten weeks. In those weeks a task force formed, sailed all the way to the Falklands and the troops had yomped from one side of the island to the other in order to recapture Port Stanley.

In all forty-four warships, twenty-five Royal Fleet auxiliaries craft and forty-five merchant ships sailed south. Two destroyers, two frigates, one landing craft and one fleet auxiliary vessel were sunk. Thirteen helicopters and nine Harrier aircraft were lost, plus the much-needed Chinook helicopters that went down with the Atlantic Conveyor. Two hundred and fifty five British troops, airmen and sailors lost their lives.

The conflict being over so quickly was obviously a great relief to everyone but it would be some months, even years, before things got back to normal. A sizeable military force would be required to remain in the Falklands for quite some time. I knew that this force would require helicopters and felt sure that task would be down to our commando squadrons.

I was quite expecting the redundancy programme to be cancelled and was, in many ways, quite happy about that because I was getting cold feet about leaving (it was only ten months away).

I had thought that I might even get a chance to remain in the Navy after my 40th birthday. If I had been able to do that, I would have jumped at it as I would have more chance of having a complete career with a considerably better pension at the end of it.

At that time, it was almost the norm in the RAF for those airmen who wished, to remain in the service to the age 50 and sometimes until 55. It was being muted that the Navy would have to come in line and offer the same opportunities but I would have to wait and see about that.

The main thing on my mind now was when would we get back to Lee-on-Solent? The move to Portland was a temporary one because of the Falklands conflict. It soon became apparent that the MOD intended to keep us at Portland permanently as shutting down completely the aviation function at HMS Daedalus would be a cost effective move.

This would mean leaving the Solent, reputedly the busiest area of water-born activities in Europe, and the two major ports either side of HMS Daedalus (Southampton and Portsmouth) without SAR cover. The nearest cover for these areas would now come from Portland on a permanent basis.

The public outcry was considerably more than the MOD expected and the local MP fought a tremendous campaign to have this decision reversed. The move to Portland had been accepted when it was obvious to all that the troops heading to the Falklands needed all the backup they could get. Nevertheless, the decision to keep the flight at Portland was not popular and people-power would make every effort to reverse this decision.

I was unable to do anything about this but I was not happy about the decision; I was to see things happen I did not like. For instance, one Senior Naval Officer gave a brief at Portland as to why this was the way forward, giving sound reasons why. Only later, I attended a meeting at Lee-on-Solent, when I heard him telling the locals that he would be fighting to keep the SAR flight at Lee. How do you deal with something like that? I was in the military and could not just stand up and say, "Hang on a minute, last week you were saying we will definitely stay at Portland." That sort of thing simply was not done.

Anyway, as the campaign grew in the Solent area, we still had a job to do; we were resigned to being at Portland and thought it unlikely they would reverse the decision.

During one week we had a spate of nasty jobs, the first during a major parachute exercise on Salisbury Plain. The winds had been quite strong and some of the paratroops had collided in mid air. Two of the parachutists even had their parachutes completely entangled and when they broke clear one dropped to the plain when his parachute failed to open correctly.

There were quite a few injured paratroopers spread over the area. We had picked up a doctor when scrambling and were very glad we did as it was chaos when we arrived on scene. The first casualty I ran to was unconscious and in a bad way; all I could do was clear his airway and pad stem the bleeding.

We quickly assessed the worst casualties - one critical and four seriously injured - then transferred them to the aircraft and flew to Odstock Hospital. We tried our best to support life with the critically-injured casualty who had now stopped breathing. I was carrying out CPR helped by the doctor Lt Cdr Sach. Unfortunately, that casualty was pronounced dead on arrival at hospital but the other four survived their injuries.

Just the day after, I was scrambled to a vessel mid-channel that had two crewmembers seriously injured after an engine room explosion. We also took a doctor with us on this scramble who was lowered to the vessel with me. One of the injured men had an amputated arm so it was quite nice having a doctor with me to share the responsibility. We did manage to get both the casualties to Dereford Naval Hospital in Plymouth and they both survived the accident.

Just as we got back from that job, John Spencer took over from me at normal crew change time. He was immediately scrambled to a man hit by a propeller after falling from a speedboat. That was awful for John as the casualty died in his arms; he had lost too much blood before the aircraft arrived.

On another occasion, we were scrambled at first light, to search for a couple who had gone missing the day before. They were both pensioners and had been last seen in a small sailing dinghy. They should not have been sailing really, as they were both quite frail but sailing was their love and for them it was a difficult thing to give up, so had continued to sail longer than perhaps they should.

When we got airborne, we felt it would be very unlikely that we would find them alive. If they had drifted away from the coast, they would have drifted into the Portland races, an area of water where the tides meet, invariably inducing very rough water, even in the lighter winds. We felt that, even if the boat was still afloat, it would be unlikely they would survive such a cold night in an open dinghy.

Lifeboats had been searching all night but nothing had been sighted. Shortly into our search we spotted the dinghy and it was still upright. When we got closer, we could see the couple cuddled up together trying to keep warm. I immediately jumped in the water and clambered aboard to find a plucky woman protecting her husband. They were both suffering from hypothermia but she could still talk; her husband was in a bad way and she was only concerned about him, asking if we could get him ashore and she would stay with the boat.

Obviously, she was confused as there was no way she could remain where she was, drifting in the Portland races. All that was keeping her going was the will to keep her husband alive. They were extremely lucky they had survived the night and within 15 minutes, we had them both in Weymouth Hospital.

Again, this job was straightforward for us but lifesaving for the couple. It was the spirit of that woman which had kept them alive overnight; the same spirit that had made them continue their hobby even though they really should not have been sailing in their state of health. A lot was said about them being foolhardy but I could not help feeling admiration for the couple.

John Spencer had completed his Petty Officers' course the year before, passing out with a top grade. He had been selected for training as a communications aircrewman, which was a sub qualification within the aircrewman's branch and only a few people were required to do this job. The role was virtually as an observer and the aircrewman would be responsible for all navigation, mainly in the fixed wing fleet of Heron and Devon's. These aircraft would fly between military airfields or airports close to establishments, often flying with VIP's onboard.

The aircrewman would sit in the right-hand seat and deal with all the navigation and communications in and out of controlled airspace, so it was quite a responsible job and required good navigational skills. For this reason and because of the high failure-rate on previous courses, the selection would now be from aircrewmen who did well on the Petty Officers' course.

John, with his rescue awards, was becoming quite a celebrity within the Navy so, being offered the training on top of all that was quite a feather in his cap. He had difficult decisions to make as like all SAR divers, he loved his job and to transfer to communications would mean it very unlikely that he would ever get back to SAR.

I felt it was stupid: the Navy had spent many thousands of pounds training him up as an SAR diver, we still had a shortage of divers and now they were moving him on to something completely different after only a few years in this role.

John talked to me at length about this and I was quite clear that I thought he would regret the decision if he accepted as I knew his feelings for SAR were as strong as mine. On the other hand, he had pressures from above; it was unlikely anyone being selected for the communications role had ever turned it down. In the main, the majority of aircrewmen who felt they could do the job would have wanted to do it.

To be qualified as a communication aircrewman had plenty of benefits and was quite a sought after-career. It would also give better prospects of continuing in aviation when he left the Navy. I had no doubt that John would pass the course and it would also lead to him picking up his Petty Officers' rate quicker, as now he had to wait for a vacancy and the wait was based on seniority and merit. Transferring would speed up that process. Having said that, I still thought it was the wrong decision for John and felt he would regret the decision later.

Nevertheless, I think the pressures from above were too strong, so John disappeared from the flight to start his course. He still had his doubts hanging over him, but was being assured that the job offered so much he would soon slot into the new role and grow to enjoy it.

The guys started returning from the Falklands and life at Portland was getting back to being a very busy base, with a lot of helicopter activity. The

SAR flight was somewhat protected from the normal bustle of the bigger squadrons, but still housed within '771 squadron' and the two could never be completely independent. This took away some of the camaraderie that we experienced at Lee.

The campaign to get the SAR Flight back to Lee was well underway with questions asked in the House of Commons regarding that decision. The situation regarding remaining at Portland was not a done deal, there could be a chance we would return. I just hoped at the time, if it did happen that we would move back before I left the Navy.

Later in the year, the RAF confirmed they would provide the majority of helicopters and crews required to defend the Falklands. This meant it was looking likely that the redundancies in the Navy would go ahead. I had tried to pull out of the redundancy program, but was only willing to do that if promised a long-term extension after the age of 40 and, of course, that was not an option as the Navy was still cutting back. The situation was to change not many years after that as all the forces came in line regarding career opportunities, but too late for me.

One morning, the aircraft was scrambled to a Catamaran wrecked in rough seas and washed up close to Sidmouth in Devon. A man had been found still alive on the beach but his wife was still missing. I was crewed with pilot Norman Lees and Dave Morris was the winch operator. It was in foul weather.

When we arrived on scene we located a lot of flotsam and wreckage in the area but no sign of the lady. The search was extended, carrying out sweeps a few miles either side of the wreckage.

On one of these sweeps, we located the possibility of a person in the heavy breaking surf but it was quite rough and the sighting would disappear for short periods. I was winched down to check what we had seen, which was indeed the missing person who we quickly recovered to the aircraft and commenced CPR as Norman flew us to the nearest hospital landing-site. We would always try our best with the resuscitation as, just occasionally, it did make a difference – we could not presume she had been in that surf line for a long time.

As the story unfolded, the trip was a retirement dream for the couple. They had purchased the very well equipped all-weather catamaran, which was to become their home as they sailed off heading for the warmer climates. They were experienced sailors and the boat should have been able to stand up to the seas that night but then suddenly disaster struck at the very start of their dream.

This was another situation that made me question the events of that night. Perhaps if they hadn't been quite so experienced they may not have started the journey in those conditions and might later have gone on to reap the benefits of that dream. I guess that's fate but still very tragic.

I am not sure if the husband survived - he was in a critical condition when located. The police later questioned Dave and me because the husband had said that when they left the stricken yacht his wife had been wearing a money belt with a considerable amount of savings in it. Unfortunately, if she had it would have been lost to the sea, probably in the surf.

At the beginning of 1983, the Navy announced that the Lee-on-Solent SAR Flight would return to Lee-on-Solent and that the original Portland SAR Flight would be reformed. That was brilliant news for me which I sincerely believed was the right decision. I wouldn't be able to enjoy being back at Lee-on-Solent for long, with only a few months left in the Navy, but was extremely pleased that I would see the Flight back there prior to my leaving.

I went on ahead with a small party of engineers and aircrewmen to get the section at Lee ready for our return and the aircraft returned on the 3rd February 1983.

Shortly after the flight returned to Lee, John Spencer called in. He had finished his communication aircrewman's course and was carrying out his probationary period on the station flight, at Yeovil in Somerset. John had done well on the course but admitted that he was having doubts about the transfer and was missing the Search and Rescue role. Life was all too serious for John in this new role. He did not say he was going to quit but it was clear he was not happy.

When John went back to Yeovilton on the Monday, he returned to the crew room after collecting the brief for the day's flying when he thought 'what am I doing here, this is definitely not the job for me' and told them he no longer wished to continue in the role.

They could not believe John's decision and tried everything to get him to reconsider, but he had made his mind up and the team at Yeovil understood his reasoning. As per normal procedure in cases like this, John was drafted to HMS Daedalus to wait for an interview with the aviation board at Seafield Park (the home of the air medical board).

Shortly after this the aviation board had contacted the flight as to our thoughts on John's decision and I heard comments from people in authority who should have known better, saying they will make sure John would never get back to Search and Rescue. It really was a witch-hunt.

My argument to the board was that I thought that John had been pushed into the course, he had registered his doubts at the time but the selection team had convinced him that this was the way forward. I also stressed that, if I could have seen the likelihood of this happening, others should also have done.

Too much was happening to John at the time, he had been exceptionally keen on his Petty Officers' course and had done well, but that was because he loved his job. A significant amount of money was invested in John's training as a SAR diver and to take him away from that after only a couple of years, especially when he was doing so well in the role, was not right. I felt it was bad judgement putting him on the course in the first place. Dave George the chief pilot backed my view.

It was amazing; John had been used by the Navy's PR machine because of his awards in Search & Rescue, giving maximum publicity for the Navy. He had also won the Navy's 'Man of the Year' award and had even been a subject on 'This Is Your Life'.

Now he was being victimised for making a decision that actually took a tremendous amount of courage to make. John knew the communication role was not for him and had more than shown he was suited to the SAR world but now they wanted to take that away from him as a punishment.

The board did meet and John was given a rough ride, the board not accepting his reasons for pulling out and in turn drafting him to a non-SAR billet at Culdrose in Cornwall. He was to prepare for a tour on a small ships flight and had been told he would not fly in SAR again.

However, whilst all that was going on the aircrew branch was still trying to get back to normal after the Falklands conflict and with the continuing shortage of divers, John found himself back on Culdrose SAR flight almost immediately.

Not too long after that, one of Lee's divers, Taff Foster, was seriously injured on a job. John returned to Lee, initially to relieve Taff until he got better but ended up staying at Lee for another year, so much for the board's decision not to let John back into SAR!

Taff Foster, the SAR diver who John relieved was injured during an incident recovering a crewmember from a fishing boat in quite rough weather. Taff had ended up entangled in the rigging, the boat going one way and the aircraft another. The result was that he very nearly had his arm severed. Taff was fortunate that they were able to have him in hospital very quickly and that the surgeons were able to save his arm. The injury was quite horrific and he was many months recovering, although he did eventually get back to flying.

Part 4

Transition to Civvy Street & North Sea SAR

Leaving the Navy

In the April of 1983, I left the Navy. That was the strangest feeling - I had served twenty-two years, it was all I had known and I was now very apprehensive about the future. I applied for several jobs but most of the applications were ignored.

The flying jobs in the North Sea had dried up so I was leaving the Navy at the very worst time. Unemployment was rocketing, anyone in work was staying put. Employers taking on staff had many potential recruits to choose from so were generally looking for younger employees.

The police force had reduced their maximum age limit to thirty-seven, the Fire and Ambulance Service even less; I think their maximum age was thirty-five at the time. The Coastguards called me forward for an interview and I was offered a posting at Stornoway in the Western Isles, which I turned down, as I was not keen to relocate to an Island off the west coast of Scotland.

I would come to regret that decision later. Dave Morris, who was leaving the Navy with me, had accepted a similar posting, in Scotland, but during his training it was changed and he ended up at Portland (his first choice) and really enjoyed the job. I am sure if I had gone to Stornoway I would have settled in and enjoyed it but, at the time I still hoped that I would find an aviation-related post.

Having joined Victory barracks in Portsmouth to commence the demob routine, the day I left was a very sad one. I was sure I had made the wrong decision and would now have loved another two years in the Navy whatever job they would have given me, especially after the rejection of my job enquiries.

The demob routine was soul destroying, trailing round different departments getting forms stamped and returning equipment. I had a list of things that I had to return and anything missing I would have to pay for. Then it was off to meet the Captain of the barracks, a person I did not know and who did not know me, yet he had to give me a quick pep talk on how useful I had been to the service. That was that and I walked out of the gate as a civilian.

I had no idea what to expect, but at that moment I felt a great sense of dejection and the full impact of leaving the umbrella of the services was rammed home. Perhaps it would have been easier if I had been leaving to go straight to another job, at least I would have had the challenge of that to look forward to but, as it was, one day I had been the Chief Aircrewman of a Royal Naval Search and Rescue flight; the next I was Mr Peel with no job or real prospects.

As my enquiries for work were ignored my expectations got lower and lower, from trying to find flying jobs abroad, to any job in the Middle East (a popular place of employment for ex serviceman) but even that had dried up. Eventually I would have done almost anything to bring home an honest wage.

Once it had sunk in that I was not going to get a job, I thought I would attempt to start a business and not having any formal qualifications other than in aviation, I decided to become a driving instructor. This only materialised because I was helping Margaret to learn to drive at the time.

I booked myself on a residential course in Bromley to prepare myself for the written exam. I took the exam and passed first time, so went back up to Bromley to train for the practical examination and went on to pass that a few weeks later. It seemed quite strange that in only a matter of about six weeks I was a qualified Department of Transport Driving Instructor. I later learnt that I was lucky, as many of the driving instructors had spent a couple of years with driving schools under a training licence before qualifying.

I bought a new car and started my business all in a matter of days after qualifying, quickly building up a client base, which was just about enough to make a living wage.

I was quite successful as a driving instructor, with the majority of my clients passing first time, hence the speed the business built up. Unfortunately, I was a rubbish businessman. If someone was having difficulty with certain manoeuvres and I did not have another lesson to go on to, I would find myself extending the lesson until they got it right. Not a sensible thing as I was only charging for the one lesson. I was so keen to see my clients pass their test that the extended lessons were becoming a regular routine.

In addition, I very quickly found that I did not enjoy the job. Often I would have to teach people I simply did not like, but would have to keep smiling, something I found difficult to do. I was now in the situation John Spencer had been in on his communication course; I was in a job that I knew was not for me.

The reasons for being so unhappy would probably seem ridiculous to most people and the majority of driving instructors I met were happy in their jobs. Unfortunately, for me, carrying out the same briefs day in and day out was not enjoyable. Most of the lessons were in the evenings and at weekends and, on top of this, I found it difficult to relate to clients I did not like.

I would and did make every effort, but leaving home to give a lesson to some young lad who thought he was Stirling Moss was no fun at all. I would of course control the lessons, trying to treat those situations as a challenge, calm them down and teach them how to drive to a standard that would get them through the test. What I would really have liked would be to have opened the door and thrown them out! I felt with this type of character that when I got them through the test, they would be straight out with the heavy boot, screeching tyres and causing havoc on the roads.

I am being quite harsh and I guess the majority of clients I did enjoy teaching, but there were enough of the others to make the job not right for me, or my nature. I could not just stop the job as it was now my livelihood but I was continuously on the hunt for something else.

About twelve months later the break came. Bond Helicopters, one of the large helicopter companies, had recently commenced a SAR Flight in the North Sea, operating from oilrigs. The first I knew about it was via a phone call from Ray Higginson, one of my pals from the Navy. Ray was a diver with me on my first two tours at the Lee SAR Flight.

Ray had left the Navy a little while before me and had secured a good job in Scotland, training people in rescue techniques from rigid inflatable rescue craft, mainly for safety boat crews operating from oilrigs.

He had now landed a job with Bond Helicopters on a SAR contract in the North Sea and was recommending that I take over his job. I was so depressed with my present job that I would have jumped at the job Ray was doing. It was with a small team of instructors and would be quite exciting. I talked it over with Margaret who knowing how unhappy I was, encouraged me to try for it. I did apply but, for one reason or another, the job did not materialise.

Opportunities were opening up in the North Sea and now I had contacts up there. All the aircrewmen taken on for this contract on the rigs were people I knew well, particularly Ray Higginson, Dave Carter (Nick) and Win Alladin. All of them would keep their ears to the ground and let me know if anything turned up.

Terry Short had also recently left the Navy and had to endure a job that he was very unhappy with (selling insurance). Fortunately for Terry, a job had come up in Sumburgh on the Coastguard SAR flight which, having experienced the insurance job, he took without any hesitation, even though it meant moving to the Shetland Isles. Terry would also ring me if he heard of any vacancies back in flying.

When Bond Helicopters had started the contract on the Norwegian oilrigs, they were using SAR aircrewmen trained in the forces as the winch operators, but had decided to train paramedics already based on the rigs as the winchmen. Once trained in the rescue techniques it was hoped they would be able to assume all the roles of the winchman.

This was not the perfect situation and poorly thought out as the medics would be coming on line too quickly. The turnover of medics would mean they would require training on a regular basis and not all the medics on the rigs would want to do the job, especially when they experienced their first moving deck or had to recover someone from a rough sea.

Anyway, quite early on in this contract, the aircraft was scrambled to an incident on one of the safety ships in rough conditions. The paramedic nominated as the winchman was a woman who was extremely efficient as a paramedic, but had only very limited experience on the winch person's role.

She was lowered to the vessel, which would have been heaving quite awkwardly and very quickly got seasick. It was quite a traumatic event for her; she did manage to prepare and recover the casualty but once back on the rig, decided it was not for her and pulled out of the programme immediately.

Realising this situation could easily happen again, Bond Helicopters decided to drop that plan and recruit two more winch operators/winchmen who had military experience in the role for the Norwegian platforms. Ray Higginson and Win Alladin contacted me immediately; Win even came round to my house to fill me in on things I should know about the company before the interview.

The interview, arranged very quickly, took place in Aberdeen and the jobs went to Terry Mooney and myself. Terry was just leaving the Navy at twenty-seven years of age (his first break point). This was a sensible move, especially having a guaranteed job to go to and one he felt he would enjoy.

If I wanted the job, I would be required almost immediately so I only had two weeks to wind up the driving school. I did not feel the need to try to sell the business as I had not been operating for long and would not have wanted anyone else trading in my name. I passed my clients on to instructors who I thought would do the best for them.

I had met one particular driving instructor, Don Blackhurst, who was doing the job on a part time basis. He had been a driving instructor in Birmingham with his own school but had recently moved south with his wife Joyce to be closer to their son and family.

Don had given me a lot of sensible advice and became a good friend when I first started. I would have liked him to take all my clients; however he was semi retired and did not want too big a workload, but he did take over the clients I felt needed his patient nature.

I left for Aberdeen the following week to do all the necessary courses before going to work offshore. Initially it was to carry out the survival drills required by all of the people working on the oilrigs such as life raft drills, lifeboat drills, dunker drills and a fire-fighting course. They were carried out at the Robert Gordon's Institute where purpose-built facilities had been set up for this training, including the first proper Underwater Escape-Trainer outside the Navy.

I was paired with Terry Mooney for these courses under the wing of Phil Strickland, who was the Senior Crewman for Bond Helicopters. Terry was a really friendly character who I instantly knew I would enjoy working with. We had a couple of flights in the helicopter we would be using and did a little bit of winching, followed by a few days off before flying out to the platform that we would be operating from.

Joining the North Sea Rig

The aircraft we were using was a French Aerospatiale AS365N Dauphin helicopter; it was quite a small aircraft capable of carrying eleven passengers in the transfer role. For the SAR role, we would remove the middle and front row of seats then fit a rack to carry a rather sparse set of SAR equipment.

The aircraft itself was state of the art; it was faster than anything I had ever flown in. Capable of 150 knots and a cruising speed of 135 knots, it had a fenestron instead of a tail rotor, the first helicopter I had flown in like that.

What was to surprise me most was the helicopter's navigation equipment; it was way ahead of the equipment we had in the Navy. This surprised me because until then I thought the military had the best equipment. When I left the Navy, we were still using charts and manual dead-reckoning plotting, relying on wind finding and radar fixes, backed up by a Decca navigator that required time to work out the position using Decca charts.

This aircraft had a system that, although still based round the Decca, had onboard computers that (in conjunction with other navigational aids) did the calculations and position-finding for us. This meant we always knew where we were. On top of that, it had a built-in SAR system programmed with all the search patterns used in SAR. The aircraft would fly these patterns at whatever height was set.

The advantages of this were not only the safety of always knowing exactly where we were, but en-route and on searches the whole crew could look outside the aircraft. In the Wessex helicopters, the search patterns were worked out by the winch operator who would continuously have his head in a chart calculating the wind drift and plotting the next leg. The pilot would have to be eyes inboard, watching instruments so that he could fly the headings and speeds given by the winch operator. This meant only the diver would be looking out continuously, limiting the chance of spotting the search target.

I did think this aircraft was too small for SAR but was completely sold by the SAR system. This equipment in a larger aircraft would be brilliant but a larger helicopter was not suitable for our role offshore; the aircraft had to be small enough to fit in the hangers on the platforms.

We were based on the Frigg field, which was a complex of five Norwegian platforms on the mid-point of a line between Sumburgh in the Shetland Islands and Stavanger in Norway.

The actual platform we were billeted on had three legs in Norwegian waters and one in British waters. Because of this, under an agreement between Britain and Norway, a small number of Brits had to work there – the helicopter team, the radio watch keepers and a few others in various other departments.

Phil Strickland came out with us for the first week to continue with a bit of training and to help familiarise us with the aircraft and platform. Win Alladin was the aircrewman onboard the week we arrived. Dave Carter the other aircrewman was returning home on the aircraft we had arrived on for his fortnight off, so we only had time to say hello and goodbye.

I had worked with Win for a short while on Lee SAR flight before he left the Navy for a job in the Middle East. Win had eventually returned to the UK and joined the MOD Police but the bug to get back to flying had taken hold and he had managed to get this job, a move he was very happy with.

Win and Dave were natural mixers who would wander round the platform getting to know the rig workers; they had soon found their feet and were very popular. That in turn had made it easier for the flight to fit in, which is something that would not have been easy, especially as Bond had just won the contract from a Norwegian company. Winning the trust of the mainly Norwegian crew was, I am sure, down to Win and Dave and certainly made life easy for Terry and me when we arrived on the rig.

We had a week settling in before Terry went back to the mainland with Phil and I completed my second week with Win. Terry would return the following week with Dave Carter. Eventually, we would stagger the routine so that each week only one aircrewman would change over, each of us staying on the rig for a fortnight followed by a fortnight off. This would mean the four of us rotating on a weekly basis providing two aircrewman on the rig at all times. We were dual trained so would swap roles as required.

The Frigg field was a gas producing complex. The platform I was based on was the accommodation platform with a further two treatment/ production platforms attached by giant covered walkways. Two more production platforms the (DP1 & the DP2) were independent and not connected in anyway, but still close to the main complex. The unattached platforms had skeleton crews with only limited accommodation onboard. The main workforce would travel over by helicopter on a daily basis, returning in the evening. This shuttle service between the platforms was the main role for the aircraft and Search and Rescue its secondary role.

The attached treatment platforms were manned by crews who operated equipment to treat the gas prior to it being pumped ashore. When off-shift, the crews would return via the walkways to the quarters platform.

The accommodation was better than I expected, certainly better than the considerably cramped accommodation I was used to on warships. The two aircrewmen shared a cabin with en-suite shower room, which was not too bad as, for the majority of the time, one of us would be on call in the ops room and the other would have the cabin to themselves whilst off shift.

The food was exceptional with snacks on hand any time of the day and unlimited soft drinks, coffee etc. The rigs were dry as far as alcohol was concerned. That was probably a good thing, as there were too many things that could go wrong, alcohol would not mix well with that environment.

It was a mixed crew platform so we had a few women onboard. The British platforms could not understand this but it was a case of the Norwegians being ahead of the Brits on equal rights, the British rigs would follow suit at a later date.

I certainly felt more comfortable than I expected on the rig and quite liked the two on and two off routine. Two weeks on the rig was not a real hardship although I was always keen to get back home to the family by the end of it.

The thing I liked the most was working with like-minded people again. It was like being on a small unit in the Navy, with a group of people that all got on with each other.

You would have the clown, the serious one, the one that continuously made mistakes, the almost professional joke teller, the nowhere near professional joke teller, the introvert, the extrovert, the one that always fell over, the observer and even a rogue. A good combination of these characters together would make the camaraderie. That recipe in my opinion is exactly why the series 'Auf Wiedersehen Pet' and other series like that worked so well.

This was obviously what I missed when I left the Navy. I have never been sure which of the traits I was, but can only guess it would be the observer as I always loved trying to analyse different people's characters, or maybe I could have been the introvert. The observer and introvert probably go together. One of my annual reports in the Navy said: "Peel is an introvert with an extrovert dying to burst out". I thought that quite comical but it was probably true.

Dave Carter, the other aircrewman I would be working with was someone I had met many times, but had never actually worked with. Dave was quite a legend in the Navy with a similar background to me changing to the aircrew branch from a general service background, having trained initially as a marine engineer. He had transferred to become a SAR diver during one of the shortages of divers when volunteers were required from the general service. Like me, he had bounced between SAR and Commando squadrons and as I mainly bounced back to Lee SAR flight, Dave would bounce back to Culdrose SAR Flight in Cornwall.

Dave went on to be the Commando and SAR aircrewman's Fleet Chief. This was quite a responsible job and the only billet available in the role. Fleet Chiefs, known as 'Mr' in the Navy were the equivalent of Warrant Officers in the RAF. As there was only the one billet for a Fleet Chief in Search and Rescue, we called him 'Mr SAR'.

He was well-respected and often talked about so, although I had never worked with him, I felt I knew him well. Dave was a hands-on type of guy; being tied to a desk was not an attractive option for him, which would have been his future had he remained in the Navy. It was great working with Dave and we got on well, soon becoming known as D1 & D2, Dave being D1.

The pilot I was mainly to work with was Pete Nordman, an ex army Pilot. He was a Major in the army and looked the part, but he was a real gentleman and a pleasure to work with. Pete had not been in Search and Rescue in the military, but army pilots being used to flying by the seat of their pants, made good SAR pilots. I soon felt confident with him and he was very responsive to our advice, realising that we the aircrewmen had a lot of experience in the role.

The engineers were all Scottish and a great bunch; the two I was to work with most were Ron Anderson (ex RAF, another real gentleman who knew his job like the back of his hand) and Bill Cruickshank. Bill had never been in the forces, he was a trained car mechanic who had originally joined Bond as a handyman, but was so handy the company arranged for his training as an aircraft engineer. He was a great big chap and well known in the highland games circuit. Like Pete Nordman, Bill was a gentle giant who would help with anything. He had to tolerate the English contingent, eventually accepting us into the fold.

The aircraft would do the first shuttle early morning about 7 am, transferring crews between the rigs and swapping the night crews with the day crews. This would occasionally include transfers to and from other complexes in the Norwegian sector. In addition, there was an unmanned rig a few miles away that was monitored remotely from our complex; if there were any problems a crew would be flown over to carry out repairs.

The helicopter needed to be returned to the hanger between shuttles because the heli-deck had to be clear for the general helicopter movements from the mainland. To achieve this, the blades on our helicopter had to be folded each time as the hanger was too small to receive the helicopter with the blades spread. It was quite an effort folding and spreading the blades, sometimes several times a day.

The blade folding was also often quite dangerous, particularly for the person on the rotor head who had to pull the pin out, while the rest of us pushed the end of the blade up. Once the pin was removed, the blade had to be manually controlled back to a securing rig attached to the tail. The blade folding was frequently carried out in strong winds, requiring all the crew to achieve it.

If we were scrambled the aircraft would have to pushed out of the hanger, rotor blades spread, seats removed, winch attached, SAR equipment and stretcher loaded. We eventually got this procedure down to a fine art from the blades-folded condition in the hanger, to being fully-kitted out in the SAR role and airborne in less than fifteen minutes, which was quite good for a helicopter not kept at immediate readiness.

The complex had a safety vessel patrolling all the time, a reasonable size vessel with further small rescue craft onboard. I felt for the crews on those vessels: the sea conditions out there could be as bad as any I had seen anywhere in the world.

Occasionally we would have winds in excess of 80 knots that continued for a few days. When this happened, the helicopter could not be used. It could fly in 80 knots of wind but it would be too dangerous to spread the rotor blades. Even if we could spread the blades, we would not be able start in those winds as the blades would sail when trying to gain momentum and could sail low enough to hit the superstructure of the aircraft.

Our limit for spreading and starting the blades was 55 knots, so when in periods of winds above that, nothing moved and the crews working on the production platforms were stuck there. If we had advance warning, as often we did, that rig would be de-manned to a skeleton crew. Any emergency requiring removal of an injured or seriously ill rig worker in these conditions would require an aircraft to come from either the UK or Norway depending on the prevailing wind. The North Sea pilots flying from and to the rigs really did a tremendous job requiring considerable flying skills, hence the high experience levels required for the pilots carrying out this job.

We also occasionally had days of thick fog when nothing moved and even the crew changes could not take place. Nothing could be done about that other than attempt a ship transfer and that was only carried out in emergencies, it was not normally practical because of the transit time required and the inherent danger of the transfers from the boats to the rigs.

Overall, it was quite a hostile environment out there but it was also quite an exciting one, which I soon accepted as the norm.

The SAR tasking was quite limited, mainly transferring injured or sick rig workers ashore from any of the platforms or safety vessels within the sector we covered. In addition, we would recover injured or ill fishermen from the fishing fleets working the North Sea. Our main SAR role was to provide cover for all the crew change aircraft that operated in our sector.

These jobs would be far fewer than I was used to at Lee; nevertheless, every so often a real nasty would come up because of the awful sea conditions that we had to learn to deal with.

Blue-Water Sailing Boat 'Sula'

9th June 1986. The weather was deteriorating throughout the day and the rig coordinator decided to evacuate the crews from the 'DP1' & 'DP2' early, before the winds increased above the aircraft start and shut down limits of 55 knots. We were close to these limits when the aircraft landed with the last crew from the 'DP1'. We quickly had the blades folded and the aircraft pushed into the hanger. All flying cancelled for the rest of the day.

Not long after we had stowed the helicopter, we had a scramble to a mayday from a yacht in our area. We decided as a crew that, although we were very close to the wind speed limit, we would get the aircraft set up on deck, spread the blades, attach the winch and load the SAR equipment in the hope for a reduction in the wind speed, even if only for a short while.

Once ready to start, the wind speed over the deck was checked and we were just within the limits so able to start the rotors and get on our way, well within the fifteen minutes even in the awful conditions.

The report was of a man overboard from the yacht 'Sula' that had capsized but had righted itself. When we arrived on scene, it was clear the crew of the yacht were in imminent danger and that we would have to attempt to get them off. My first thoughts were that it could not be done; the movement of the vessel in the mountainous waves was too erratic.

The Captain was Steve Westoram, a very experienced ex-Navy Sea King pilot who also had quite a number of years flying the North Sea under his belt. The co-pilot was John Masters an ex-army Sergeant pilot building up his hours for North Sea Command. Dave Carter was the winch operator and it was my turn to be winchman. I was very pleased that Dave was on the switch as he was the most experienced out of all of us, plus Dave and Steve had worked together as a crew considerably longer than I had. I was still in the early stages of joining this team so was pleased that it had worked out this way.

I mentally questioned my own ability as a winch-op to achieve a successful transfer. In all honesty, I would not have relished attempting it; getting me onboard safely would rely on the skills of Steve and Dave and it would not be easy.

We studied the movement of the yacht, briefed all the hazards and decided to give it a go using the hi-line technique, then briefed the crew of the yacht on what to do when they received the hi-line weights.

This was one of the times, which fortunately do not happen too often, when I would leave the aircraft wondering what on earth I was doing. I do not remember too much about the winching. I entered the water several times but expected that, as the sea was so rough. I also know I had to fend myself off the rigging a few times but was not injured so was willing to keep trying. Eventually, I hit the main mast and was able to slide down as Dave lowered the winch wire. I hit the deck with some force as the boat came up on a wave to meet me but relieved to be in one piece.

I started the recovery of the casualties immediately, sending the first survivor up to the aircraft. This was an easier procedure than getting on board as, if necessary, they could be dragged away from the vessel and I could control the swing with the hi-line, one end being attached to the winch hook and the other controlled by me.

When I was sending the second person up I noticed one of the crew only had one arm, (not lost during this incident), who I assumed was an amputee, possibly after a previous accident. I had not come across this before and realised we would not be able to use the normal strop method. The single strop is positioned around the casualty's back and under the arms and it is the arms hanging down which secure the strop in place. There was also no way we would have been able to get him into a stretcher in those conditions. I was wearing a four-point harness as normal, so quickly took this off and briefed a crew member on how to get him into it while I continued with transferring the third person.

I was thinking that I would throw myself over the side when I had sent the last one up; I could then be recovered from the water using a single lift strop. In hindsight this was a daft thought as the yacht was trailing a lot of ropes and debris from when it had capsized. I was comfortable with the thought of entering heavy seas (something I had done before on several occasions) but on this occasion it may have been too heavy and I could see myself entangled in the lose rigging.

I could not go up with the last man as I did not have a harness and the lift of the last casualty would be much safer if I controlled the hi-line. Dave, being one-step ahead, sent a single lift strop back down for me. I put that on, disconnected the hi-line and let Dave drag me clear. The aircraft felt quite the safe haven.

We dropped the survivors at the nearest rig then went back to retrace the track of the yacht to search for the missing crewmember. The search continued until we required fuel, which we took from the rig that we had dropped the survivors on. By then it was dark and, not being a night-equipped aircraft, we returned to the Frigg platform. The Coastguard aircraft from Sumburgh, which was an all-weather aircraft with night capability and infrared camera, had arrived on scene and continued the search. The man overboard was not located.

We all felt quite elated after this rescue. It was tempered by the sadness that a man had lost his life, but we had managed to recover the remaining crew from a truly horrendous situation.

A few months later, an article by the skipper of that yacht appeared in the magazine 'Practical Boat Owner'. This was quite nice to see, a survivor giving an account of the other end of a rescue and his graphic account of the rescue actually made me feel quite proud and highlighted to me the job satisfaction I took from this role. We do receive a few thank you letters, but for me this was a rather special account.

In the article William Bryce, the skipper of the boat, explained that 'Sula' was a very sturdy 33ft ferro-concrete, immensely strong double ender of Colin Archer design; she was a 'no nonsense' heavy displacement blue-water sailing boat.

They had sailed from Inverness and were heading directly to Bergen, expecting to take a week for the crossing and then a week to explore the fjords. They had a crew of six, all friends and one of the crew was the skipper's wife. They had developed engine problems and felt it wise to call in at Wick for repairs before proceeding again. I will take up his log and account of the rescue from midnight on the day of the rescue.

Monday 9th June

0000 hours. *Sailing at 7/8 knots towards Bergen. Little sea running clear sky, no shipping Barometer steady.*

0110 hours. *Wind eased. Hoist full main and jib.*

0400 hours. *Wind increasing steadily still logging 7/8 knots.*

0800 hours. *There was by now a definite change – barometer dropping rapidly and the main was double reefed and the jib dropped and lashed to the bowsprit.*

We estimated the wind to be approaching 25/30 knots with a wave height of 4/6 metres. 'Sula' was sailing well and completely under control. The only concern was we were continually bearing away off course to 030T.

1000 hours. *Sea was building up dramatically Wave height had increased and was now blowing well in excess of 30 knots. Called for deck crew to assist in dropping main. Harness to be worn. The main sail was dropped on deck and lashed This was a precaution as with the motion I did not want a boom flying round supported only by a topping lift. The Decca gave out a screech and suddenly went haywire giving a fix nowhere near our position. Contacted oil supply ship, which passed close at hand for fix 59° 07 N 0° 22 W. We were now running dead before large sea Wind 35/40 knots.*

1400 hours. *Wind now increased to between 50/60 knots (this figure was obtained later from the oil platform) Sea state was high 12 metres with large overhanging crests. Huge lump of water was observed breaking the high crest. Decided to close all hatches including main, which on 'Sula' was very small.*

On deck were myself, P Holden – both with harnesses on. We were running at between 6/8 knots under complete control with towering waves astern. Fell off wave and strained shoulder. Change watch after reducing staysail. While putting in double reef it was noted that 'Sula' was still charging downhill at 7 knots but I still felt the speed gave me control of the situation.

1500 hours. *Changed watch to V Scott and David North. I went below for a rest. The remainder of the crew were all lying on the cabin sole as nowhere else was much use. Spoke to everybody about how well the boat was sailing and that there was no need for concern as this was the type of weather that she had been designed to cope with. Cannot tolerate being down below.*

1530 hours. *Relieved Victor and once again asked David to please go below and either put on a lifejacket or harness. Having sailed with David for eight years,*

I have had this constant argument regarding harness and he has always said 'No'. I was clipped onto the port running backstay deadeye. Locked main hatch. The sea was now extremely dangerous with high hanging crest. Wind full storm but we had time to remark how blue the sea was.

1600 hours. *We had just roared down the face of a gigantic wave when on my starboard side a sight that will remain with me forever' – a vertical wall of water with the top five metres curling above Sula's mast. Even at the time, I found it difficult to believe how this wave was there. We had just sailed down one it should not have been there.*

The next few seconds are lost as the wave broke above and over Sula. My first thoughts were of anger what a stupid situation to find myself in. I immediately ducked for what reason will remain a mystery. The wave struck just aft of the mast.

I must have been thrown completely out of the cockpit with David I have no recollection whatsoever of leaving the yacht. I was now under or on top of the boat but do remember reading the name upside down, as I actually saw from as if I was an observer the yacht roll completely in front of me. A second or a minute passed and Sula righted herself and I was still attached being dragged along the port side with the staysail set on self-tacking traveller the boat just started sailing downwind at 4/5 knots.

Climbing back on board was only made possible by determination and I effectively grabbed hold of the boom, which had been lashed to the deck. Holding on I was physically catapulted back in the cockpit, which was empty.

David had gone. There was no possibility of changing course. The boat was still charging forward.

All the cockpit seats had been ripped off, the engine access hatch had gone and the complete port bulwark had been severed to deck level. It was observed that the starboard lifebuoy was now hooked around the aerial at the top of the mast. I immediately started pumping the main bilge pump and I tried to steer at the same time. I am able to describe this hellish state of both me and the boat but the conditions down below must have been beyond human appreciation. A feeling of despair is quickly replaced by one of anger as the survival instinct in us takes over. How long you can force yourself to super-human tasks remains unanswered.

On opening the hatch the four remaining crew including my wife gazed up with staring eyes Victor, my engineer was bleeding badly from a deep head wound. The devastation below done in such a short time was difficult to register. What had been an orderly seamanlike ship was now completely destroyed. Engine hatches had been smashed drawers food equipment etc. was flying round the main cabin.

To make matters worse smoke was billowing from the engine. An electrical fire was brought quickly under control but we were now without any power whatsoever. I stayed at the helm while Roger Holden a doctor and my stepson, carried out repairs on Victor.

It is at this time that Victor, even though injured and concussed, using surgical clips and some spare wire rigged up a supply from our emergency battery into the radio. This superb piece of work possibly, saved our lives. Within minutes, we had made contact with a tanker and through the Coastguards and rescue services; we were able to determine our approximate position.

2000 hours. *The last four hours were spent with Victor and Arthur helming and myself conducting the search procedures through the tanker till air sea rescue helicopter was sighted at 2010 hours overhead.*

With great determination and bravery the winchman was lowered on deck and my crew were lifted to safety.

2015 hours. *All safely aboard the helicopter and being taken to the oil production platform Beryl 'A' where we were received with great kindness. No words can describe the assistance given to us on the rig and we will be forever in their debt.*

The following morning in fair weather we were airlifted to Aberdeen to be met by press and TV to both of whom we declined to speak.

The article then went on to give an account of the rescue.

This is a report on the helicopter rescue of the Gaff 'Sula' in the North Sea on the 9th June 1986.

At 2000 hours *approximately, a red Bond helicopter appeared above us but to me as skipper, this appearance did not mean rescue, as I could not see how on earth we were going to be physically transported from the deck of the yacht into the helicopter. The sea state at this time was horrendous with large breaking crests to the sea approximate wave height 15 metres, wind speed well in excess of 45 miles per hour. After consultations over the radio the pilot informed me that he was going to attempt to lower a line to the boat and I was in no way to attempt to attach this line to anything. I was asked to repeat these instructions, which I did.*

The winchman then performed the most amazing acrobatic feat by lowering himself from the helicopter and after being totally immersed in the sea numerous times and once being thrown against the mast of the boat, which is solid wood. I am amazed that he did not suffer some serious damage to himself. We were still steering the yacht on an approximate course 025° dead before the wind to minimise any sideways rolling. After great difficulty and at no concern to his own personal safety he eventually landed on the deck of my yacht by sheer determination and courage. I will never forget his smile it will stay with me for a long time.

We then air lifted the crewmembers one by one up into the helicopter. As one of my crewmembers has only one arm, the winchman took of his own full harness and strapped Mr Scott into this then raised him to the helicopter. I was last to leave and it was with great relief.

Through these, trying times the concerns shown to us by the helicopter team was very encouraging and full praise must be awarded to them in my opinion as the acts which they carried out were totally without regard to their own personal safety. On reaching the Beryl Alpha, the same degree of comfort and concern was awarded us. As it was only at this time that me and my crew realise how near death we had come.

Reading that report again I can almost relive it. That of course was the skippers view as he saw it, but obviously I did not lower myself to the yacht – that was achieved by the skill of Dave Carter and Steve Westoram. If I did have a big smile on my face when I landed on deck, it was probably because I was so relieved to be down there safely! Nevertheless, this job is one of those tucked away in the back of my mind, surfacing occasionally as a scary memory, but mainly as a good memory of a job well done.

I had settled into life on the rig and the fortnights at home allowed me to get a lot done on the DIY front, I used to be able to plan a job during the time on the rig then carry it out when I got home building conservatories and en-suite bathrooms etc.

I did not miss anything about the driving school. I could have kept doing that job, keeping my licence in date by working for someone else during my fortnights off, but I was quite happy with my situation and could not bear the thought of giving even one more lesson. When my check ride for being a Driving Instructor came round I let it lapse with no regrets.

The only worry I did have was that the offshore SAR contract had to be fought and renewed on an annual basis; this would always be a worry as the deadlines approached. By the end of that first year and just prior to a new contract being awarded, the Norwegians decided they wanted to utilise the SAR aircrewman more effectively. We had a lot of standby time with little constructive work to do, so they wanted to use us for additional duties on the rig.

The company had little choice but to agree with this and, after consultation between ourselves, the company and the client, we were sent to Montrose in Scotland for a helicopter deck fire-fighting course, so that we could cover as relief fire crew during shuttles and the arrival and departure of the crew change aircraft. I was quite happy to do that; it was yet another string to the bow if we ever lost the contract and we received an extra allowance for the additional qualification.

Bond Helicopters had another SAR contract which was in the Forties oil field, with the aircraft and crews billeted on a semi submersible Emergency Support Vessel called the 'Iolair'. The Iolair looked similar to an exploration rig without the derrick and could be attached to any of the rigs in the field by a most impressive telescopic walkway, the 'free' end of which was capable of staying in one position against a fixed platform to allow a safe evacuation if required.

That may not sound impressive in itself until one realises that the production platforms are fixed and this safety semi–submersible was floating. The 'free' end of the walkway remained in exactly the position it had been placed by a computer dead reckoning system, while the safety vessel from which it extended was moving up and down even in heavy seas. It was quite a feat of engineering.

The original SAR crew on this vessel were Ray Higginson, who had contacted me about taking on his previous job on the rescue inflatable and again when this job came up. The second aircrewman was an aircrewman called Alex Knight also ex-Navy; Alex had been working for Bond Helicopters for a while.

The Bond contract on the 'Iolair', being in the British sector had a different routine inherited from the previous contract holders. They operated with just two military trained SAR aircrewmen working back-to-back and used a small group of volunteers locally trained as winchmen. It was a secondary role for the winchmen, who also had other important full time jobs on the platform. The fact that their other role was their main job made it difficult for them to get enough training to keep them fully proficient as winchmen although, having said that, they had carried out some very good rescues over the years.

After the Frigg field incident with the paramedics, Bond decided too many risks were being taken by this routine so three more ex-Forces aircrewmen who could operate in either role were recruited for the 'Iolair' and, as leave and sickness relief for the two fields, all ex–Navy: Pete Mesney, Mike Cockerill and Ted Wilkinson. Occasionally we would rotate round the two fields, not on a regular basis but often enough to help break the monotony of being on one platform.

This was quite good really; it gave us all the chance to work with each other and the opportunity to meet other people. I was also interested in the way the fields operated. The Forties was an oil-producing field and the Frigg a gas-producing field so there were many different procedures.

Both rigs had a gymnasium with reasonable equipment and quite good running machines. I used to spend hours on the running machine on the Frigg platform, trying to keep my fitness levels up for the marathons. I had taken up road running mainly as a way to keep fit when I left the Navy and actually managed to get to a reasonable standard close to the three-hour mark for a marathon. I was striving to crack the less than three hours barrier. However, training on a machine is nothing like running on the roads in nice scenery and I never enjoyed running on this machine, with just a small window to look out of.

The window on the Frigg platform faced the walkway to one of the treatment platforms and very little happened there as it was normally only used at shift change times. Occasionally a seagull would stop for a rest on the walkway and I would play stupid games like increasing the speed of the running machine until the bird took off again, cursing it if it rested for too long.

One day through the window, I saw a Norwegian running round the walkways. It had never entered my mind that we would be allowed to do that. I then used the walkways for running; I could get quite a good circuit going between the three rigs, taking in a few sets of steps between decks as well. This was much more enjoyable than the running machine, although not the same as running along the sea front at home.

SAR training was not as frequent as I felt it should be. That was a shame really; we only had the aircraft for dedicated training once a week and that in my view was not enough. We would try our best with lots of wets, practising on a very heavy dummy that we would take turns to recover from the water in whatever conditions the aircraft could fly in. We also practiced the winching skills (hi-lines etc) with the safety boats. The training sessions we had were valuable as the weather was invariably quite rough but really, we should have trained more than we did. That is the way it was back then; offshore SAR was not taken quite as seriously as perhaps it should have been.

When we had a job, it was likely to be quite a nasty one because of the weather conditions in the North Sea. If it was an injured fisherman or crewmember from a safety boat for example, the injury was likely to have happened because of the rough weather and would require some challenging winching. Conversely, we had several medical evacuations from the rigs which were normally straightforward as often we could actually land on to transfer the casualty.

Occasionally the transfer would take place in conditions just about suitable for getting airborne, but not suitable to shutdown afterwards. The shutdown limits were the same as for starting up and the wind-speed may well have increased while we had been airborne. In these conditions, it was sometimes safer to keep burning and turning and with a suck of fuel from the rig fly ashore to shut down, normally to the coast of the North Sea that would provide the most favourable conditions.

For normal shuttle-flying, the aircraft had to have enough fuel to fly ashore in case of any emergency which may have made it dangerous to carry out a rig landing. For instance, following an engine failure the aircraft would be able to continue flying on the remaining engine, but it would be rather foolhardy to attempt a landing on a small area with just the one engine.

Occasionally there were short periods when we were unable to carry out the routine shuttles to the production platforms, perhaps because the wind was out of limits for us to spread and start the blades albeit within limits for flying, in which case aircraft would fly from Stavanger, approximately 290 miles round trip, simply to carry out a 100 metre shuttle between the rigs. Extravagant as this sounds it was cheaper to do that than lose production for the short period.

Flight Deck of the Frigg Platform 'AS365N' (Dauphin Helicopter)

Offshore crew with Albert the wet winching dummy

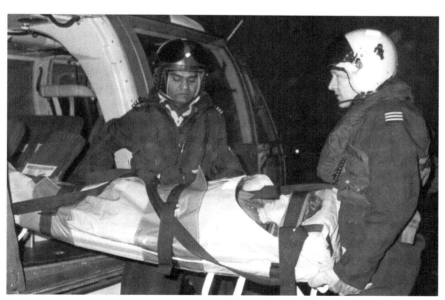

Win Alladin   **Dave Peel**

Part 5

Coastguard Search & Rescue

Rumours about the Lee-on-Solent Coastguard Contract

Eighteen months into the Frigg contract, rumours were circulating that the Navy might discontinue operating the SAR Flight at Lee-on-Solent. The possibility had been broached during another round of defence cuts.

The rumours, if there were any truth in them, would be devastating for the naval crews based on the flight at Lee, most of whom I still knew. I also knew they would probably be fighting a rear-guard action to prevent the closure, but nothing much could be done from crew level, especially as it was only rumour.

I had experienced this situation before, when they tried to keep the Lee-on-Solent flight at Portland. Public demand saved the flight that time, maybe this would win the day again, but if the Coastguard were to replace the military flight with a Coastguard-contracted flight, that may also be considered acceptable.

At this stage I felt as though I was in both camps. When I was in the Navy, I was adamant that civilians could not do this job; it was simply inconceivable. A non-military SAR helicopter flight had been operated for a short while, in the early seventies, when Bristow Helicopters replaced the RAF SAR flight at Manston in Kent. Bristows had been contracted by the Coastguards because the RAF required the Manston aircraft elsewhere.

Manston was the next base to the east of the Lee-on-Solent aircraft and at the time we did not believe they would be able to carry out the job so were expecting to end up covering many of their taskings.

We were wrong; they coped well and recorded many very difficult rescues. The crews of that aircraft were mainly (if not all) ex-military SAR crews with considerable experience behind them. The RAF eventually moved back to Manston, but the concept of the Coastguard providing their own contracted helicopters had been proven.

Although essentially military, the flight at Lee-on-Solent was considered a Coastguard asset and was partly funded by the Coastguard. They covered the cost of operational tasking, had financed the refurbishment of the buildings and employed the two full time Coastguard Officers attached to the unit. Even then, it was a partnership with the MOD and had been since its formation in 1973.

By this time the Coastguard had contracted a commercial, civilian-operated SAR flight based at Sumburgh in the Shetland Islands. The Sumburgh flight was formed to cover the increased activity in the Shetland basin due to the oil exploration and production carried out to the east and northeast of the Shetland Islands. A second Coastguard flight was in the process of forming to cover a blank spot off the west coast of Scotland; this flight would be stationed at Stornoway on the Western Islands.

Bristow helicopters, the same company that had run the short-term contract at Manston in the early seventies, had won both of these Coastguard contracts. Bristow had selected the Sikorsky 'S61N' helicopter for their SAR aircraft; quite a large aircraft with revolutionary avionics and equipment dedicated to the Search and Rescue role installed. I had read quite a lot about the capabilities of this aircraft but at the time did not quite believe it.

I had even considered applying to join the flight forming at Stornoway, but that would have meant relocating and I was not sure that I wanted to do that. I was happy with my routine on the rigs but would have loved to be back on a dedicated SAR flight. Anyway, I decided to stay put; I was enjoying the job and there was a possibility that my dream job at Lee-on-Solent may become reality.

I felt that if the flight at Lee-on-Solent was replaced with a Coastguard-contracted helicopter, I would have a reasonable chance of selection. I knew I would be at the upper age limit or even past it being over 40, but I was as fit then (due to my marathon running) as I was when I did my original SAR divers' course, if not fitter. My background of being an ex Chief Aircrewman of the flight at Lee was likely to hold me in good stead, plus I was still current as a SAR aircrewman and my home was in Lee. All in all, I was hopeful that I would be accepted if Bristow Helicopters won the contract and a certainty if Bond Helicopters won the contract.

Anyway, they were only hopes and dreams and it was all speculation, so I put it to the back of my mind while I got on with the job, which I was lucky to be doing; I just couldn't help dreaming about the possibilities of a job that I would enjoy even more.

Living with the Norwegians was quite comical; their sense of humour was so different from ours. We could all be watching a movie together but laughing at very different things. I also found them to be quite serious people. If there was a problem onboard they would huddle in groups to discuss solutions, even for things that we Brits would think quite trivial and probably have a laugh about. However, they were exceptionally efficient so perhaps they did have the right attitude.

An example of something that I found amusing was the night of the Eurovision song contest. Coming from a nation that generally belittles the contest, with many of our population watching just to listen to Terry Wogan's often-hilarious comments, I had not really thought of anyone taking it too seriously.

On the rig, it was like a national holiday, even to the extent that the production on the rig was reduced so that the maximum number of people could be off shift to watch the contest. Special food was laid on and there was absolute silence during the contest. The Brits, well and truly outnumbered by the Norwegians would get a crescendo of Shh! Followed by the dirtiest of looks, when we could not contain our amusement at some inane comment or during voting when Norway was not getting any points.

The Norwegians would work two weeks on the rig followed by three weeks off. This made us Brits (who worked two weeks on two weeks off) feel a little like second-class citizens, especially as we also earned considerably less than the Norwegian crews, even if doing the same job.

I could accept that really, because the cost of living in Norway was far higher than Britain. The reason for their different work patterns, which obviously took more manpower than our fortnight about shift pattern, was down to the Norwegian policy of keeping the maximum percentage of the population in employment.

That was not such a daft idea; it would considerably reduce the numbers of people out of work and I guess the additional cost to make that happen would be balanced against reduced benefits having to be paid out to the unemployed. The biggest advantage in my opinion, however, was that the Norwegians did not have large numbers of people who had simply lost their work ethic, learning to live on benefits as was becoming a culture in our country.

Lee-on-Solent SAR Contract

Another six months or so went by before we heard that the situation at Lee-on-Solent was no longer a rumour. It was happening: the Navy was to pull out and the flight would be replaced with a Coastguard contracted civilian operation.

The tenders had been published and Bond Helicopters was going to bid for the contract. There was some doubt as to the size of aircraft required and the actual positioning of the aircraft such as whether the new flight would remain on the site of the naval squadron at HMS Daedalus, or be positioned at another airfield in the area. We felt that, if they went for the smaller aircraft, Bond Helicopters would get the contract and, if not, it was likely to go to Bristow Helicopters. Nothing was guaranteed though as the other large operator at the time (British International Helicopters) would also be bidding.

When I went off for my next break after this announcement, the local papers were full of it and there was quite a strong campaign underway to keep the Navy at Lee, which again I fully understood. However, I guessed that it was all too late, as the decision must have been made for it to reach the stage of tenders going out.

Terry Short contacted me and although he had relocated to Sumburgh with his family, he was quite excited as he still had his house down south. It was clear that Bristow Helicopters were ahead of Bond Helicopters with their bidding process and had already nominated all their key personnel for the contract so that the experience of these crews could be included in the bidding process.

Terry had been selected as the Chief Aircrewman if they won the contract and wanted me onboard if that happened. Terry was not assuming that the contract was in the bag, as he also felt that if the Coastguard went for the smaller aircraft it was likely to go to Bond helicopters because of Bond's experience with the AS365N.

This put my hopes up higher and, of course, I would be trying to get Terry across to Bond if we won the contract. Sounds like nepotism but it was not quite like that; there were so few people around with our experience. It was also clear that companies would want crews they knew were reliable in the role.

It was also inevitable that quite a lot of us would already know each other, whoever got the contract. There would be some recruitment from the military plus movement between the SAR flights already in operation.

The majority of the aircrewman working for British International Helicopters (BIH) were people I knew from my Navy days: Billy Deacon, 'Stokes' Garland and Brian Johnstone, all ex Navy SAR and apart from 'Stokes' Garland, people I had worked with.

Another good friend of Terry and myself was Mike Walton (Wally) who had worked with us on the Lee SAR flight in the seventies and had also worked for BIH. Mike was the aircrewman onboard the British International Chinook that plunged into the sea off the Shetlands in June 1986. There were forty-four oil workers and three crew onboard: only two people survived.

It was soon apparent the only survivors were the co-pilot and a passenger, who had both been recovered from the sea very shortly after the incident by the Sumburgh Coastguard SAR helicopter. They were airborne on a training sortie when the incident happened and arrived on-scene within minutes. They had actually come across the oil slick on the surface at the same time as the incident was declared recovering the two survivors immediately.

Terry Short had been involved in looking for survivors and recovering bodies from the incident, a very difficult job. At the time, Terry did not know Mike was on board but he did know all of the aircrewman working for British International so knew one of them would be involved and was dreading the thought that he may have to recover their body.

Terry had to recover bodies mainly from fishing vessels whose crews had recovered them from the sea. At one stage, while hovering alongside the Lerwick lifeboat, Terry could clearly see Mike laid out on the deck. This was quite a jolt for Terry, who had to continue the recoveries with all sorts of thoughts running through his mind.

When I heard the news, I was devastated. Mike had been my winch operator for quite some time at Lee and I could not imagine what his family must be going through. Clearly, our thoughts were with all the casualties and their families. It was a terrible tragedy, which would also play on the minds of all the North Sea oil workers as helicopters were the main mode of transportation between the rigs and a way of life for all of them.

I was very keen to join the Coastguard flight at Lee-on-Solent and talked through the prospect of leaving Bond Helicopters at length with Dave Carter, both of us trying to work out if other military flights would be transferred to the Coastguard, plus the likelihood of Bond winning the contract.

Dave knew that I would apply, especially as I lived at Lee-on-Solent and he had also considered applying to the other operators as well but had decided it would be awkward (being settled in Cornwall), as the job would almost certainly require having to live at or close to Lee.

I sent my CV to both Bristow Helicopters and British International Helicopters, keeping all my options open; however, I did warn Phil Strickland (our Senior Crewman) that I had applied to the other two operators.

My company did not appear to have a plan as to how they would crew the aircraft if they won the contract – or maybe they had but information was certainly not coming our way. There was a rumour they may rotate the offshore flights with the flight at Lee which, if true, would not have been the way forward. Trying to run a dedicated SAR flight with rotating crews between offshore and onshore contracts would not have been safe.

The logistics to achieve that rotation would have been enormous; it would have been quite nice for the crews but would simply not have been practical. The Coastguard flights operated twenty-four hours and required crews living locally. The rig flights operated two weeks about, requiring increased crewing levels and relying on special CAA dispensations to operate the way we did.

In the middle of this contract procedure, I went to the annual Aircrewman Association's reunion, held at a hotel in the New Forest. The functions were always well attended, with good entertainment, good food and a chance to meet up with old mates.

This year it was buzzing with the news of the up and coming contract and the vacancies elsewhere that may open up because of it. Bond, BIH and Bristows all had representatives there, aircrewmen who would have been there anyway including Terry, who had come down from Sumburgh. It turned out to be one of the most memorable functions and was made even better by an ex aircrewman called Tony Campbell.

Since leaving the Navy, Tony had become a Thomson Holidays rep and decided the night needed livening up. He took over the evening's entertainment – something Tony tended to do, but only when well-oiled and he was well-oiled that night!

This was quite impromptu and the official entertainment that had been organised for the evening soon realised they could not compete, so Tony stole the show. Anyway, the evening was hilarious and is still talked about today. Tony was not to know it but that evening was going to lead to a new career for him and not in entertainment.

Bristow Helicopters, being ahead of the game, were starting the interviews for the Lee-on-Solent contract in a few weeks time. They hadn't won the contract or been given a heads-up but it was the way they did things so they could swing into action very quickly if they were awarded the contract.

Terry was going down to Redhill in Surrey, Bristow's headquarters, to assist in these interviews, but I would be offshore while they were taking place and the announcement for the contract was only a few weeks away. Terry arranged for me to have an interview at Redhill en-route to my return to the rig. I had my interview with John Follis who was management level and the man in charge of the SAR contracts.

Not knowing the outcome of that interview, all I could do was to carry on doing my job, still with no idea which way all this would go. I told Phil Strickland I had been for an interview and would, if offered, accept the job if the contract was won by Bristows. Phil understood this and was quite pleased that I had warned him.

I had another two weeks back home and the day I arrived on the platform for my next tour, I had a phone call from Terry to say they had won the contract and the job was mine if I wanted it. Calls from shore-side were very limited back then so I could not get any more information than that.

I was so keen to take the job that I accepted without even knowing my full terms and conditions. I sent a telex to Phil resigning and giving my month's notice, which in effect meant just completing the fortnight offshore, as I would be off for the second two weeks anyway.

The lads on the rig understood my decision and fully supported it. Win Alladin, who had also been for interview, was also hoping to join the flight but had not heard anything. He was still pleased for me and of course, if I could have any influence I would be looking out for him. I was not able to get hold of Terry again while I was offshore so knew nothing more for the rest of the fortnight.

On the way back from the rig I was able to call into Bristow Helicopters base at Aberdeen where I met Chris Bond who was also joining the Lee team. Chris was the Senior Aircrewman at Sumburgh but had requested to join the Lee flight even though it would mean giving up that position. He was busy getting all the safety equipment packed up and ready for the Lee contract. I was able to gain a little more information on the contract and was measured up for my flying clothing while I was there.

The day after getting home I drove up to Redhill where Terry was preparing the aircraft we would be using. This was to be a standard Sikorsky 61N with winch and infrared camera fitted and would be our start-up aircraft. The main aircraft would arrive later after being prepared with all the special Search and Rescue avionics that would make up the SAR system, bringing it to the same standard as the Sumburgh & Stornoway aircraft that I had heard such a lot about.

I carried out a joining routine, which included a medical held at Gatwick airport and then a talk with Terry about the finer details. I also had the opportunity to meet the Chief Pilot of the SAR flight **Peter Thomson**, who gave a first impression of being a dynamic enterprising person, probably picked for his leadership skills. He was an ex-RAF SAR Pilot and had been one of the pilots on the Sumburgh SAR Flight with Terry and Chris. Terry assured me that Peter was a very good SAR Pilot and would be a good boss.

The aircrewman that had been selected, seven of us in all, were all ex-Navy with a SAR background; five of whom I knew well. The other aircrewmen in addition to Terry and myself were:

Chris Bond: Chris, an ex Navy aircrewman, had been with Bristows for ten years or more and had considerable civilian SAR experience in the North Sea. He had been on the Forties field when Bristow Helicopters had that contract and was appointed Senior Aircrewman at Sumburgh when that flight was formed. Chris had decided that he would like to move down south and was happy to accept that Terry would be the Senior Aircrewman. He would be moving down with his family as soon as he could find suitable accommodation.

Mick Rowsell: Mick was my mate from Lee SAR who had been my winch operator on many a job, including a few precarious cliff rescues. I had probably been crewed with Mick more than any other aircrewman and was pleased he was coming back to Lee.

When Mick left the Navy, he had contacted me for advice about working in the North Sea; he had been offered a job on the Bristow

Helicopters operated SAR flight on the Brent oil field. Knowing Mick's views on SAR were much the same as mine, I had advised that he take it. I had been through the experience of doing a job I did not like and felt he should go straight in to this, rather than try something else closer to home and risk not getting a chance again.

Mick took that advice joining the SAR flight on the Brent oil field. Within a year of being in that job the Coastguard contract at Stornoway came up. Mick's wife Christine was born in Stornoway and her mother still lived on the Island, so they felt that they could move back up there, especially to a job that Mick was going to enjoy. Mick, already working for Bristows, had transferred to the Stornoway flight when it formed.

Mick and Christine were bringing up two children with cerebral palsy (Jason & Victoria) as well as their own children Ivan and Catriona and it was proving difficult to relocate from Gosport to Stornoway. The problems they were facing made them question whether they were making the right decision, as the move would probably be quite traumatic for Jason & Victoria.

When the rumours about Lee started, Mick decided to hold off moving in case there was a chance he could get a job on the Lee Flight. If he was able to transfer from Stornoway to Lee the family would not need to move; indeed Mick was selected, making an internal move within Bristows.

Don Sowden: I had worked with Don for a period in the Navy and he had carried out his very first job as an SAR aircrewman with me as his diver. The job was many years ago in the seventies, a quite unusual task on a cliff in Devon right on the edge of our endurance and by coincidence he was standing in for Mick Rowsell that day.

Don had left the Navy and joined the ambulance service; he was one of the first paramedics in the Portsmouth area and was considered quite a catch for us, as he may well be able to advance our medical skills. Don had to work his notice with the ambulance service but was allowed to start his refresher training when off shift.

Tony Campbell: He was the odd ball because he had been away from flying for a while doing his Thomson Rep bit in Spain. It was known that he was a good aircrewman in the Navy but obviously a slight risk as to whether the skills would still be with him.

Consequently, in Terry's desire to have a good mix of skills and characters (and after seeing Tony's entertainment skills at the aircrewman's association social!), Terry had pushed for him to join as it was felt his up-front skills would benefit the flight, it would just take a little longer to bring him back on line as a SAR aircrewman. Tony would join us at Lee after some extra refresher training with the SAR flight in Sumburgh.

Nick Horst: The final place went to a crewman still in the Navy. The company's reasoning behind this was they had to employ the main group of crewmen from an age group a little higher than they would have liked. This was important as the flight would be scrutinised and any mistakes or accidents jumped on by the media.

The idea of SAR being carried out by a civilian company was perceived by many not to be the way forward and the military crews would be watching events very closely. Bristow Helicopters clearly wanted to make this work, so had made every effort to bring in a wealth of SAR experience. This had its problems because the average age of the crews was quite high. Pete Thomson, the chief pilot, was very keen to bring in a young SAR aircrewman still getting to grips with the job who could continue his training with us.

Nick was that aircrewman; he was working on his first tour at Lee-on-Solent SAR flight prior to the decision that the military SAR flight would be disbanding. He had applied for an interview knowing that he wouldn't be able to leave the Navy for at least another four months, but had thought it would be worth a try, if only to get his name on the books for a later date.

He had impressed at the interview and being the right age, Bristows had decided they would fill his position with aircrewmen from the other units and Aberdeen, until he could leave the Navy

The pilots were a mix from all the services, seven in total with four Captains and three co-pilots; the chief pilot **Peter Thomson** I had already met.

John Whale: would become the deputy Chief pilot. His background was a Royal Marine, trained as a pilot and attached to the Navy. John later became a North Sea pilot and, prior to moving to Lee, was the Chief Pilot of the Tiger fleet at Aberdeen. Although John was a Chief pilot at Aberdeen, he did not have as much SAR experience as Peter Thomson so had accepted the deputy position.

Peter Nicholson: Ex-Naval SAR pilot who had almost certainly been on the team at Brawdy SAR, when I had my first trip in a SAR aircraft, which had led to me transferring to aircrew. Peter had, since leaving the Navy, spent several years as a North Sea pilot. He was also a Qualified Helicopter Instructor and civilian Training Captain and would be in charge of training and procedures on the flight.

Rob Flexman: Rob was an old school mate of mine and rather bizarre that so many years later we would end up working together. We both went to a naval boarding school at Holbrook, close to Ipswich, in Suffolk. My parents had sent me there because I had failed my eleven plus and they hoped Holbrook would sort me out.

Rob was bright and had gone there purely because his parents considered it a good school, which it was. I knew Rob well at Holbrook and we had both been in the school gymnastic team.

The brighter kids at Holbrook generally joined the Navy as Officers, average groups joined as artificer apprentices and the less academic as ratings. I was one of the latter, hence ending up joining as a rating.

Rob had joined the Navy as a pilot and, on leaving, spent a few years flying in the Middle East before joining Bristows specifically for this contract.

Graham Sorge: Ex-army NCO pilot. Only the army and Royal Marines allowed soldiers from the ranks to be trained as pilots. The Navy and the RAF did not follow this practice and ratings who wished to become pilots, were first selected for commission as an officer and only after qualification and receiving their commission could they proceed for pilot training.

Graham had also become a Helicopter Instructor while in the forces. On leaving, he became a North Sea pilot and later a Training Captain (pilot examiner) for Bristow Helicopters. Unfortunately, there was only one slot for a QHI/Training Captain at Lee.

Graham, although military trained was not an SAR trained pilot so, although he was an excellent pilot and a qualified North Sea Captain, he would have to take a co-pilot's position while receiving SAR training to build up his hours to meet the Coastguard's contract requirements. It was not at this stage necessary to have Graham as a SAR command pilot, but was certainly desirable as operating with only four Captains made rostering quite difficult, particularly around leave or sickness and the company had to look to the future.

Mike Roughton: Mike was a Royal Marines pilot who like Graham, had been a rating pilot. On leaving the Marines, he had joined 'British Caledonian Helicopters,' transferring to Bristow Helicopters when Bristows took over the company. Mike was a first officer coming up to command in the North Sea and had joined the Lee team even though he knew it would hold up his command for a while. The original compliment was to be four or five Captains and two or three co-pilots. It had been established the fifth Captain's slot would eventually go to Graham, who was already a North Sea Captain.

Mike would have to build up the hours and training in SAR before being offered training for SAR Command. The rules regarding all our qualifications had been set by the Coastguards and were even more stringent than the forces. I had flown with many a pilot in the Navy in Search and Rescue with far less experience than Mike already had.

Rob Torenvlied: Rob was a Dutch pilot trained by Bristows and had been flying the North Sea as a co-pilot. He had volunteered for Lee because he felt it would benefit his piloting skills. For Rob, the posting was to be just for a few years. The plan with the co-pilots was to build up SAR skills from the left hand seat for two or three years. Then they would go somewhere else like the North Sea, where they could build up hours much faster than in SAR.

Occasionally, someone considered suitable would go back to SAR for a second tour still as a co-pilot. It was hoped by then the Coastguards would agree that these second tour co-pilots would have enough experience to progress and train as SAR Captains. Obviously, Bristows would only put forward the ones deemed suitable for the role and, even then, the training would take another couple of years.

It would be no easy route to SAR Command for anyone who was not military trained and at that stage it was not possible because the Coastguard were insisting that all SAR command pilots were military trained. Provisions had to be made for the future as the experience base in civilian SAR progressed; after all, we now represented a fifth of the UK SAR fleet and it was becoming difficult to recruit crews who already had the necessary experience.

The flight would be forming at Lee on the 13th May in just ten days time; and we would go operational on the 15th. That was quite a commitment but Bristows had the back-up to make it happen. The Chief Engineer at Sumburgh (Sean Skeffington) was brought in to set up the engineering side.

Sean was quite a taskmaster with the ability to get things done, a good motivator, the ideal person to control the start-up of an operation. He would make sure the aircraft was ready and that the right choice of engineers for this type of role selected. He also had a way of putting us uppity aircrew in order.

Extra crews loaned from Sumburgh, Stornoway and Aberdeen were brought in to assist in setting up the flight while Don, Tony and myself were brought up to speed on the 'S61'. Don and I would also go up to Sumburgh to work with the crews up there for a few weeks to familiarise ourselves with Bristow standards and practices.

Among the new boys to Bristows I would be the first brought on line in the dual role (winch-op and winchman) as I only had to convert to the 'S61' helicopter type, being in date on all other SAR practices. Don and Tony would come on line later first as a winchman and then dual–trained, reflecting the time they had been away from the role. Terry, Mick and Chris were already on line, having transferred from Stornoway and Sumburgh. It was all very professional and first impressions exceeded anything I was expecting.

I had mentioned when I joined Bond Helicopters, how impressed I was with the avionic fit and to put that equipment into a bigger aircraft would be brilliant. Here we had that combination in the 'S61N', configured as a nineteen seat aircraft, with a large work area.

Even in this interim aircraft (G-BCLC), we had a SAR fit that would take us to a given datum and carry out the search patterns selected. The selected search pattern had to be manually flown by the pilots who were following instruments, as there was no autopilot in the interim aircraft (there would be in the main aircraft). 'LC' also had a Forward Looking Infrared Camera fitted (FLIR) which was really quite revolutionary at the time. It was a camera that could see in the dark and to me was quite astonishing.

At the time, FLIR was only being used by the United States military and I believe on a few American SAR flights. Its use had been championed by Bristows, after they had trialled it on the Brent oilfield SAR aircraft. The trial had been organised by Shell oil as a way forward to improve safety in the North Sea. It had been so successful that the Coastguard had the foresight to make the FLIR a contract requirement for the Coastguard aircraft.

Sumburgh and Stornoway at this stage had the first generation of this system. This had limitations, as it required recharging with a gas after only an hour or so and charging the unit could only be carried out on the ground. We were getting the second generation, which did not require recharging and had improved picture definition.

I was impressed with this aircraft as it was, despite it being the interim aircraft and looked forward to seeing the main aircraft when that was ready.

The 13th May soon arrived and I was tremendously eager. It was the strangest sensation because I had never been so enthused about anything previously: the whole situation just felt right to me. I had contacted Mike Rowsell who was as chuffed as I was, although he had already been working on the similar contract in Stornoway. For both of us it was like going home, back to the unit we had enjoyed so much in the Navy – quite surreal!

We arranged to meet each other at the main gate of HMS Daedalus before going over to the flight, a very strange feeling going back into the base. As soon as we walked in the gate a voice shouted "Dave you old F***!" I was quite taken back and the last thing I expected; I turned round to see Charlie Charlton, one of the first people I had ever worked with in SAR. Charlie had been the comedian on the flight back then in the early seventies. For Charlie's sins, he was now the Chief of the gate at Daedalus; it was great to see a friendly face on the gate.

Having Charlie on the gate could only help us as there was quite a lot of dissention over a civilian-run flight operating from a military airfield, especially as we were taking over from a military flight. Charlie being in charge of the gate staff would ease the tension as we were subject to car and personal searches for security reasons. I knew these searches could have been enforced a little too enthusiastically if they had wanted to make things more awkward than necessary.

The flight was using different hangars and buildings than those we had used on the Navy SAR flight because our aircraft was just a few inches too tall to fit through the hangar doors. We had been given the old '781 squadron' building on the opposite side of the airfield, so that was where Mick and I were headed; arriving just after the aircraft had flown in.

It was a sunny day and everyone was getting themselves involved with setting up the flight. It was so hectic that there was only time for quick introductions to those we did not know and straight into helping with the setup. Ops desks to set up, maps and charts to organise, communications, radios and telephones to sort out, furniture to source by whatever means, some provided by Bristows, some by the Coastguards and some sourced from the Navy via contacts that Terry, Mick and myself still had in Daedalus. The whole building, ops room and offices also needed painting.

Everyone just got on with it and it was quite incredible to see our achievements in the first few days prior to going operational. It was clear that everyone wanted to be there and more than happy to put in whatever it took to build a good operation.

Peter Thomson and Sean Skeffington should have made a career of setting up flights and operations, because it was down to them that everything went so well, the pair of them working as hard if not harder than everyone else.

Not all the engineers had yet been selected for the flight: we had a full compliment to carry out the job, but some were on loan from other units. The Engineers we knew were staying with the unit were:

Derek Hapgood: Derek, ex–Navy, had joined Bristows for this contract from British International Helicopters, where he had been working on the S61 'shuttle helicopter' that was operating between Heathrow and Gatwick at the time. Derek would be taking over as Chief Engineer when ready to do so; he still had to familiarise himself with Bristows' procedures so would be shadowing Sean.

Dave Savage: Dave, ex–RAF, was an airframe and engines engineer. He was the comedian of the unit, always wore a stupid hat and caused quite a few problems in the early days as the Navy came to terms with him being in the camp! Dave was billeted in the Chief Petty Officers' mess and they did not know what had hit them; however, after a few weeks he had won them over and through that helped the unit get a lot of backing from the Navy lads.

Daryl Edwards: Daryl had not long finished his apprenticeship as an airframes and engines engineer. He was a local lad but had been working at Bristows base in Redhill prior to hearing about this unit starting close to his home. Daryl had volunteered not really knowing what to expect and would become the 'Mr Fix it', with his fingers in so many pies – a very useful guy to have on the unit.

Mike Townend: Mike was the licensed avionics engineer. Mike had been working for Bristows at Aberdeen; he was one of the few engineers who had completed the course on the SAR auto hover system that we would be getting in the main aircraft. Mike had been working on the 'S61' fleet in Aberdeen so was snapped up when he volunteered to move south.

Dave Gash: Dave was also ex–RAF, an airframe and engines engineer who had transferred from a Bristows contract in Yarmouth.

Some funny things happened during the set up of the operation, which for some, having to live and operate on a naval base for the first time and for others returning to a naval base, was quite a culture shock. There was, initially, an unwillingness to accept the camp rules and the Navy in turn had trouble dealing with or accepting us.

One day Dave Gash was walking round the inner boundary of the airfield, heading to the unit, when a military patrol wagon pulled up beside him. The Naval Regulator got out of the vehicle and insisted that Dave ran (not walked) across the end of the runway. This was a military procedure probably left over from when it was a busy airfield. In some camps, you even had to run across the parade ground which was just one of the things you expected, more as a little discipline than anything else.

Dave was not going to run anywhere and nobody was going to order him to; the regulator did not know how to deal with this. Dave was taken to the control tower to be re-briefed on procedures – which missed the point for Dave, as he was simply not going to run across the runway! The situation grew out of all proportion; Pete Thomson had his work cut out calming everything down.

Another of the engineers on loan to the unit, Spud Murphy, also had trouble settling in; he would not run across any runway thresholds either, as silly rules like that were exactly the reason he had left the RAF. Spud was Irish and, with long hair, looked completely out of place on a military camp. Eventually Spud, with Dave Savage and Dave Gash, were all accepted because of their personalities. The lads in the mess they had been billeted in loved it; they found it refreshing to see these guys getting away with things and enjoyed watching the reactions they occasionally got from the officers.

Spud started a major security alert one day that went on for hours and meant that no one could leave or enter the camp. The alert started because it had been reported that a strange looking guy with an Irish accent was walking round the camp. Eventually, someone put two and two together and enquired where the man had been at the time of the sighting. That was the end of the security alert when they realised it was only Spud.

Another time, the Navy decided to test our fire fighting drills, taken quite seriously in the forces, as they should be. They made these drills quite realistic by sneaking up to a building and throwing a smoke marker into the room. The normal reaction if this happened would be to raise the alarm, abandon the building, group at a known point and carry out a head count etc.

This time Daryl was walking down the passage when a smoke marker popped through the window. Daryl thought 'what is that silly beggar doing throwing this dangerous looking thing in the building', so he picked it up and threw it out of the window again then carried on with his work. The Fire Officer went loopy shouting at Daryl "You can't do that!" Daryl replied with, "Of course I can, I just have!"

These were a few examples of the cultural problems Peter had to sort out since we were on military premises and would have to abide by their rules, within reason. The Navy never succeeded in getting Spud or Dave to run across that runway and it was agreed that we would not be subjected to the sneak smoke bomb attacks. They still conducted fire exercises by walking in and shouting Fire, Fire, Fire, which they did considerably more frequently than I remembered in the Navy.

Commencing the contract at Lee

We had quite a few SAR jobs in that first month, the first being a military rescue, which was quite unusual as over 95% of the SAR incidents carried out in the UK were civilian related (one of the reasons why the Ministry of Defence had decided to pull the SAR helicopter from HMS Daedalus). It was understandable that the MOD would want their SAR assets based at operational military airfields where they could be utilised more effectively in both roles. That very first job was to recover an injured seaman from the warship HMS Nottingham.

Another couple of unusual jobs happened in the first two weeks; we were scrambled twice, on separate occasions, to Manston in Kent as a back up to the RAF aircraft. In both cases, we were tasked to take fire fighters out to cross Channel ferries which had suffered fires onboard, straight away justifying the Coastguard's decision to use the larger aircraft.

The Coastguard had sought advice from the RAF on how much training the crews should carry out each month to keep in date and the RAF had recommended fifteen hours per crew. We worked a three-crew system so forty-five hours a month flying training was allocated within the contract. All operational flying on incidents would be additional to the training hours.

Pete Thomson insisted that the training was as realistic as possible and, quite honestly, this pressure for realistic training would be kept indefinitely. The continuation training was actually better than I had been involved with in the military. When I was on the Lee flight in the Navy we only trained with MOD vessels, Police launches, lifeboats, local rescue craft and very occasionally, with a military-owned yacht. Now we could train with any vessel we chose, obviously subject to approval from the vessel.

The company had taken out a massive indemnity to cover against any possible accidents.

This allowed us fantastic flexibility with training; we would pick vessels on a suitable heading to train with, approach the vessel, hover alongside and show them a blackboard with 'Channel 67' written on it. The majority of vessels had radios onboard and would go to the frequency requested, we could then ask permission to winch to their vessel. It was rare that anyone turned us down. If the vessel accepted we would brief and carry out the intended exercise. This was a procedure being used by RAF crews but for some reason not cleared at that time for the Navy crews.

As the runway at Lee led directly onto the Solent, we never had any difficulties finding suitable vessels. It soon became the norm to winch to three or more vessels on each training sortie, plus possibly a cliff or some other exercise required for our monthly training records.

We were able to get plenty of practice winching people from the water as we would carry out the winching for the naval survival courses and life raft/boat winching carried out for the maritime training college at Warsash.

If we had strong winds, Pete would insist we went out into the channel to take advantage of winching to larger vessels in the rougher sea conditions. We were to become so used to this that our skills grew to a standard way above those I had when I joined; on occasions we winched to vessels for training in conditions I had seen medals awarded for on jobs. With Pete, everything was a challenge. He believed if we trained enough in these conditions the majority of problems we were likely to face on jobs would be made safer.

This was all obvious stuff but there had to be limits to reduce that risk of injury in training. In later years as the Civil Aviation Authority (CAA) got to grips with SAR, plus pressures from health and safety, standards etc. we gradually had to curtail some of the riskier training as safe training limits were introduced; nevertheless, they were exciting times and pushed us to a different level of capabilities. We would find many ways of producing the realism needed to keep the standards high as the safety limits were introduced.

The 'S61' could start up in winds of up to 47 knots but we were not limited to that as we could start up in the lea of a hangar hence strong winds were unlikely to curb our training or the ability to respond to tasks.

One thing that took me completely by surprise was that I was not as good on the winch operating side as I thought I was. We had now been dual-trained (or would be eventually) so that all seven aircrewmen would be able to fulfil the role of winchman and winch operator, rather like the way we worked on the oilrigs.

This would make running the rosters much easier and would enable us to continue a task if one of us was injured (depending of course, on the seriousness of that injury). The other major advantage of this dual training made for better decisions as to the best way to tackle a job, as both of us were fully aware of all the problems.

In the Navy, the divers were trained for both roles, but on all tasking the diver acted as the winchman so the majority of our practice as a winch operator was carried out on training flights, normally in better weather than we might expect during scrambles. The winch operator carried out the winching during jobs.

As a diver, I had rarely experienced the concerns of the winch operator under these circumstances on the difficult jobs, when he really did have the life of the winchman/diver in his hands. The winch operator had to make the decision as to the right time to put the winchman on deck.

The timing required in getting the winchman safely onto a deck in strong winds and rough seas would never be an easy call. The winchman could be trailing well behind the aircraft on a long wire (forced behind by the strong winds), especially when working with vessels with high masts or superstructure. The winch operator would be working out when the winchman would lose that windage due to the superstructure and suddenly swing forward. At the same time, he would be keeping an eye on the movement of the ship. In rough weather, it was likely to be cork screwing from side to side, as well as heaving up and down by as much as three or four storey houses. While processing all this information in order to pick that right moment to put the winchman on deck, he has to keep a cool and controlled voice as he cons the pilot towards the contact.

In those circumstances it really is a difficult job, something that even in all the years I had been doing the job, I had not fully appreciated. Even when working on the rig I had somehow ended up being the winchman during the more awkward jobs, probably because I had defaulted to the role I felt most comfortable doing.

Now there would be a definite demarcation once we were all dual trained, we would be the winch operator one shift and winchman the next. I was now experiencing these more difficult conditions, even during training, as we would actually go looking for difficult decks to work with in stormy conditions.

As winch operator, you also had additional pressures en-route to a tasking; liaising with the Coastguard and vessels you had been scrambled to, keeping track of the aircraft's position, planning search patterns and generally trying to keep ahead of the game. Anticipation was required, such as determining where the nearest or most suitable hospital for the casualty would be, digging out the maps and information about any danger areas that required clearance to cross to get to the incident or hospital, checking obstructions on the approach to the hospital, etc.

I knew it could all be quite a workload, but now I was experiencing it all first hand and realised that I had been taking a lot of the winch operator's work for granted; now I was genuinely doing both roles. This in turn helped the two aircrewmen in the cabin work better as a team: if we were en-route to a tasking (as winchman) I would take some of the workload off the winch op once my equipment was ready and vice versa. In time, we learnt to read each other's minds – it was definitely the way to work.

Another thing Peter and Terry insisted on was the rotation of crews so that we were all used to working with each other, rather than one crew working together all the time. The one crew system worked well but had limitations as a crew working together all the time may change procedures slightly, so a new member joining the crew as a relief (perhaps for sickness or leave), could miss something that would normally have been done automatically by the person he had relieved.

Swapping crews round regularly ensured all procedures were standard and any changes felt necessary were assessed by the whole flight. I preferred the one crew system but, in time, had to admit that Peter and Terry's way was best as we all learnt to work with each other and it helped the flight to bond together as a unit much quicker than normal.

Nick Horst joined us in the July, having managed to arrange early release from the Navy. Nick would be our seventh aircrewman so we were up to full strength. He was already a qualified SAR aircrewman and was soon on line as a winchman; he would be trained as a winch operator over the following year. It was not possible to change straight from military procedures to Bristow procedures because of differences in aircraft and the new systems that would be on the main aircraft when that arrived.

In the September, our main aircraft 'G- BIMU' arrived. It was like a brand new aircraft painted in the Coastguard colours, new trim inside and all the avionics fitted to make it a true SAR helicopter.

The equipment that was fitted was a complete SAR package partly developed for the SAR Bell 212's operating in the Brent oil field and further enhanced for the SAR S61's based in Sumburgh and Stornoway, Now, with a few slight improvements like the second generation of Infrared Camera, it was ready for our operation. This was 1988 and 'MU' was way ahead of anything else offered for SAR at the time.

The following was from the press release at the time and for me as a user the aircraft was simply something else. I am not saying everything performed quite as well as the sales pitch but it was certainly streets ahead of anything I had flown in and it was clear that a considerable amount of research and best use of equipment available in the 1980's had been put together to make the 'S61' a brilliant aircraft for the SAR role. The equipment would be further enhanced as required over future years.

Bristow Helicopters Press Release:
Bristow Search and Rescue System

Search and Rescue operations have routinely been carried out by conventionally configured helicopters but to enable the crew to carry out the Search and Rescue mission in adverse weather conditions, the following systems have been developed and incorporated into the aircraft:-

Chelton Radio Homing System
This equipment allows homing on the following frequencies:-
VHF/AM 121.5 MHz plus fully diallable on VHF/AM
VHF/FM channel 16 plus fully diallable on VHF/FM
UHF 243 MHz
2182 KHz may be homed on by the aircraft Automatic Direction Finding equipment

Racal Avionics R Nav Area Navigator
This area navigation equipment uses three separate input sources. The GPS is backed up by VOR / DME and Doppler to compute three separate navigation plots. The most accurate plot will be used, normally to an accuracy of <1/4 nautical miles (nm). The system's database holds 100 waypoints and 30 routes. It also incorporates the following search patterns:-

Box or expanding square search
Creeping line ahead search
Sector search
Expanding spiral search
Interception of a moving target

Bendix RDR 1400c Weather Mapping and Search Radar

The unit, fitted as part of our SAR system, is one of the most modern, advanced capability multi-mode radars available. It is optimised to search for small targets in rough seas where its processing capability allows the highlighting of targets against a background of sea clutter. It incorporates the choice of two weather modes, three search modes and a beacon mode whereby it can interrogate, receive and display signals from fixed transponder beacons on all ranges. It also incorporates an interface unit enabling navigational data to be displayed by itself or superimposed over beacon, weather or search displays.

FLIR – Forward Looking Infrared Unit

An Infrared camera is mounted on the port side of the fuselage under the co-pilot's window, this can be rotated 120° either side of the aircraft's heading. The monitor screen is in the cabin aft on the port side. There is a control with the monitor that allows the winchman to point the camera in the desired direction. Heat sources are shown either as white areas on a dark background or vice-versa. The winchman, on seeing a target, can trigger a switch to enlarge the target by four times. This equipment has been used successfully to locate survivors in dinghies or small boats at sea and is particularly useful in searches overland, on cliff faces or in the mountains.

Rescue Hoist

The aircraft is equipped with a variable control rescue hoist that has 300ft of cable, a load capability of 600 lbs and incorporates an electric motor with variable speed control. The hoist has a maximum speed of 150ft per minute.

Flight Path Control and Auto Hover Equipment (LN450)

Prior to the development of the Bristow SAR System, the location of a survivor did not always lead to a successful rescue. Keeping a helicopter in a steady state of hover over a survivor whilst he is being winched to safety is difficult enough in perfect conditions due to the aircraft's inherent instability. To attempt such a manoeuvre at night or in bad visibility, with the lack of visual cues and peripheral references, is virtually impossible.

The Bristow SAR System enables a steady state of hover to be maintained over a target by the fitment and use of the Louis Newmark LN450 flight path control and auto hover equipment. A digital microprocessor system translates information from a variety of aircraft sensors that control the autopilot. As the autopilot makes all the control inputs, the pilots only have to monitor the flying controls and take over in the unlikely event of a system failure.

The system includes an innovative feature called the 'Overfly'. On locating a survivor, this mode is selected and the helicopter then flies over the survivor at search height, around a modified 'racetrack' pattern and brings the helicopter into wind at a point from which an automatic 'Transition Down' takes place.

During this phase, the helicopter's height and speed are progressively reduced until it comes to an automatic hover near to the survivor. All this happens without the need for the pilots to have any external visual references. Indeed, as long as the location of the survivor can be determined, the rescue can be completed without the pilots seeing anything outside the helicopter throughout the entire procedure.

To Summarise

The Bristow SAR System comprises equipment that can assist and enable the location of survivors. Without the crew having external references, a rescue can be carried out at night or in adverse weather conditions, which could otherwise prevent such location and rescue.

The system is fully approved by the UK Civil Aviation Authority and is in service in Bristow operations throughout the UK

In October 1988, The Coastguard aircraft at Stornoway ditched while carrying out a low-level search in the early hours of the morning. I have never been quite sure as to the exact cause of the ditching but the back seat crew were Vic Carcass as the 'winch operator' and Cy Rogers as the 'winchman'. Vic had quite a chequered past of ditching, I believe this was his fourth. The three previous ditches were while he was in the Navy; his second was quite nasty and resulted in a serious back injury that very nearly ended his flying career.

Vic not only got back to flying but he continued as an SAR diver for some years afterwards, finishing his naval career as a communications aircrewman, but not before a third ditching (this time in a fixed wing aircraft en route to Ireland). This goes to show that some people just never learn the right time to give up!

The winchman Cy Rogers was an ex RAF aircrewman; both he and Vic had a lucky escape. In Vic's case, he was at the open doorway attached to his dispatcher harness when the aircraft ditched. The force of the impact twisted him round, putting the quick release for the dispatcher behind him. It took a while for Vic to work out why he could not release the harness; he was under water unable to get out. It was his diving training that kept him calm enough to work out what had happened; enabling him to release the tension on the harness and twist it round. He could then reach the quick release fitting and make his way to the surface.

For Cy Rogers, the situation was even worse. He was operating the FLIR camera towards the back of the aircraft when they ditched and forced all the way to the back by the influx of water. He must have gone to hell and back during the next few minutes, as the aircraft was filling up with water. At the time, the four windows in the tail end of the 'S61' could not be jettisoned. There was one quite large emergency exit with a life raft attached just forward of these windows.

The water had almost immediately pushed Cy behind this emergency exit and he was trapped in a very small (and reducing) air pocket. He attempted to swim down to the emergency exit but could not get it open, I can only guess, having to accept his fate as he was forced further back.

In the meantime, the remaining crew had made a successful escape. The two pilots plus Vic had joined as a group (normal ditching procedure), soon realising Cy was nowhere to be seen. At the time, I believe they thought he had not made it thinking he may have been knocked unconscious on impact. There was no way they could attempt to get back in the aircraft as it was clearly sinking. The tail of the aircraft was still accessible and the rear emergency exit still visible. At the time, Vic already thought it would be too late for Cy Rogers, but there was just a chance if they could get the emergency door open that Cy may be stuck in the tail.

If they could open this door, it would also give them access to the life raft, which would give them a better chance of surviving until their own rescue. Attempting to open that exit would not have been the safest thing for them to do as the aircraft was sinking and there would have been considerable snagging hazards around the tail pylon and tail rotor.

However, they managed to get the door open and out popped the life raft followed almost immediately by Cy Rogers. He had virtually given up hope at this stage and you can only imagine what was going through his mind, when he suddenly saw a larger area of light. He dived down towards it suddenly ending up on the surface with the others. Because of that incident, the windows in the back were made jettisonable in all the North Sea 'S61's and on the rest of the Coastguard SAR fleet.

The loss of the aircraft left Stornoway without a fully coupled all weather aircraft. Because they had operations that could take them to the edge of their endurance, way out into the Irish Sea, it was felt their requirement for the fully equipped aircraft was greater than ours was at Lee-on-Solent.

The Coastguards decided to replace Stornoway's ditched aircraft with our new aircraft 'MU'. We went back to the basic 'S61' 'LC' until another aircraft could be prepared with all the SAR systems. I am quite sure this was the right decision, but it felt pretty awful losing 'MU' just as we were beginning to get used to all its advanced capabilities.

Incidentally, Vic still did not consider his fourth ditching to be an omen and continued flying at Stornoway, even surviving a further serious incident when the helicopter's blades struck a cliff during a rescue. Vic became our standards aircrewman, until a rather unusual flying-related injury, caused by static discharge during a winching incident, grounded him just a short while before his retirement.

In the November of 1988, Nick Horst had a difficult job: they were scrambled to the yacht 'Shadana' which was in difficulty 18 miles south of St Catherine's point, the southerly tip of the Isle of Wight. The crew were: Captain Lemmy Tanner (a pilot who was on loan to us during the start up phase), co-pilot Graham Sorge, Terry Short was the winch operator. The incident was at night in rough weather, in a non-coupled aircraft so it was never going to be an easy tasking.

The yacht was at risk of breaking up in very rough seas and the crew needed evacuating. They managed to get Nick on board the yacht using the hi-line technique but the area Nick had to work in was tight, just a small cockpit area cluttered with rigging.

Because of the unpredictable movement of the yacht, Nick found it very difficult getting the three survivors winched back to the aircraft. He prepared the first two for transfer planning to send them up as a multi-lift with both of them on the wire. Unfortunately, as Terry was about to lift them from the yacht, a sudden movement put the two casualties either side of a stay. Terry had to winch out quickly and abandon the lift. The casualties fell back, landing heavily on Nick. He was able to send them up to the aircraft safely on the second attempt.

After that narrow escape with the rigging, Terry signalled for Nick to get the remaining casualty into a life raft, having decided that would be the safest way to complete the rescue. Nick was now injured quite badly from the casualties falling on top of him. He knew what had happened to him, but also knew that no-one could help him where he was, so opted not to say anything and get on with the job in hand.

He prepared the life raft and held it alongside as the casualty jumped in Nick had no choice but to jump in himself, knowing that with his injury, this was going to be difficult. Nick ended up in the water after landing awkwardly in the life raft, but managed to scramble back onboard, completing the rescue by sending the survivor up to the aircraft before being recovered himself.

Once everyone was safely onboard the helicopter, Nick turned round to Terry, flopped his lower leg around in his immersion suit and gave Terry a snapped signal. Terry did not need to be told, he could see it. Nick's leg had been broken when the casualties had fallen on him while still onboard the yacht.

Nick was flown straight to Haslar Hospital where he was met by an ambulance. The survivors were taken back to the unit to warm up and have a coffee. This was the first time the casualties were brought back to the unit, while a crewmember was dropped off at hospital.

Nick genuinely accepted the incident as just one of those things that happened, almost as though it was part of his job. He did everything possible to get back to work as soon as he could.

I felt he had done a brilliant job; it would not have been easy continuing a rescue with a broken leg, particularly in those conditions and having to jump into a life raft as well. Nick says he had no choice and he probably did not have; nevertheless, it must have taken considerable will power to help sort the casualties out once back in the aircraft, before making Terry aware that he had a problem.

Nick was the only crewman not to have ever worked with any of us before the flight had formed. He was the last to join the flight so had his work cut out settling in, but this incident sealed his position; we now knew we had another good, solid member in our team.

Don Sowden, who had been trained as one of Portsmouth's first paramedics, hit the ground running when he came back to flying. One of the reasons Terry wanted him on the unit was he thought Don would be able to advance our first aid skills. Don was keen to see this happen as he knew there was room for improvement; very little had moved forward on the first aid side of our job from his previous time in the role.

Don arranged for colleagues from the ambulance service and doctors from the Portsmouth hospitals to visit the flight to help us improve our skills gained in the forces. He was also trying very hard to push the borders further and had identified the skills he felt would be of benefit to our advanced first aid such as intubation, cannulation, the use of defibrillators etc. This was all black magic to us back then and even the programme to train ambulance paramedics in these skills had not been running for long.

Achieving this was not going to be easy as it would require additional courses plus time in hospital theatres to gain these skills, but we had to start somewhere and we felt as a group that if we kept chipping away slowly, we would eventually improve things.

The first thing Don managed to move forward was for us to carry a defibrillator. He had managed to arrange training with the Hampshire ambulance service, who were willing to train us providing we passed a self-learning module, prior to the actual course.

At the time defibrillators were both very expensive and complicated and not even carried by all ambulances. It was not a contract requirement to carry one of these and getting approval was not easy; however, it was agreed that if we could raise the money to purchase a defibrillator, the Company would pay the costs to gain CAA approval for its use in the aircraft.

Getting this approval would run to thousands of pounds, as it was thought the operation of a defibrillator in an aircraft may affect the avionics. Many tests had to be carried out operating one during different stages of flight and the trial would have to be supervised by the CAA.

A few air ambulances had been fitted with defibrillators and had been through a similar process, but the CAA insisted that each aircraft type would have to be separately tested.

The challenge to raise funds for the defibrillator (approximately £6000) was taken up and a charity fund formed, which the whole flight got behind. Mick Rowsell became our charity champion; this was because of his already considerable experience with charity work raising funds for disabled children, obviously close to Mick's heart, bringing up two children with cerebral palsy.

All the local sailing clubs and maritime related businesses were approached and many charity events taken up by the flight. In only a few months, our target was met much quicker than we expected.

We had agreed to carry out all the training and continuation training in our own time. All seven aircrewmen became qualified, the CAA trial was conducted and approval to carry and use the defibrillator given. That was our first breakthrough and, in time, all SAR flights would carry defibrillators.

This achievement was the first of many and had quite a noticeable effect on the flight. Not only was it the start of advancing our medical skills, it was the start of a charity fund, which would go on to help many people in the future. Everyone was doing their bit and some daft challenges would be set over the years.

Presentation of our first Defibrillator after raising money for purchase and training with the Hampshire ambulance Service (1990)
Left: – Don Sowden- Mick Rowsell-Chris Bond
Centre: – Chief Ambulance Officer Gordon Adams & Paul Smees
(Training officer)
Right: – Terry Short-Nick Horst-Dave Peel-Tony Campbell

GBDIJ-(India Juliet)

Fortunately, we did not have too many scrambles during the four months we had to wait for our new fully fitted aircraft; experiencing only a few situations that were difficult for us to carry out in 'LC'.

Now we had experienced the benefits and capabilities of the main aircraft, even though only for a short period before it was sent to Stornoway, we were looking forward to its replacement and all stops had been pulled to make this as quick as possible.

In May 1989 the aircraft arrived, registration: 'GBDIJ' ('IJ'). It was every bit as good as 'MU' with all the SAR System as promised. We could now settle into our role with a brilliant aircraft and the prospects of a good future ahead of us.

We were getting extra training to continue our familiarisation with the new systems. It was quite strange relying on all this black magic, letting an aircraft take you to a given position, fly a search pattern then on the press of a button take the aircraft down to a winching height of 40ft. All this being carried out by computers, while the pilots' hands hovered over the controls in anticipation of things going wrong...and the crew in the back hoping they would react quick enough if anything did go wrong!

Our time with 'MU' before it went to Stornoway was not long enough for us to be fully confident with the SAR Systems, but everything on this aircraft was responding the same way. We got through this stage after many hours of additional training until we all accepted its considerable capabilities and had mastered the few shortcomings.

We were finding the Infrared camera very useful: not only did it have the capability of finding someone in the water at night, it was also proving to be a real time saver on searches, at times quite considerably so.

The old procedure for a night time search would be to proceed to the datum, select a search height for the target we were looking for and commence the actual search required for that target. If something was sighted visually like a light, or if a target was picked up on the radar, the pilots would have to let down low enough to creep towards that contact or light, until we could focus our flood lights on the target. This was quite a slow procedure at night, as the pilots would not have any visual references and were likely to fly the aircraft into the water if not very careful.

Often, once the aircraft's lights were on the target, we would find it was not what we were looking for, so had to get back up to search height until the next target was located. The FLIR saved all that delay; we could now stay up at search height, moving towards the target until it could be identified on the monitor. If, for example, we were looking for an overdue open fishing boat with three people on board and we could see on the FLIR monitor that the target was a yacht, the original search pattern could be continued with minimal delay.

One of the more unusual incidents, which was not maritime related, was a night time stabbing that had taken place at a burger stall on Hayling Island. The chap who had carried out the crime had been last seen running towards the sea so the police requested our assistance and the man was quickly located hiding in bushes close to the shore. The police were conned onto the contact and the chap was arrested. It was accepted that he would easily have got away if we had not picked him up on the camera.

The stabbing victim died, so it then became a murder case and as a result of that, the Hampshire police aircraft was fitted with a FLIR camera. They had been assessing the possibility of FLIR but this incident helped to seal that decision. We were told at the time that had the man not been located so quickly, a murder investigation team would have been set up and the investigation costs could have rapidly risen to the million pound mark. The FLIR camera would eventually be accepted as an essential tool, fitted to the majority of police helicopters and fixed wing patrol aircraft.

Being the only SAR aircraft fitted with the FLIR camera South of Scotland meant that we would be tasked out of area for many jobs at night when it was confirmed that people were missing or wreckage had been located. These jobs would take us as far afield as Wales, Cornwall, East Sussex, Kent, plus France and the Channel Islands.

Not all jobs go to plan and very occasionally, mistakes can be made just by a slight oversight or wrong assumption. Mistakes happen in any profession and hopefully lessons are learnt from them, but some can be extremely comical, providing no one is hurt by the mistake.

In this particular incident Chris Bond was the winchman en-route to a yacht south of the Isle of Wight, the weather was foul and the sea rough; the yacht had an injured crewmember onboard. This was never going to be an easy task as getting on to yachts in heavy seas is always difficult. Chris was busy preparing his equipment en-route and, when the aircraft pitched up alongside the distressed yacht it was time for him to be lowered.

The yacht was the only one in the area at the position given. 'Rescue IJ', approached the yacht, had a crew brief on the task in hand, lowered the hi-line which was taken in hand by the crew, then Chris was lowered. The yacht was moving all over the place in the heavy seas so Chris took a few knocks on the way down – something we learn to live with in these circumstances.

It is always with some relief when you finally land on deck, but then you have to get straight on with the job in hand. Chris thought it rather strange to see the looks of amazement on the faces of the crew. When he asked where the casualty was they did not know what he was talking about; no one was sick or injured onboard.

It was the wrong yacht! The crew were surprised when a helicopter appeared alongside and lowered a line but they simply did what was natural to most sailors; if given a line they will pull it inboard. When Chris appeared from the door of the aircraft they continued pulling, wondering why anyone would put themselves through that, in those conditions.

At that stage, Chris would not have been able to see the funny side of the error, as it now meant he would have to be recovered to 'IJ', find the right yacht then go through the whole procedure again.

The mistake was understandable, although avoidable; a catalogue of events had led up to this incident. First, the initial position of the yacht in distress was wrong; secondly, there was a radar contact in the position given; thirdly, when the yacht with the injured crewmember was called on the radio it had acknowledged all the instructions. Finally, when 'IJ' arrived on scene, the yacht in that position matched the description given and was on the heading that the distressed yacht had been asked to be on.

The correct yacht was located by homing in on radio transmissions and the casualty was recovered to 'IJ'. Fortunately, the delay had not made any difference to the casualty's condition.

The situation caused a few red faces. We all knew we could have easily been drawn in to the same situation. The serious side of the incident was addressed first, with many debriefs and discussions as to the best way to avoid a situation like that happening again. For example, asking the yacht to fire a flare when they had the aircraft visual, or signal by some other means if they did not have flares; checking the actual name of the yacht when visual. Whilst en-route gain as much information as possible about the vessel e.g. colour, size, type; checking with the homing device that you are heading towards the vessel etc.

It also caused considerable amusement; I know exactly what I would have felt if I was Chris that day because he was not in any way responsible for what had happened, yet had to carry out two awkward winches as winchman. I also know that I would not have been able to contain myself once the job was over.

Towards the end of 1989, we had quite an awkward job after an accident in the Solent when several sailors ended up in the water, leaving two of them seriously injured. When we arrived on scene, both these casualties had been recovered from the water by separate yachts. One casualty was unconscious and the other was being resuscitated by the crew of a rescue craft that had also arrived on scene.

It was an awkward scenario with several decisions to make; neither yacht would be easy to winch to and the casualties were in very awkward positions on the yachts. We opted to get the seriously injured person into the helicopter first so that we would both be available to keep the resuscitation going when we winched the second casualty onboard.

Nick Horst was the winchman, I was the winchop and Pete Thomson was the Captain. We managed to get Nick and stretcher down to the first yacht using the hi-line technique and he got the survivor onto the stretcher as quick as he possibly could, but the casualty would need looking after once recovered to the aircraft, in particular making sure his airway was maintained. We could not really just run with this casualty, as that would give no chance to the other person being resuscitated on the yacht. Recovering the second casualty would require both of us to get Nick onto the second yacht and again for the recovery of Nick and the casualty.

We quickly discussed this as a crew and decided to use Rob Torenvlied, the co-pilot to look after the person already recovered to the aircraft. It was simply one of those situations where a calculated risk had to be taken and Pete felt he could manage without the co-pilot as it would be virtually the same procedure as for the first yacht and he knew the power requirements he had used for that.

Hence, Rob climbed out of the left hand seat to receive a quick brief from me on how to maintain the airway and then we got on with the recovery of the second casualty. This was done as quickly as Nick could prepare him for transfer and the hi-line was simply ditched as we did not want to waste any time recovering it, we then departed immediately for Haslar helicopter landing site, radioing ahead for a resuscitation team to meet us.

Nick and I continued CPR on the second casualty, while Rob looked after the first casualty who was starting to regain consciousness but needed reassurance to stop him from trying to move around.

When we landed at the helicopter-landing site, the crash team came on board and soon had my casualty intubated and prepared for transfer to hospital, whilst Rob's was taken by a second ambulance. The back of the helicopter looked like a bomb had hit it with equipment all over the place!

This incident, although extremely tragic, was the second breakthrough to our efforts to advance our first aid skills. The leader of the crash team was a Royal Naval anaesthetist, who took the trouble to write to the flight saying how well he thought we had managed the situation, praising the way we were managing the casualties even while they were working round us. Whilst we always do the best we can, it is always nice to get some praise.

Shortly after this incident the anaesthetist, who had considerable experience in trauma situations, had been talking to another senior consultant anaesthetist, Surgeon Lt Cdr Sean Tighe. Sean was at the time thinking about carrying out a trial to help medics in the field in the event of multiple casualty situations.

The trial he wished to carry out was related to airway management, and designed to see how quickly medics could be trained up to carry out intubations compared with the time it would take to train the medic to carry out a fairly new procedure using a laryngeal mask. Both procedures provide a casualty with a good airway but required special skills, the intubation being more difficult than the laryngeal mask.

He contacted Peter Thomson to see if our team of seven aircrewmen would be willing to take part in this trial, which of course, we jumped at. The trial took place over several weeks with us attending classroom instruction, followed by time in hospital theatres practicing our newly-acquired skills on servicemen prior to operations, permission obviously having been obtained from the patients.

The trial went well and it was clear we could be taught to use the laryngeal mask quicker than intubation, which was the object of the trial. As we had also successfully learnt to intubate, it was agreed that we could continue with this skill – intubation probably being the better route for us as, once inserted, it completely protected the airway. This was subject to us getting approval from an official medical body and keeping up to date with these skills, which would require a number of successful intubations a year.

Don Sowden, who had been trying to move this forward, had already started talks with a consultant called Gary Smith, who was a consultant anaesthetist, helping to shape the way forward for paramedics in Hampshire.

Gary worked at Queen Alexander Hospital in Portsmouth and was willing to act as our medical authority. Another anaesthetist, Bruce Taylor, was willing to help us to keep our newly learnt skills in date. He would also train us in cannulation skills, which would allow us to set up infusion of fluids and enable the availability of an intravenous line for drugs if required on arrival at hospital. At that stage, we would not be allowed to administer anything other than fluids.

Many meetings took place as to whether this was the way forward, it was not a requirement of the contract and there would obviously be a cost to all of this. The company decided to give us full backing but it would really be more like a trial on our unit and would again, have to be done in our own time.

I was not to know it at the time, but meeting Gary Smith and Bruce Taylor would make a major difference to me several years later, when I would face quite possibly the most difficult challenge of my life.

This extra training proved a very good step toward our aims. At that time we did not want to be full blown paramedics: there was already quite a high workload to stay current in the aviation aspects of the crewmens' role which involved ongoing currency and annual assessments. To achieve additional competency as a paramedic would require off-base continuation training which would have to take place outside of the SAR roster and that meant the manning level would have to be increased – and that was seen as unlikely to happen.

We knew from our own experiences that the additional skills gained were an advantage, the benefits being clear almost immediately with vastly improved advance first aid skills which lead to greater confidence in the role.

We were now some way towards achieving the level that Don, with his paramedic experience, felt would be advantageous to us and would continually assess these requirements over the years ahead. We also hoped that once these advantages were proven, all the SAR units (including the military) would take them up.

This indeed proved to be the case and it was not long after we started our training that the RAF had an incident that made them review their SAR winchman medical training and decided to increase their own skill levels. Once the RAF had taken it on board, we hoped it would become a Coastguard requirement rather than a voluntary one as it was on our unit. At the next contract renewal, the Coastguards had accepted the new extended skills as the way forward plus the inclusion of defibrillators as part of the Coastguard SAR helicopters' equipment, so these changes were written into the contract.

All the Coastguard SAR aircrewmen would have to learn the skills, which meant official courses would be required. The course was set up at Queen Alexander hospital in Portsmouth, under the guidance of Gary Smith. Even the northern units came down for their initial training, backed up by a refresher course carried out every two years. Don had previously been to evaluate the RAF course, then being held in Newcastle, to ensure we were all covering the same syllabus.

The relationship between the military and civilian SAR flights would prove to be quite strange. We would, over the years go through stages of openness and other stages of silly arguments about who had the best kit, procedures etc. However, I think we all benefited from this, as improvements on the first aid side could be made to both fleets.

Over time, the military SAR aircraft would be fitted with equipment that we had, like the infrared camera and the Automatic Manoeuvre Control (AMC), which enables the winch operator to control the aircraft with the aid of computers linked to the auto hover-system. This was used to recover casualties from the sea in positions where the pilots had no visual references (mainly used at night).

In turn, we would notice equipment they had like night vision goggles, which is one area where they were (and still are) ahead of us. We will continue to push to be equipped to the same standard as the RAF regarding their advanced night vision capability and special cockpit lighting and I am sure will get that capability. I am also sure that we will continue to push for any future equipment we find valuable to the role.

The charity side of the flight was in full swing during all of 1989 which was pushed along by an offer from our company who promised to double any charity funds (up to £5000) raised during the year. This was because of our success with the fundraising carried out in the first year of the flight forming.

The flight had decided to form an official charity fund with Mick Rowsell as the fund chairman, the benefits going to handicapped children and adults in the local area. We had already provided a number of special 'Supa Bikes' for disabled children in the area with money left over from the defibrillator fund. These were purpose designed sturdy bikes with special gearing plus the facility to make the children secure on the bikes when being used. They were very successful and we even had a few children's races on them in the hanger: seeing the children's faces was something else.

The main project for 1989 was to provide a 'Snoezellen' room for Furzebrook School in Sarisbury Green (between Fareham and Southampton) which was a school catering for handicapped children from all over the area. The 'Snoezellen' was a specially prepared room that would provide a restful environment designed to reduce stress and promote a sensation of well-being. The room would contain fibre-optic boards and cascades, water tubes filled with bubbles that changed colours and projectors creating gentle patterns.

The company challenge was taken on, with all the flight involved. We took the 'Standby' aircraft to outside functions at the weekends and individuals would carry out sponsored events. Terry Short carried out a couple of long distance cycle rides, including one round the coastline of the Isle of Wight at breakneck speed.

I did a couple of sponsored runs and a sponsored swim from the Isle of Wight to the mainland and was joined on this by Nick Horst and Sandra, our cleaner. The training alone took us several months; we were reasonable swimmers but a five-mile sea swim was a little more than we originally felt capable of doing. Others did daft things: for example, Dave Savage not only shaved off half of his moustache and beard but he then walked around like that for a week!

Many events were held, culminating in a Miss SAR competition involving Lifeboat-men, Coastguards and the SAR crews treading the boardwalk in drag. It was an incredible night. We had been to France for the booze and had made a catwalk inside GAFIR's (Gosport and Fareham's Inshore Rescue) boathouse. All the contestants had been drinking quite heavily to gain the Dutch courage required to get dressed in drag and walk the catwalk, and the 'Dutch courage' helped make the competition hilarious.

The cheap booze had everyone else lubricated enough to dig deep in their pockets towards the charity. The atmosphere was electric, making the event so successful that the same format was used for fund raising at later dates. This event was a Pete Thomson idea and he was most upset not to win the title, which went to Don Sowden, but the challenge was set.

By the end of 1989, we had exceeded the £5000 promised by the company raising a total of £14200, including Bristow's donation.

To make the money go further, we prepared and fitted the special room ourselves, leaving a balance of funds for further causes. The 'Snoezellen' room was opened in early 1990.

The spare time the lads on the unit were devoting to get the fund underway during those early years would prove unsustainable; we worked unsocial hours anyway and would normally have only one weekend a month off. That weekend off plus many of our off-shift days were being utilised for carrying out charity events or training for sponsored challenges.

Those frantic levels at the early stages of the contract, although quite hard work, were extremely satisfying and went a long way towards cementing the camaraderie that was and would continue on the unit. The fund would continue and everyone would remain active with varying events and challenges, just not at the frenetic rate we had been working at.

Winching view from the door (Photo Mick Rowsell)

Leaving the door during winching sortie

India Juliet at the Needles (Photo Mick Rowsell)

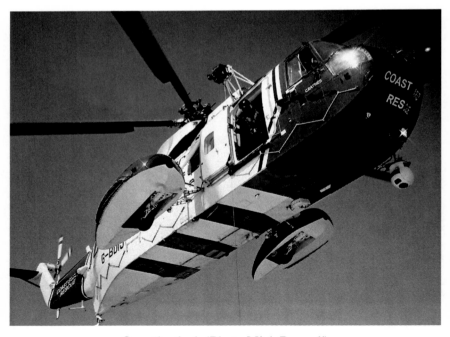

Over the deck (Photo Mick Rowsell)

Part 6

Lee SAR 1990 – 1996

1990/1991

The beginning of 1990 saw hurricane force winds in the south reaching 100-mph. 'IJ' was called out for a search at the peak of the storms, to search for the crew of a boat that had been reported adrift off the Isle of Wight, with no crew onboard.

Once the search was fully underway, involving both 'IJ' and lifeboats, it was ascertained by the coastguards (after locating the owner of the vessel) that it had broken away from its moorings and had drifted out to sea with no-one onboard. So, fortunately, no lives were lost but it was quite something to know we could get the aircraft airborne and operate in those conditions.

Towards the end of January, we had one of the most tragic incidents in the Solent when a Greek cargo carrier the 'Flag Theofano' sank with the loss of nineteen lives.

The vessel was carrying a cargo of cement between Le Havre in France to Southampton. The weather was force 6 to 7 and the vessel was intending to shelter off St Helens, near Bembridge on the Isle of Wight. This was normal procedure for vessels waiting for pilotage into Southampton and the pilot boat was planned to come out in the morning to assist them into

Southampton. The vessel was seen approaching St Helens and the weather should not have been a problem to a vessel of that type.

In the early hours of the morning the aircraft was scrambled and Bembridge lifeboat launched to the report of a person seen walking into the water at Southsea near Portsmouth which turned out to be a false alarm. Both aircraft and lifeboat were searching within a couple of miles of Flag Theofano's last known position, unaware that a major incident was unfolding.

The first anyone was aware that something had happened was when the pilot boat went out to assist the 'Flag Theofano' in the morning. The vessel was nowhere to be seen, clearly unusual as boats of that size don't just disappear especially in sheltered waters.

Shortly after the pilot boat reported this phenomenon, a ship's lifeboat was reported washed up at Hayling Island, which sparked a major search. Two bodies were found washed up in Bracklesham Bay, so it was quite clear something tragic had happened to the 'Flag Theofano'. Our aircraft soon located a large oil slick off St Helens. The conditions were too bad at the time to put divers down so a naval Sea King helicopter was called in to search with Sonar, quickly locating a large object on the seabed.

All that could be done then was to continue a surface search for any possible survivors. The search went on for the rest of the day involving many coastal search teams and lifeboats backed up by SAR helicopters but nothing further was located. We carried out first-light searches for the next few days mainly checking the coastline during which another body was spotted by Rescue IJ and recovered by lifeboat and I recovered another body fourteen days after the incident. All the crew lost their lives that night: eleven Greek crewmembers, one Egyptian and seven crewmembers from the Maldives in the Indian Ocean. It was thought the incident must have happened suddenly, possibly as the cargo shifted when the vessel was manoeuvring round a buoy and was likely to have been during the time we were airborne on the false alarm search.

The crew must not have had time to react as no distress call was made, nor flares fired, so it can only be assumed that the majority of the crew were unable to get clear from the vessel. The vessel remains on the seabed on the approaches to Portsmouth harbour marked by a group of wreck markers – a very tragic incident.

In the summer of 1990 the annual Round the Island race took place, in which over a thousand yachts set off from Cowes on the Isle of Wight to sail the fifty miles or so around the Island.

This event is a fantastic sight, watching all the sailing craft of various sizes and classes, an absolute mass of sails and colourful spinnakers. The spectacle provides a lot of pleasure to crews on the boats taking part and the spectators taking in the wonderful sight from viewpoints on the coastline overlooking the Solent.

An event of this size will always have risks and I feel quite confident that it was well organised by the race committee. Many safety vessels were put in place including volunteer and RNLI Lifeboats. For this year's race there was even a Royal Navy warship acting as guard ship, plus MOD vessels and Police launches.

This particular year the weather conditions were perfect for the start of the race, but the wind increased to a force 5 to 6 as the main group started to head round the Needles, to commence the easterly run around the south coast of the Island. The seas were quite choppy with wind against tide; a significant change from the conditions faced during the first part of the race while in the sheltered Solent. Many of the yachts had been having a good run, the conditions perfect for using their spinnakers.

Unfortunately, the conditions rounding the Needles were not quite so friendly; the yachts were at considerable risk of broaching, particularly those trying to continue using their spinnaker. A bad broach had the potential to knock a yacht flat, or a sudden jibe giving increased risk from boom injuries. This is exactly what happened, with many of the yachts becoming damaged and crewmembers injured.

I was duty winchman that morning with Chris Bond as the winch operator; Graham Sorge was the captain and Peter Thomson acting as co-pilot. We were initially on a training sortie shadowing the race and enjoying the sight of all these yachts. We knew all wasn't well at the Needles after the report that an ex French Admirals cup yacht the 'Xeryus' had sunk after hitting a well known wreck just off the tip of the Needles. The crew of the 'Xeryus' had been rescued by safety boats.

Quite a few vessels including very large yachts were limping back into the Solent with broken masts or booms, torn sails etc. so we expected a busy day.

Our first scramble was tasked while airborne to an 'Ultra' racing yacht capsized with nine persons in the water. The Ultra is a high performance yacht not suitable for the conditions to the south of the Island. The crews on this class of yacht would mainly be very experienced sailors, as was the case this time. On scene, all the crew were alongside the yacht and it was not too busy at their position, as they were one of the leading yachts.

I was lowered to the water alongside the vessel but the crew refused to be recovered by the helicopter. This was quite understandable as it was possible for them to right this type of yacht and continue with the race, although I did not think they would succeed in those conditions.

Once it was clear these guys were all wearing suitable gear with lifejackets and also knowing Bembridge Lifeboat would soon be with them, I was recovered to the aircraft as we had been re-tasked to the second incident; another capsized yacht with three people in the water.

All three in the water were recovered to the aircraft; one was transferred to the Bembridge lifeboat in the hope of helping in the recovery of his yacht and the other two were taken back to base.

Rescue 'IJ' was re-tasked, after dropping off the casualties and refuelling, to the report of people in the water from the yacht 'Alexa' that had sunk after a collision. It was absolute chaos when we arrived on scene with hundreds of yachts bearing down on the incident, unaware of the people in the water.

Other yachts were trying to protect the people in the water, two had already been recovered and we could see the difficulty in attempting to recover others. The conditions were too rough for easy recovery by other yachts and most of the rescue craft were dealing with other incidents or too far away. Six survivors remained in the water.

We decided to run in for the pickup, hoping that the yachts would be more likely to bear off if they saw a large helicopter in front of them, which fortunately was the case. It was very disturbing for the pilots, watching the mass of yachts approaching, slowly parting either side of the aircraft.

I was lowered into the water to act as a surface swimmer, preparing each of the survivors for recovery to the aircraft, sending up the ones I felt were fit enough to go on their own and going up with the ones I felt needed help. The important thing in this situation was to get them onboard the aircraft and away from this quite ridiculous situation as quickly as possible.

As soon as we had them onboard, we were scrambled to another yacht 'Athene' with a casualty who had a suspected heart attack. Fortunately none of the casualties pulled from the water were seriously injured, so it was easy to move them around the cab to make room for the next casualty.

At this stage, after recovering the casualty from the 'Athene', it was clear we would have to drop the casualties we had onboard to hospital but many more incidents were happening. The Royal Naval aircraft from Portland was tasked to assist and we headed off with our casualties.

We arrived at the helicopter-landing site before the ambulances had arrived and knew we were required back on scene with further reports of people in the water and injuries on yachts, so again a decision on priorities needed to be made.

The casualties in my care were all aware of the situation and just happy to be on Terra Firma. With their approval, I ended up leaving them with a couple of security guards, having quickly briefed the guards regarding the care required and been assured by the Coastguards that the ambulances were on their way. This was a very difficult decision and one I feel would not be possible today, as we have to be so much more conscious of litigation. However, I really felt none of the injuries to be life threatening, yet the incidents happening out there could well be.

Our next tasking was to two casualties with head injuries from two different yachts, the 'Roller Coaster' and 'Monsoon'. One of the casualties was reported to be quite badly injured. Both these lifts were extremely awkward given the conditions and the fact that they were in close proximity to all the other yachts. I was so busy I gave very little thought to the risks. The real pressure in these situations, I feel, lies with the winch op and captain as it is not an easy job getting the winchman onboard yachts in these rough seas.

In all, fifty-one people were to be rescued that day with many boats damaged and escorted or towed back by lifeboats and other vessels. Even with all that happened during the race, over thirteen-hundred boats finished the race with more than nine-thousand crewmembers onboard. Unfortunately, one man lost his life after a boom injury.

Having witnessed and being involved in many of the rescues that day, quite honestly I was surprised that many more incidents did not take place.

Shortly after this, on a much calmer day, we had a rather unusual incident when a man and his stepson were enjoying some dinghy sailing just off Ryde Sands (Isle of Wight). They had capsized a few times but had righted the boat and continued sailing. The next time they capsized the stepson (a young man and a good swimmer) suddenly disappeared.

We were on scene within five minutes and immediately came across one man clinging to the bows of a sinking dinghy. I was the winch op, with Mick Rowsell the winchman. Mick was lowered to recover the survivor but there was no sign of his stepson. It was a clear day and a huge search was carried out. We even utilised the stepfather as an extra pair of eyes for the first part of the search. Later, as it began to look unlikely that there would be a happy conclusion we dropped him off to be met by Coastguards before continuing with the search.

The missing young man wasn't wearing a lifejacket as he was a strong swimmer and so close to the shore, but this highlighted that things could still go wrong and lifejackets should be worn at all times. I never knew exactly what went wrong; his body was recovered a few days later after returning to the surface some miles away.

The family, although obviously having to come to terms with the tragic incident, still found time to appeal for people to wear lifejackets at all times, in the hope they may prevent other families going through their pain.

This was the first of several tragic incidents in the Solent area. Two more people drowned that month in the Solent in separate incidents involving small dinghies. One was an incident that occurred just off Cowes (Isle of Wight) after a dinghy collided with a ferry and the other, a 21-year-old man, who had fallen out of a rubber dinghy only 30 yards offshore at Hill Head on the mainland opposite Cowes.

Don Sowden had a traumatic time when he had to be winched down to the scene where a woman with her two children had driven over the cliff at Beachy Head. There was little Don could do other than assist the police and fire fighters who required winching to the scene; nevertheless, to be involved in something like that especially when children are involved will always take its toll.

Tony Campbell picked up another woman who had attempted suicide by jumping over a cliff and a yachtsman who had a fatal heart attack was winched from a yacht off Yarmouth by Nick Horst.

Billy Deacon, the aircrewman who had worked with me in the helicopter escape trainer, had joined Bristows from British International Helicopters and was now employed as the leave and sickness relief for the Coastguard units.

It was good to see Billy again but he could not have felt too good in this short spell on the unit, as the majority of his jobs were tragic. He had to recover bodies from three separate incidents and was involved with Tony

Campbell on the search for survivors when a fishing vessel capsized south of Brighton, with the loss of a further five lives.

All this happened in our patch over a couple of months which was fortunately not the norm, otherwise the job would be very hard to cope with. I have mentioned before that many of our jobs have happy results, normally far outnumbering the tragic ones but, just occasionally there is a run of nasty jobs, one following the other. These unusual incidents are experienced by most SAR aircrewmen and I guess to others in the emergency services at one time or another. In our case, that nightmare scenario is when a particular winchman or crew gets a run of tragic jobs; you start to feel jinxed when that happens.

Later in the year, we were involved in the rescue of Daisy the cow! Daisy had managed to wander on to mud flats and had got herself well and truly stuck. Fire fighters and coastguards had been trying for some hours to release the cow but were not getting anywhere. The tide was coming in as well as darkness so they were running out of time. It was thought that a vet would have to put her to sleep before the tide came in but, as a last resort, we were asked if there was any way we could help.

At first, we thought it wouldn't be possible as the cow would be heavier than the safe working load of our winch. We had quite a long debate about this and Peter Thomson, the captain that day, felt it might be possible if we could rig up load lifting slings under the aircraft.

The aircraft had a load lifting capability but all the equipment to achieve this was removed for the SAR role and only the hard points for this equipment remained. We had a 200ft rope as part of the SAR equipment and I knew the breaking strain of this rope was greater than the weight of a cow. I thought it may be possible to utilise that in some way from the remaining hard points.

Being an ex seaman and therefore used to messing around with ropes, I went out with the crew to check if it was feasible. With the aid of some karabiners and a few canny knots, I tied four equal lengths to the strong points and joined them together at the central point under the aircraft, with at least a further 100ft that would hang down from this central point.

We felt that if I could get two of our extended strops normally used for hypothermic lifts positioned under the cow and, with the use of Karabiners, join the four ends of the two strops to a central point, we could then attach it to the rope dangling below the aircraft and hopefully lift her out.

There has always been a dispute about the practice of lifting people out of the mud as it is perceived that the suction properties of the mud might cause damage to the casualty as you try to pull them clear using a vertical lift. So it was becoming normal practice to try to dig the casualty out and only use a helicopter in situations where the casualty was at immediate risk from incoming tide or hypothermia etc.

During my early days in this role, when there were only a few mud teams available, we did the majority of these mud rescues. I found that trying to dig them out while on the end of the wire often made the situation worse as the casualty normally sank deeper as you tried to dig around them which a vertical lift on the winch would prevent. Having said that, if there is no helicopter available they have to be dug out if being rescued by teams working from mud sledges and the casualty has to be slid out virtually sideways – the mud teams have varying techniques to achieve this safely.

When I have had to be used in these situations, which was quite often in the early days, it always proved quite easy to winch the casualty out of the mud. I have never had any difficulties when being lowered into the mud alongside a casualty (entering the mud alongside the casualty helps to break the suction holding the casualty); the strop that I put round the casualty is attached to my harness via a quick release fitting. At this stage I am now firmly in the mud with the casualty but, providing the aircraft remains in an accurate position above the casualty and the winch-op provides a slow smooth lift, the pair of us will slide out quite easily. I am being eased out of the mud with the casualty and will feel similar discomfort to the casualty during the lift and can signal for the winch-op to stop winching if necessary.

I cannot comment on the rights or wrong of this, as it is likely that the mud will have different consistencies in other parts of the country, but this method has never been a problem to me.

With this conviction, I felt it would be no different with Daisy, providing that we could get the strops around her. It was dark when we arrived on scene, there were dozens of fire fighters and Coastguards all covered in mud and hoses all over the place that had been used to try to drag the cow out of the mud.

I was lowered into the mud with my two strops and karabiners. The fire fighters helped me feed the strops under the cow, one just behind the front legs and one just in front of the back legs. The cow was motionless, all its energy drained, so it only took a few minutes to achieve this. We tied a couple of guide lines to the strops and passed them to people ashore so they could steady her as she came free from the mud, hopefully keeping Daisy clear of myself and the fireman helping to guide her out.

When ready with the strops now joined to one fixed point I called the aircraft in. Terry Short lowered the rope by hand to me and, once I secured it to the lifting point, he commenced the con for a slow climb of the aircraft, keeping it vertically over the top of the cow (not that easy, as the visual references in the dark were minimal). Daisy slid out smoothly until she was airborne, mooing away, wondering what on earth was happening to her!

Terry conned the aircraft towards firm ground and slowly lowered her to the ground. The fire fighters immediately surrounded Daisy when her hooves touched the ground, to stop her trying to run off before being released from the strops, quite crucial as something that weight suddenly dashing off while attached to the aircraft, could be quite dodgy.

This was another of those jobs that would be considered too dangerous today. Risk assessments would have to be carried out, making it difficult to justify the job without proper load-lifting equipment and quick-release fittings.

We all felt great to have achieved it, a good exercise of initiative requiring accurate flying at night. We were successful and the result was a very happy farmer plus of course Daisy, who, although completely confused, lived to have a lot of loving care and notoriety.

On the 10th April 1991, a vessel reported that they had been in collision with another vessel in fog approximately twenty miles south of Newhaven.

The ship reporting the incident was a Cypriot cargo vessel. Unfortunately, the vessel did not report the collision immediately. They had suspected they might have hit something and had carried out a search of the area, only notifying the coastguards two hours later after finding the aerial from a fishing vessel embedded in its bows.

This was to spark a huge air and sea search. We were scrambled shortly after 4 o'clock in the morning, the crew was: Captain Rob Flexman, co-pilot John Bentley, winch-op Don Sowden and myself as winchman. The Coastguards also launched Newhaven and Shoreham lifeboats and the warship HMS Norfolk passing through the area at the time had joined the search along with other fishing vessels in the area.

All the vessels known to be in the area were contacted and it was soon apparent that the fishing vessel 'Wilhelmina J' out of Camber docks in Portsmouth was possibly missing; no contact could be made with her.

En-route we flew into quite extensive fog – patchy in places and very thick in others. It was hoped that the FLIR camera would be of assistance in the foggier conditions, although at times the fog was too thick for even the infrared to be effective. The fog was almost certainly the reason that the accident had happened although the 'Wilhelmina J' was thought to be fishing away from the shipping lanes.

While en-route we were informed that two unmanned lifeboats had been located by vessels helping in the search. When on scene we quickly located debris and a large oil slick but no sign of life. We also located a distress beacon, the type designed to break away from a vessel if it has a catastrophic accident.

The beacon would normally transmit on emergency frequencies so that rescue aircraft or lifeboats could home in to the beacon. In this case the transmitter on the beacon had not worked, possibly damaged in the collision. It was just fortunate that we located it visually along with a couple of lifejackets. I was lowered to recover these items and other pieces of debris to the aircraft. By now, enough debris had been recovered and information gathered to confirm that we were looking for the 'Wilhelmina J', which was missing with six persons onboard.

A huge search was now underway, with lifeboats plus up to thirty small fishing vessels heading to the area to help in the search. We remained on scene for close to seven hours, refuelling onboard HMS Norfolk before having to return to base for maintenance reasons.

The surface search continued throughout the day and our aircraft carried out another search the following morning, but nothing further was found making it very likely the fishing vessel had gone down with all six crew.

This was a very tragic incident and felt even more so with it being a local crew that was missing, bringing the incident close to home. We would read so much about it in the local news, almost living the grief their families and friends were going through.

Considerable effort was made by the families and the fleet owners of the 'Wilhelmina J' to try to get answers as to the cause of the incident and why there was such a delay after the collision before anyone contacted the

Coastguard. The 'Wilhelmina J' was located on the seabed and salvage was arranged in an attempt to get the answers but even this was thwarted at almost every step by weather and sea conditions. However, after approximately three months the vessel was recovered to the surface.

Two bodies were recovered, one from the crew sleeping cabin and one in the starboard access space to the wheelhouse. It was clear that they were fishing at the time and, with the nets out, and the remainder of the crew were likely to have been on deck at the time of the collision. This likelihood must have been even more tragic for the families as, had the search been commenced immediately, a survivor or survivors may have been located still on the surface.

A survey of the 'Wilhelmina J' was carried out by the maritime accident team before the fishing vessel was slowly lowered back to the sea bed with at least some questions having been answered. The vessel that collided with the 'Wilhelmina J' was already known and further action taken regarding the incident and the delay in reporting it.

This was the year that we noticed a considerable increase in the number of diving incidents but we were not sure as to the reason. We felt that it may be because the diving equipment was improving and getting more affordable, on top of the fact that the wrecks in shallower water had been dived on so often they were no longer of interest.

The incidents we had been attending recently were in deeper water, which considerably increased the chances for things to go wrong. I had picked up several divers that year, mainly with decompression problems that required rapid transportation to a recompression chamber. Some of these had tragic results.

One particular tragic incident occurred when Nick Horst was winchman. They had been scrambled to the FV 'Michelle Mary' which was being used as a dive platform and had reported two divers missing.

A lengthy search had been carried out including a search by other divers already at the scene but nothing was found. When the shot line (the line from the dive boat to the seabed used for divers to descend and ascend on) was recovered to the boat the bodies of the two missing divers were still attached to it. They were recovered to the aircraft and flown to Haslar hospital. I am not sure if the cause of that incident was known, but it was clear these incidents were on the increase and would continue to do so.

The next trend that would create several jobs for us over future years was the increase of hang gliding and paragliding; the gliders operate from hills and cliffs to to use up drafting air. Unfortunately, this meant that any accidents often made it difficult for ambulances to get close to them and we were often called to help recover them in the event of accidents.

My first one was in the May of 1991 when we were scrambled to the report of a paraglider over the cliffs at Freshwater on the IOW. I was expecting the worst from this but he had made a safe landing in the sea close to the bottom of the cliff. The paraglider pilot had managed to scramble on to a ledge clear of the water and was casually trying to repack his parasail by the time we arrived.

We found this quite amusing, it was as though he did not have a care in the world, but his position would require recovery and it would make for a difficult winch. Rob Flexman was the captain and Terry Short was the winch-op. They managed to get me alongside him where I had to prise the casualty's treasured parasail out of his hands and wedge it in the rocks - our downdraught could have caused havoc, possibly allowing the pair of us to get airborne independent of the aircraft.

That was a good result – the guy was uninjured and totally unfazed by the incident. So much so that, when we were scrambled to a second incident, (a man suffering a heart attack on a yacht) we were able to place him back on the cliff top with no medical assistance required, allowing us to proceed to the more urgent task. This was to be the start of more incidents like this, some with serious consequences.

In the August, we had an amusing tasking. Well, amusing for me but not for Don Sowden who was the winchman that night! We were scrambled from home about midnight to the report of a small boat stolen from Cowes (IOW). This would not normally have involved the aircraft, but someone presumed to be under the influence of drink had been seen boarding it and drifting into the Solent. Lifeboats had been searching but could not locate it.

We eventually located the boat with the FLIR camera quite a way from the nearest lifeboat, just drifting on the tide with no lights or anything. Being concerned for the person in the boat, we decided to winch Don down to check on him before the lifeboat arrived. I could see that he was holding a pole up which I thought was an oar, so carried on winching, concentrating on getting Don onboard, just a little bemused why the guy was holding the oar.

The next thing I could see was him jabbing at Don, while Don was bouncing around on the end of the wire gesturing for me to pull away, which of course I did. When Don was recovered to the aircraft he was rather perturbed, as the guy had been trying to stab him with a pitchfork!

How a pitchfork ended up in a stolen dinghy, I have no idea. We remained on scene until the guy drifted ashore where he was met by the police. A few cartoons appeared recording the incident and Don still today 'tongue in cheek' has a go at me for laughing, when I recovered him to the aircraft.

Another incident about the same time was after a light aircraft ditched into the sea south of the Isle of Wight. The report had come from a fishing vessel that had witnessed the ditching, so we were scrambled immediately.

The crew of that aircraft were extremely lucky; the pilot had suffered a nasty head injury and a broken leg, while his passenger had been knocked unconscious in the ditching. The pilot had still managed to pull the passenger from the sinking aircraft obviously ignoring his own injuries. The fishing vessel that witnessed the ditching was soon alongside and rescued both of them from the sea.

When we arrived on scene, Terry lowered me to the fishing vessel to prepare the guys for recovery. Both of them were in quite a lot of pain, I administered Entonox (the same gas and air pain relief given to expectant mothers during childbirth). When trying to move people who are in a lot of pain I would try to get them to take deep breaths of the analgesic – the deeper the intake, the greater the pain relief, which at times resulted in some very funny comments from the casualty.

Once I had both the casualties recovered to the aircraft, the Entonox was continued as required, especially for the pilot who was already in considerable pain having rescued his passenger, then pulled out of the sea on to a fishing vessel, followed by recovery to the aircraft, all with a broken leg. He had recognised the benefits of the Entonox and was taking deep breaths of the analgesic. He looked Terry in the eyes and asked, "What's a silly old bugger like you doing in a job like this." Terry was ribbed for months after that.

I had another Entonox moment the same year when a lucky young man had survived having his arm badly mangled by a propeller after falling overboard. Don Sowden had lowered me on to the vessel to prepare this casualty for recovery. This was one of the more difficult jobs, trying to stem the bleeding and at the same time having to get the casualty into a stretcher while in the confines of a small space. He remained very calm and was even trying to reassure a couple of pretty girls on the boat that he would be alright. I thought he would be very lucky if the surgeons managed to save his arm.

Again, I was relying on the entonox to help with the pain relief during the preparation for recovery to the aircraft, when he suddenly started fitting (or that is what I thought). He quickly calmed down from that and I cannot really repeat his exact words, other than to say he was "checking he had not damaged his ******* arm"! I found his comment and actions to be so comical it helped me to relax as I was calling on my reserves to complete the very awkward job. Once recovered to Haslar hospital his arm was saved by surgeons.

1992

In 1992, rumours were circulating that the flight may have to move from Lee-on-Solent another fifty miles or so along the coast towards Brighton. This was due to a review of helicopter SAR cover and the possibility of HMS Daedalus closing down, a casualty in the latest round of defence cuts.

Having been through this before when the MOD tried to keep us at Portland, I was feeling quite vulnerable. Being completely settled for the first time in my life, the prospect of further disruption was not something I would relish. Daedalus would not be closing for another four years but the move of the aircraft, if it was to go ahead, would be well before that.

This time, it was an MOD review obviously with Coastguard involvement planned around overlapping circles encompassing the coastline on a map of the UK. These circles, in my opinion, did not appear to be taking into account the areas of vulnerability. If account was being taken it was on mis-information regarding the risk of individual areas and, as usual with reviews and re-shuffles, it would ultimately mean less actual cover. In this case, it was rumoured that at least two out of the fifteen SAR bases would be axed.

As with the last time they had tried to move us, I would hear absolute lies or mis-interpretations regarding incidents in the Solent area and as to why the aircraft would not be required here.

Peter Viggers, our local MP, still armed from the previous fights to keep a SAR flight at Lee, found himself yet again at the forefront of another battle to keep the SAR Flight in the area and there was considerable local and media support backing him up. We were contractors so had absolutely no say, so just had to keep our fingers crossed that public opinion would save the day.

If the move was to happen, I had decided that I would move with the unit, as would the majority of the crews (if not all of us). The job was too important to us, but I can put my hand on my heart and say I thought it would be a terrible decision and would cost lives.

I could accept that it may well save a few lives in the area we might move to. Clearly if a maritime incident happens close to a rescue facility then the prospects of a satisfactory rescue will be greater. Nevertheless, I am also quite confident that the SAR flight at Lee was ideally located to respond to the possibility of numerous maritime incidents.

I have already mentioned my reasons that I base these views on, let alone the fact that the aircraft was sandwiched between the two major ports of Portsmouth and Southampton, the Solent being a hive of waterborne activity and the busy shipping lanes south of the Isle of Wight.

The Dover straights I would consider the next most vulnerable stretch to the east, which was, at the time, covered by the RAF at Manston in Kent.

This year was proving to be another bad year for diving incidents; after the increase last year the signs of even more incidents this year made the Coastguards put out a safety statement, backed up by a report from a senior medical officer in diving medicine who was based at the Institute of Naval Medicine in Alverstoke, Gosport.

He was picking up the pieces of these diving incidents. The institute had treated thirty-five patients during the previous year and that figure was overtaken by the July of this year. The majority of the divers were treated in the chamber at Alverstoke. There was another chamber in Portsmouth at the naval diving school that was used in absolute emergencies but, ideally, that chamber should be left available on standby for the Navy divers.

I had picked up two divers from separate incidents in the past few months; neither of them survived. I had also picked up others who would suffer long-term injuries. On a few of the weekends, both chambers were in use and the divers were flown to Poole in Dorset, which was the next chamber down the coast. On one occasion the diver was flown all the way to Plymouth, as even Poole was in use.

The next problem was a sudden increase in yachting incidents, including tragic incidents during the 1992 Cowes week the annual sailing regatta in the Solent. Several of the yachting incidents happened on one day, at the peak of the racing week during quite squally conditions. Two people lost their lives and several others were injured.

Mick Rowsell got the bulk of these: he had come on shift slightly earlier than normal and as soon as he had taken over from the morning winchman we were scrambled. I was the winch operator that morning and had not yet been relieved. The scramble was to a race yacht that had a casualty suffering a suspected heart attack. This was quite a difficult job because of the conditions but the casualty was successfully recovered to the aircraft, using the hi-line technique and flown to hospital.

We had no sooner landed back at Lee and started sorting out the back of the aircraft, which had equipment all over the place from the previous job, when the aircraft was scrambled again. The new crew was: Captain Rob Flexman, co-pilot Mike Roughton, winchop Don Sowden. They had time to take over from the morning crew while the aircraft refuelled, Mick remained, as he was the afternoon crew anyway.

The second scramble for Mick was to the yacht 'Mefisto' and the report of a yachtsman who had been knocked overboard by a huge wave. By the time the aircraft arrived on scene another yacht in the area had recovered the casualty from the water and he was being resuscitated when Mick arrived onboard.

Transfers from yachts can be awkward due to the very limited space and the vessel movement in rough seas. Additionally, the resuscitation would need to be continued while preparing the casualty for transfer. This casualty was flown to hospital where the helicopter was met by a crash team. As soon as the transfer was complete, they were re-tasked to another incident. Don and Mick again did not have time to get the aircraft back in order and an amazing amount of equipment had now been used on the previous jobs.

The third tasking was to a person who had suffered a serious boom injury on the Yacht 'Valdemar'. She was a doctor and had become tangled in the mainsheets before being pinned to the hull by the boom. Once released when the wind changed she had fallen to the deck. It was a tragic accident with awful consequences. Her husband and father in law were also on the yacht; they not only witnessed the tragic incident but they then had to carry out CPR. I cannot imagine the thoughts that must have been occupying their minds at that awful time.

Mick now found himself involved with the transfer of a casualty from a third yacht, all difficult transfers and two of them whilst carrying out resuscitation. Once the casualty was recovered to the aircraft, Don and Mick continued the life support until the crash team took over at the helicopter landing-site. I am quite sure that busy couple of hours will remain with Mick and Don forever.

The Duke of Edinburgh and Prince Edward were also sailing in the same race along with a further six hundred yachts associated in Cowes week races.

An unusual number of yachting incidents were to happen over the next few months, more boom injuries, lost fingers in winches and suspected heart attacks.

I picked up a very lucky family – mother, father and child – who had been floating in the Solent for three hours in the dark after their dinghy had sunk, the child holding on to a buoyancy aid. They were very fortunate as no emergency had been declared; they had been spotted by an alert yachtsman transiting the Solent and were suffering from severe shock and hypothermia by the time we arrived.

Don Sowden and Mick Rowsell picked up four survivors when their boat sank suddenly south of the Needles. They had only managed to grab a waterproof bag of flares, the eventual sighting of those flares undoubtedly saved their lives.

Terry Short and Tony Campbell recovered seven crewmembers, from the sinking yacht 'Misty Ocean' southwest of the Needles.

Nick Horst and I recovered another seven crewmembers and a lifeboatman, from a youth training yacht that had run aground in a force nine gale. That day had started with us being called in from home to the report of a man missing overboard from the 45ft yawl 'Aelian', which had been knocked flat in winds up to 80 knots. The crew was: Captain Graham Sorge, co-pilot Mike Roughton, winch-op Nick Horst and I was the winchman.

When we arrived on scene in the Western Solent, Yarmouth lifeboat was in the process of recovering the casualty from the water. A second lifeboat was heading towards the damaged yacht. I was lowered immediately to Yarmouth lifeboat and resuscitation commenced on the casualty. We recovered him to the aircraft using the hypothermic lift, continuing life support as we flew him to St Mary's hospital (IOW) but unfortunately, the man did not survive.

Later that morning and the weather still atrocious, we were scrambled to the report of a large ketch aground off Chichester Harbour entrance. When we arrived on scene, we could see the yacht taking a terrible hammering while being forced onto a sand bank by the sea. The Hayling RNLI lifeboat had managed to get a lifeboatman onboard the ketch and a second lifeboat was approaching.

The lifeboatman now onboard the 'Donald Searle' was trying to get some of the seventeen survivors into the lifeboat; not an easy task, as the lifeboat had to try to sneak alongside between breaks in the huge waves. The conditions were actually out of limits for Hayling's 'Atlantic 21' (which was a rigid inflatable used for inshore rescues) but the crews were totally ignoring the conditions because of the seriousness of the situation.

Nick managed to get me onboard using the hi-line, which was handled by the lifeboatman once he had transferred as many of the casualties as he could to the lifeboats. Having him onboard to handle the hi-line probably made the difference between me getting onboard and not. It was a procedure we practiced with the lifeboat crews, even this particular scenario of them getting someone onboard a yacht to handle the hi-line.

Standing up on the vessel was almost impossible as the yacht kept lifting and then smashing onto the seabed. I sent the remaining seven survivors and the lifeboatman up to the aircraft two at a time then ditched the hi-line as I was winched off at the end. This was a job well done and I had nothing but admiration for the achievement of both the Hayling Islands lifeboat crews: it was a tremendous piece of boat handling. The skill of the coxswains was always something we would marvel at as we often witnessed them in action when the chips were down, unfortunately something that is very rarely recorded.

Later that year Pete Thomson remarried after quite a surreal meeting with his partner which was totally unexpected for the pair of them, leading to a whirlwind courtship which must have left them wondering what was happening. This must have been especially true for Peter who was still coming to terms with the loss of his wife Jan early the previous year and was not yet feeling ready for a new romance. They were both caught up in a bit of magic beyond their control.

This came about in the September of 1991, when the aircraft was scrambled to the report of a woman having suffered a boom injury on the yacht 'Scot Free'. The incident had happened at the entrance to Portsmouth harbour. The crew was: Captain Peter Thomson, co-pilot John Bentley, I was the winch-op and Don Sowden the winchman.

On scene, I lowered Don to the yacht with his first aid equipment. The injured lady was starting to come round but had a very nasty head injury, which Don dressed and bandaged before they were recovered to the aircraft using the hypothermic lift.

As I pulled them into the cabin, the lady had a huge bandage on her head and a cervical collar around her neck; all I could see was a lovely pair of eyes. They were so striking I commented on that fact to Peter who replied that he had noticed when he had glanced in his mirror as she was approaching the door.

Mentioning that was also a bit of friendly banter that had been going on for a few months with the lads on the flight trying to cheer Peter up by bringing any pretty women rescued to his attention. He would play along but was certainly not ready for any of this banter to be taken seriously.

A few months later, the lady contacted the flight to thank the crew for our part in the rescue. She had been in hospital for a while after the accident and had suffered quite disturbing headaches and other problems from the injury for several weeks afterwards, but was now making a good recovery.

Peter rang her back to invite her to visit the flight, which was a normal response to this type of call; it is always nice to hear from people you have assisted. Quite honestly, I think the romance started with that phone call, during which Peter had remembered he was talking to the lady with the lovely eyes.

The phone conversation lasted quite a while, talking as if they had known each other for years and that was something both of them later admitted to being surprised by. Anne was a member of a sailing club and asked if she could invite some of the club members to the flight with her, in particular those who were with her on the day of the accident. Peter invited them all along and found himself looking forward to the visit and meeting the lady he had enjoyed talking to so much.

I was on shift with Peter when they came round and we all met Anne. Pete went for a meal with the group after the visit and that was it. Anne was as shocked as Pete was: she was in a long-term relationship at the time but this meeting with Pete was simply something spontaneous that could not be stopped.

Peter was still coming to terms with his own life after his tragic loss and Anne had her own huge decision to make. Not many months later, they were officially an item and even that announcement was unusual. I was on shift with Peter when he received Anne's decision regarding their future together – it arrived in the form of a fax and actually read along the lines of 'Yes I guess this now makes us an item'! I found this particularly amusing as I often asked Peter if they were an item yet.

All the flight was pleased for Peter and Anne: it had all happened quite fast but we certainly understood why and wished them all the best. It was nice to see Peter back to his normal self and Anne was the ideal partner for him.

Another job that year was in the early hours of the morning, again in atrocious conditions to the report of a Dutch sailor on the yacht 'Lt Harry'. He was sailing single-handed approximately thirty miles south of Portland and had fallen in the cabin knocking himself unconscious. When he came round ten hours later, he contacted Portland Coastguard and it was clear to them that the man was completely confused. We were scrambled and Weymouth lifeboat launched with a doctor on board.

The crew was: Captain Rob Flexman, co-pilot Pete Thomson, winch-op Don Sowden and myself as winchman. When we arrived on scene, it was apparent we would not be able to get any help from the yachtsman and could not even get him to manoeuvre the yacht onto the heading we required to attempt getting me onboard.

In this case, as the lifeboat was proceeding towards the incident, we thought it would be safer if the lifeboat could get alongside and transfer the casualty to the lifeboat, or put a lifeboatman onboard to manoeuvre the yacht onto a safe heading and to handle the hi-line for us. However, we were not sure at that stage if even the all weather lifeboat would manage to get alongside in the sea conditions.

We were able to provide good light from overhead with our searchlights as the lifeboat eased alongside the yacht, waiting for the right moment to make contact. A few attempts were made until the lifeboat could nip in and secure the yacht, another of those times we as a crew feel privileged to witness the tremendous skill of the coxswain and courage of the men as they jumped across to secure the yacht.

Even the doctor went on board; they then decided that they could get the casualty onto the lifeboat, from where it would be safer for us to transfer the casualty and doctor. Once the transfer between the yacht and lifeboat was complete, Don lowered me to the lifeboat to prepare the casualty for recovery to the aircraft.

During the recovery of myself and the casualty from the lifeboat, we went into the most horrendous squall of horizontal wind-driven rain which suddenly reduced the visibility. As the aircraft tried to maintain station with the lifeboat the weak link on the hi-line broke, but luckily, I swung clear from the lifeboat with the casualty who was now in a stretcher. The loose end of the hi-line was wrapped round the sponson: 150ft of rope with 15 lbs of weight on the end was trailing behind the aircraft.

Fortunately, the lifeboat crew spotted the rope, as we would not have been able to see it. The consequences could have been awful if we had flown away like that, the rope could easily have ended up in the tail rotor. We managed to cut the hi-line clear but decided it would be too dangerous to go back onboard for the doctor. I am sure he would have taken that risk, but our decision had to be for the safety of the aircraft, especially when we already had the casualty safely onboard.

Towards the end of 1992, the Coastguards announced that we would be staying at Lee-on-Solent, but the euphoria was quickly snatched away at the MOD announcement that three RAF Search and Rescue bases had been axed. At the same time we were informed that the next contract at Lee-on-Solent in one years' time might well be with a smaller aircraft. The Aerospatiale Dauphin, the aircraft I had operated with in the North Sea was the front-runner.

I could not believe this; we were going round in circles yet again. I had started my flying career in Whirlwind Mk 9's, which had a cabin smaller than the interior of an ambulance. We did a good job in that aircraft but only the best that it was capable of and it had many shortcomings. We then changed to the Wessex; a bigger, better and more powerful aircraft with the luxury of two engines but still limited on size. However, the Wessex was a step up from the Whirlwind and at least it had the room to work round a couple of injured casualties laid out on the floor.

At the time this decision was being made, the military were in the process of changing their fleet from Wessex to Sea King helicopters, which was quite a quantum leap. The Coastguard contracts had selected the 'S61', which was slightly bigger than the Sea King and a good, proven aircraft in its role as the workhorse of the North Sea. The decision to replace the 'S61' with the Aerospatiale Dauphin would, in my view, be for economic reasons, not capability, no matter how it was dressed up.

Having worked in the Dauphin, I was convinced this would be a wrong decision; the interior was even smaller than the Whirlwind. The Dauphin was a nice modern aircraft and just about adequate for the SAR role it was carrying out in the North Sea. However, I am sure that if the oil platforms and rigs had had large enough hangars, the operators would have preferred a larger helicopter, one that could at least pick up nineteen passengers plus crew from a ditched crew change helicopter.

A Dauphin would run out of space when carrying six survivors, who would have had to sit on the floor around an equipment locker that was only big enough to carry basic SAR equipment. This of course assumed those casualties were not injured in a stretcher or lying on the floor. Even to achieve that arrangement would require that we operate without a FLIR or a winch operator's station.

Once I had worked in the larger aircraft, I was completely sold on the advantages. A large area allowing us to work on more than one casualty at a time, plus we were able to carry enough equipment to suddenly go from a maritime role to the cliff role or help in a land-based job.

We carried a defibrillator, aspirator, oxygen and entonox packs, spare oxygen and entonox bottles, airway management pack, bulky first aid bags, splint packs, blankets, our rescue harnesses and strops, hi-line packs with weights, two different types of stretchers plus a scoop stretcher used for possible spinal injuries. Other immobilisation equipment was also carried for situations when there was no room to use a stretcher i.e. on the smaller vessels.

This equipment alone, plus the infrared camera station, (which I could not imagine the contract would leave out), would fill the Dauphin. To get round that problem would require role changes, taking just the equipment required for the one situation we were tasked for. That would not be very helpful when tasked again while airborne to another incident requiring different rescue equipment.

We even had room in the 'S61' for additional equipment not mentioned above, equipment we knew from the history of our jobs was advantageous to us but not considered mandatory for the role. We would no longer have the luxury of carrying this extra equipment. I felt quite strongly that the change would be a backward step, particularly for a full time dedicated SAR Unit.

In December, we were scrambled to the Lulworth range Safety Control Vessel 8124, which had run aground and was at risk of breaking up on rocks in Chapmans Pool, very close to Lulworth cove on the coast of Dorset.

This was a night time scramble, in atrocious conditions, poor visibility in heavy rain. The captain was John Whale, Co-Pilot Mike Roughton, I was the winch-op with Tony Campbell as winchman.

En-route we could hear over the radio that the lifeboats were attempting to rescue the crew. The vessel was high on the rocks, being battered by the sea and badly damaged. The lifeboats had attempted to get a line to her but all the attempts had failed. The three crewmembers were well and truly in serious trouble.

The weather worsened as we approached the scene with severely reduced forward visibility in driving rain preventing us from keeping visual contact with the sea. Our only chance of continuing was to try to gain visual contact with the cliffs in the vicinity and then try to feed ourselves into Chapmans Pool.

We made a couple of approaches to the cliff using radar and Tony trying to pick up the cliff with the FLIR camera which had limited effectiveness in heavy rain. The first couple of attempts failed and we all knew that if we could not make visual contact with the cliff we would have to return to Lee. To return would have been the most horrible decision and one no crew would have wanted to take, especially in this case, it was quite obvious we were the only hope for the three casualties. It was beginning to look like this was going to be one of those rare occasions when that decision would be made.

We decided to keep trying at least until we had to return for fuel, this time creeping in at a much lower height and using all the aids we could, finally picking up the coastline just about on our break-off point. We then discussed the situation as to whether we should continue. Hoping that we could keep visual contact with the cliffs, we all agreed to proceed.

Easing into Chapmans pool was no joke particularly for the pilots, the wind sheer quite disturbing and knowing we had to remain visual with the cliff. The lifeboats had their spotlights on the stricken vessel, which we could see to be on the rocks at the base of the cliffs and was already breaking up. The wind direction made things awkward and required us to back in toward the vessel. It would have been nice to have a lot more time to assess the best way to achieve this but we did not have that luxury.

We had to treat the approach as the dummy run; slowly edging backwards towards the cliff trying to judge the clearance of our rotor blades against the cliff face. On a night like that, the pilot has to rely totally on the winch operators' judgement. Tony was lowered and must have been wondering what the outcome of this would be.

We positioned Tony onboard and although it was virtually impossible for him to stand up, he managed to send the first two survivors up to the aircraft before coming up himself with the third crewmember.

Our relief at the end of this rescue was indescribable. The task had taken advantage of all the avionics making up the SAR system and we felt quite sure the rescue was successful that night because of that equipment.

Receiving Chief Coastguards commendation for Rescue of the crew from the range safety boat in Chapmans Pool

Presented by Chief Coastguard Derek Ancona

John Whale – Dave Peel – Mike Roughton – Tony Campbell

1993

In the February of 1993, we had a spate of incidents caused by a somewhat deranged young lady and her friend. They would spark a total of five scrambles for our aircraft and further rescues by lifeboats.

The first two scrambles were because the pair had been seen going into the freezing sea close to the pier at Southsea. On each occasion, they had left the water and disappeared by the time the aircraft arrived. On the third occasion, one of the ladies was still in the sea when the aircraft arrived and was not attempting to get out. Don Sowden was the winchman and Chris Bond the winch-op. While Chris was trying to position Don alongside the casualty she was swimming away from him.

When Don got hold of her she put up quite a struggle; he managed to get the strop around her having to be quite forceful as she continued to struggle all the way up to the aircraft. Once onboard the aircraft she had to be physically restrained while she was flown to the hospital landing-site where she was handed over to a waiting ambulance.

Ten days later the aircraft was scrambled again to the same report as the last time. Unfortunately for Don, he was the winchman yet again, so was concerned as to what she would try to do this time. When he was lowered to the water alongside the casualty, she was so cold that she was quite subdued and she did not struggle so it was a straightforward lift. For the second time she was flown to the helicopter landing-site to be met by an ambulance.

A further ten days went by before we were scrambled again to a woman in the water off Southsea pier. This time I was the winchman. She started to swim away from me as I approached but her wet clothes were dragging her below the surface, any strength she had swiftly disappearing in the cold water. I was trying to place her into the two strops for the hypothermic lift when her eyes rolled back and she went unconscious and began sinking below the surface. I was able to get one strop round her, clinging on tight for the recovery to the aircraft.

As soon as I pulled her into the aircraft, it was clear she had stopped breathing. I had almost certainly witnessed post rescue collapse, caused by the body closing down due to the cold water shunting the blood from the extremities to the core of the body. This as mentioned earlier is a natural defence mechanism where the body tries to provide oxygen to the major organs as hypothermia takes hold. In this case, that process was being assisted by the hydrostatic pressure of the sea. Suddenly removing that hydrostatic pressure, especially when being lifted from the water vertically lets the blood back to the extremities and away from the core; the shock of this can be catastrophic.

We did not have time to get the airway management kit set up before this rescue. Therefore I immediately started mouth to mouth while Chris Bond prepared the rest of the kit: oxygen, bag and mask then it would have been on to intubation. By the time we started using the bag and mask on her, she started breathing again. This time I was hoping they would be able to keep her in hospital or section her, but apparently they could not and she discharged herself the next morning.

I heard several months later that she did eventually succeed in taking her life, I believe from a bridge onto a road. If one of those cries for help had been taken seriously, even if it did mean sectioning her perhaps someone may have got to the root of her problems.

Another serious concern I had from that incident was that she was a known drug addict and was main lining the drugs. This put her in the high-risk group for hepatitis 'B' or HIV; having just given mouth to mouth, it did leave me feeling some concern. On the way home I called into Haslar hospital for advice regarding the possibility of being infected, but was assured I would be OK. They did give me a tetanus booster and I think that was just to make me feel as though something was being done.

We changed our procedures after that. The winchmen would normally carry a pocket mask in his immersion suit used for initial resuscitation, the mask could also be oxygen assisted and be used while the rest of the kit was being prepared. We also placed one of these by the doorway so we could grab it if required as we came in the door.

On the charity front, we had decided to support a local disabled group who were trying to raise money to send a member of the group on a sail training adventure onboard the Lord Nelson. The ship was a tall ship 180ft square-rigger owned by the Jubilee Sailing Trust.

The Lord Nelson had been adapted for handicapped people to join able-bodied people aboard the vessel to learn how to sail; it had even been adapted to cater for wheelchairs. It was felt by all of us that this would be a worthwhile appeal, the sail trainer was a vessel we winched to quite regularly for training and were quite intrigued with the concept of it being able to carry out the task it was doing.

The flight decided that the person selected for the trip should be someone who would really benefit from the experience and, volunteers from the flight would have to escort the person the flight sponsored on this very special adventure. Rob Flexman and his wife Mich were the first to take on this challenge taking the young man the club had being trying to raise the money for. The trip proved so successful it was continued in future years

Michael Keat is one of the young men who I can remember; he was a spina bifida sufferer and also a member of the local disabled group. Michael was a courageous young man who was making the best of his situation, also raising money himself to help others by competing in wheelchair marathons - at the time he was preparing for the London Marathon. It was felt by the flight that he be given this rather unusual experience in thanks for his own personal efforts.

Nick Horst and his wife Jane volunteered to host the trip with Michael. The plan, like the previous year, was to carry out their own charity event with the person they were sponsoring for the rather special trip. They would raise as much money as they could and the balance of the trip would come out of the flight charity fund. The idea was that the sponsored person was also involved in the fund raising and in Michael's case it was a challenge that he relished.

The trip would not just involve sending Michael; able-bodied helpers were required to go with him, not only to help him but also to act as crewmembers on the tall ship. The ship had a skeleton crew of professional sailors, the rest of the crew were made up from the disabled volunteers and their helpers. They would fly out to the Canaries to join the ship for the seven days adventure, flying back to the UK from the Canaries on completion.

This was not by any means an easy adventure, all the disabled participants had crew and watch-keeping duties, which they had to carry out to the maximum of their abilities. Michael found himself doing everything from peeling potatoes, lookout duties, steering the vessel, handling ropes, trimming sails and even being hoisted up the mast. He was a working member of the crew on a very special vessel that the majority of adventurously-inclined people could only dream of being on.

The trip was a great success and not only for Michael. It also cheered up the entire disabled club that he belonged to when listening to stories about the trip from the returning recipients. Michael even gave a presentation of the experience with all his exciting photographs.

Nick and Jane had not appreciated how hard they would have to work as Michael's helpers onboard the 'Lord Nelson', but they thoroughly enjoyed the challenge themselves, having to be involved in all the ships chores.

The first six months of 1993 saw a number of quick reaction jobs mainly involving small numbers of casualties who had rather sudden incidents such as fires onboard, hitting rocks, swamped boats and collisions between small speedboats. The majority of these had resulted in the casualties being recovered from the water, some hypothermic and requiring hospital treatment, others very lucky that they had a rescue unit so close.

One of these lucky rescues involved a speedboat towing a water skier. The man driving the speedboat carried out a tight turn that threw him, the only occupant, out of the boat, forcing the water skier to let go. This left them both in the water with a speedboat circling them at full speed.

The aircraft was on a training sortie close to the incident, so was on scene within a few minutes and quickly located the two casualties who were clinging to a navigational buoy in Southampton water. As the aircraft approached, the crew noticed that each circuit of the now unmanned speedboat was getting closer to the casualties. It was plainly a dangerous situation with the threat of the boat colliding with the two casualties in the water, possibly resulting in serious injury from that collision or from the propeller.

Chris Bond was the winchman and Mick Rowsell the winch-op. Chris was immediately lowered to the casualties, the unmanned boat having just missed them. Chris had taken two strops down intending to lift them one at a time in the hypothermic lift. Realising the seriousness of the situation as he approached, he slipped one strop onto each of the casualties and remaining on the hook himself, all three were winched clear.

This proved to be a very wise decision as the next circuit of the boat actually hit the buoy they were clinging to prior to Chris lifting them clear. It was not a normal practice to winch three people on the wire as the safe working load was 600 lb and three adults in wet equipment could exceed that. We had discussed scenarios like this in the past, situations that may require three on the wire and these discussions had led to approval from our standards team to carry three on the wire but only in life saving situations and providing one of the three was the winchman; this was one of those situations.

In May, it was announced that Bristows had won the contract for another five years. The news was a tremendous boost. We were quite confident that we were providing a good service; nevertheless, there had been many rumours going around regarding the use of smaller aircraft and other companies putting in strong bids etc.

Contract renewal time will always be a really worrying time, particularly for anyone employed in services that require a bidding process periodically. When I was in the North Sea that process was every year and there was always one group of workers on the rig in fear of losing their jobs.

Diving incidents reduced a little this year, although we still had several decompression recoveries and several searches for missing divers, one of these involving five divers missing after they had surfaced some distance from their broken down dive boat but all were located safe and well. On two separate occasions, the divers were missing because they had surfaced out of sight of the dive boat in fog which made for very difficult searches as crawling around low level in fog is not healthy for helicopters, even with our infrared camera and autopilot. Fortunately, these occasions had successful outcomes.

In the October, the Coastguard decided to change the rescue call signs of the Coastguard aircraft. Previously the dedicated helicopters around the British coastline had nominated call signs. Our aircraft was 'Coastguard IJ' when training – taken from the last two letters of aircraft registration 'GBDIJ' and when we were on a rescue our call sign was 'Rescue 174'. The stand-by aircraft was 'Coastguard VA' when training and 'Rescue 175' on tasking. The rescue call signs would be consecutive around the country, so that at any time the Rescue Coordination Centre would know which aircraft was on which job.

It had now, been decided that the military would keep their nominated numeric call signs and the Coastguard flights at Stornoway, Sumburgh and Lee-on-Solent would keep the last two letters of their registration. When we were training, we would be 'Coastguard Helicopter India Juliet' and when on a callout we would be 'Coastguard Rescue India Juliet' ('R-IJ') or if in the standby aircraft 'Coastguard Rescue Victor Alpha' ('R-VA').

This was just a small change in procedures that would later lead to the aircraft becoming characters in their own right. I was never sure as to why this decision was taken but it was to make a difference in our local area. The main aircraft, which carried out the majority of our tasking 'Rescue-India Juliet', was always reported on after jobs by its call sign, becoming affectionally known as 'Rescue India Juliet'.

On one occasion, I was on the beach in Brighton on a day out with the family when the aircraft flew past returning from a job. Lots of people were waving at it and talking about 'Rescue India Juliet' even using the phonetic letters. I was quite taken aback as I had no idea it was building up this following, I was more used to the noise being a nuisance. I knew the locals at Lee-on-Solent were referring to the aircraft, as 'Rescue India Juliet' but Brighton was sixty miles away from our base.

We had a couple of high profile jobs towards the end of the year, both on the same day and involving the same crew: Captain Graham Sorge, co-pilot Rob Flexman, winch-op Don Sowden and the winchman Nick Horst. They were scrambled to the Ferry 'Norman Commodore', which had a fire onboard while on passage between Portsmouth and Guernsey.

The Royal Navy helicopter from Portland had also been scrambled and, being closer, would be on scene before 'R-IJ'.

En-route 'R-IJ' was tasked to continue to Guernsey to pick up a team of fire fighters and equipment. The Portland aircraft would take passengers from the ferry leaving the crew to fight the fire. They had to be winched off the vessel in very heavy seas, all successful lifts. One of the ladies was a sixty-eight year old pensioner who had been writing a journal about her exciting holiday just prior to the emergency, then found herself being winched into a helicopter on a stormy night. She reported later that it was quite the dramatic ending to her journal!

'R-IJ' picked up a team of eight fire fighters and equipment from Guernsey and transferred them to the stricken vessel. Fortunately, the fire was virtually under control when our aircraft arrived on scene but a team of fire fighters was lowered with breathing apparatus to check the vessel was safe before it limped into Guernsey.

Once the situation was under control, 'R-IJ' refuelled at Guernsey and then headed back to Lee. En-route they were re-tasked to the report of a woman trapped inside a capsized catamaran. As with the last job, Portland's aircraft was also en-route with a diver onboard.

When 'R-IJ' arrived on scene, Don lowered Nick to Yarmouth lifeboat, which had a line attached to the capsized catamaran. The SAR diver from Portland's aircraft had already attempted to get into the yacht's cockpit but it was completely blocked by a mass of sail rigging, ropes etc. and, in the limited visibility, it was impossible to gain entry; the diver would have to wait until a back up team of Navy clearance divers arrived.

They were able to talk to the trapped woman, Heidi, through a hole by the side of the keel and had ascertained that she had managed to get herself out of the water by sitting on oars that she had jammed across the cabin, cramming herself clear of the water in a 2½ft deep pocket of air. She was aware of the rescue attempts being made and unbelievably, was remaining calm.

The next problem was that the vessel was taking a pounding in the open sea and Dave Kennet, the coxswain of the Yarmouth lifeboat, knew this would make for a difficult rescue for the divers. He was also worried that the heavy sea would cause even more damage to the yacht, leading to the possibility of it sinking.

Dave decided to tow the capsized catamaran into calmer waters. The four-mile tow was carried out extremely carefully, initially to Allum Bay on the Solent side of the Needles. Unfortunately, the bay was still too rough, even a boat taking a doctor out to the lifeboat was swamped by the waves and the doctor himself had to be rescued.

The tow was continued to Totland Bay where the rescue was carried out; three Navy divers went down, cleared the debris to gain access to Heidi, gave her a mouthpiece from a breathing set and guided her out. She was then hypothermic lifted into our aircraft and flown to Hospital. 'R-IJ' then returned the doctor to the island before picking up the divers for their return to Portsmouth.

Heidi had been in the capsized hull for six hours in the middle of December. I was not on that rescue, but all the crews involved had nothing but the utmost praise and admiration for her for remaining calm throughout the ordeal.

1994

I had an awful experience this year that was to provide a flash back to 1977, when I had the unusual inner ear problem which had grounded me for a short while. The spinning had returned only for a short time with visual disturbances and a bout of sickness exactly like the last time. I had told Peter Thomson what was happening. I was worried that it would affect my work and it was important I found out what was causing it.

Peter arranged through the company for me to see an ear nose and throat consultant, which was booked within a couple of days. The consultant was Dr Peter West, who I saw in a hospital in Portsmouth. He carried out several tests that pointed towards me having a disease called Meniere's. I knew straight away that if it was true it was likely I would be grounded. If I was a pilot I am sure I would have been.

Dr West arranged for me to have an MRI scan to rule out another possible cause before he would confirm the diagnosis. He arranged the scan quite quickly for me and that ruled out any other likely cause. I feel I was very lucky to see Dr West as he believed in keeping people with this disease in work, even in the type of work I was doing (This was contrary to many other doctors' opinions). He felt I might be able to keep it under control with drugs and diet and suggested we try this first. I started the treatment straight away and Dr West would monitor the results on a regular basis.

I had also been very lucky in that, if this had been the diagnosis seventeen years earlier when I was in the navy, it is unlikely that I would have been allowed to remain flying as less was known about the illness then. I felt extremely fortunate I had gone so long without any serious reoccurrence, but I am convinced that the illness I had back then was Meniere's as the symptoms on those previous occasions were the same as this time.

Meniere's can be quite a debilitating disease without a definite answer to what causes it. Pressure builds up in the inner ear, which periodically tilts the balance mechanism, causing the spinning and sickness bouts. The Meniere's attacks can be of varying ranges between sufferers. Some have no warning of attacks and can have what they call drop attacks, others have attacks that can last for up to 24 hours leaving some feeling constantly off-balance and in the worst cases having to give up work all together.

I was in the lucky band, I had plenty of warning of the attack coming on, warnings that I was to get used to and sometimes I could stop an attack from happening by focussing on a fixed point. The medication also helped to reduce the attacks and control the dizzy spells.

I only missed a few shifts through this and that was only during the tests and diagnosis. I was pleased about this as I took pride in not having days off work. I could easily count on one hand the days I had been off work through illness since the last time this had happened to me seventeen years earlier.

It was still very worrying as it meant that the tinnitus I was getting in my left ear would be permanent and my hearing would deteriorate in that ear, both already noticeable symptoms. The tinnitus was something I had been learning to live with for a while and there was a possibility I could get the Meniere's in both ears, which would certainly be the end of my career. Fortunately, my hearing was still perfect in the right ear. I did have a few more attacks but the medication was increased until I found the level that worked for me.

One of the early scrambles of 1994 involved two friends who lived on the Isle of Wight. They had left Gosport on the mainland at 8:30 in the evening in a rigid inflatable, returning across the Solent back to the Island. It was a calm night and they were experienced sailors who had made this particular trip on many occasions and had adequate equipment for the crossing.

'Rescue IJ' was tasked while airborne on a training sortie when the family of one of the men had reported that they had not returned home. Shortly into that search a rigid inflatable was located washed up on a beach at Calshot, near Southampton.

Terry Short was lowered and was able to confirm that it matched the description of the missing inflatable and that it looked as if the boat had hit the beach with the engine still running. This would indicate that the occupants were likely to have been thrown or fallen overboard at some stage during their trip.

A huge search was to build up involving several lifeboats, 'Rescue-IJ' and the Portland aircraft, but nothing untoward was sighted during that first search. When 'R-IJ' required fuel we changed crew. I took over from Terry as the winchman and Chris Bond as the winch-op. We had only been on the search a short while when a ferry leaving Southampton reported that a passenger had sighted a body floating in the mouth of Southampton Water.

We soon located the body and I was lowered to recover the man from the water. Although he was wearing protective clothing and lifejacket, he had not survived his time in the water. He was taken to Haslar HLS for transfer to a waiting ambulance before we returned to the search for the second casualty and, although the search went on all afternoon, nothing further was sighted.

Eventually the search was stood down due to fading light and the fact it was now many hours after any possible survival time. Lymington Lifeboat (while returning to their base) came across the torso of the second casualty when entering Lymington harbour. We were re-tasked to recover the torso from Lymington Lifeboat – I can only imagine he had been hit by a hydrofoil or a large propeller.

I am not sure if the investigation team ever got an explanation as to what had happened. Clearly a very tragic incident had occurred and we could only surmise that they had collided with, or been knocked overboard by, the wake of a larger vessel.

Terry approached me one day explaining he had a desire to carry out a triathlon and thought that as I was still running regularly, he was still cycling regularly and we were both reasonable swimmers, that I might join him. He felt he would have a better chance of achieving it if I joined him, as we would be able to push each other along with the extra training we would require.

Like the fool I am I agreed! This would mean I would have to improve my cycling and Terry his running and we would both have to get swim fit again. I had not done too much swimming since the Solent charity swim and, to be truthful I needed a challenge.

Terry was 51 and I was 49 at the time. It was always on our mind that we should maintain a reasonable standard of fitness to continue in the role that we were lucky enough to be doing. This would be a brilliant way to maintain an edge and help to raise money for the flight's charity fund.

The training virtually took over our lives, as we did not want to enter unless we thought we could do reasonably well. We bought good bikes and managed to get free admission to a military swimming pool during specified lane swimming sessions, so started our training in earnest.

Not all the training was fun and I had one very embarrassing experience when I progressed to the proper click-in racing pedals. I was on my first serious cycle ride with the click in system believing I had mastered the technique when I suffered my first injury and considerable loss of pride. I had stopped at a traffic light but had not managed to click out of my special cycle shoes. I simply fell to the left unable to put my foot down and landing with the bike on top of me.

A lady, who was in a car next to me also stopped at the traffic lights, thought she had knocked me off the bike and had dashed to my aid. In my embarrassment, I almost let her believe she had knocked me off. I did come clean though thanking her for her concern while trying to hide the pain of hitting my ribs on the kerb. The injury took a few weeks to get better, but I was able to train through it apart from the running (but as that was my best discipline, it was not too serious a problem).

Apart from that hiccup, the training went quite well. I enjoyed the cycling, Terry got on top of his running and we hit the pool on a regular basis. Terry's suggestion had become reality and we achieved a competitive standard for our age group, initially on a short course triathlon and followed later in the year with a medium course triathlon.

We also raised a reasonable amount for the flight's charity, including another donation from the company. It had proven to be more enjoyable than we expected so we vowed to keep up the training, aiming for even better times next year.

Strangely enough, I found while doing the training that it stopped the effects of the Meniere's in its tracks. The tinnitus remained and the fullness in the ear but I had no experience of feeling unsteady at any time during the extra training and was steady enough to remain within inches of Terry's back wheel even when cycling at speeds of greater than 20 mph during training.

In the May, 'R-IJ' was scrambled to the report of a collision between two vessels twenty-two miles southeast of Beachy Head. The crew was: Captain Pete Thomson, co-pilot Mike Roughton, I was the winch-op and Mick Rowsell the winchman. En-route it was ascertained an eight thousand ton refrigeration vessel the 'Ariake Reefer' had collided with the thirty thousand ton container vessel 'Ming Fortune'. The collision had happened in foggy conditions and the two vessels had twenty-one persons between them.

An RAF SAR aircraft (R166) was also en-route from Manston in Kent and a P&O Tanker the 'Steersman' was heading towards the two vessels. In addition, three lifeboats from Eastbourne, Newhaven and Hastings had launched to the incident.

When we arrived on scene, it was apparent the 'Ariake Reefer' was stable although it had a massive gaping hole in its bow just above the waterline; the crew had elected to remain onboard. The Container vessel 'Ming Fortune' was not so fortunate. Although it was still afloat, it had a hole in the side below the water level and was unstable. Some of the Chinese crew were being transferred to the P&O tanker 'Steersman' by the 'Steersman's' lifeboat. The rest of the crew were preparing to board the container ship's lifeboats.

We lowered Mick to the vessel to assess the situation and to ensure that no one had been injured in the collision; the evacuation was continued by lifeboats transferring the remaining crew to the MV 'Steersman'.

Once all the crew were safe, 'R-IJ' was tasked to recover the first group of survivors now onboard the MV 'Steersman' and take them to Lydd airport, where a reception team had been set up to receive them. 'Rescue 166' picked up the remaining ten survivors.

'R-IJ' was kept on standby at Lydd in case further assistance was required. We were later tasked to put a maritime accident investigator onboard the 'Ariake Reefer' who would carry out the initial assessment of the causes and assess possible environmental damage from leakage of oil and fuel from the vessels.

The following morning when it was apparent the 'Ming Fortune' had stopped taking on water we recovered the MAIB officer. The captain and mate returned on board with a North Sea pilot and the vessel was taken in tow to Le Havre. The 'Ariake Reefer' was taken in tow to Rotterdam.

If this collision had taken place in rough seas and strong winds, I feel the outcome would have been quite different as it would have been virtually impossible to stop the inflow of water to the 'Ming Fortune'. The lifeboat evacuation may not have been possible, so the outcome would more likely to have been a case of how long the vessel would stay afloat, making the evacuation of the crew considerably more difficult.

MV 'BARD'

In June, we had the celebrations for the 50th anniversary of D-Day commencing with celebrations taking place in Portsmouth and Southsea, with Heads of state and government from fifteen different countries attending, including President Bill Clinton. On completion of the celebrations in Portsmouth, an armada of vessels led by the Royal Yacht Britannia sailed from Portsmouth to the main celebrations in Normandy in France.

I not only had an aerial view of all these ships gathering, I was lucky enough to be in the crew that had to fly a TV cameraman to film the fly past of a Lancaster bomber over the armada, mid channel between Portsmouth and Normandy. The Lancaster bomber would drop two million poppies representing one for each person who took part in the original landings, a sight I will never forget.

Late evening on the 7th June, we were scrambled to recover a 78-year-old man, who had suffered a heart attack onboard the MV 'Bard' thirty-six miles south of the Isle of Wight. The crew was: Captain John Whale, co-pilot Mike Roughton, winch-op Tony Campbell and I was the winchman. The vessel was familiar to us: it was a lovely old Buchan fishing vessel owned by an enthusiast who had restored the vessel and at that time operated it in the local area. I had winched to it on a few occasions previously.

The vessel had gone across to Normandy as part of the armada with a group of World War II veterans who had hired the boat for the crossing. I feel they were re-living the actual event and had probably taken part in that invasion, hence wanting to go across on a boat representing those times.

The 'Bard' was returning after the celebrations, the weather had blown up to become quite nasty but the boat was well capable of handling the weather. This would turn out to be one of the more difficult jobs I would experience.

It was a dark night in heavy rain when we arrived on scene; the 'Bard' was moving around too much to attempt a standard winch, so we briefed the crew on using the hi-line. The crew was the skipper and his son who was about fourteen years of age, the skipper would have to remain on the helm to steer the vessel during the winching, which would require as steady a course as possible into the heavy sea and winds. This meant the fourteen year old boy would have to handle the hi-line, anyway I need not have worried he handled it well, pulling me on board as Tony winched out.

I immediately went down to the cabin, which I had to enter through the wheelhouse and down a steep ladder. Below decks, a group of veterans faced me all completely washed out from the extremely exhaustive few days and now suffering from seasickness.

The man who had suffered the heart attack was conscious and could not move but he did not seem too worried about his situation. I am sure he had resigned himself to it and could not see a way out; he was even apologising for causing all this trouble, his manner had won my admiration within two minutes of meeting him. His son had gone along on the trip to help with the veterans and I can only guess to experience something of what his father had been through during the war.

My initial assessment of the situation was that there would be no way to get the casualty out of the cabin. He could not move and would have to be put in a stretcher, which would have been impossible to manoeuvre up the vertical ladder and through the tight turn in the wheelhouse. There was a small watertight hatch in the roof of the cabin about two feet square but I didn't think there would be any way that we would be able to pull him vertically through that, especially with the jolting movement of the vessel.

I went out on deck to look at the other side of this hatch just to see if there was any way we could hoist him through, I was hoping for some form of gantry system just to get the casualty on deck. Unfortunately, part of the hatch was obscured by a big heavy steel boom lashed to the roof of the cabin; it could not be moved in these weather conditions.

By this stage, I was resigned to having the oxygen and the defibrillator sent down to me. I would have to remain onboard with the casualty until we could make port which would be many hours later. When I mentioned this to the casualty, he was still apologising and totally understood; however, his son who was so concerned his father would not survive the trip that he persuaded me to have a go at getting him through the hatch in the roof. I felt it would take super human strength to achieve this but was also impressed with the determination of the young man.

I decided that I would at least get the casualty strapped into the stretcher, take it one-step at a time and see what we could achieve. I was also pressured by time, as 'R-IJ' only had thirty minutes left on scene. If I could not achieve anything by then I would have to stay with the casualty, but perhaps the aircraft could return after refuelling and maybe with a doctor to help me.

Tony sent down the empty stretcher and it was a struggle getting it down to the cabin, again making me feel this would be an impossible task. There was a bench table across the centre of the cabin, which we laid the stretcher on while the skipper's son and the casualty's son helped me transfer the casualty to the stretcher. I soon had him strapped in; it was a Neil Robertson stretcher – just about the best stretcher for this type of operation with its horizontal and vertical lifting capability.

Once I had him secure in the stretcher, I went back on deck to check again as to how this might be achieved. The skipper had to stay on the wheel, which was an old type large spindled wheel needing total control and strength to keep the heading into sea.

I had decided that there would be just enough room to squeeze the stretcher through the hatch and past the boom lying across the corner. This would mean pushing and pulling the stretcher up through the hatch vertically and I would need to set everything up ready for one attempt. The young boy had already proved his strength when he pulled me onboard and the casualty's son was going to have to use all the strength he could possible produce and more. The rest of the veterans were unable to assist as they themselves were incapacitated through either exhaustion or seasickness.

First, we jammed the stretcher in the vertical position between the table and the edge of the hatch. Two of us went back on deck and pulled while the other pushed, until we got the stretcher about two thirds through the hatch. We were able to jam the stretcher again while the casualty's son came on deck and the three of us managed to lift it vertically the rest of the way while struggling to maintain our own balance. I could hardly believe we had achieved this and felt a sudden surge of relief when we were able to lay the stretcher and casualty onto the upper deck.

I sent the casualty's son up to the aircraft first in a straightforward lift, as I could guide him over the guardrail with the hi-line. Lifting me with the stretcher would be more difficult because I could not position the stretcher clear of the guardrail. Tony would have to pick the right moment to pull us clear, which of course he did and we were able to transfer father and son to Haslar hospital in the early hours of the morning. Another job that remains vivid in my mind, even sending shivers down my spine, but also a good memory of a successful job carried out in very awkward conditions.

In July 94, a television crew joined us for the late summer to carry out a fly on the wall documentary, following us on jobs and even occasionally, during our off watch time. A company called Chameleon had been commissioned to produce six thirty-minute programmes for Meridian television.

We were getting used to having TV crews around, with several 999 re-creations, a feature with the "Blues and Two's" series and occasionally the media would descend on us when we had been involved with high profile rescues.

Nevertheless, I found this quite intimidating. Chameleon had picked a very good production team who would fit into our crewing system and gain our acceptance, but it was still daunting coming under such scrutiny. We did, as a team, learn to live with it and on actual jobs would often forget they were there, but I would never find the interviews afterwards easy.

The series became quite popular and would continue for the following two years with the crew joining us for a six-week period during the summer months. The only advantage to the flight other than PR was that the production team would turn up every morning with cakes and other goodies, which we felt was great until we started putting on weight. That problem was sorted by almost non-stop volleyball while the TV crews were here, the extra people enabling us to have two reasonable size teams.

Another job that year, one that I class as a real lifesaver, was from the report that a man on the South Coast of the Isle of Wight had noticed a puff of smoke on the horizon out to sea. The smoke he thought he saw did not last long, but he did report it and a Coastguard team was despatched to the area, but they could not see anything even with binoculars. It was a day with misty low-level cloud and a rough sea with lots of spray, so it would have been easy to deceive the eye.

John Trill, who was the Coastguard sector officer and had worked on the island for some years knew the person who had made the report and had a strong feeling that this person would not have reported it if he was not sure in his own mind that something was not right. John insisted a search was carried out.

'R-IJ' was scrambled the crew was: Captain Peter Nicholson, co-pilot Mo Wilson, winch-op Tony Campbell and Terry Short was the winchman. They were tasked to carry out a sector search three miles south of St Catherine's point, which would have been as far as someone could have seen that day.

The search was very nearly called off after the first sector search had been completed and nothing had been seen; the original sighting had not been a positive sighting, the sea state was force seven to eight with lots of white caps and sea spray, which could easily have looked like smoke. The aircraft's sector search was in the right place, watched from the shore by the original informant, the aircraft itself disappearing into the horizon on some of the sector legs.

Just to be sure, a creeping line search along the line from shore towards the sighting was commenced. This would involve a search either side of the line and continuing a few miles beyond the point that the aircraft was visible from the shore. The crew were coming to the end of the search, on the last couple of legs, when two men were spotted clinging to a capsized hull. Terry was lowered to recover the men who were both showing signs of hypothermia and finding it difficult clinging onto the hull.

They were two Dutch sailors on a sailing holiday and were extremely lucky for lots of reasons. If the only person who caught a glimmer of their smoke had not stuck by his guns, even though he must have had some doubts, as it was only a short sighting or if John Trill had not known the first informant so well and had such trust in that person, it could have ended very differently. The casualties were in a position that would not have made any chance sightings from other boats likely and they were on a sailing holiday, so it would have been quite some time before anyone would have reported them missing. The most likely outcome would have been that they would have succumbed to the cold within an hour had they not been found.

The relief shown by the Dutch sailors was highlighted for us as the rescue was captured by the TV crew shadowing the flight at the time; they had a wonderful shot of the two survivors in the back of the aircraft immediately after rescue. They were clinging to the flectalon blankets that Terry was covering them with, when one of them gave a huge sigh. That sigh told the whole story.

Another quite unusual task shortly after the Dutch Sailors rescue, 'R-IJ' was scrambled just after midnight to the report of three divers reported missing. Crew: Captain Peter Thomson, co-pilot Rob Flexman, winch-op Mick Rowsell and Don Sowden was the winchman. The position they were given was in Lyme Bay, off the Dorset coast and was based on the last known position of the divers.

That position would have to be the starting point of the search as it was all the Coastguards had to go on. The search had commenced after worried families had reported that the divers had not returned home from their diving trip.

As 'R-IJ' was coming to the end of the original search, they were tasked to investigate a rigid inflatable spotted on the horizon by one of the shoreline search teams. On investigation, it was apparent that it was the missing divers' boat, complete with diving equipment but no divers. It was subsequently found to have the engine kill cord still attached and the vessel had run out of fuel. This indicated that the divers had possibly fallen overboard while the craft was underway and the craft had simply run on until the fuel ran out.

This meant they could be anywhere. The next search would be between the boat and the original datum and it continued until the aircraft had to go to Portland for a refuel. The break off point was marked in preparation for 'R-IJ's return to the scene or for another aircraft to take over.

While 'R-IJ' was refuelling the report came through that the divers had been located by a fishing boat, the position would have been within the next few legs of the search. An aircraft was tasked to pick them up from the fishing vessel. At the time of their rescue, the divers had been in the water for sixteen hours.

It was their story afterwards that would spark considerable conversation and will act as a reminder that searches will rarely be straightforward due to many 'ifs and buts', we can only rely on information known, backed up by tidal and wind information, followed by clues as the search progresses.

In this case, the divers had left home that day intending to dive on a particular wreck, telling their families they would not be sure as to what time they would return home so not to worry if they were late, something their families were used to when the divers went on these trips.

In the meantime, the divers changed their minds and decided to go to a different wreck, so the original search datum was wrong. Once the divers had completed their dive they headed home, the wind was increasing and the sea was getting up. About 4:00 pm one of the divers who was sat on the tube of the rib, found himself tipped out into the water. He thought the others would soon return to pick him up then noticed his two mates in the water as well. The boat was continuing on its own eventually disappearing into the distance.

They got together as a group as they watched the boat disappear. It was not very comfortable in the sea with ten-foot waves but they kept their spirits up at that stage, hoping one of the returning fishing boats may see them. As it got darker, they realised the likelihood of being seen was less likely and had to cling to the hope that their families would report them missing and a search for them would take place. They even deliberated on how long it would be before their families reported them missing, cursing themselves for always telling them not to worry.

As it was, the worried families held out until midnight before reporting the divers missing, that being the moment 'R-IJ' was scrambled. At one stage, the divers had seen a helicopter come very close to them before changing direction so they now knew a search was taking place, but also knew the reasons the search was likely to be in the wrong area.

During the night, after several hours in the water, one of the divers had noticed a split in his suit under the arm, caused, I believe, when they had tried to swim towards the lights of Lyme Regis. He tried his best to keep the split closed knowing he would not survive the cold water and that the water entering his suit would take his buoyancy away. He thought that he would eventually disappear below the surface.

When he could no longer stop the water entering the suit, he swam away from the other two as he did not want them to watch him die; he had completely come to terms with his fate. The remaining two divers knew the consequences of their friend's predicament and encouraging him to remain with them; however, they had been in the water for thirteen hours themselves and were close to accepting that none of them would be found alive.

The diver that had swum away had decided he would keep swimming as best he could towards the shoreline, using one arm until he sank. During this last ditch effort, he saw a boat quite close to him and, having started waving to attract attention, he soon found himself being pulled out of the water. He was then able to tell his rescuers that there were two more divers in the water somewhere south of his position. The remaining two divers were quickly located and hauled onto the boat. They had all survived their ordeal after a total of sixteen hours in the cold water.

All those search aids, lifeboats, coastal patrols and three helicopters had been involved in the search, yet they were finally located by a fishing vessel heading out for a day angling. The crew of 'R-IJ' was quite sure that they would have located them when the search was continued after the refuel, as they were located along the track of that last search pattern, but that may well have been too late for one of them.

The next high profile tasking was to a fire onboard a cross channel ferry. I had been on call at home overnight and was having a cup of tea prior to heading off to work for the rest of the shift. I was watching the news and the headline was of a ferry, the 'Sally Star', on fire in the Channel six miles East of Ramsgate close to the Goodwin Sands.

I was thinking to myself that we might be called for this job; the report mentioned helicopters had been scrambled from Wattisham in Suffolk to RAF Manston in Kent to pick up fire teams. A further SAR helicopter was scrambled from Koksijde in Belgium direct to the 'Sally Star' and lifeboats were heading to the scene. As I was watching the news report, the phone went; we were tasked to head for the ferry 'Sally Star'.

As soon as we arrived at work, we received an update prior to proceeding towards the stricken ferry. The crew was: Captain John Whale, co-pilot Mike Roughton, winch-op Nick Horst and I was the winchman. En-route we were tasked to relocate to Manston, to be on standby from there in case the fire fighters and remaining crew needed evacuating from the vessel. On arrival at RAF Manston, we were tasked to take 1400 lbs of fire fighting equipment to the 'Sally Star' and uplift 1900 lbs of equipment plus a fire fighter from the ferry and return to Manston.

We quickly loaded the equipment and were soon alongside the vessel. A tug was spraying water on the ship's side, acting as boundary cooling and we could see from our FLIR camera that there was still a considerable heat source from the area of the boundary cooling. I was lowered to the vessel to receive the equipment, recovered our load and then we returned to Manston to await further instructions.

At this stage, the non-essential crew and passengers had been evacuated from the ferry by lifeboats and were being taken ashore; one injured crewmember had been airlifted to Manston and approximately fifty fire fighters had been flown out to the Sally Star.

'R-IJ' was then tasked to take six fire fighters and 300 lbs of equipment to the 'Sally Star' and uplift six fire fighters plus 800 lbs of equipment from the ferry to Manston, then return to the ferry for a further ten fire fighters.

I remained on the Sally Star during these transfers by 'R-IJ' and the RAF aircraft. At this stage, the fire was pretty well under control, so the initial fire fighters were being taken off and a smaller relief team put onboard, to keep the situation under control and prevent a further flare up. I was recovered on completion and 'R-IJ' was released from task.

On returning, we were re-tasked to a small boy trapped in a gulley on a cliff that provides the backdrop to the eastern end of Hastings. This was more awkward than expected, Nick had to lower me to a ridgeline then guide the aircraft while I walked the ridgeline, still attached to the wire until he could drop me into the gully. We soon had the boy onboard and delivered to hospital, just suffering from shock but otherwise all right.

The irony of the job that day was that the RAF aircraft had recently moved from being based at RAF Manston in Kent to RAF Wattisham in Suffolk, part of the latest reduction and repositioning of SAR flights around the coast of the British Isles. In this case, the fire fighters had to wait for pick up. There would be a lot made of this incident and many questions asked but the decision was not reversed. Again, the day was saved by good weather and the fact that the vessel was close to shore.

After the success of the last Miss SAR charity thrash, we decided to have another at the end of the summer season to top up our charity fund, helped by a donation from the TV crew who would sponsor the event. It was time for Don to sharpen his nails, choose his outfit and defend his crown.

The event would take the same format as the last time hoping we would get the same support. The event would be filmed as part of the fly on the wall series so would possibly bring more people out of the closet. They filmed a scene showing Don choosing his outfit and it was hilarious but it was a good job his wife Mandy was helping him choose it otherwise we would have had to wonder about him!

There was a challenge this time, between Don Sowden and Pete Thomson who had vowed to take the crown from Don. Quite a few lifeboatmen and Coastguards wanted to steal it away from the flight altogether, so the fight was on.

We took over 'Gosport and Fareham Rescues' boathouse again, built the catwalk and a few of the lads did the France run to stock up with booze. The French duty free booze was supplied free as part of the entrance fee; I think that was legal at the time.

The night was so successful that it was clear we should have used a much bigger venue. The contestants had excelled themselves – some enjoying it a little too much! I was the greeter that night and had so much to drink that I fancied half of them myself.

Don had worn a Miss Whiplash outfit revealed after he had stripped from a pair of orange flying overalls in a rather seductive scene. Pete Thomson made a very nice 'Madame', spending hours on his makeup and nails. Other contestants tried to steal the show.

My wife Margaret had to organise the catwalk and suffered the most hilarious abuse, especially from entrant Miss Betty Swallocks. Margaret had to use all her skills from her work in the solicitors to keep this unruly lot under control.

Bob Woodwark, the Coastguard District Controller was the leader of the panel of judges and we believe bribed by Pete Thomson who was crowned Miss SAR 1994. The real winner of course was the flight's chosen charity and if we can have a bit of fun achieving that, it is icing on the cake.

The film crews were to return the following year and we noticed that through the screening of the programmes we were able to see the outcome of the casualties we had rescued. The first series had been successful and was quite a revelation even to us in seeing the other side of the situations that had involved us.

The production team covered the tasks from the Coastguards receiving the 999 calls and the problems they had gaining enough information to decide what course of action to take. They also followed the auxiliary Coastguards, RNLI and volunteer lifeboat crews whenever possible, to get a good mix of the maritime incidents happening in our area. They then followed up the after care in hospitals, often finishing with an interview with the casualty.

1995/1996

One of the unusual jobs during 1995 was to a young man stuck in the rigging of a tall ship the 'Kaskelot'. It was in the central Solent, midsummer, with hundreds of yachts in the area, plus a large sailing race taking place near the incident.

'R-IJ' was scrambled. The crew was: Captain Graham Sorge, co-pilot Gary Queen, I was the winch-op and Tony Campbell was the winchman. When we arrived on scene, there was very little wind and the vessel was stationary. This would make for a difficult winch, as we were using a good deal of power and the downdraught would be directed straight into the rigging.

We decided to lower Tony to a police launch that could provide us with a heading into wind, once Tony was onboard the police launch he would be taken with his equipment to the 'Kaskelot'. This procedure only took a few minutes and was by far the safest way to get Tony onboard the tall ship.

Tony was immediately faced with having to climb the rigging to get alongside the casualty. Once with him he had the dilemma of what to do next. The casualty was in so much pain he could not be moved back down the rope ladders.

It was an unusual situation; the young man had recently had an operation on his leg requiring a steel pin to give the leg stability. The operation had been successful and he could get on with his life as normal. Unfortunately, this pin had become dislodged while he was up the rigging and any movement was causing excruciating pain.

Tony tried relieving the pain with entonox but still could not move the young man, even with the help of a group of lifeboatmen who had arrived onboard to help. Eventually, Tony asked us over the radio if there was any chance of us winching him straight out of the rigging. This was not an option while the vessel was stationary as they were in the rigging of the forward mast and the spars and rigging on the mast behind them would make this impossible.

We felt we might be able to achieve it if we could get the vessel underway, but we would need plenty of sea room into wind and the vessel on a very steady course. There were two problems with this: firstly the number of yachts in the area and secondly that we only had about ¾ mile of sea room into what little wind there was. We mulled it over; deciding that as we had a team of lifeboatmen on board whom we knew would operate the hi-line correctly, we could ask the lifeboat and police launch to travel ahead clearing the yachts that would be in the way. The captain of the 'Kaskelot' also assured us they would be able to keep the vessel on an accurate course, although it was a tall ship sailing vessel it did have an auxiliary engine.

With all this in mind we decided to give it a go, making sure everyone was briefed and aware of the point at which we would have to ditch the hi-line and pull away if not achieved. The hi-line, when lowered to the vessel was taken to Tony. I kept the inboard end of the line in hand, so that I could ditch it if it snagged on anything, which it did at one stage on the central spar but we managed to pull it off by guiding the aircraft to the left.

When we were happy as a crew that we were positioned correctly, I attached the weak link to the hook and sent the hook down to Tony. Graham was able to keep Tony visual while I winched out the winch hook and in turn, the hook was pulled onboard by the lifeboatmen. Once the hook was onboard, it was taken up the rigging to Tony.

Tony had the two strops on the casualty both attached to his harness so that he and the casualty would come away from the rigging together. He would have to protect the young man's leg as best he could. As soon as we had the thumbs up from Tony, I started the con to move the aircraft to the on top position. Graham was now relying on visual references from other structures on the ship to gauge my instruction against because he would lose sight of Tony as we moved in. When in a position where we could safely swing Tony and the casualty clear of the rigging I winched in and the lifeboatmen guided Tony and casualty clear with the hi-line.

As soon as Tony was clear of all obstructions, he cut the weak link of the hi-line, which was recovered to the vessel as it turned back into deeper water. We spent a bit of time easing the casualty into the aircraft as his leg was still unstable but had him in hospital only a few minutes after that. This was a very unusual piece of winching, almost certainly only achievable by complete crew cooperation and understanding of each other's intentions, but above all the unrelenting practice we do carrying out hi-lines with yachts in varying weather conditions. I had to accept the ability to achieve what we had just done was down to Peter Thomson's drive in making sure we all kept on top of realistic training.

This enthusiasm Pete had for training and keeping standards high was the source of considerable light-hearted humour. One cartoon in our scrapbook was of a view of Pete, looking through the cockpit towards the lead yacht of the Whitbread round the world race, entering the Solent at the end of the last leg of that race. The yacht was being escorted into the Solent by a welcome home flotilla of boats following along. The cartoon shows Peter asking if the yacht will come round onto port tack to carry out a practice hi-line, the yachts reply was 'Yes and I will do a lap of honour after that'!

Joking aside, Pete was right and it showed itself over and over again on difficult jobs that we would all face from time to time, in particular the number of yachting incidents we were required to assist with in our patch. We all knew he was right.

Also in 1995, the Navy had decided to close down Portland Naval Air Station and, as part of this process; they would be pulling out the Search and Rescue flight by the end of the year. There was quite a lot of deliberation as to whether there would be enough helicopter cover for the south coast, as this would leave only the Lee-on-Solent flight and the Royal Naval flight based at Culdrose in Cornwall.

The Coastguard decided that the gap was too wide and put out a tender for a fourth Coastguard flight. That contract was awarded to Bristow Helicopters.

Pete Thomson, Mike Roughton, Tony Campbell and our Chief Engineer Derek Hapgood would move down to Portland to help set up the new flight.

This left a space for another aircrewman at Lee. John Spencer, the aircrewman who had carried out the rescue from the capsized barge in the late 70's, was about to leave the Navy and had been offered a place on the Portland flight. John's family lived at Lee but the company could not offer him a position here as it was not sure whether Tony would be coming back after setting up Portland and even if not, the post would be offered internally first.

In the meantime, we managed to get John here on a temporary basis, to fill in for Tony when he first went down to Portland. Later Tony decided he would be staying at Portland as the Senior Crewman. No-one from the other units wanted to move to Lee so John managed to get a permanent post on the team. This suited us at Lee, as we all knew John and his capabilities, so wanted him on the team.

We were sorry to lose Tony; he had kept us amused at Lee for seven years doing exactly what Terry had hired him for, being the entertainment king. He had also slotted back into the aircrewman role extremely proficiently.

We in turn had helped to change Tony's life around; since joining, he had managed to calm down from his holiday rep days and was now a happily married man and proud father. The job at Lee had added much needed stability to Tony's life. I reckon leaving the flight would have been a wrench for him but probably worthwhile with his promotion and Tony needed new challenges.

Once the flight was set up at Portland, Mike Roughton stayed down there as the Chief Pilot. Derek Hapgood stayed on as the Chief Engineer and Tony Campbell as the Chief Aircrewman. Pete Thomson returned to Lee – he had made it clear at the start that he would only remain at Portland until the flight was operational with all the crews selected. Jaffer Dharamsi took over from Derek as the Chief Engineer here at Lee and Dave Thomson joined us as the seventh engineer, Dave had recently returned from working overseas.

The diving incidents were on the increase again this year with twenty-one divers requiring assistance by our aircraft alone, including some fatalities. These diving incidents were clearly a problem that was not going to go away. The sport was getting hugely popular and more affordable; I guess that the problem will continue to increase as more people pursue this form of recreation.

Another noticeable trend was with serious and even fatal head injuries from booms on yachts which was possibly because of the increase in people taking up the sport as it was becoming more assessable for anyone wanting to give sailing a try. There was a noticeable increase in the number of sailing facilities and schools opening up in the Solent area.

In early 1996, Anne Braggington our secretary was reading an article in the office while Terry and I were sorting out a SAR Report. The article was about difficulties a children's hospice at Sutton Scotney was having, regarding reaching financial targets required to keep the brand new purpose-built building open. The article was quite upsetting. To think that a place like that, offering such an incredible service to children who are suffering terminal illnesses and providing considerable help and support to the children's families, would so soon after being built be struggling for funding.

Terry thought that even if it did not come under the flight's fund remit; we could use this coming year's sponsored triathlon money towards the appeal. We had kept our training going over the winter and had already applied for two more events this year, but had not yet sent out the sponsor forms.

Terry then thought we would raise a bit more sponsor money if we did a longer challenge and suggested that we swim the Solent, then immediately get on our bikes and cycle to our sister base in Portland. That would be, approximately, a five mile tidal swim, followed by a ninety mile cycle ride. I had swum the Solent before with Nick & Sandra; Terry had covered ninety miles on his sponsored cycle rides on a few occasions so again we just had to tie the two together.

The next thing we knew, we were not just talking about it but I was looking at the feasibility, sorting out tides and searching for volunteers. Safety boats would be required to cover us on the swim and a back up vehicle would be needed to shadow us to Portland.

We would still do the triathlons, as they would help with the training; however, we would have to increase the training we were doing, increase our pool training, adding some sea swims and increasing the cycle distances.

Don Sowden and Gary Queen (our new co–pilot) volunteered to look after the trip to Portland and Don and Rob Flexman would crew the flight safety boat for the Solent swim. 'Gosport and Fareham Inshore Rescue' crews would provide a second safety boat, plus a canoeist for each of us. They were used to helping with cross Solent swims supporting several attempts each year, which in turn had helped raise many thousands for charities over many years. Now it was just a case of making sure we could achieve it or at least give it our best shot.

In the May of 96, 'R-IJ' was scrambled to a speedboat that had reported being in difficulty between Shoreham and Littlehampton. The crew was: Captain Peter Nicholson, co-pilot: Richard Norris, winch-op Mike Rowsell and I was the winchman.

The initial report had been following a mobile phone call between an occupant of the speedboat and a friend saying the speedboat had broken down and was taking on water. The friend had contacted the Coastguards and initially we thought there were two people onboard.

As the picture built up it was apparent that there was a small white speed boat missing and that there could be four young men aboard it. The search soon built up to being a major one as nothing further was heard from the mobile phone. The search area was between Shoreham and Littlehampton (the intended route of the speedboat) and our first search revealed nothing.

We refuelled at Shoreham airfield and continued with the search, during which we spotted a body in the water floating face down with no lifejacket on. I was lowered to recover the body and we immediately called the Selsey lifeboat to concentrate on this area. We also recovered a jacket floating on the surface, initially thought to have been another person in the water.

Selsey lifeboat recovered a second body shortly after arriving in the area; we took our casualty ashore to waiting police before returning to the search. The search was continued until the next refuel was required – by then we had been airborne for nearly six hours. Another crew had been organised to relieve us at the next refuelling, continuing the search with fresh pairs of eyes.

The search continued throughout the following day, but the other two missing persons were not located. It was all very tragic and the two bodies recovered turned out to be brothers.

I was called to be present at the inquest of this incident and found it quite harrowing as the details of the build up to the incident had become known. It was apparent that it was a group of young men out to have a good time. There were many lessons to be learnt from the tragic incident, the boat was not that seaworthy, with a shallow draft making it only suitable for calm water, it had a history of engine problems, lifejackets had not been worn and other problems were discussed at length during the inquest.

Unfortunately, these things do happen and we can only hope that lessons are learnt that may prevent loss of life at some date in the future. However, I had to accept I have done some daft things in my life so find it very hard to criticize and was pleased that, in this case, it was not my duty to do so.

The thing that got to me the most in this incident was that one of the young men who lost his life had only just met the other three men in the pub that day: he had volunteered to help launch the boat and in turn was invited along on the trip. That extra person in the boat quite possibly made the difference to the draft of the boat, making it easier to be swamped; he would have been totally unaware of that. I felt that to be awful, he had left home that morning just to enjoy a few drinks without any intention of going out in a boat.

The day of the swim and cycle ride had come round rather quickly. All the arrangements had been made and now all we required was good weather. Terry and I had a leisurely swim in the Solent the day before the actual challenge, just a winding down swim after all the training. The weather was perfect that day, but the forecast for the next day was mixed, a weather front was approaching but it couldn't be forecast whether the weather would turn before the swim or not. We were not too worried about the cycle ride, as we could plod through that even if the weather was bad, it would just take longer to finish.

On the morning, the wind was twenty-five knots and increasing with white caps starting to form on the sea. We should have had the sense to put it off to another day, but too many people were involved in this and the TV crew, who were with us for the third year, had decided they wanted to film the event. We had put too much effort into this one day and the weather was not going to put us off. Rather a stupid attitude, especially for the role we do.

'Gosport and Fareham Inshore Rescue' decided to put four canoeists in with us as well as their main boat. Our flight boat launched with Rob and Don as crew. Even the Coastguard boat had come along to support us; it would be like a mini flotilla crossing the Solent.

This gave us the security to go ahead, so we climbed into the flight boat to be taken across the Solent to Ryde (Isle of Wight). That was the first point we realised we hadn't been too smart; we had arranged the swim during a neap tide meaning the low tide was at its highest, adding approximately ½ a mile to the swim. The previous time I had carried out this the swim we started about ½ a mile from Ryde sea front whereas this time we were starting from the front itself.

When we climbed out of the boat to commence the swim the water was freezing. It was amazing the difference a day had made. Anyway, off we went, heading in the right direction towards the mainland. We soon lost sight of each other and by the time the first thirty minutes had past, the winds had increased to forty knots and we were swimming in a moderate sea. I could not see anything ahead of me let alone the mainland; this proved a very difficult thing to cope with. I had to rely on the canoeist alongside shouting directions that I could not hear too well with my earplugs in and the waves thrashing around me.

The last time I had carried out the swim I found it relatively easy and I was not as fit then as I was now, but in these conditions it was a different ball game. We expected to complete the swim in less than two hours yet at that point; we had not even reached the half way mark, which would mean missing the tidal flow that would have given us the advantage for the second half of the swim.

After three hours, I realised the canoeist was no longer with me and it was Don on the flight boat, who was shouting instructions at me. The canoeist had been pulled from the water because they were becoming hypothermic; they were getting the full wind chill, making them worse off than we were in the water.

Gosport Rescue's Lifeboat was guiding Terry. After four hours and within ¼ of a mile of the mainland, it had become clear to the crews of the rescue boats that, having missed the favourable tide, we were virtually standing still, just being driven by the strong flooding tide towards the Western Solent. At this stage, I was just head down and plodding on, completely unaware that I had now been in the water more than four hours. A boat suddenly came alongside and dragged me inboard depositing me on top of Terry who was lying in the boat with a huge flectalon blanket over him. The boats had taken the decision for safety reasons, to pull us out of the water.

The despair we felt being pulled out of the water was unbelievable and by the time we reached the shore we were both shivering beyond control. We were taken to the boathouse for a hot shower thinking to ourselves that it was the end of this attempt.

Once warmed up, we had a chat and decided to give the cycle ride a go. We thought there would be no chance of making it all the way to Portland, as we had used up too much energy trying to battle through that moderate sea. We now faced a ninety-mile cycle ride into a forty-knot headwind. Terry said if we could make it halfway, it would still be an achievement on a day like this so, off we went; my family had decided to follow us to Portland as well as the support pickup truck.

After an hour and with lots of energy drinks, bananas etc. our energy started to increase, the thrill of the challenge returning. I was even enjoying heading into the wind. Both of us were quite elated that we were regaining our energy.

When we reached the halfway point, we stopped for a short break. Unfortunately, our support truck had not caught up with us. They had backtracked thinking they had missed us and we became separated. This might have proved a problem as they had our lights on the truck, which we would need before Portland. However, we decided we would crack on and hope that they would catch us up before it got dark, which fortunately they did along with the TV crew.

As though we had not had enough hassle that day, Terry thought he knew a short cut as we approached Weymouth, but I soon knew something had gone wrong as we were cycling up quite steep hills when I was sure we should have been on level ground. Terry realised his mistake too late and it added seven miles to our journey. I forgave him when we did eventually see the lights of Weymouth. The feeling, cycling across the causeway between Weymouth and Portland, which was the only time on the trip that we had the wind behind us, could only be described as euphoric, we had made it!

The despair at not having completed the swim was washed away. It was disappointing, but we could and did take pride in what we had achieved in the conditions that had prevailed. In some ways, it had added to the challenge. We both felt it was far harder than anything we had ever done and probably would do in the future as we were both in our fifties. Terry said it would be time to throw in the towel but I knew he would be planning something else within the week.

Terry rang his wife Hazel to reassure her that we had arrived safely, finishing off the call by saying we had decided to cycle home. That statement was captured by the TV crew and used to finish the series.

1996, was to be another year of uncertainty with the flight under threat of being moved yet again. This time it was because of the closure of HMS Daedalus and the threatened closure of the airfield. The MOD was planning to sell off the land and it looked almost certain that we would have to move...but where to? The main rumour was that we would move to Shoreham in Sussex. This was going round in circles yet again – the fourth time I had witnessed a fight to keep the aircraft in the local area.

The campaign took off with vengeance, a regular topic on the local news, petitions set up by various interested groups who felt strongly the aircraft was needed in this locality and Peter Viggers again asking questions in the House. The campaign would roll for many months and we could only wait for the outcome.

I mentioned earlier that occasionally, in extreme circumstances and only in life threatening situations, we would winch with three people on the wire i.e. the winchman and two survivors. We had another situation this year when that had to happen. We had been scrambled to the report of two men stuck on Culver cliff at Bembridge. The crew was: Captain Peter Thomson, co-pilot Peter Nicholson, I was the winch-op and Don Sowden was the winchman.

Don had decided to take two strops down with him. Using two strops as for the hypothermic lift (one under the arms the other under the back of the knees) would make it more comfortable for the casualty so we had started doing this whenever possible. The casualties were about 125ft from the bottom of the cliff, so I walked Don on the end of wire from the top of the cliff keeping him in contact with the cliff face as I winched out. The initial winch was carried out down-wind from the casualties. When Don was horizontally level with casualties we walked him across the face of the cliff towards them. We had a good wind for this procedure and it would keep the downdraught away from the casualties on the approach.

When Don arrived with them, they were perched on a precarious ledge with very loose screed making it difficult to get a safe foothold. Don was worried as to whether the remaining boy would be able to hold on, especially if the downdraught caught him as 'R-IJ' pulled away from the cliff with the first survivor. Don, thinking on his feet, decided to use one strop on each boy and all three came off together.

I am sure that was the right decision and perhaps one we may have discussed at the brief prior to winching, but it is often difficult to assess the condition of the area you are being winched to until you arrive there. It is the same in the sea, it's not always easy to assess how high the swell is or the height of the waves until you are about to enter it on the end of the wire.

In the November, 'R-IJ' was carrying out a search at Folkestone in Kent after a car had been located at the bottom of a cliff. On scene, it was established the car was empty and nobody was in the vicinity. We were returning to Lee after refuelling at Manston when we were re-tasked to a yacht in difficulty eighteen miles south of Bembridge. The crew was:

Captain Pete Thomson, co-pilot Richard Norris, I was the winch-op and Mick Rowsell was the winchman.

The yacht 'Scorcher' was reporting two people onboard both suffering from severe seasickness and one hypothermic. The sea was extremely rough and the Coastguards had also launched the Bembridge Lifeboat to the incident.

On scene, it was apparent that neither of the people onboard would be able to handle the hi-line and, without the hi-line it would be very difficult getting Mick onboard in the very rough sea conditions. It would have been difficult even with the hi-line unless we could get the yacht underway into wind so we decided to wait until the lifeboat arrived.

We lowered Mick to the lifeboat as it was approaching the scene in the hope that they could get Mick onboard the yacht, which they achieved along with two lifeboatmen. One of the casualties was unconscious and it would have been impossible to transfer him from the yacht to the lifeboat.

I was able to pass our stretcher via the lifeboat to Mick who was able to use the lifeboatmen to help get the casualty into the stretcher, but it would still be a risky recovery from the yacht in those conditions unless we could get some stability.

Pete Thomson came up with the idea of the lifeboat taking the yacht in tow. Once under tow the lifeboat could head into wind with the yacht behind it and the two lifeboatmen could remain on the yacht to handle the hi-line, preparations were quickly made to secure the yacht, the lifeboat got under way into wind and it did the job perfectly. We had not expected to stabilize the yacht completely but it reduced the mast from slewing around, enabling us to carry out the safe recovery of Mick and the casualty in the stretcher.

Another yachting incident that proved very awkward that year was to a yacht 'Racy Lady', in extremely rough conditions. The yacht had met with disaster on the shingles bank, between the Needles and Hurst Castle. We had been scrambled while airborne some forty miles away from the incident. The crew was: Captain Pete Thomson, co-pilot Richard Norris, I was the winch-op and John Spencer was the winchman.

En-route the visibility had reduced considerably in torrential rain and low cloud. We had to locate the yacht using our direction finding equipment to home in on transmissions from the yacht and Lymington lifeboat.

When we arrived on scene, a crewmember from the Lymington lifeboat had somehow managed to get onboard the yacht. How he achieved this is beyond me as the vessel was taking a pounding, being bounced heavily on the bank and moving rapidly from side to side. The lifeboat crewmember had managed to attach a line to the yacht and the lifeboat was attempting to pull the yacht off the shingles. This proved not to be possible, the situation was getting worse and the reducing tide was making it impossible for the lifeboat to recover the crew of the yacht or their own crewmember.

We had problems in the aircraft, as the torrential rain had managed to seep into our intercom. This, as it turned out, was through a faulty external lead-connection point. The fault had wiped out the intercom and made making radio communication difficult because of a loud background howl. At the same time, my helmet packed in completely, having been soaked during some winching which we had carried out earlier.

After messing around with the emergency intercom and using extension leads, we managed to rig up a system that would allow Peter to hear my instructions during the winching. I would have to wear a standard headset.

It was not easy getting John onboard, even with the lifeboatman handling the hi-line, as the yacht kept bouncing from side to side. This unfortunately meant John taking a few knocks and a battering from the sea, which was whipping off the yacht and the shingles bank.

Once John was onboard, the recovery of the casualties was an easier procedure. John prepared them for the lift two at a time and we were able to pick the right moment to swing them away. We recovered the three casualties and the lifeboatman to the aircraft then returned the lifeboatman to the Lymington lifeboat. The three casualties were flown to Haslar hospital.

In December 1996, the Department of Transport announced that the SAR flight would remain at HMS Daedalus and that there were no plans to review the service again. Politicians, sailors, sea rescue groups and the public had campaigned hard to keep us here, a campaign that had rolled non-stop from the announcement that we would be required to move.

That was brilliant news, this being the fourth reprieve for the SAR aircraft to remain at Lee since its formation in 1973. I found the statement 'there were no plans for the service to be reviewed again' a little hard to believe as the airfield would always be under threat. Every year rumours would rise to the surface and we would see many surveys carried out on the airfield, with proposed uses from gravel pits to open prisons. Still, this was another reprieve and we could get on with our work without all the uncertainty that we had become accustomed to over the years (Until the next time!).

Part 7

Lee SAR 1997 – 2001

1997

In the April of 1997, we were tasked to the report of an injured jet skier with a possible broken back half a mile south of Langstone harbour. The crew was: Captain Peter Thomson, co-pilot Mark Robson, I was the winch-op and Nick Horst was the winchman.

When we arrived on scene, the casualty was lying in the water supported by members of the Portsmouth lifeboat alongside a small speedboat. We immediately lowered Nick to the Portsmouth lifeboat, as we did not want our downdraught causing any further problems. The lifeboat dropped Nick in the water alongside the casualty.

Nick quickly assessed that they would have to attempt immobilising the casualty in the water. Between Nick and the lifeboatmen, all in the water, they managed to put a cervical collar on the casualty, followed by a spinal board that would secure his back and neck. They then floated him onto the aircraft stretcher. Nick was then able to strap the casualty into the stretcher and prepare the lifting strops while the lifeboatmen held the stretcher afloat.

When Nick was ready with the casualty's spine and neck immobilised and firmly strapped in a stretcher, we ran in to recover them from the water to the aircraft for onward transfer to hospital.

This may sound reasonably straightforward but it was actually quite tricky and it was the first time I had seen a spinal immobilisation of a casualty in the water. Nick was good at sorting out the unusual incidents; in this case, it was with the aid of the Portsmouth lifeboat crew. As with all these combined jobs, the lifeboat crews always made our job easier, without them, the casualty would have had to be recovered without full immobilisation.

Margaret

In the May of 1997, I had to face the biggest challenge of my life. It was quite unexpected and a huge shock. This account, although nothing to do with my work, was positively life changing. I mention it because aspects of my job and the people I work with helped get me through this and the change in lifestyle is almost certainly the reason I am writing this memoir.

Margaret and I had gone to bed on Sunday 4th May 1997 with Margaret feeling as though she had started another migraine. She had suffered from migraine attacks from her teenage years, often quite severe.

Early in the morning, it had developed in to a full migraine with sickness. Margaret has so many migraines we considered it to be another attack and she tried to sleep through it. A few hours later however, I heard a crash and found Margaret sat on the end of the bed and everything had been knocked off the dressing table.

She had picked up a miniature picture of our grandson Michael that she was carefully wrapping in a lace doily. It was blatantly obvious that something serious was wrong and that she did not appear to know who I was. I immediately phoned an ambulance, which rushed Margaret to Haslar hospital in Gosport.

As soon as Margaret arrived at hospital, a team of doctors and consultants built up around her. She clearly had cerebral confusion and was fighting off everyone's attempts to help. She had to be put into an induced coma and onto life support prior to being a given a CAT scan, which showed she had a particularly nasty cerebral haemorrhage.

The results of the CAT scan were wired to a consultant at the Wessex Neurological Unit at Southampton. After discussions between consultants at Haslar and Southampton, a doctor came to see me informing that it would be unlikely Margaret would survive because of the extent of the bleed and her conscious level at the time of admittance.

This was the first of many negative responses I was to receive over the next few months. Margaret was now on a ventilator in intensive care and remained stable for the first couple of days. The first attempt to take Margaret off life support failed – the agitation she was showing was increasing the chances of a further bleed. The movements she was making when coming off life support they said were just low-level brain activity.

Our daughter Kerry was virtually living at the hospital with me and sharing all my anguish. We were never given any hopes to cling to, every report or update was pessimistic, it was awful for Kerry seeing her mum like this and I was barely coping, so was very little help to Kerry.

Because of bed shortages at the intensive care unit at Haslar, one of the patients required transferring to another hospital. This was required because during the night, our aircraft at Lee had picked up a casualty with severe carbon monoxide poisoning. Haslar was one of the few hospitals that could treat this casualty as it had a special hyperbaric chamber.

Being in a hyperbaric chamber helps a casualty with carbon monoxide poisoning by allowing the oxygen to be absorbed in the tissue much quicker, helping to stop further damage and speeding the healing process; however, an intensive care bed was required for this casualty between treatments in the chamber.

Margaret, being the only one stabilised on life support was the one chosen to be moved. In effect, a tasking carried out by our helicopter had resulted in my wife having to be moved to another hospital even while on life support.

Fortunately, the move would be to Queen Alexander (QA) intensive care. This was a move I quite welcomed, not that I thought Haslar ITU were not doing their best for Margaret, but because of the flight's association with the unit at QA. At the time, our medical courses were being run with the help of a few intensive care anaesthetists from the hospital, so I felt it would be easier to ask questions.

Indeed the first face I saw on arrival at QA was Bruce Taylor, the anaesthetist who had taken the flight under his wing with our extended medical training. Gary Smith, the consultant anaesthetist who had formulated our medical training course was the head of the intensive care unit; he came along to see me shortly after our arrival.

Although the prognosis was not good, being at QA intensive care made me feel more secure. On the fifth night, we were told that the signs and symptoms including the pressures in the skull showed no signs of improvement and were gradually deteriorating. The stabilizing drugs were no longer having any effect and they expected Margaret to pass away overnight. Family and friends came down as we prepared ourselves for the worst.

This was to be our longest night, an absolute nightmare, listening to the ventilator and watching the pressures fluctuating. I was aware of the parameters of the various readings on the monitors and had to watch as they approached the upper limits then dropped back only to go up again later; however, I am sure that Margaret's will and all the prayers and hopes from friends and family helped to pull her through the night.

The next day the consultant decided to try again to take Margaret off the ventilator. If she did wake up, they would make her as comfortable as possible, but still expected her to pass away.

We were at that stage given one shred of hope to cling to when I was advised by one of the consultants, (who would later become part of the team instructing our extended skills courses) that there was a slight chance of the swelling being reduced by large doses of steroids. This was a treatment used a few years earlier in brain injuries, but later it was decided to be of little benefit so no longer used as a standard treatment. However, in Margaret's case he felt it was worth trying.

I was also warned that, if she was to pull through, she would be very disabled with little (if any) standard of living. I could not let go and felt that if Margaret could get home one day, even if bed bound, providing she regained awareness of her surroundings we could make her comfortable and she would be able to watch and enjoy her grandchildren growing up. Kerry was in full support, so we asked them to go ahead and prayed that we would not make things worse for Margaret by prolonging life, with the possibility of her being in a vegetative state.

When they weaned Margaret off the ventilator, she did breathe for herself but there were no other signs; she was not responding to any stimuli. Later a doctor took Kerry and I aside to tell us nothing had changed; the brain activity was still low, the pressures were still fluctuating and he advised us that it would be kinder to let Margaret go.

We were expecting that, as all the vibes had been negative and all the tests and results had been pointing that way, but I was in denial. Talking it over with Kerry and the family, we decided we should not allow Margaret to suffer. They had decided to administer diamorphine by an automatic pump to assist with pain control, as it was not sure if she would feel pain. Pneumonia had already set in and it was now expected Margaret would drift off slowly but comfortably, with no further treatment given.

Kerry and I discussed a wish Margaret had always expressed and that was to donate her organs. We conveyed that wish to a doctor who explained in these circumstances that may not be possible; nevertheless, she went off to check the possibility. All I could do now was give considerable thought to positive thinking, still not able to take in that this was happening. I guess this to be a normal response for the majority of people facing a situation like this.

Shortly after they had started the diamorphine pump, Margaret's brother Terry, who lives in London, came in for his second visit that day. In between these visits, he had been to see Margaret's dad who was in a rest home. Terry being extremely busy at work had not visited his dad for a while, something Margaret had been trying to get him to do for some time.

Anyway, Terry was in the room with Kerry me and other family visitors, having our last moments with Margaret. We were talking about Terry's visit to dad, when Margaret's eyes suddenly opened wide. She immediately looked round, directly at Terry just staring in to his eyes, a really magic moment that stunned us all. The nurse dashed out to get a doctor who asked us all to leave while they did another assessment.

After a short time, which felt like hours, a consultant called us back to say that there was some improvement. He warned us not to expect too much, but they would continue assessments over the next few hours.

This was the moment that I knew Margaret was going to recover and no one was going to tell me differently. The diamorphine pump was stopped, as that would mask any further signs of recovery. Indeed, had she been on it a few hours longer, it is very unlikely that she would have opened her eyes at all and we would never have known there was a chance.

At this stage, we had discussions with the consultants about the possibility of an operation, not to make Margaret better but to prevent a further bleed that would obviously be catastrophic. However, Margaret was so low down the coma scale that the neurological surgeons at Southampton did not consider it safe for her to have the operation.

By now, I was having other responses from Margaret: simple things like she would stroke my hair and I felt sure she knew who I was. I was adamant that Margaret would pull through and wanted anything that could prevent a further bleed to be attempted, making this clear at every opportunity.

One of the things which had kept Margaret low on the coma scale, was the fact that she had made no attempt to speak since coming off the ventilator and would not respond to any verbal commands. Eventually, the consultant who suggested trying the steroids, argued the case for Margaret, saying that it was quite possible the speech mechanism of the brain was damaged; the same area of the bleed may also affect quite a few thought and understanding functions.

After discussions with Kerry and me, he managed to convince the neurological unit at Southampton to go ahead with an angiogram, to see whether the operation would be possible.

Margaret was transferred to the Wessex Neurological Unit at Southampton on the 15th May. The angiogram showed a large aneurism. This had caused the first bleed and it was very likely to bleed again but fortunately, it was in a position where they would be able to reach and clip. They confirmed that, if they could get Margaret clinically strong enough to take the operation, they would go ahead.

Unfortunately, the move to Southampton put Margaret back a step. Just prior to the move it was becoming clear she knew who we were, but now she was back to how she was when she first showed signs of waking up, just opening her eyes occasionally and looking around.

The next two weeks were to be a continuation of the nightmare so far. Margaret was in the Neurological Unit at Southampton, being looked after in a high dependency unit in the hope the pressures would reduce enough to carry out this operation. During that time we knew that she would be sent back to QA hospital in Portsmouth if there was not any improvement over that period.

There was a serious likelihood of that happening anyway because of severe bed shortages in the unit. I did not want her moved again as the move to Southampton had put her back considerably. During this period, Margaret was very distressed, even though she had no movement on the right hand side she was continuously trying to turn from side to side, making it a continuous battle to keep her lines and oxygen connected.

On the third day at Southampton, the surgeon on one of his visits told me it was very likely that Margaret would remain as she was at the time of his visit, just opening her eyes occasionally, with no real comprehension of anything. Before I could ask any questions he was called away, leaving me devastated. I would be knocked back every time I allowed myself hope.

When I saw him again, I questioned his view and he explained that by this stage, it would have been expected to get some normal type responses, Margaret still couldn't respond to any instructions nor show any signs of awareness, even her response to stimuli wasn't as expected. I counter argued that things were happening and that she was responding to me, but this never happened when a consultant or doctor was around. He then said, "If that was true then there was hope," but I felt he thought I was imagining things.

A few days later, I was having one of what I considered the magic moments with Margaret. I was sure she was responding to me and she was stroking my hair, when I noticed the surgeon standing behind me. He had been watching us for a while and agreed that Margaret was more alert than he had thought. He assured me that they would keep Margaret at Southampton until she was able to undergo the operation.

Eventually the surgeon decided that Margaret was well enough to have the operation and we even managed to get some signs from Margaret that she understood what was happening, by blinking twice for Yes and once for No.

That consultation was another story in itself, it was also the first time we were sure that Margaret knew who Kerry was. We had tried this Yes & No technique many times but had never been sure if she really understood us. Until then, the only person she had been responding to was me, this was on the Sunday and she had the operation on the Monday 2nd June.

Kerry and I waited in the rest room for the eight hours Margaret was in theatre, both of us going through yet another nightmarish session waiting for the all clear; we could hardly believe it when they told us that they had been successful. We knew this was not a cure but at least knew there would be no more bleeds.

On the 10th June, it was considered Margaret was well enough for transfer back to QA in Portsmouth to start rehabilitation.

This was another stage I was not happy with as she was put in a medical ward, not a rehabilitation ward and very little was done for her. Not that I am saying she was neglected because the nurses were wonderful, but they were definitely short-staffed and doing the very best they could, but it was a medical ward not a rehabilitation ward and I was expecting much more.

Eventually I ended up looking after her during the day: washing, toilet etc, because I could not take all the delays when things needed doing. Very little physiotherapy was carried out; they would come in, decide Margaret was not responsive and leave. There was one physiotherapist who gave me hope but she then went on holiday.

On the fifth day a consultant with his entourage came in, spent ten minutes with Margaret, asked her to poke her tongue out and touch her nose, Margaret did not do either. He then took me aside and more or less told me I was setting my hopes too high and that the likely outcome was that Margaret would not get well enough to go home and that, if she did get home she would need so much care that it would be very difficult,

246

particularly if I intended to continue working. I was being encouraged to look for a nursing home for her.

I was now getting so much response from Margaret that I simply refused to believe what he was saying. I had listened to so many negative views from people over the weeks that I was losing faith in the various consultants' decisions and was considering most of them to be born pessimists. A few days later Margaret said her first word "Yes." Shortly after that, they were able to take out her feeding tube. Another few days later, they removed her catheter and she was managing to cope with that. She was also able to sit in a chair for a few minutes.

By now, I was pushing hard to get Margaret to a proper rehabilitation unit. Eventually a young doctor stuck his neck out, suggesting that a rehabilitation specialist from another hospital was bought in to assess Margaret, as no one at Q.A. seemed able to make the decision.

The specialist arrived later in the week; he was from St Mary's hospital in Portsmouth and was a rehab specialist. I was worried that he would be pessimistic like the rest and decide that Margaret would not be suitable to go to a proper rehabilitation unit.

When the specialist arrived, he breezed in like a breath of fresh air. Margaret was in one of her more alert stages, still only responding to me but the consultant could see it was a proper interaction and said the sooner Margaret went to a rehabilitation unit the better. In addition, I was able to persuade him to approve that she came home with me until a place was found (thanks to the help of a nurse who spoke up on my behalf). He agreed that providing I could get enough help, she would do better at home than in a medical ward, so arrangements were made for me to take Margaret home.

There was quite a delay getting Margaret home. The social services had to be involved regarding the suitability of the house and arranging home help, the delays continued and scheduled meetings cancelled. In the meantime, nothing was being done with Margaret, so I decided to take her home anyway, obviously against the hospital's advice but I had lost faith in the system.

Terry Short and Nick Horst came round to help me convert a room downstairs into a bedroom. I borrowed a wheelchair and other aids I felt I might need from the Red Cross centre and brought Margaret home in the afternoon. I had arguments with the hospital staff, who I felt were trying to delay me taking Margaret home. I said we were going and they had no choice but to accept that.

My mother stayed with us to help, she had looked after my stepfather for ten years after he had a stroke and had encouraged me to get Margaret home as she thought the time in hospital was not helping Margaret, especially as she was receiving very little physiotherapy. My mother was and continues to be a tower of strength.

The first few days proved very difficult. Margaret needed constant care and I was too stubborn to go for outside help. I simply did not want any more dealings with doctors and felt sure they would arrange to send Margaret back to hospital.

My mother eventually got the district nurse involved when we were promised all sorts of help that never materialised. If I wanted things to happen I would have to go and bang tables but I did not want to do that as I had accepted in my own mind that perhaps I had been silly bringing Margaret home early, so felt it was my responsibility and was willing to continue on my own.

I felt sure I would never get back to work again so was accepting this was my future. After those initial few days at home, Margaret started responding in a big way, taking an interest in her surroundings and improving on a daily basis. She was sitting up in a chair for longer periods, directing us by pointing at areas that had not been dusted or cleaned properly, fussing over ornaments being in the wrong place etc. These were the sort of things Margaret always fussed over but to me it was like a miracle because I knew I was getting Margaret back.

Later the next week we were informed that Donald Wilson House, the rehabilitation unit would take Margaret for a week's assessment on the following Monday. At this stage, Margaret was becoming aware of what was happening and did not want to go. In addition, I was beginning to feel we could do more with her at home; the improvements since coming home were so great.

However, I also felt she must go if there was a chance of any serious rehabilitation. For that reason, we turned up at Chichester feeling rather apprehensive and with considerable doubts that this would be right for Margaret. I felt it would be another round of people telling me that I am expecting too much.

Once settled into Donald Wilson house, I began to feel at ease with the situation and Margaret was getting the sort of rehabilitation I had been hoping for from the day she left Southampton: it was apparent that, if anything, she should have gone there earlier.

The staff even admitted that Margaret had been let down badly by the NHS; ideally she should have gone there from the moment she started to show signs of awareness. The normal procedure for someone Margaret's age would have been several weeks in a proper rehab unit, followed by weekend trials at home once the rehab unit thought she was ready and after alterations had been made to the home to meet Margaret's needs.

Margaret went on to spend several weeks at Donald Wilson, receiving physiotherapy, occupational and speech therapy backed up with considerable TLC from all the staff.

During the time that Margaret was in hospital I was losing control of the Meniere's and getting quite regular attacks, the first of which was only a few weeks after Margaret was taken into hospital and continued once or twice a week. Each attack would last a couple of hours when I could not do anything followed by a few hours getting over them.

These attacks had, almost certainly, been induced by the stress I was experiencing at the time. After a few more weeks of the attacks getting worse, I contacted Dr West's secretary explaining what was happening and that I was in the hospital with Margaret the majority of the time. I just hoped that I might be able to have a short notice appointment with him.

I was very fortunate, managing to get an appointment the next day. He could see that the attacks had become a major problem to me; not only was it likely I would have to give up my job if they continued like this but that I would also have difficulties looking after Margaret.

At the stage when I saw Dr West, I couldn't see any further than looking after Margaret, accepting if I ever managed to get Margaret home she would need full time care, so I felt quite sure I wouldn't get back to work.

The appointment with Dr West was only days after I had the awful discussion with Margaret's medical team when they had said that it was unlikely she would be able to be cared for at home.

Dr West had been looking at a relatively new treatment for Meniere's disease; it was not a cure but would, if successful, take away the spinning attacks and sickness. The treatment was to destroy the balance mechanism in the affected ear by perfusion of the antibiotic gentamicin through a small incision in the eardrum to the inner ear.

This was not as drastic as it sounded as our balance relies on other factors as well as the balance mechanism in our ears. The brain still provides spatial awareness and balance by processing all the sensory information from the undamaged ear, the eyes, position of joints and sensors in the feet, this is called proprioception, so to take away the balance from one ear is not a major problem.

I met all the criteria to have this operation. Furthermore, there was a surgeon in the hospital who had recently started to carry out the procedure, it all sounded too good to be true. Dr West arranged an appointment with the surgeon within days; he was able to do that because I was in the hospital all day anyway.

I had my appointment with Mr Pringle, the surgeon, who agreed I was suitable for the treatment, which would be carried out in day surgery once a week for four weeks. He explained the possible effects after each treatment, I would find it strange on the balance side for a while and that there were no guarantees that it would work. The cases he had done so far had a high success rate in the short term, the long term was not yet known.

I jumped at the chance and was fortunate enough a few weeks later to be offered a cancellation, commencing my treatment in September. By then, I was happy that Margaret was being looked after at Donald Wilson rehab unit so was very happy to take that cancellation.

The first operation was in mid September and I had further ops on a weekly basis for four weeks. The procedure only required me being in the ward for the morning and in theatre for just ten minutes, followed by an hour's rest on a bed lying in a set position, then a few balance tests. I was extremely lucky as, by the second op, the attacks stopped altogether and it really did not take me long getting used to the balance side of things.

The worst time would be in the dark, when the visual senses were taken away, but I could still cope, it just required extra effort and, in time, I was noticing little difference. Another problem in the first few weeks was that I felt disorientated if I turned suddenly. I used to do that regularly as an exercise and quickly had that under control.

In October, I had the last of the series of four operations. Travelling to see Margaret afterwards was quite uncomfortable so I had arranged for Margaret to be at home on the day of the last operation. This day proved to be a big turning point for Margaret.

The plan was for my daughter Kerry to pick me up when the hospital phoned because I was not allowed to drive for 24 hours. However, shortly after I had left home to go to the day surgery at Q.A. Hospital, Margaret made it clear to Kerry that she did not want to wait until the phone call and virtually insisted they went over to wait.

When eventually allowed to go home, I asked the nurse if they had phoned my daughter and the nurse informed me my daughter had been here all morning with a lady in a wheelchair. Kerry then walked into the ward pushing Margaret in the wheelchair with our granddaughter Jessica on Margaret's lap. Kerry was clearly enjoying having some time on her own with her mum, Margaret was smiling away looking a million dollars and Jessica was grinning at me. It was all I could do to stop the tears from flowing; we really had come a long way since the 5th May.

The next day I took Margaret back to Chichester in the morning, spending the rest of the day with her. When I went in on Wednesday, it was to find Margaret rather agitated and gesturing for me to take her. I thought she meant to the toilet but, as I passed her room, she jammed the brake on the wheelchair and I saw that her bag was packed.

It turned out Margaret had decided she had been there long enough and had managed to get the cleaner to get her bag down from the top of her wardrobe and had immediately started to pack the bag. The cleaner went off to tell the staff sister what was happening and the occupational therapist, a lovely lady, took Margaret off to the café at the main hospital in an attempt to calm her down.

Margaret stuck by her guns and was adamant that she was going home – a difficult thing to portray when you cannot talk! Consequently, the unit had a meeting with the team responsible for looking after Margaret and decided that if she was showing so much determination then perhaps the time was right. That night we went home together, both of us like all our Christmases had come at once.

Once home, Margaret continued to improve in leaps and bounds. She still received plenty of Physiotherapy and Occupational Therapy from a wonderful team at Haslar Hospital until they decided she had reached her potential.

We have had many more happy moments like the day she met me at QA Hospital. Probably the icing on the cake for both of us was the visit to her surgeon on the 2nd of December. The Surgeon, Mr Brooks, was visibly surprised to see Margaret so well and once he realized Margaret understood everything he was saying, told her that he would not normally have operated on someone presented to him in her condition, but expressed that he would have to revaluate patients presented like Margaret in the future.

Margaret would not make it any plainer that she thought that was a good idea, with a loud 'YES' she slapped her thigh, moved the foot rests on her wheelchair and stood up! She demonstrated in the best way she could, that it had all been extremely worthwhile and that more people should be given the chance.

Margaret would go on to walk indoors and be a wonderful grandmother. The talking would not return, other than a few basic words, but she has no difficulty in getting a message across. To say she would never have a reasonable standard of living couldn't be further from the truth and I'm sure many of the people who suggested those things would feel terrible if they saw what she has achieved.

Margaret still cannot poke her tongue out or touch her nose on a verbal instruction, although she can do both if mimicked. This is something we now find quite amusing, especially as she can now do so many other things, yet this inability to respond to verbal commands in hospital was stopping them recommending rehabilitation, a decision that was clearly wrong. I was assured that the failures in Margaret's care would be looked at and, hopefully, lessons learned. The various things that Margaret has learnt have been taught by repeated demonstration and Margaret's personal determination.

Getting Back To Work

During the first couple of months of this quite traumatic experience, I withdrew into myself, my only concern being Margaret. I could not think about anything else and found it very difficult talking to people: they may have been wishing to pass on their best wishes etc, but in my mind, if I was spending time on a phone or talking to someone in person, then I wasn't looking after Margaret's concerns. Quite irrational, but that is how I was. Other members of the family had to take the messages.

I had managed to explain this to Terry who would ring Kerry or my mother daily and keep the flight informed as to what was happening, requesting no one rang me at hospital. I was very rarely at home, so my mother or Kerry would take most of the messages from other people and from Margaret's colleagues, plus we had many letters and cards.

When I told Terry that I could not really see a way of getting back to work, he urged me to wait a little longer before making that decision. My position at work was being filled by Billy Deacon, Tudor Davies & Mike Langford, taking it in turns on loan from Aberdeen, so the company was keeping my job available and I knew between Pete Thomson and Terry, they would fight to keep it open as long as possible.

I also had to accept reality; if I left work, it would be a complete life style change. I would have to move house, as I would be living on benefits and a small pension so would not be able to afford my mortgage nor the upkeep of the house I was in. I also knew that I would miss the job and the flight who were like a family in themselves. I simply could not see any other way.

When Terry felt it was right, he suggested I try fitting in the odd shift, to see how that would work. My mother felt I should try and she would look after Margaret while I was at work. Kerry and my sister-in-law Lynne (who was a nurse) would help when my mother was not available. I started those tentative steps, worried sick that something may go wrong at home.

My return to work was quite straightforward. I had to carry out a few check flights before going back into crews. The first few shifts went well and the lads worked their shifts around my requirements for Margaret's physio and hospital appointments.

Absolutely everybody was bending over backwards to help me back to work, it felt like I had never been away. The lads carried on as normal only bringing up my situation when I did, which was exactly the way I wanted it.

My mother moved in with us while she sold her house in Bolton: she had decided she would move down south, eventually buying a flat close by. This was something she had been thinking of doing anyway because my brother also lived on the south coast in Bournemouth.

This was quite some commitment on my mother's part, as prior to this she would spend the majority of the winters in Spain. She got on very well with Margaret and really thought I should get back to work. Margaret was happy with the situation; she felt my mother to be a friend and companion and had complete trust in her when I was out. I am quite sure that if it had not been for my mother, I would not have stood any chance of getting back to work.

After a couple of months, I was back at work full time, just requiring the odd swap to meet appointments. Eventually, I was able to arrange the physio and appointments around my shift patterns.

Fortunately, our work routine and shift system made it easy to juggle our requirements around. My mother moved into her new apartment about six months after Margaret came home, but would still stay at our house whenever I was on shift and Kerry would help as required.

Bristow Helicopters had, just prior to my returning, been given another five year contract. I could not see that far ahead and was still struggling with what my future would hold. It would take time to see if I would be able to cope with work and my situation at home; however, it was great news and I was pleased for everyone on the unit.

One job that was going to stretch our decision-making was towards the end of the year. It was to the report of a person over the cliff at Ventnor on the Isle of Wight, at night and the wind not in a favourable direction.

The crew that night was: Captain Rob Flexman, co-pilot Simon Hornsby, I was the winch-op and Dave Brown was the winchman. Dave (Bomber) was the diver who had helped John Spencer with the rescue of the man in the capsized barge all those years ago and the Chief Aircrewman I had taken over from on my last tour in the Navy.

Dave had been a SAR aircrewman on the offshore contract in the North Sea, working from the Brent platform. He had recently retired when he reached the company's normal retirement age for SAR Crew. However, he was still exceptionally fit, (Dave was an ex naval field gunner so fitness had remained extremely important to him). Because of this fitness and his SAR experience, the company had asked him to stay on as a contractor filling in as winchman for the Coastguard units.

When we arrived on scene, cliff teams had already been lowered to the bottom of the cliff and were still looking for the casualty. We were tasked to help search with our lights and the infrared camera. When the search parties located the casualty amongst trees in a wooded area close to the base of the cliff, they reported that our assistance would be required.

We immediately had a number of problems; we could not see the casualty as it was a wooded area at the base of the cliff and all we could see with our floodlights was the canopy of the treetops. In addition, because of the wind direction, the aircraft would have to hover with the left side towards the cliff. This would mean the aircraft being flown by the co-pilot.

The co-pilot, Simon Hornsby, was on his second tour at Lee-on-Solent and a pilot destined to be a SAR captain. It was not going to be an easy job and would require very precise flying. We could have tried to find somewhere to land and for the pilots to swap round, but we all agreed that we were happy for Simon to carry out the task.

The next problem was that we could not winch Dave down through the canopy of the trees so he opted to be winched to the cliff top and then lowered down the side of the cliff by the cliff team. This way he could assess the situation and see if there was any way that we would be able to recover the casualty to the aircraft.

Dave soon disappeared out of sight then shortly afterwards called for the stretcher, which was sent to him via the cliff team, his radio had failed so his messages were being relayed through a Coastguard. Dave had located a small clearing in the canopy and felt he could move the casualty, once in the stretcher to that winching position.

We asked for one of the cliff team to mark the clear area by flashing a torch from the clearing so that we could hover over the position. This would be a practice run, to see whether Simon would be able to maintain enough visual references to hold a hover and for me to check if there was enough clearance for Dave and the stretcher. After the dummy run, we decided it would be possible and Simon was confident he had enough visual references to remain in position.

When we received the call that Dave was ready, I lowered the hook through the canopy to the torchlight while Simon kept a steady hover. I had to rely on the Coastguard to tell me when Dave had hooked on then started to winch in.

Dave and the casualty were on the end of the wire, 250ft below the aircraft and I had completely lost sight of them. I thought the aircraft had moved so I stopped winching for a moment and checked with the ground crew as to whether Dave was clear of the canopy. They assured me he was almost clear so I continued winching in and it was with considerable relief that I saw them come clear of the trees and firmly into the beam of the aircrafts lights.

The casualty was transferred to St Mary's hospital on the Island. Later we were re-tasked to take the casualty plus a medical team to the John Radcliff hospital in Oxford.

Another task that November was to the container vessel 'Rosa M', whose crew were abandoning the ship after the cargo had shifted. This was threatening to capsize the vessel fifteen miles northeast of Cherbourg. The tasking was in French waters and a French helicopter plus lifeboats were proceeding. Our aircraft had been tasked to back up the much smaller French helicopter. The crew was: Captain Graham Sorge, co-pilot Simon Hornsby, winch-op Chris Bond and Dave Brown was the winchman.

When 'Rescue India Juliet' arrived on scene, 'Rescue Bravo Xray' (the French helicopter) was winching five survivors from a life raft. A quick visual search located two empty life rafts plus a ship's lifeboat with a large number of crew onboard. The MV 'Meleri', who was assisting in the search, went alongside the open lifeboat and commenced transferring the survivors.

Dave was also lowered to the lifeboat to gain further information as to how many people had been on the 'Rosa M', soon establishing that there were thirty-two crewmembers onboard. Twenty-seven were in the lifeboat and five had been recovered from the life raft, so all crew were accounted for. Three of the crew were unable to climb the ladder onto the 'Meleri' so were winched to the aircraft. 'R-IJ' was then tasked to standby while a small crew plus the captain of the 'Rosa M' attempted to return to their vessel to assist with salvage.

'R-IJ' was relieved from this task by a salvage vessel and further tasked to recover seventeen of the rescued crewmembers from the MV 'Meleri' making a total twenty survivors on board who were all flown to Cherbourg where they were handed over to the French authorities.

Bill Deacon

Early in the afternoon the 9th Nov 1997, I had a telephone call from Terry. He was ringing round before we saw or heard the news, which would be reporting a winchman was missing after being washed overboard during a rescue by our Sumburgh aircraft. Terry had rung me straight away; the missing aircrewman was Bill Deacon.

Bill had been in Sumburgh as the relief aircrewman, the same role as he carried out at Stornoway, Portland and on our base, as and when required. Bill had covered many shifts for me when Margaret had been in hospital and was a good friend of both Terry and myself from our Navy days.

Bill was rescuing the remaining ten survivors from a vessel in heavy seas close to shore in the Shetlands. Shortly after he sent the last two survivors up to the aircraft, a huge wave washed Bill over the side of the vessel. At the time I received the phone call, he was still missing. It was an awful time in which we could only wait for news and reflect on what Bill's wife Lorna, son Alan and daughter Emma would be going through.

Everyone was trying to get information but there was not too much coming out of Sumburgh at the time. They were swamped by the media, something they could have done without at that tragic time, especially as the search was still going on. We mainly had to rely on news reports.

As the story unfolded, it was clear that Bill had carried out an exceptional rescue in the most horrendous conditions. He had succeeded in saving the lives of the ten crewmembers, who he had prepared and sent up to the aircraft from the stricken freighter the 'Green Lily' which had suffered engine failure off Bressay (one of the Shetland Isles).

The Bahamian registered freighter 'Green Lily' with fifteen crew onboard was approximately 14 miles southeast of Bressay in storm force winds when at 0644, the 'Green Lily' reported they had main engine failure. The problem was not declared as a full emergency until some two hours later, when it was clear they were drifting towards the rocks at Bressay. The first tug on scene managed to attach a tow but, unfortunately, that tow parted when they got underway.

When the tow parted, the Coastguard helicopter was scrambled from Sumburgh. The crew was: Captain Norman Leask, co-pilot David Gribben, winch-op Paul Mansell and Bill Deacon was the winchman. Bill was dual trained, but it was his turn to be winchman that day. Lerwick lifeboat was also proceeding and both were tasked to standby to evacuate non-essential crew.

When 'Rescue LC' arrived on scene, the 'Green Lily' was lying with her starboard beam to the sea and swell. After attempting evacuation of non-essential crew, it was established that the winching area was not suitable in the heaving sea so the first attempt was aborted.

The tug was still attempting to establish a tow, so the crew decided that it would be safer to wait until the tow was established; the tug would then be able to pull the ship's head into wind. A safer winching position could then be assessed prior to evacuation. Unfortunately, the second tow broke leaving the vessel drifting even closer to the rocks.

'Green Lily' was now dangerously close to the shore and was told to drop its anchors, both anchors were dropped and the starboard anchor held with the effect of pulling the head closer to the wind. Shortly after this, the lifeboat coxswain felt he had an opportunity to move in on the lee side of 'Green Lily' and commence evacuation. The lifeboat then approached the vessel and, in extremely difficult conditions, managed to recover five crewmembers before having to pull away as they ran out of sea room.

One of the tugs managed to manoeuvre itself close enough to the 'Green Lily' to snag one of the deployed anchor cables making it possible to pull the head further into wind giving 'Rescue LC' the opportunity to move in to attempt recovering the remaining ten casualties.

The crew would have known the hazards they faced, the anchor was holding but the freighter was pitching dangerously close to the rocks. I am sure Bill would not have hesitated at making the attempt; he would have known that 'R-LC' was the only hope for these people.

They managed to winch Bill onboard and he immediately started the evacuation. At some stage during the winching the anchor cable separated. The ship was now drifting towards the rocks making it increasingly more difficult for the aircraft and with the sea sweeping over the deck even more difficult for Bill. Shortly after he sent the last two survivors to the aircraft, a giant storm driven wave forced the 'Green Lily' onto the rocks.

While returning the winch hook to Bill, the hi-line snagged on the superstructure. The snagged hi-line was now threatening the safety of the aircraft as the vessel tossed around on the rocks. At the same time, a huge wave swept Bill overboard. In the subsequent actions to prevent the aircraft from being pulled into the 'Green Lily', the winch wire was damaged making the winch unserviceable. It was subsequently noticed that a bite of the hi-line had snagged on the winch hook preventing the weak link from working.

The search for Bill was continued by the second aircraft based on the Shetlands, backed up by an RAF helicopter. Bill was wearing full survival clothing and lifejacket so we could not give up hope, but we knew that in those conditions, the longer the search went on the more our hopes would dwindle.

Bill's body was located at the bottom of the cliffs the following afternoon and recovered by the RAF helicopter.

Terry and I, Tony Campbell from Portland (who was another very good friend of Bill) along with colleagues from Sumburgh, Aberdeen and Stornoway were able to join Bill's family and friends at the funeral in his hometown, Ellon, near Aberdeen.

Many moving tributes to Bill were made, including a tribute from Kieran Murray an aircrewman from Sumburgh and a close friend who summed up Bill perfectly as we, the aircrewmen, knew him. Kieran also read out a tribute from Prince Charles sent to Lorna and family which read:

"I was so desperately sorry to hear the tragic news about your husband and wanted to send my heartfelt sympathy.

"As Honorary Commodore of Her Majesty's Coastguard, I am only too well aware of the commitments and the dedication shown by those who maintain a constant watch of our coasts.

"I have been profoundly impressed by Mr Deacon's heroic efforts to save the crew, regardless of his own safety, in the best traditions of the Coastguard service.

"My thoughts and prayers are with you at such a sad time for you and your family."

That tribute from Prince Charles would have embarrassed Bill; however, I felt it was a wonderful tribute and I am sure would be treasured by Lorna, Alan and Emma.

Alan Deacon, Bill's son who was 24 and a serving Petty Officer Artificer in the Royal Navy, gave a personal tribute to his father saying:

"My Father would have been surprised by all this attention. He did not believe in all this 'hero crap', as he would call it. Ever since I was young he has been a hero to me, it did not need him to die to prove that. I am only in this uniform because of him. I only hope I can be half the man he was. He did not deserve for this to happen to him, he was too busy trying to prevent this happening to others."

The story that summed up Billy in my mind and mentioned in Kieran Murray's tribute was nothing to do with work or rescues, but a report from the secretary of the McDonald golf club, where Bill was a keen member. He had been a friend of Bill's for thirteen years but was totally unaware that Bill was a Search and Rescue aircrewman; he knew Bill worked in helicopters but that was all.

Only months before this happened Bill had won a prestigious award, when he was crewed with Tony Campbell while standing in at Portland. The award was for a rescue carried out recovering a casualty from a rather awkward cliff incident.

I would very much doubt that many people in Bill's hometown, other than his family, would have been aware of that award; he would have shunned publicity on that when back home.

I can fully believe he would enjoy his rounds of golf with friends, only mentioning he worked with helicopters but not expanding on what his actual job was and I can imagine him telling his son "he doesn't believe in all this hero crap!" That was Bill.

Bill went on to receive posthumous awards for the 'Green Lily' rescue including the George medal.

In memory of Bill and his ultimate sacrifice on the 'Green Lily' rescue, an annual award has been set up, sponsored by Bristow Helicopters and Breitling UK. The 'Billy Deacon SAR Memorial Trophy' is awarded to the Winchmen/Winch Operators from the Coastguard, Royal Air Force and Royal Navy for meritorious service during SAR helicopter operations from UK SAR bases. The award is presented annually at the Air League's Annual Award Ceremony at St James Palace, London.

Many tributes would be made to Bill over the years and it was nice to see that even six years after the incident the incredible sacrifice was still being remembered when the Coastguards named a new state of the art training simulator after Billy Deacon in honour of his bravery.

The building, built at the Coastguard training centre at Highcliffe in Dorset incorporates the latest digital communications, command and control technology. Designed to help Coastguards learn and practice the skills of Communications and Search and Rescue co-ordination. The simulator will go on to host students from all over the world. The Chief Executive said when opening the building, "that it would serve as further recognition of Bill's work and life. It will also serve to remind students of the importance of the skills they will learn when they come here."

Another tribute that I thought was special, as it will remain indefinitely, was a stone Cairn built by the people of Bressay to commemorate Billy's bravery. The Cairn was built at Grutwick on Bressay close to the Green Lily incident.

1997 Continued

In December, seven crewmembers were rescued from a coal-carrying coaster 'Paulina B' after a cargo explosion. One burns casualty was recovered to the aircraft followed by multi lifts of the remaining six crewmembers. They were flown to Haslar hospital.

On Christmas day, 'R-IJ' was scrambled to search for a missing French fishing vessel with five persons onboard off Milford Haven. The crew was: Captain Rob Flexman, co-pilot Mark Robson, winch-op John Spencer and the winchman Don Sowden. Dave Savage had also gone along; an engineer may well be required as the tasking was way out of our area and Dave would also act as an extra pair of eyes during the search.

The RAF Sea King based at RAF Chivenor had been involved in this search for some time, so 'R-IJ' was relieving them on scene. The initial search was carried out with nothing untoward sighted. On completion 'R-IJ' returned to Chivenor for fuel, then was re-tasked to a second search when some wreckage was sighted by one of the surface search boats. This wreckage included an emergency beacon that had unfortunately not operated. There was no sign of any survivors.

A further search commenced as per the Coastguard's instructions, the search being planned around weather and tidal information in the area and based on the sighted wreckage. 'R-IJ' continued the search until relieved from task by Chivenor SAR flight. 'R-IJ' then refuelled at Chivenor prior to returning to Lee-on-Solent after 8 hours and 55 minutes flying time.

Christmas dinner or festivities would no longer have been on their minds, having been involved in a very long search and finding only wreckage, which would have left them only with thoughts of those missing fishermen on their minds.

1998

By the start of the New Year, I was settling into being back at work full time. I had managed to arrange for Margaret's physio and medical appointments to be during my off shift times.

This was very important to Margaret as she did not feel comfortable going to these appointments with anyone else. We had, between us, developed ways of coping with the situations we faced, simple things like transfer methods from wheelchair to car, which was quite awkward for Margaret when someone else tried to do it.

Not being able to speak was the most difficult thing for her. Everyone we saw would be asking her questions, which of course she couldn't answer, but even worse her Yes and No's would be confused. Often if a question like "does it hurt if I press here?" Margaret's reply would be something like "well yes err no." She actually knew she was doing this but could not do anything about it.

I was obviously learning to understand what she actually meant and we could even laugh about these things; nevertheless, it was understandable that she would want me with her whenever she had to meet or see anyone else.

One of the funny things was that, being ex forces, I had many daft sayings picked up over the years. When I first met Margaret I had plagiarised a phrase used by one of my mates, Lou Armstrong, and introduced myself as "Dave Peel all round good egg" – stupid as it was, Margaret had found it amusing. After we did get together, last thing at night she would say "Good night Dave Peel all round good egg." Now she could not say my name without adding the "all round good egg," even if she was trying to say her own name it just went automatically when she said the word 'Peel'. This was clearly embarrassing for her but all we could do is laugh and try to explain. Other word association things would be said in response to key words and it would invariably be some silly thing I used to say.

I never had any problem looking after Margaret. It soon became a way of life and in time we would both get used to the changes and find ways round problems with the support of my mother and Kerry. We did not seek any outside help as Margaret felt insecure if anyone she did not know tried to help, no matter how nice or friendly they may be. To be quite honest I did not like strangers in the house either.

The only thing I found very difficult was all the shopping, washing, cooking and housework; it all seemed never ending. I was now finding out how little I used to do in helping towards running the household, too occupied in DIY and leisure activities, all of which had now become meaningless as priorities changed.

My mother would have done many of the household things and even prepare meals etc. Nevertheless, I felt quite strongly about that. I felt she was doing so much for us as it was, so strived to keep any further jobs from her and I would always have everything in order for when she came round to look after Margaret.

It would all eventually become a way of life, just different to how it used to be. At the time of writing Margaret is still here and I am still in a job I enjoy very much, working with colleagues I enjoy being with and who do not pussy foot around me. After going through the roller coaster of events over the previous nine months, reaching real despair at times, it all now seems unreal and has in fact left me feeling very lucky to get to this point as it could have been so different.

In the February of 1998, we were scrambled to the fishing vessel 'Emma Jane' 26 miles south of the Isle of Wight. The crew was: Captain Rob Flexman, co-pilot Steve Buckland, I was winch-op and Don Sowden was the winchman, Dave Savage the engineer on shift, had also decided to come along.

The fishing vessel had a crewmember with an allergy problem causing his throat to swell. The transfer of the casualty to the aircraft was straightforward with Don recovering him to the aircraft using the hypothermic lift. The only thing we could do for this casualty (at the time) was provide oxygen and reassurance, the important thing was to get him to hospital as quickly as possible.

Unfortunately, fog had started to roll in as we approached the mainland. We did manage to get into Haslar hospital landing site, carrying out a well-practiced poor visibility approach using all the aids in the aircraft. The casualty was transferred to ambulance and we took off to make the short hop back to the airfield, thinking that the poor visibility approach to the airfield would be easier than it was into Haslar.

However, the fog suddenly thickened, severely reducing our visibility so the first approach to Lee failed. This was going to cause quite a problem as we were reaching our safe minimum fuel level, which was 800 lbs of fuel calculated for such an event. Our base at Lee had no landing aids and even with all the aids we had on this aircraft, we would not be able to land in visibility as bad as it was.

To prevent being caught out in that situation, we would always carry enough reserve fuel to enable us to fly to another airfield that offered an instrument approach facility to enable a safe landing in very poor visibility, hence the 800 lbs. The airfields in our region were Southampton and Bournemouth, as a last resort we would just be able to make Gatwick airport.

Rob had calculated that we had enough fuel for one more attempt. It would be easy to be sucked into continuing the attempts until suddenly you do not have enough fuel to divert. The second attempt failed, so off we went to Bournemouth. We tried Southampton first as some evenings they remained open beyond their normal closing times but that night they were closed.

We had been assured previously that, although Bournemouth airport had reduced manning for short periods during the night between mail aircraft coming in to land, they would still be able to provide an instrument landing service at short notice if required in an emergency.

This was one of those situations but things did not quite work out that way. A controller was there but at first turned us away because he said he could not offer an instrument landing (ILS) because the emergency services were not manned up. Rob had to tell him that we only had one shot at this and that we would have to attempt the approach with or without the ILS; we were coming in. We got our instrument approach, the controller quickly providing the excellent service they carry out, just a little different from his usual night shifts I guess and without the backup he would normally have.

We spent the night in the airport's fire station lounge until the fog cleared the next day, when we were able to refuel and return to Lee.

Later that year the aircraft was scrambled to a diving incident from the dive vessel 'Voyager'. The crew was: Captain Peter Nicholson, co-pilot Graham Sorge, winch-op Mick Rowsell and Terry Short was the winchman. When they arrived on scene it became apparent that five divers had been involved in the incident. One casualty was not breathing and four possibly needed recompression.

Terry had quite a job on his hands; he would have to check that the divers onboard were carrying out the resuscitation correctly, while breaking off at each winch cycle to send the other divers to the aircraft. When the four divers requiring recompression were onboard, Terry was recovered to the aircraft with the casualty being resuscitated. Once onboard both Mick and Terry could concentrate their efforts on that casualty en-route to hospital.

All five divers were transferred to Haslar hospital. One diver was unfortunately declared dead on arrival while the other four were taken to the hypobaric chamber.

The accident had happened while eight divers (six of them trainees) were on a training dive to a depth in excess of ninety feet. One of the divers was taken ill and was found lying on the seabed unconscious, and without his mouthpiece, so was taken to the surface by an instructor. Unfortunately, in the confusion, three other divers had returned to the surface also missing their stops.

While the winching was taking place, 'R-IJ' developed engine problems, the automatic power control had failed to the number one engine. Graham had to control the fuel to the engine manually while Peter continued with the winching. Afterwards, Terry said he was just thankful that he was unaware of that happening. 'R-IJ' was replaced by the standby aircraft as soon as they landed back at base, but was fixed and back on service the next day.

In the August, Margaret and I attempted a holiday. We needed to see whether it was possible and were encouraged by my mother, again doing everything she could to make us live as normal a life as possible. She was using all the lessons she had learned through looking after Roy (my stepfather) after his stroke.

My mother had an apartment in a village called Nerja in Spain, a place we liked and had been to for several holidays in the past. We would not be able to stay at my mother's apartment because it had a large set of steps at the entrance that would be impossible for Margaret to get up.

We booked into a hotel for a fortnight and my mother stayed in her apartment. She booked the same flights so she could help us with the travelling, which would make it much easier, especially for that first trip – navigating airports with a wheelchair and baggage is no joke. I am not sure if we would have gone abroad if it were not for her convincing us we could do it.

In addition to my mother's help and encouragement, a serendipitous meeting with a couple in the hotel helped both Margaret and I enormously: both Mona and Arthur made such a fuss of Margaret and were such good company that they made our holiday a complete success. That meeting was the start of a very special friendship which would continue back home and on future holidays.

Mona and Arthur extended that friendship to their family, all of the same caring nature, making us so welcome on our visits to their home in Sheffield. Margaret was spoilt rotten when we visited and, of course, we would enjoy their visits when they came to our house.

In the October 'Rescue IJ' was called to the tall ship 'Eendracht', a Dutch sail trainer that was being driven aground by gale force winds at Newhaven, East Sussex. The crew was: Captain Rob Flexman, co-pilot Iakapo Ferrachi, winch-op Mick Rowsell and John Spencer was the winchman. Iakapo was an Italian pilot trained by Bristows and doing a tour as a SAR co-pilot.

There were fifty crew and passengers onboard the tall ship so Portland's aircraft 'Rescue-HL' was also scrambled to assist.

When 'R-IJ' arrived on scene, they carried out the crew brief as to how they would conduct this rescue, deciding the quickest way would be to get John onboard using the hi-line. Once there he could brief and prepare the casualties then attach two people at a time to the winch. Mick would winch them clear of the vessel, then transfer them (still on the end of the winch wire) the short distance to the beach. Rob was confident he could achieve this and still keep visual references with the vessel.

John would be able to control any swing by the hi-line, the inboard end would be controlled by John from onboard the 'Eendracht' and the other end would remain attached to the hook. Once the casualties were safely on the beach and met by Coastguards, the aircraft could move left, returning to the winching position ready for John to pull the hook onboard. The system worked well, it was quite hard work for John but he successfully transferred thirty-nine survivors to the safety of the beach before 'R-IJ' had to go to Shoreham for fuel.

'R-HL' took over the rescue, lowering 'Buck' Rogers to the 'Eendracht' to assist John who was still onboard. Between them, they transferred the remaining survivors and themselves ashore. John was later picked up from the beach by 'R-IJ' on return from its refuel.

This was a successful transfer in awful conditions and no-one was injured, just one person taken to hospital to be checked out and released the same day. The rest of the survivors, all Dutch, were looked after at the 'Stena Sealink' accommodation centre at Newhaven.

During 1998, the Coastguard Agency joined with the Marine Safety Agency to form the Maritime and Coastguard Agency (MCA). This would make the UK Coastguard a worldwide model for Search and Rescue co-ordination. They would concentrate on rescue co-ordination, prevention of incidents, minimising pollution and raising maritime safety awareness, targeting by education the most common causes of maritime accidents. They would focus on using the best available technology to achieve these commitments.

Although I was not a Coastguard, I had been involved directly with them since I had started flying, having spent the majority of my career to date on UK SAR both in the military and as a civilian. Therefore, I had always felt considerable loyalty to the service and I was interested in any changes being made and in what they hoped to achieve. During the following year the combined agency would face many issues in connection with its commitments mentioned above, not just the incidents I will be mentioning in our area, but all around the coast of Britain.

1999

This year turned out to be one the busiest years with a series of high profile incidents, at least four of which had the potential of being major environmental incidents. However, these incidents were contained by well-rehearsed plans controlled by the Counter Pollution Response team (a unit attached to the MCA) and the equivalent French authorities.

Many of these incidents would involve considerable flying time for our aircraft at Lee-on-Solent, involving all the crews at various times. The first was in February when the Ro-Ro car ferry 'Picasso' had engine failure shortly after leaving Boulogne bound for Folkestone. It was in a north-westerly gale with forty-four passengers and crew onboard. The crew was: Captain Graham Sorge, co-pilot Steve Buckland, winch-op Nick Horst and the winchman was Chris Bond.

By the time 'Rescue India Juliet' arrived on scene, French helicopters had taken off twelve passengers and non-essential crew, leaving a skeleton crew of sixteen men onboard.

The 'Picasso' had dropped both anchors but they were not holding too well, so the ferry was under threat of being forced onto the sands. 'R-IJ' was tasked to stay on scene to take the remaining sixteen men off should efforts to secure the vessel fail.

In the meantime, the MCA tug the 'Far Turbot' was en-route. 'R-IJ' remained until the tug arrived and commenced passing a tow; once the tow was established, 'R-IJ' was released to refuel at Le Touquet in France. On returning to the incident, the crew reported that they had repaired the engines and the 'Picasso' was going to continue under its own steam escorted by the 'Far Turbot'. 'R-IJ' was released from task after five hours flying.

The second of these potentially serious incidents was a fire onboard the cross channel ferry 'Pride of Le Havre', twelve miles south of Portsmouth. The crew was: Captain Peter Thomson, co-pilot Peter Nicholson, winch-op John Spencer and Don Sowden was the winchman.

Fortunately, the ferry was on sea trials, ready to go back into service the following day. The onboard fire crews had contained the fire in the engine room and sealed the area, hoping to starve the fire with Halon gas, a system built into the engine room for such an event. Unfortunately, it was only partially successful.

'R-IJ' was scrambled to pick up teams of fire fighters and equipment from Newport on the Isle of Wight and transfer them to the ferry. The transfer was achieved in three sectors between the Newport helicopter landing-site and the ferry, in visibility down to 200 metres in fog. On completion, 'R-IJ' was tasked to standby at Lee.

Later once the fire was under control, 'R-IJ' was tasked to recover eight of the fire fighters and equipment. The rest remained onboard until the vessel was safe to enter harbour.

In the August, there was a collision between a Taiwanese owned cargo vessel the 'Ever Decent' and a luxury cruise liner the 'Norwegian Dream', eighteen miles offshore in the Dover straights. Fortunately, no one was seriously injured in the collision and the 'Norwegian Dream' was able to limp back to Dover with a huge gash in the bow. Later it was confirmed that twenty-one passengers and crew had been slightly injured.

The 'Ever Decent' was holed below the waterline and the collision had sparked a fire in one of the three thousand containers she was carrying. This clearly had the potential of being a major pollution incident, especially when it became clear many of the containers contained toxic cargo.

Tugs, some with special fire fighting equipment, were proceeding to the incident. The fire was spreading by the time the tugs arrived. Boundary cooling commenced and specialist fire fighting teams had been put onboard.

The vessel would remain offshore until the fire was under control and it had been assessed by the MCA that the hole below the waterline was not serious enough to cause the vessel to sink. The fire was the major problem and hopefully that would be under control in the coming hours.

Unfortunately, the flames were fuelled by paint and paint hardener that was carried in some of the containers. This was making the fire extremely difficult to bring under control and the seat of the fire was in the lower layers of containers.

The following day 'Rescue IJ' was tasked to fly to Dover to pick up three MCA personnel for an assessment flight around the incident. The crew was: Captain Graham Sorge, co-pilot Steve Buckland, winch-op Don Sowden and I was the winchman.

We picked up the MCA team then flew to the 'Ever Decent'. On scene our infrared camera clearly showed the seat of the fire and that it was still burning. We had also been tasked to film this for analysis onshore. Once that was carried out an MCA surveyor was winched to the 'Ever Decent' prior to 'R-IJ' being tasked to search for containers that had fallen overboard in the collision.

Two more flights were made to the 'Ever Decent' on successive days to carry out similar assessments, each time putting an MCA surveyor onboard. A total of eleven hours flying time was carried out by 'R-IJ'. When the fire was brought under control, the 'Ever Decent' was towed to Zebrugge to offload the remaining cargo and for repair. It was estimated that a million tonnes of water had been used to get the fire under control. The MCA deserved praise for the successful conclusion of that incident.

Only a few days later, on the 1st September, the cargo vessel 'Sonia' had just departed from Southampton for Greece when the engine room started to flood six miles south of the Isle of Wight. The crew were unable to get the situation under control, so opted to head to Sandown Bay on the east coast of the Isle of Wight to anchor while they carried out repairs.

Later that day, all attempts by the crew had failed and the engine room continued to flood. When the Coastguards became aware that there was a problem, it was much later in the day and the vessel was already low in the water.

Portsmouth and Southampton port officials together with the Coastguards attempted to assist the vessel, but the ship's officials had initially been reluctant to seek help. The MCA eventually had to instigate their intervention powers, which hastened the assistance of specialist equipment, required to prevent this incident from being a major environmental hazard in Sandown Bay.

The situation was brought under control and the 'Sonia' was towed into Southampton the following day.

'Rescue India Juliet' was called out five times during that incident, including the rescue of a crewmember from the tug 'Powerful' who had fallen overboard between the tug and the 'Sonia'. He was initially picked up by Bembridge lifeboat suffering cold and shock and we then recovered him from the lifeboat and flew him to Newport HLS. We also transferred teams of divers to the vessel plus special cutting equipment from Newport on the Isle of Wight.

On the 4th December, there was another major incident when the Liberian registered refrigerator vessel, the 'Dole America', collided with the 'Nab Tower', a ten-thousand ton fixed platform that marks the deep-water channel into the Solent.

The Dole America was leaving Portsmouth harbour under pilotage and the pilot disembarked to the pilot boat about two miles north of the Nab tower. The 'Dole America' continued, now under the command of its captain, who set course to pass the tower about two cables to the east. On approaching the tower, the captain saw a red light that appeared to be on a collision course with his vessel.

During the subsequent actions of that sighting, the 'Dole America' collided with the Nab tower, bounced off then made a second impact. She was damaged forward on the Starboard side below the waterline and aft below the main deck above the waterline. She started to take on water and soon developed a 12° list to starboard.

The captain requested assistance and the pilot was tasked to return onboard. With the approval of the captain, he took the only preventative action possible and ran the vessel into shallow waters where it would rest on the seabed away from the main channel. That decision almost certainly prevented a disaster and quite possibly to the life of crewmembers who may not have abandoned ship in time, plus the environmental problems that would have resulted from the sinking of the vessel.

'Rescue-IJ' was scrambled and, once it was clear the vessel was safe with the bows firmly on the sands, was tasked to film the extent of the damage.

Between the 7th and 13th Dec, the aircraft carried out ten sorties relating to that operation mainly in support of MCA surveyors who stayed on the vessel throughout, making it safe and assessing the pollution-prevention measures that may be required.

The 'Dole America', was made safe and re-floated over a six-day period then towed into port for repair. The vessel had 440 tonnes of heavy fuel oil onboard; 40 tonnes of lubricating oil did spill into the sea and the slick was monitored. Fortunately, it caused little environmental impact; the 440 tonnes of heavy oil would have been a serious problem had that leaked into the sea.

This was also another bad year for diving incidents, with five fatalities in our area. One of these incidents commenced with 'R-IJ' being tasked to search for a missing diver, after a diver's marker was found between Newhaven and Selsey Bill. On completion of the first search (when the aircraft returned for refuel), Terry Short and myself took over from Chris Bond and John Spencer.

After only forty minutes on search, we were re-tasked to recover a diver with possible decompression sickness from the dive boat 'Channel Diver'. 'R-IJ' had to jettison 1000 lbs of fuel prior to recovering the diver, because we were too heavy for the winching having taken on full fuel for the search. Terry was lowered to the vessel to recover the diver who was then flown to Haslar hospital. Once we had transferred the diver to the waiting ambulance, we returned to Lee for running rotors refuel prior to returning to the original search.

En-route to the original search area we were re-tasked back to the dive boat 'Channel Diver', who was now reporting that they had a missing diver. The search for the original missing diver was continuing by surface search vessels, while we were tasked to search for the 'Channel Diver's' missing diver. This search was continued until we required refuel when a relief crew took over as another full fuel search would have put us well over our allowed flying hours.

The relief crew searched for a further six hours overnight using the infrared camera. By now, many ships and lifeboats were involved in the search including the warship HMS Fearless. 'R-IJ' was able to land on HMS Fearless to refuel during their six-hour search. On completion of their second search, still nothing sighted, they returned to Lee for refuel and crew change.

We took over again and on completion of our search, still nothing sighted went to Shoreham for refuel. En-route back to the search area, we were re-tasked to the report of two more missing divers off Selsey Bill. On scene, the fishing vessel 'Page Three' reported they had picked the divers up safe and well. The search for the divers still missing was scaled down for varying reasons; 'R-IJ' was relieved from task and returned to base.

These incidents involved four separate diving tasks, two divers located, one diver requiring a recompression chamber and two still missing, involving a total of eighteen hours and thirty minutes flying by our aircraft alone.

Another incident in August, searching for two missing divers from the dive boat 'Spartacus' would involve another two crews and over 12 hours flying again with nothing found.

The aircraft had also been involved in another unsuccessful search in French waters for a missing diver in the July. I was to recover a further fatality from the dive boat 'Woodpecker' in August. Don recovered two divers (one a fatality), from the FV 'Bessy B'. This was probably to be our worst year for diving fatalities and, with my diving background, the incidents left me feeling exceptionally sad. Questions, as to why there had been so many accidents would need to be asked.

We obviously had all the normal type jobs in 1999 and most with happier results; however, the year was marred by these tragic diving incidents and the sudden increase of the large ship incidents.

I feel it was quite amazing that all the large ship incidents were resolved without any loss of life or major environmental damage. A lot of that was down to the MCA and their advanced planning for such events. Nevertheless, the actual collisions the MCA had no control over, they happened and it was down to the design of the vessels and a considerable amount of luck that all the vessels remained afloat and no one was injured or killed.

The MCA does, however, have a continuing involvement in monitoring and analyzing why incidents like these happen and publishing recommendations to help prevent future incidents. They are also responsible for checking the sea worthiness and safety equipment of vessels that enter our ports and have the powers to stop unsuitable vessels from going to sea.

2000

One of my jobs in 2000 that was slightly out of the ordinary and a lesson to me was a tasking while airborne on a training sortie; it was to the report of a speedboat taking on water one mile south of Selsey Bill. The crew was: Captain Graham Sorge, co-pilot Steve Buckland, winch-op Terry Short and I was the winchman.

We were on scene within minutes and, after a short search of the area came across three men in the water; one clinging to the bows of a speedboat without a lifejacket on, the rest of the boat submerged. Two more people were in the water close by with lifejackets on.

I immediately opted to go for the one clinging to the wreckage. As Terry winched me out, I noticed that he was an older man and looked in quite a precarious situation, clinging to the bow of the boat; however, he was signalling for me to pick the two in the water up first. I opted to continue towards him as my thoughts were that he was elderly, had no lifejacket on and that the speedboat could disappear below the surface.

We quickly recovered him to the aircraft using the hypothermic lift and I was lowered to the remaining two, who were clinging together in the water a short distance from the wreckage.

I managed to get a strop onto one of them with difficulty but was unable to use the second strop as a hypothermic lift because they were holding onto each other so tightly. It is obviously difficult to communicate with the noise of the aircraft, so I had signalled to the one I would be leaving in the water that I would be straight back down for him.

As Terry started to winch in I noticed the one left in the water starting to flip over and was looking at me in sheer panic, I knew instinctively that something was wrong so I signalled to Terry to put us back in the water. Terry was doing that anyway as he had also noticed something was not right. I had kept a firm grip of the one I was about to leave in the water from the moment I realised all was not well.

Now all three of us were back in the water, I quickly assessed his predicament: his lifejacket was only partially on and soon pieced together what had happened. When the boat sank, one of them had managed to get his lifejacket on correctly and the other had only managed to get one arm into the jacket, subsequently being supported by the other. Being a non-swimmer he needed both hands to hold on to his friend, so had never managed to get the jacket on properly.

I had come along and was about to take his life support away i.e. the friend he was holding on to. This was now another situation for three on the winch, (the procedure we could only use in an emergency) so I quickly slipped the second strop on him and all three of us were recovered to the aircraft.

This simple tasking helped to show that even after years in the role, we can still make the wrong decisions when things look straightforward, but are not necessarily as they appear.

This may have been a difficult one to call, but the signs were there. In particular, the man clinging to the boat making it quite apparent we should pick the others up first. I should have noticed the lifejacket not being secure on one of the two left in the water but that was not quite so easy as they were holding on to each other tightly, I was still angry with myself that I hadn't noticed.

Fortunately, I was able to rectify the mistake when we realised all was not well. We would take lessons from this, in particular to be more observant of the incident that is presented to us. Normally we brief the situation but this looked so straightforward we had run straight in to the one clinging to the wreckage.

Nick Horst was to carry out a transfer of a badly injured jet skier from the water, like last time that Nick had recovered a casualty with a possible spinal injury from the water. He again managed to package this casualty into a spinal board and stretcher while still in the water, this time with the aid of Cowes Rescue lifeboat and crew.

In the job prior to this, Nick Horst and Mick Rowsell had recovered a man face down in the water and had successfully resuscitated him.

The flight had another flourish of fundraising this year including charity flights and a Grand Summer Ball held in the hanger. This was the third Charity Ball, the first two having been arranged by Peter Thomson and his wife Anne. They had been extremely successful but involved a tremendous amount of work and preparation over a few months prior to the event from all of the flight team.

This time it was to be backed up by the Coastguards from Lee-on-Solent MRSC, in particular Kathy Henderson, a Coastguard watch officer who was very keen to make this a joint event with the flight.

Kathy's aim was to help boost both the flight's and the Lee-on-Solent Coastguard's charity funds and for part of those proceeds to go towards purchasing an electric wheelchair and speech synthesizer for Margaret, plus a special computer for Mick Rowsell's disabled daughter Victoria. Kathy (with the help of the flight and Coastguards) had carried out considerable research on different speech synthesizers for Margaret and the requirements for Victoria.

She had started the ball rolling by contacting many companies and requesting prizes for the grand draw and auction that would be held on the night. She had also started on all the other preparations required: contacting caterers, entertainment, sourcing materials for decorating the hanger, tables and table decorations etc. Unfortunately, Kathy was transferred to Sumburgh Coastguards in the Shetland Islands before the actual night of the ball; this was a promotion for Kathy, which she felt she had to take.

Dave Thomson, the engineer who had recently joined us from working overseas took on Kathy's role. Dave had a lot of experience in this type of thing running many charity events over the years he had been working overseas.

Dave's organising skills showed on the night. The ball commenced with a beat the retreat by a Royal Marine Band, followed by a very professional meal with silver service and wonderful entertainment, including table performers. The main entertainment for the night was Tony Hadley, former Spandau ballet, who had waived his own fee for the event. Dave even held a very successful auction on the evening, which he pulled off as though he had been an auctioneer all his life. This proved to be another exceptional evening.

Margaret was completely overwhelmed when she heard she was to receive these items. The flight arranged for her to visit a unit to select the best speech unit for her situation and to select the most suitable wheelchair. Victoria was equally overwhelmed, the special computer was something recommended by her school and one she had been hoping to get for quite a while.

In the July, my family was hit by another awful medical problem when our grandson Michael was diagnosed with leukaemia. Michael was ten years old when our daughter Kerry had noticed a lump on his neck. It did not seem to be causing Michael any problems but he seemed a little listless, so she had decided to get it checked out. Initially they ran checks for glandular fever that came back negative.

A couple of weeks later Michael woke up with Bells Palsy to the left side of the face and was admitted to hospital where further tests for glandular fever were carried out. At this stage Michael started to get quite poorly, making us all start to suspect something more sinister. The tests still came back negative and a few days later the doctors explained they were suspecting lymphoma and that Michael needed moving to a specialist unit in Southampton for further tests. After carrying out these tests, he was diagnosed as having Acute Lymphoblastic Leukaemia (ALL).

We could not take this in. Margaret was now absolutely convinced she had survived against all odds to get Michael, her pride and joy, through this ordeal. Margaret was the most positive out of all of us that he would get through this. This was a double whammy for Margaret as her brother Nigel was just finishing a course of chemotherapy after being diagnosed with Myeloma. This had been an awful worry for Margaret and now Michael was to start his treatment for Leukaemia.

The treatment would prove to be quite brutal, with chemotherapy and steroids making Michael very ill, then a period of building his strength up to make him strong enough for further rounds of chemo; this would go on for three years. The doctors assured us that the success rate in children was quite good and if the three years of treatment failed, there was still a chance of a bone marrow transplant, providing of course that they could find a suitable donor. Even so, the thought of him having to go through all this quite barbaric treatment was difficult to cope with.

I was angry, simply wanting to challenge why all this could be happening. I felt I was reliving the nightmare of three years previously when Margaret had the cerebral bleed. Since turning the corner on that awful episode, she had lost her father and her aunt (who had been her guardian since Margaret was only 7 years old after her mother had died), then her brother had developed Myeloma and now our grandson was desperately ill: life seemed so unfair. Clearly, anyone would question a situation like this. We had to accept that it was bad luck and awful things like this can happen to other families, it was not just us, but it was difficult.

Margaret had huge inner strength and, even though unable to speak, she was able to give enormous encouragement to Kerry and her husband Richard, adamant that there could only be one outcome from this which was that Michael would get better. Kerry and Richard soon took on that conviction and, in time, I would find my anger replaced by hope. Incredibly, Margaret never displayed anger. She loved Michael so much she really did believe she was only here to see Michael through this trying time.

Kerry had decided to explain everything to Michael from the day of the diagnosis, passing on everything she was being told. Michael was very brave, and, being an intelligent little boy, already understood a lot of what was happening, perhaps even more than his mum who was struggling to take it all in.

It is quite amazing how children cope with this sort of information and how they manage to accept all the hurdles they will have to face during the treatment. Michael was no different; one day he was a normal happy child doing all the things a ten year old boy would be doing, the next day he was that same ten year old boy, who now had to face losing his normal childhood for three years or longer while having to face up to a life threatening illness. Where does that strength come from?

This would be life changing for the family. Kerry and Richard had to spend so much time at the hospital even having to stay over on many nights. Jessica, Michael's four-year-old sister visited so often she became part of the furniture. She would play in the hospital children's playroom, often with children her own age going through the same sort of treatment as Michael, even joining in the school lessons they have in hospital. It became like a play school and was very much part of her life. We would worry that she was missing a lot of her childhood but she, like Michael, would cope brilliantly.

For the second time in three years, I would find another side to the job I do. When I went back to work after Margaret's CVA, the camaraderie on the unit was just what I needed to stop me dwelling on my problems and the satisfaction gained from the work we do would put everything back into some sort of order in my mind. I cannot explain this other than that is the way it was, the lads just knew me so well. The same would happen with this latest scare, they would only bring up the situation when they sensed I needed to talk about it. It was just something magical as far as I was concerned.

The other 'out-of-the-normal' jobs for us that year included tasking due to serious flooding in Dorset and Sussex caused by heavy rain. The first call out was to a man clinging to a door in the river Uck in Sussex: the river had burst its banks and the man was being washed downstream. The crew was: Captain Rob Flexman, co-pilot Dave Gibbs, winchop: Don Sowden and John Spencer was the winchman.

When they arrived on scene, rescuers had pulled the man to shore, but he would need air transport to hospital. The area was a tree-lined strip of land with the river one side and a swollen stream the other. The rescuers were unable to carry the casualty to the ambulance and there was nowhere for the helicopter to land. John opted to be winched through the tree canopy followed by the stretcher. This was successful: John and the casualty in a stretcher were recovered to the aircraft and flown to Haywards Heath helicopter landing site for transfer to an ambulance.

Shortly after they returned to base they were tasked to a man spotted on a first floor balcony of a building to the south of Tunbridge Wells with water flooding around the house. When they arrived on scene, Don lowered John to the balcony to find the man refusing to be winched. John must have felt like winching him anyway especially after the difficulty getting onto the balcony. However, the crew had no option but to recover John and leave the casualty there. 'R-IJ' remained on scene until fire fighters managed to secure ropes to the house to gain access.

Returning from that job 'R-IJ' was re-tasked to two people and two small dogs trapped in their boat, which was being forced against a bridge parapet by the raging floodwater on a river to the north of Lewes, East Sussex. On scene, John was lowered with two strops and the child valise in the hope he could get the dogs into that (the child valise was a carrying system we had developed for lifting very young children and babies).

John managed to get both dogs into the bag and went up to the aircraft with the lady plus the dogs in the valise, then returned to double-lift the man.

John would have one more quite unusual task due to further floods a couple of weeks later this time crewed with Captain Pete Thomson, co-pilot Dave Gibbs and winch-op Nick Horst.

They were scrambled from home to the report of a man stuck in a car due to flooding on a bridge at Bagber near Sturminster Newton. On scene, a police helicopter was illuminating the scene and acting as a communication link. The car was pinned to the side of the bridge by the force of the water. Nick lowered John to the top of the car and managed to winch the casualty from the rear hatch of the vehicle.

Dave Gibbs, the co-pilot on these tasks, had joined us at the beginning of the year as a Bristow trained co-pilot. Dave's story was slightly unusual in that, having been very keen on aviation, he had applied for work experience with the flight when he was only fifteen and had spent a fortnight with us at Lee. At the time, he was a member of the gliding club that operated from the Lee-on-Solent airfield. He went on to gain his solo as a glider pilot shortly after his sixteenth birthday, remaining attached to the gliding club during his time at university.

When he had completed his degree course, he had applied and was accepted for a place on a Bristow Helicopters training course, gained his hours required to become a SAR co-pilot in the North Sea and achieved the dream he had as a fifteen-year-old lad of joining the Lee SAR flight. We still introduce him as the work experience lad and I consider that to have been quite an achievement.

Paul Mattinson was our other new co-pilot with a similar background to Dave. He learnt to fly with the RAF whilst at school, continuing to fly privately through university. On graduating, he worked as a research scientist and then took up a place to be trained as a helicopter pilot by Bristow Helicopters, gained the required hours in the North Sea, then requested to come to Lee. Paul had moved down with his wife Kate and lovely Dalmatian, Ben. Both Dave and Paul, being natural pilots, had no problem fitting in and being accepted by the unit.

In the November of 2000, we were scrambled from home by Portland Coastguard to the Ro-Ro car ferry 'Britta Oden', which had lost power to both of its engines and was drifting thirty miles south of Portland Bill.

The crew was: Captain Graham Sorge, co-pilot Steve Buckland, winch-op Don Sowden and I was the winchman.

We had been scrambled to stand-by while the tugs 'Anglian Earl' and 'Anglian Duke' were making their way to the scene. Being a Ro-Ro (Roll on –Roll off) ferry, it was very vulnerable, with its cargo of cars in danger of moving as the force nine gales battered it. The Coastguards had transmitted a mayday relay, which resulted in other nearby vessels proceeding, including the warship HMS Kent. The Coastguards had also launched three lifeboats from Exmouth, Weymouth and Alderney. The rescue helicopter from Chivenor was airborne at the time and had been redirected to the incident: it was already standing by the vessel when we arrived.

The ferry only had sixteen passengers onboard plus crew and it had been decided that, for the time being, they would be safer remaining onboard.

The weather was horrendous and several attempts at passing the tow had failed, but eventually the 'Anglian Earl' managed to establish the tow and started heading towards Portland. The tow to Portland was into the sea and wind so it was decided that it would be safer to head for Southampton. While manoeuvring to commence the heading towards Southampton, the tow broke. The other tug the 'Anglian Duke' took over, established a tow and continued towards Southampton, escorted by the warship and lifeboats.

'R-IJ' was tasked to return for refuel and remain at immediate readiness. The Chivenor aircraft remained on scene until towards the end of their endurance when we returned to remain on stand-by until the vessel was in the calmer waters of the Solent before finally being released to return to base.

This was another situation that could have been much worse had it not been for the quick reaction by the Coastguards in getting tugs and other vessels to the scene so quickly. In these situations, virtually all vessels in the vicinity respond to a mayday relay and that was certainly the case that night.

The Coastguards task the lifeboats, helicopters and coastal search teams etc. They also arrange or contract the tugs as required, but the vessels closest to the incident may well be the ones that can make a difference. We are very fortunate regarding maritime incidents that masters of vessels respond the way they do; it is almost a universal rule of the sea for vessels to respond to a Mayday relay. The Coastguards can then task the vessels that have responded and release them as and when the distress situation improves or is brought under control.

Towards the end of the year, I was presented with a situation I was not really expecting. Terry Short was approaching our normal retirement age of 58. Quite a few people at the time considered 58 to be too old for a job like ours. However, Terry was proof that, providing you keep fit and work hard at keeping up professional standards, it would be possible to continue even beyond that age.

Terry was almost certainly the fittest person on the unit and in my view the most professional aircrewman. No one on the unit had any doubts that Terry was more than capable of continuing, but those were the company rules and our pension entitlement had been calculated around that retirement age. The same rules applied for the pilots.

There was lots of talk about who would take over from Terry as the Chief Aircrewman. Most of the aircrewmen expected me to take over, probably because they knew I would be a soft touch! Nevertheless, I had decided that being so close to retirement myself, I really didn't want the hassle. I would have loved the job earlier, especially as I had been the Chief Aircrewman on this flight when it was a Royal Naval flight.

However, I had joined this flight knowing Terry was to be the Senior Aircrewman and had absolutely no problem with that. He was one of the few crewmen with more experience than me and someone I had looked up to from the day I first met him.

Terry had tried to talk me into applying but I told him I would not be doing so. Then, only a couple of weeks before the applications had to be in for the position, Terry happened to mention that Peter Thomson thought it was probably best I didn't apply, because of my situation with Margaret.

This was like a red rag to a bull for me! I had worked consistently around my situation at home from the day that I had decided I would try to continue working. I had managed to sort a routine to achieve this and my situation at home had not affected my work one bit.

I arranged everything around the job, as I felt I should only continue on the flight if I was able to do the job without affecting the flight's routine and rosters. I had gone out of my way to achieve this and had not had one day off work in over three years. Margaret, my mother and family supported me totally in achieving this.

This situation did get me thinking; perhaps it would be nice to finish my career as the Chief Aircrewman. I was confident that I would be able to do it, I also questioned the fact that although I had no problem working under Terry, I might not feel the same way if I was working under someone with less experience than me. I had been controlling a lot of the administration side of the flight anyway along with one of the pilots, Graham Sorge. This was something I had simply inherited because I had become quite knowledgeable on computer systems, purely because I had found computers to be the way around my dyslexia. Between Graham and me, we produced and maintained the majority of forms, spreadsheets and databases used on the flight at the time.

Perhaps for all the wrong reasons I put in for the job. On paper, I had the most experience and having previously been the Chief Aircrewman of this flight when it was military would give me an edge. Nevertheless, I was acutely aware that, if Peter did not want me to do the job, I probably would not get it; there would be three people on the interview board but Peter was a persuasive character.

When at the interview it came to the question of "should I be considering taking this role with my situation with Margaret?" I simply said, tongue in cheek, "off course my situation at home will affect the role and I may not be able to put as much into the role as I would like to. What it does mean is, without that situation, I would probably be the best Chief Aircrewman in the company; as it is I will have to settle for being just a good Chief Aircrewman."

Anyway, I did get the job and it was a unanimous decision. I am also quite sure I had taken Peter's remark the wrong way: he had only been thinking of Margaret and that I was doing enough already.

There was a twist to this. At some stage the following year the company was hoping to win a contract to conduct a SAR trial in the North Sea. The contract would be to equip a helicopter with state of the art equipment, then to evaluate that aircraft for its suitability regarding a newly proposed rescue concept for safety cover in the North Sea.

British Petroleum was financing the trial and a team of SAR aircrewmen, pilots and engineers would be required. Chris Bond was nominated for the trial if it went ahead, which would make us two aircrewman short at Lee. Terry's relief had already been selected but we would, if Chris went, need one more.

Chris was very keen to come back to Lee after the trial so the obvious solution was to ask Terry to remain on as a contractor until Chris returned;

Peter Thomson thought that to be the ideal solution and managed to get the company to agree.

Terry was pleased, as he had always wanted to stay on. I was over the moon not only had I always thought it was a real waste letting someone like Terry go, but he would still be around if I had any problems as the Chief Crewman.

This would be a year with several changes. John Rooney came in as a SAR captain to replace Peter Nicholson who would be retiring later in the year. John was an ex Royal Navy pilot and had, since joining Bristows, operated in the North Sea before joining the SAR flight at Sumburgh in the mid 90's. John joined us at the beginning of the year, moving from the Shetland Isles with his wife Debbie and their family.

Towards the end of the year, Rob Flexman would be taking early retirement, something Rob and his wife Mich had been planning for years. That plan was to buy a yacht and sail leisurely around France and Portugal's coastlines visiting the many nice harbours and ports, followed by a few years in the Mediterranean. They already had their yacht and for the previous few years had been carrying out trips on the south coast and across to France.

Mark Jackson would replace Rob. Mark was also a SAR captain based in Sumburgh and was one of the first Bristow trained pilots to be qualified as a SAR captain. He had served at Stornoway and Sumburgh as a co-pilot and had even carried out a few relief shifts at Lee-on-Solent. Between the co-pilot slots, he had operated in the North Sea, the Falkland Islands, Africa and other places abroad before returning to Sumburgh to be trained as a SAR captain. Mark would be moving down from Sumburgh with his wife Tracy and their family.

However, it did not quite work out as planned as Peter Nicholson was offered an extension as a contractor, the same deal as Terry and virtually for the same reasons, extra SAR pilots would soon be required for the North Sea contract. Consequently, John relieved Rob but Mark still joined us as planned; he would now relieve Peter Thomson during the next year.

Peter was doing the same as Rob, taking early retirement. He had been preparing a retirement adventure with his wife Anne for some years. They planned to sail on their yacht 'Muskrat', initially in the Caribbean, then wherever their mood took them.

Our grandson Michael's treatment was slowly becoming a routine of hospital stays, periods of sickness, hair loss etc. He had a central arterial line implanted in his chest called a Hickman line. Michael called it his wiggly; it would remain for quite some time and be used to introduce all the drugs he required during his long-term treatment.

He was able to spend the odd day at school but so many things were affecting him: bright lights gave him headaches and he had sudden bouts of violent sickness, so Kerry was on constant call to pick him up. The school was fully aware of the situation and the majority of the children were supportive. A few silly ones laughed at his hair loss but Michael retaliated to that by saying something along the lines of "You are very silly and quite cruel. In a few years I will be well and my hair will grow back, but you will probably still be silly and cruel."

The treatment was carried out in scheduled blocks, alternated between chemotherapy and steroids both having different side effects. In between these, he would have lumber punctures and courses of injections into a muscle in his leg that he did not like at all.

We had to stay strong, avoid showing too much worry and resist the temptation to molly-coddle Michael; it was important that he led as normal a life as possible. Yet inside we wanted to spoil him rotten and keep him protected; at the same time, we were fighting back the anger as to why this sort of thing can happen to a child. Nevertheless, in time Michael's strength would rub off on all of us, we had to accept that, if he could handle it so well, we needed to be just as strong. This was very hard for his mum and dad, who had to give him control over what he wanted to do or try to do, he knew himself when things were not possible.

Kerry and Richard monitored him perfectly, making sure one of them was always available when he needed them, remaining with him during his hospital stints, yet holding back when he wanted to achieve something on his own. They had a long haul ahead of them but all very positive.

2001

This year, apart from the changes on the crewing side, was to be a reasonably quiet one for the unit. One of the jobs that created a bit of fuss at the time was a very straightforward job for us, but was unusual in the way the rescue services had been alerted to the situation. The tasking was a canoeist in difficulties between Milford on Sea and the Needles. The crew was: Captain Graham Sorge, co-pilot Paul Mattinson, winch-op Terry Short and I was the winchman.

We were approaching the Needles returning from a flight to Portland when tasked and located the casualty within a couple of minutes. Terry lowered me to recover the casualty to the aircraft, the canoeist was reasonably well and we were able to drop him off with Coastguards at Milford. Yarmouth lifeboat recovered his canoe.

As it turned out, the casualty (who was a doctor) had set off on a four-day, single-handed kayak trip round the Isle of Wight. Unfortunately, on his first day the weather had turned nasty, the seas were quite rough causing him to capsize a few times. Eventually, through cold and exhaustion, he was unable to make it back into his canoe.

He was a fit young man wearing the right clothing and lifejacket but the sea was rough and very cold. The cold sea will soon sap the strength away, as was the case that day. He had with him a mobile phone and a mobile GPS; the mobile phone was in a waterproof bag and his fingers being very cold made it very difficult for him to press the keys, but he did manage to ring some pre-programmed (single button) telephone numbers. The first call was to his father in Dubai in the Arab emirates, the second to his brother in Cambridge and finally his mother who was somewhere on the UK mainland.

His father phoned Swansea Coastguard from Dubai and his brother phoned Thames Coastguard both of which relayed the call to Solent Coastguard. His mother got through to Solent direct.

Solent was able to task us straight away and, as we were in that area, it was a very quick rescue. If he had not been able to get through to anyone, his location meant it would have been unlikely that he would have been spotted unless he had managed to get back into his canoe or had been fortunate enough to drift ashore before he succumbed to the cold sea.

The lesson that was learnt from this was that if he could press his emergency numbers, and if he (and others in similar situations) had realised or been made aware, he would have been able to press 999 and ask for the Coastguard and he would then have been put through to Solent Coastguard direct. Still, all ended well and I am sure the message was taken onboard; next time he will be taking a waterproof radio.

Other benefits do come out of situations like this, as the story struck a chord, especially as having been relayed from Dubai, it made the news headlines. He was willing to be interviewed so a serious safety message was passed on to many thousands of people. The message may well have made a difference to someone in the future.

The main message, strangely enough, was for people to be aware that the Coastguards are part of the 999 system and have many rescue assets available to them. I say strangely because, despite all the adverts and publicity, many people still do not recognise that or they simply forget it.

The other message is that mobile phones may well get you out of difficulties but they are unlikely to be waterproof and suffer from poor signal areas. Most people carry one now, but (unfortunately) some seagoers consider it as a replacement to a radio.

I feel mobiles should only be used as a back up to a good quality waterproof radio having been to several tragic incidents where the initial call was made on a mobile phone but, before the casualties had been located, the mobile signal had been lost because the phone got waterlogged, battery ran down or they had drifted too far offshore to pick up a signal. In addition, we cannot yet home in on a mobile phone signal.

Another incident was quite comical and although ended well could have been tragic. The aircraft was scrambled to the report of a missing dory with one person onboard who, it was reported, was under the influence of alcohol. The crew was: Captain Peter Thomson, co-pilot Dave Gibbs, winch-op Terry Short and John Spencer was the winchman.

They had been tasked to search from the Needles to Yarmouth, then into the Western Solent and up Southampton Water. They started the search from the Needles and soon located a boat on a beach above the waterline where it had run aground. Initially they thought it was empty.

John was lowered to the beach alongside the boat to assess the situation. When he approached he found someone was laid in the bottom of the boat fast asleep. When John woke him, he had no idea where he was; he thought he was alongside at Southampton where he had climbed into the boat for a rest after a few drinks!

It is unlikely that he would have survived the night in the middle of November while laid in the bottom of a dory. He was also very lucky that the dory had managed to travel several miles without mishap and had run up the beach at a safe point.

Another job I was to attend that year was to the yacht 'Emlee' with a lady onboard who had suffered some form of fit after a fall in the cabin. We were airborne at the time so were soon on scene. The crew was: Captain

Peter Nicholson, co-pilot Dave Gibbs, Terry Short was the winch-op and I was the winchman.

I was lowered to the vessel which was south of the Isle of Wight to find the lady on a bunk in the cabin. I felt immediately that she had had some form of cerebral trauma and did not think it was as a result of her fall. She was confused, but trying her best to keep composed.

Her husband was clearly extremely worried and the situation took me right back to 1997 and the day that Margaret had her cerebral haemorrhage. This lady had more of a conscious level than Margaret had, but I knew she needed to get to hospital as soon as possible.

There was absolutely no way I would be able to get her into the stretcher and out of the cabin into the cockpit with only her husband to help; it was just too tight, especially with the movement from the rough sea. I requested that the Coastguard launch the Bembridge lifeboat, which meant I would have to remain with them for 40 minutes or more. I had all the equipment that I might require sent down and prepared the stretcher.

I was very conscious of how both of them would be feeling, it was important to keep the lady as calm as possible and to provide reassurance for her husband. At the same time, I was reliving my own experience.

Somehow, I must have achieved this. He sent a thank you letter to the Coastguard later to explain that his wife was still in hospital, but he was thanking all involved in the rescue. He also explained how I had reassured them both (in his words) "as if by magic" while waiting for the lifeboat. The letter was so sincere that I did feel humble because I was genuinely so concerned for the lady and I really was re-living my own experience.

I often came across situations that took me back to 1997, especially in hospital transfers, as many of the casualties we transferred were experiencing cerebral problems.

In this incident, when the lifeboat arrived three lifeboatmen came on board to help me transfer the lady (in a stretcher) through the cockpit hatch and across to the lifeboat which would provide a safer transfer to the aircraft. I opted to take her husband as well, the lifeboat crew agreeing to tow his yacht back to Bembridge harbour; they would find a safe berth for the yacht until he could pick it up later.

Another problem raised its head this year when the Company announced that the pension scheme was running into difficulties and that consultations would be commencing with the staff as to ways to correct the situation.

This would be the start of a few years of absolute worry for many of the staff, in particular for those close to retirement. It would also lead to mistrust of the Company. The consultations would become quite explosive: until then no one believed that pension agreements thought to be integral to our terms of employment could be reneged on. Many private companies were having the same problem and the rush to get out of the responsibilities of Defined Benefit pensions would roll through the private sector rapidly over the following few years.

The problem was highlighted by a new accounting rule and the Government's raid on the pension funds, tied in with the sudden drop of shares at the end of the dot-com boom and the problems in the Middle East. In addition, other stock phrases such as 'we are all living longer' etc. would start this ball rolling.

I could understand that the problems were real but I felt additional advantages were taken by many companies to restructure pensions from being the company's liability to being the employees' liability. The combination of the above problems emerging at the same time gave many companies the perfect opportunity to make this happen.

This is not the place to air this sort of problem but it was a major change to our employment terms and references and, for someone who was required to retire early on a suddenly reduced pension, it was very worrying.

I was to become quite vocal in the discussions, in particular protecting as best I could the rights of the aircrewmen. In the meantime, we could only carry on with the job and follow the consultations as they were unveiled. Some terrible mistakes were made during the so-called consultations and transition stage. I was to learn a great deal about pensions during that period and I was able to spot a few of those mistakes and have them rectified.

Part 8

Lee SAR 2002 – 2007

2002

Michael our grandson, was well into his second year of treatment and coping very well. He had to face up to many problems and there had been a roller coaster of worries, particularly for Kerry.

There were so many side effects from Michael's treatment, it was very difficult to know what to expect. Whenever anything out of the normal happened and he got poorly, she thought it was further symptoms of the leukaemia. So many worries and scares, but invariably these scares would prove to be side effects of the chemo or steroids and she grew to recognise and even expect them.

Michael himself learnt how to control the side effects; he would take himself off if he knew he had to rest and worked through the ones he could.

Early in 2002 'R-IJ' was scrambled to three missing children last seen on cliff paths close to Allum Bay on the Isle of Wight. The crew was: Captain Mark Jackson, co-pilot Dave Gibbs, winch-op Chris Bond and I was the winchman.

We had been scrambled at night, tasked to commence the search at the coastline east of Alum Bay towards the Needles. The cliffs started as rather muddy slopes with vegetation still growing on them, the occasional landslide leaving a very soft muddy screed then becoming firmer leading up to sheer chalk cliffs as we closed on the Needles lighthouse.

Only three minutes into the search, I located a heat source on the infrared in the muddy sloping area surrounded by small trees. As we got closer I was quite confident from the infrared camera that it was the boys and was able to con the aircraft close enough for Chris to confirm it using the night vision binoculars.

We had to jettison 1000 lbs of fuel as there was very little wind. This meant flying away from our present position, but we remained close enough to keep the boys identified on the infrared.

We then made the approach until we were able to get the boys in the spotlights. Two of them were trapped firmly in a thick mud screed, while the third boy was clear. He had been sensible, staying where he was because he could easily have slipped over the edge of one of the quite sheer drops.

It was not too difficult to pick the boys out of their predicament. I recovered the one not stuck in the mud first, as I did not want the downdraught to cause him further problems and the two in the mud were not going anywhere. I had to recover them to the aircraft one at a time; I could not have sent them up on their own as they were too small, making it unlikely they would have remained in the strops.

The boys had been cycling round the coastal paths prior to deciding to be a little more adventurous and head down a little dirt path towards the cliffs, eventually having to abandon the bikes when they had realised they were lost. They then stumbled into the mud while trying to get out of their predicament. The boys were flown to hospital now covered in mud and very cold, where they were reunited with their very worried parents.

Jobs like this will always be extremely rewarding. The boys had been located quickly and then rescued from the situation without too many problems, a happy conclusion with the children having a story to tell.

Yet, in the back of your mind, you know that if it was not for the infrared camera or night vision binoculars, they may not have been located until daylight the next morning. By then the headlines may well have been telling a totally different story.

In the June, Peter Thomson was coming up to his retirement and had his last job at the end of his last shift. They were scrambled to an unconscious diver from the dive boat 'Michelle Mary', who had missed his stops,.

It was a warm day with no wind and good visibility at Lee. The weather reports collected in the morning had not shown any problems. Peter was the captain, Pete Nicholson was in the left hand seat, Chris Bond was the winch-op and Mick Rowsell was the winchman. They headed off to carry out what they thought would be a straightforward tasking.

As they approached the scene, they were flying into a fog bank with the visibility reduced to less than 200 metres. They had a vessel on the radar in the position given and were able to get the 'Michelle Mary' to make transmissions to home in on with the aircraft's equipment, so decided to continue with the approach. The fog was too thick for the infrared to be of any assistance.

The first approach failed but the crew decided to make a second attempt before calling the job off. On the second approach, they caught a glimpse of the vessel just at the point they would have had to break off. The rescue was then completed as tasked.

The majority of the flight's compliment were at the base that day for Peter's last landing, a training flight having been planned so that he would be airborne when we all arrived for a sneaky reception as he landed on. The real scramble had been very timely, finishing Peter's career on a successful job and this could not have been better for someone who had been in Search and Rescue as long as he had.

When they landed, we could tell the crew had frightened themselves. When things are not quite right, we all tend to leave the aircraft looking a little vague as we are running through what has just happened in our minds.

They had taken off in perfect weather and visibility, unprepared for suddenly ending up in fog. Pete had felt like the fog was sucking him in on his very last flight! It really had been on the limits but the tasking was achieved and the diver left safely in medical care, probably unaware of how difficult the job had been.

Peter had his final leaving do on HMS Victory in Portsmouth dockyard – quite a special venue. Only a few weeks later Peter and Anne were on their way to begin their retirement dream, with exciting times ahead for them.

The flight would feel unusual without Peter. I did not always see eye to eye with him, but I recognised the many benefits he brought to the flight. I had never come across anyone who stuck up for his lads quite like him. He looked after the welfare of the flight in every respect, if he thought something was wrong he made sure it would not happen and no one would convince him otherwise. He had great drive and energy, I always felt he should be running a company or certainly a large operation like Aberdeen with dozens of aircraft and crews to control.

Graham Sorge took over as Chief Pilot so I was confident the flight would continue to run well. I also knew that I would be able to work well with Graham; we had always worked well together and would approach problems the same way, hence the reason we tended to look after a lot of the admin and databases for the flight and had done so for some years.

Richard Norris was the next pilot to join the flight; he had already carried out a few years on the unit as a co-pilot before leaving to build up the hours required for command. Richard had completed tours in the North Sea, Falkland Islands, and on a United Nations contract in Kosovo, before returning to Lee. He had returned to fill a co-pilot slot for the time being, replacing Steve Buckland who had recently left to work in Unst in the Shetland Islands. The intention was for Richard to be trained as a SAR Captain and eventually replace Peter Nicholson when he retired.

Around the same time, the company had won the SAR trial contract in the North Sea and Chris Bond would leave the unit to join the trial team. Chris would be returning in about a year's time, assuring another year at Lee for Terry. Alf Kitwood, an aircrewman previously based in Stornoway, would join as Chris Bond's relief initially, then Terry's relief when Chris returned.

Alf's background was much the same as the rest of the aircrewmen. He had been a Search and Rescue diver in the Navy, reaching Chief Petty Officer. Alf had also qualified as an anti-submarine aircrewman and a qualified helicopter aircrewman's instructor. He had joined Bristow on leaving the Navy, working on the SAR contract at Stornoway for a few years prior to transferring to Lee.

Alf's wife Sharon lived locally in Gosport. They had met when Alf was working on the flight at Lee when it was a naval flight, pre 1988. They had settled and bought their house in Gosport where they still lived, so this transfer was ideal for Alf.

I knew Alf before he joined but had never worked with him. He was from the next generation of naval-trained aircrewman after me but it was clear that the Navy was still producing aircrewmen who were characters in their own right. He is a true Yorkshire man and proud of it, very much his own person with a wealth of tricks and jokes up his sleeve. He had no difficulty catching me out, so much so that I had to get him to use the codeword 'safeguard', when he was on a serious topic as I was never sure whether or not he was joking.

Nevertheless, Alf would wake us all up at Lee and bring a few more laughs to the unit. If you put him and John Spencer together, the rest of the crew on shift would wonder what had hit them!

It is quite amazing really: Alf was only the second aircrewman to come into the unit since 1988 the last being John Spencer, who replaced Tony Campbell when Tony moved to Portland.

Diving incidents raised their head again this year, with one particular week that would involve several diving incidents. It started with 'R-IJ' being tasked to the report of a dive boat that had broken down with two divers missing. The crew was: Captain Mark Jackson, co-pilot Paul Mattinson, winch-op Mick Rowsell and I was the winchman.

When we arrived on scene, nothing was located in the position given. The dive boat had moved after repairing its engine. When we located it, they reported that they had recovered one diver but the other was still missing.

We soon located the missing diver and I was lowered to recover him and his equipment from the sea. The diver was fine and no medical help was required, so we lowered him to the Newhaven lifeboat that had also arrived on scene, they would return him to the dive boat and escort them back to shore.

On arrival back at base, we were re-tasked to refuel and return to the incident to escort the Newhaven lifeboat back to base as it had sprung a leak and was at risk of flooding, an extremely unusual situation for an all weather lifeboat as they are so sturdily built. They had managed to get the leak under control but could not make it back to Newhaven. When we arrived back on scene the lifeboat was entering Eastbourne harbour escorted by Eastbourne lifeboat.

Two days later the aircraft was scrambled to an unconscious diver, thirty miles southeast of the airfield. The diver was recovered to the aircraft and flown to Horsea landing site. He was conscious again by arrival at the hypobaric chamber.

The next day 'R-IJ' was tasked to the report of two divers in difficulties twenty-three miles southeast of Selsey Bill. The crew was: Captain Graham

Sorge, co-pilot Dave Gibbs, winch-op John Spencer and Alf Kitwood was the winchman.

The divers were on the dive boat 'Earl Grey.' One was conscious and the other was being resuscitated. When on scene, Alf was lowered to the vessel to prepare the casualties and recover them both to the aircraft: it is always a difficult job to deal with two casualties, in particular if one is requiring resuscitation.

Once recovered to the aircraft they were informed that all the hyperbaric chambers in the local area were in use. The aircraft was re-routed to Brighton hospital HLS to be met by a crash team for the casualty being resuscitated, before flying the conscious diver to a hyperbaric chamber at Whipps Cross hospital in London.

The next morning the same crew were scrambled to the report of two divers missing from the dive rib 'Wycombe Diver' four miles south of Goring. Soon after arriving on scene, the divers were located on the surface safe and well so they were picked up by the dive rib and Littlehampton lifeboat.

The following day 'R-IJ' was scrambled to the dive boat 'Voyager' twenty miles south of Selsey with another unconscious diver who was being resuscitated. Nick Horst was the winchman and recovered the diver to the aircraft where, with the help of Don Sowden, they continued the resuscitation until they were relieved by a crash team at Horsea HLS.

A few days later, I picked up another diver and his 'dive buddy' from the dive boat 'Channel Diver'. That was quite a number of diving incidents including two fatalities in a very short period, again, just in our area of coverage.

In September during a period when 'India Juliet' was undergoing a major refit and we were operating with Portland's aircraft 'Whisky Bravo', it was scrambled to a roll-on-roll-off container ferry with a fire onboard eight miles south of Eastbourne. The crew was: Captain Peter Nicholson, co-pilot Paul Mattinson, winch-op John Spencer and Chris Bond was the winchman.

When the aircraft arrived on scene, the ferry was leaving the shipping lane and intending to anchor. The infrared camera showed the hotspot to be at deck level below a stack of containers. 'R-WB' was then tasked to pick up East Sussex offshore fire teams and fly them to the vessel. Fourteen fire fighters plus eight 250 lb equipment pods were flown out and winched to the vessel. The Coastguard tug 'Anglian Monarch' and the Newhaven lifeboat were also proceeding to the scene and it was reported that the vessel was carrying 532 tonnes of cargo of which 20 tonnes were known to be dangerous.

The position of the fire was not easily accessible so proved quite difficult to bring under control. Once under control the vessel was re-routed to Southampton for damage assessment. Unfortunately, a second fire flared up so the vessel was re-routed into Portsmouth harbour and docked where eight fire engines and forty-five fire fighters assisted the crew, in getting the fire under control.

This was the second major incident in the channel in twenty-four hours as the day before, a tanker carrying 15,000 tonnes of molten sulphur caught fire. The fire had started in the engine room of the tanker 'Kaliope' as it sailed thirty miles north of Dover. The on-board fire fighting system was activated and proved successful in bringing the fire under control; none of the ship's eighteen crew were injured. Again, these were situations that could have easily been much worse.

In October, Alf Kitwood had a cliff rescue that was to prove quite awkward. They had been scrambled to the report of a man stuck a third of the way down a cliff at Warren Bay near Hastings. The crew was: Captain Peter Nicholson, co-pilot Richard Norris, winch-op Chris Bond and Alf was winchman.

This was a night tasking and, when 'R-IJ' arrived on scene, the man was seen by Alf on the infrared camera. He was still trying to climb the cliff in a very precarious position so Chris lowered Alf to recover the man to the aircraft.

It had not been easy getting Alf to the casualty, as they had to approach him by walking Alf along the cliff just below the casualty then, once in position, winch Alf up to the casualty; all calculated to minimise the downdraught and to prevent knocking screed etc. onto the casualty. When Alf arrived alongside the casualty, he was completely uncooperative and refused to allow Alf to place the strop around him.

Because of the precarious position both Alf and the casualty were in, Alf was obliged to take active action to pacify the man. He succeeded in that active action and called for the aircraft to climb then deposit them both on the cliff top, where Alf had to restrain and calm the casualty down until Coastguard assistance arrived.

That was clearly the right decision for Alf to make; it would have been unwise to recover the man to the aircraft, as a flying helicopter is not the environment in which to have a struggling person.

2003

In February 2003, 'R-IJ' was tasked while training to the report of a woman and child in the water having fallen off Bognor Pier in Sussex. The crew was: Captain John Rooney, co-pilot Dave Gibbs, winch-op Mick Rowsell and Alf Kitwood was the winchman.

When they arrived on scene, the child was being supported by a man (both still in the water at the end of the pier) while the mother and another man were also holding on to the end of the pier. On seeing the helicopter, the man with the child swam into the open water, holding on to the child to make it easier for the helicopter recovery.

Mick lowered Alf to the water to recover the child, a five-year-old girl, who they took to a waiting ambulance on the beach. After transferring the child to the care of the ambulance, they returned to recover the man who had saved her. A lifeboat that had now arrived on scene was recovering the lady and the other man while 'R-IJ' recovered the man who had been supporting the little girl, who by then was extremely cold and close to being hypothermic.

Due to a low fuel state 'R-IJ' had to fly to Goodwood airfield having radioed ahead for an ambulance to meet them there. The casualty was then transferred to the ambulance on arrival.

It transpired that the man was a police officer who, with a member of staff from Bognor pier, had swum out to the woman and child, supporting them until help arrived. It was February and the sea temperatures were very low. Without doubt, the police officer and the pier worker's quick response to the call had made the difference to the outcome of that incident.

In the April, 'R-IJ' was tasked by Dover Coastguards to another fire on a car carrier 'Oriental Highway' in the Dover straights. The Crew was: Captain Peter Nicholson, co-pilot Paul Mattinson, I was the winch-op and Mick Rowsell was the winchman.

On scene, we were tasked to standby the vessel until the first lifeboat arrived as the crew thought they had the fire under control. This proved not to be the case so, once the lifeboat arrived; we were re-tasked to pick up fire teams from Tide Mills in Sussex.

Nine fire fighters and 900 lbs of equipment were picked up and flown to the 'Oriental Highway'. On completion, 'R-IJ' was tasked to return to Lee, refuel and return with another team of fire fighters and equipment. Shortly after picking up six fire fighters for the return trip, 'R-IJ' was informed that the fire was definitely under control and the aircraft was stood down.

These sorts of incidents can easily turn into very serious life threatening ones but, thankfully, the majority are brought under control. Much of this damage limitation has to be attributed to the ships fire fighting systems and fire teams who attend these fires. The offshore fire teams are made up from serving fire fighters attached to fire stations close to SAR helicopter bases or recognised helicopter pick up points.

The fire fighters that are called to go offshore are all volunteers and undergo quite comprehensive additional training to carry out the offshore role, including helicopter briefings, helicopter winching, dinghy and helicopter underwater escape drills. They have special equipment that can be loaded into accurately marked bags showing the total weights of the equipment inside (the weights being very important for our calculations). In addition, the fire fighters have to wear special offshore fire/immersion suits and survival aids. All this equipment is kept at immediate readiness close to or at the likely pick up points.

This system was already in operation in Hampshire, Sussex and Kent. Over the next few years, we would see a national standard established under the initiative called 'The Sea of Change Project' which led to the 'Maritime Incident Response Group', with the volunteer offshore fire fighters trained and equipped to the same standard.

In the March we had been called in from home to the report of a crewmember having had a suspected stroke on the fishing vessel 'Opya' ten miles south of Hastings. The crew was: Captain John Rooney, co-pilot Dave Gibbs, I was the winch-op and Pat Holder was the winchman. Pat was being trained as the south coast relief aircrewman. He was another ex Navy SAR diver, already on line as a winchman and part way through his conversion to our aircraft as a winch-op.

En-route the weather worsened the further east we went and the cloud base was forcing us down until we reached the point when we had to decide to climb to a safe height. This would mean the pilots flying on instruments, in itself not a problem, but it would mean letting back down to the surface when we arrived on scene. That would only be possible if there was suitable clearance below the cloud at the scene of the incident.

On closing the area, we had to request that the 'Opya' transmit a countdown on his radio so that we could home in to those transmissions to the actual position. This was a French-speaking vessel and we had difficulty getting them to estimate the cloud base. There were a number of vessels in the vicinity and we would not know the height of them, so they would all need to be avoided when we attempted the descent.

John and Dave, using the aircraft's over-fly facility flew over the top of the contact we believed to be the 'Opya' and pressed the 'on top' button which allowed the aircraft to enter a circuit that would automatically approach the contact into wind. John would descend to 200ft whilst in the circuit and, if we were not visual with the surface by then, we would climb back up to a safe height.

At 200ft, we were getting glimpses of the surface so we continued towards the contact on Radar. We had asked the vessel to put all the deck lights on and picked them up visually on the latter part of the approach, allowing enough visual references for John to continue his approach.

The next problem was that the 'Opya' was heading out of wind; it was a beam trawler and had its trawl out. We tried to get him heading into wind but he was not able to do that in the time we had on scene. The conditions were very rough and the vessel was moving up and down considerably, although we noticed that having the beam trawls out was preventing it from corkscrewing.

We decided as a crew that we could attempt the lift on this heading and, providing we could get the hi-line onboard, we would give it a go. Pat who would be going down on the vessel was in full agreement. We were successful in managing to get Pat onboard where he prepared the casualty for the recovery. Both Pat and the casualty were recovered to the aircraft safely.

When we had the casualty in the aircraft, John had to climb to a safe height as he lost visual references as soon as he pulled away from the vessel. The low cloud base made it impossible to take the casualty to either of the nominated hospital landing sites at Hastings or Eastbourne, so we opted to take the casualty back towards Lee because the cloud base was improving towards the west.

As we descended on the approach to Lee, the cloud base was high enough for us to divert to the Portsmouth hospital HLS, where we were able to transfer the casualty to a waiting ambulance. This was not an easy job and letting down to the vessel in those conditions was only made possible by the SAR avionics we had onboard.

In the June, one of our jobs was to a man overboard from the container vessel 'Patricia Delmas' twelve miles south of Eastbourne. The job was late at night and the crew was: Captain Mark Jackson, co-pilot Paul Mattinson, I was the winch-op and John Spencer was the winchman.

En-route the story was unfolding that the man was a stowaway found onboard; he had been apprehended and was being kept in detention until the ship arrived at its next port.

However, the man had escaped and had run through the accommodation onto the upper deck, grabbed hold of a lifejacket (which he had quickly put on) and then jumped overboard. That in itself was extremely dangerous, in particular with the type of lifejacket he had put on. He also had the risk of being sucked into the propellers. Apart from all that, there was no way he could make it twelve miles to shore (even in June) and he would soon succumb to the cold water.

The warship 'HMS Lindisfarne', which was in the area at the time, had responded to the Mayday relay and was commencing a search. The ferry 'Dieppe' was also joining the search and the Eastbourne and Newhaven Lifeboats were proceeding to the scene.

En-route 'R-IJ' was informed that the warship had located the casualty and that the crew of their rigid inflatable sea boat was in the process of recovering him from the water.

When we arrived on scene the casualty was onboard the warship and resuscitation was being carried out by some crewmembers. John was lowered to the warship to recover the casualty to the aircraft. We flew him to Eastbourne hospital landing site, continuing life support until relieved by a waiting crash team; the man did not survive.

I often reflect on this incident, as does John. It simply seemed so tragic; he was clearly a fit young man, who for whatever reason had deemed it necessary to leave his homeland on the Ivory Coast in Africa. He had managed to make some landing point in Europe then made it by whatever means to Rotterdam, eventually boarding this vessel illegally, probably unaware that it would not be stopping at a British port.

He had obviously expected to end up in the water at some stage, as he had his personal possessions in a clear plastic waterproof bag attached to him. Witnessing such a fruitless and desperate attempt to get to the UK, certainly made us look at the immigration problem in a different light. I can only guess as to the reason for that attempt, probably to achieve a future for himself and possibly to help his family back home.

In the July, Peter Nicholson retired. Being the training captain on the flight, he was instrumental in keeping standards high at Lee-on-Solent. He was always extremely professional and someone the company listened to. Personally, I always considered Peter to be the voice of reason, providing a lot of stability on the unit. It was a shame seeing the people that I had worked with, liked and respected leaving the flight; this was all an unwanted reminder that it would soon be my turn.

Richard Norris, who was now qualified as a SAR captain, took over Peter's slot and another returning pilot, Simon Hornsby, who had rejoined a few months previously took over Richard's position. Simon had a similar background as Richard; he had carried out two tours at Lee-on-Solent as a co-pilot and had worked in the Falkland Islands, the North Sea and Den Helder in Holland. Simon would be trained as a SAR Captain as it had been decided that the flight should operate with five captains and two co-pilots allowing for greater flexibility in running the rosters.

Michael was coming to the end of his treatment for Leukaemia. The three-year regime that he had to endure was quite traumatic for him and for Kerry and Richard who had to cope with the worry of it all; they were constantly available for Michael, while at the same time, making every effort not to let Jessica miss out on a normal life.

Margaret and I lived every step of the way, fighting constant worry, but were now reaching the end of that awful journey and were very proud of how well they managed as a family unit.

Everything was looking fine for Michael with the tests showing him clear; he would still be monitored and tested for a few years on a scheduled follow up programme. The main thing was that he would soon be able to get back to a normal childhood; he was now thirteen-years-old and fortunately still doing well at school despite his many weeks of missed classes. We were hopeful that he would catch up and his teachers were very positive that this would be the case.

For Michael himself, he was looking forward to his football and other sporting activities. He had been warned that it would take a while to get back to full fitness as his body would have to adjust to being without all the medication he had been on. It all seemed very strange that, on the 1st September he would go from taking a whole collection of powerful drugs to the next day taking none.

Michael, Kerry, Richard and Jessica managed to have a well-deserved holiday in Florida, taking in all the sights that Kerry had been able to enjoy when she was Jessica's age. The trip was a nice pick-you-up for them.

It would seem that I could not cover a year without some major diving incident. This year would have the now familiar run of divers requiring recovery with decompression problems, perhaps no more than the yachting fraternity with boom injuries or rescues on cliffs, but each year we would get one or two incidents that were way out of the norm.

This one was in the July when 'R-IJ' was scrambled to the report of an unconscious diver plus another who had missed twenty minutes of stops, both divers were onboard the dive boat 'Michelle Mary', fifteen miles south of Shoreham. The crew was: Captain Richard Norris, co-pilot Dave Gibbs, winch-op Don Sowden and I was the winchman.

On scene, Don lowered me to the dive boat to find one diver presumed dead with no sign of life. As I could not confirm that, life support was continued and I sent the second diver (who was not showing any signs of decompression sickness) up to the aircraft as he would still need to go to a recompression chamber. Once I was recovered to the aircraft with the unconscious diver, the life support was continued with Don's help until we were met by the paramedics at Horsea (Portsmouth) helicopter landing site.

On returning to base, we were re-tasked to refuel then return to the 'Michelle Mary' as the dive boat had reported more divers missing. The afternoon's crew were waiting to take over when we landed so 'R-IJ' refuelled then headed back to the dive boat. The new crew was: Captain John Rooney, co-pilot Paul Mattinson, winch-op John Spencer and Nick Horst was the winchman.

On scene, the dive boat confirmed that just one diver was missing. He had failed to surface at the end of his planned dive so he could still be below the surface or may have made surface somewhere out of sight of the dive boat. The search commenced with Shoreham lifeboat and other vessels assisting. 'R-IJ' continued the unsuccessful search for six hours including a refuel at Shoreham airfield before being released. The final outcome was tragic; two fatalities and one diver who required decompression, and this from two separate incidents from one boat. The second incident possibly had something to do with the first, but either way the incidents were among a small group of divers, highlighting the possible dangers.

In the November, we had a tragic incident on the day the England rugby team had won the World Cup. 'R-IJ' was scrambled to the report of a man having fallen or jumped off the end of Brighton Pier. The crew was: Captain Graham Sorge, co-pilot Simon Hornsby, winch-op Nick Horst and I was the winchman.

Initially we had thought that 'R-IJ' would be released from task before we arrived at Brighton, fully expecting the man to be recovered from the water before we arrived.

However, en-route the Coastguards reported that the man had been seen clinging to the end of the pier, but he had failed to grab any of the life rings thrown to him by security men working on the pier and had disappeared before anyone could get to him.

When we arrived on scene, Nick spotted him almost immediately floating in the very heavy surf, the sea being moderate to rough at the time. I was lowered to recover him from the surf and carried out resuscitation en-route to Brighton hospital landing site for transfer to a waiting ambulance.

The young man was a rugby fan and had been celebrating the victory on the end of the pier when the accident happened. I do not know if this young man had been drinking, or whether he had jumped into the water as part of the celebrations, but he lost his life as a result and it doesn't get more tragic than that.

I would reflect on this and other similar incidents, because I used to be one of these strange people who always felt the need to jump into water as a prank, especially when celebrating, and I have a number of friends who did the same. Some of them are still working with me now fortunately; we have grown out of the strange habit.

Winching to Calshot Lifeboat (Photo Mike O'Brien)

Approaching the deck (Photo Mike O'Brien)

Yachting incident in the Solent (Photo Mike O'Brien)

2004/2005

2004 was supposedly my retirement year, but I was still incensed about our pension being reduced; we had just come to the end of two years of wrangling involving two different consultation sessions. The first was (in my view) a deal forced on us under the guise of it being implemented by consultation, which was really an exercise in anger management, with few employees able to control that anger and the process simply bulldozed through regardless. As soon as things started to settle down, the company then announced that the fund was still in trouble and commenced a second round of consultations to reduce our entitlements even further.

After all that, I was given a chance to remain in the job after my normal retirement date if I wished, but as a contractor with many of my rights as an employee taken away (even though I would be expected to do exactly the same job). This was before the new legislation regarding age discrimination had come in. If my pension had not been messed around with, I would have been happy to remain as a contractor as Terry had done.

However, I now felt after the awful things that had happened to the pension fund over the last two years, that aircrew who wanted to should be given the opportunity to continue past the age of 58 and remain under their present terms and conditions. This would at least give us a chance to recoup part of the shortfall in our expected pension. Our managing director had hinted during the consultations that they may allow this, but I was the first to put it to the test.

The argument about this went on until just a couple of weeks prior to my retirement, when the company eventually agreed to keep me on under my present terms and conditions, allowing me to extend rather than becoming a contractor. This would make a major difference to my pension and, in my case, would allow me to recover some of the pension I had lost.

It was my intention, if allowed to extend, to stand down as the Chief Crewman as I did not feel it was fair to continue in the role after my normal retirement date. However, Graham asked if I would stay in the role and the lads also thought I should, so I was fortunate enough to keep that job as well.

I felt extremely fortunate. I wanted to remain working, I knew I was still fit enough to carry out the role and still enjoyed the job. I worked hard to keep an above average level of fitness that I felt was required for the role.

I also kept on top of my job in the many other factors required, making a special effort to achieve this. I would not have remained if anyone on the unit felt that I should not.

The year had commenced very quietly with very little out of the ordinary for the first few months, just standard type jobs that had included hospital transfers, yachting incidents, a few divers, a few cliffs jobs and plenty of searches. One of the searches in the June had involved one of our crews for over seven hours flying.

The crew on that search was: Captain Simon Hornsby, co-pilot Paul Mattinson, winch-op Nick Horst, Alf Kitwood was the winchman. They had been searching for a missing lone yachtsman reported overdue, his yacht the 'She'll Do' had been located washed up on the beach, fully rigged at Hengistbury Head in Dorset.

This search involved two helicopters, seven lifeboats and shoreline search teams, with nothing untoward sighted. Jobs like this will always be frustrating as you always hope to find the casualty safe and well. Even if the result of the search is not what you hoped for, recovering a body will make a major difference to a family, at least there can be closure to the situation and the family is not left wondering and possibly clinging on to false hope.

Don Sowden and Terry Short located three lucky men who had been missing overnight on cliffs near Charmouth. The men had managed to light a fire enabling them to keep warm and although the fire had gone out, it was still warm enough for the infrared camera to acquire the embers. The three men were located on a path alongside a 300ft drop and winched to safety.

Mick Rowsell and Terry Short recovered our first casualty from the 'Queen Mary II'. We had been wondering when our first transfer with the cruise liner would be, having carried out several medical transfers with the 'Queen Elizabeth II' over the years.

Another unusual task this year was a tasking to search for a missing 89-year-old gent at Milford on Sea. The crew was: Captain Simon Hornsby, co-pilot Paul Mattinson, John Spencer was the winch-op and I was the winchman. On completion of the unsuccessful search 'R-IJ' was stood down and on our way back to base we flew over what John thought was a person sat in the water of a dyke close to Lymington.

We decided that we should check it out so circuited back to the position only to find a situation that would require a helicopter to resolve. A man and his wife had been cycling alongside the Dyke when the man had slipped in, still on his bike and was lying injured in the mud half-in and half-out of the water. I was able to recover him to the aircraft and we were on our way to hospital only minutes after his accident. He was unlucky to have the accident but extremely lucky he had timed the accident to match a rescue helicopter flying overhead.

In the October, while operating with Portland's aircraft 'R-WB' we were scrambled to an angling boat with two people onboard that was taking on water south of the Nab tower near Portsmouth. The crew was: Captain Mark Jackson, co-pilot Paul Mattinson, winch-op Nick Horst and I was the winchman.

On scene, we located the boat semi-submerged with the two casualties sitting on the bow of the boat. Nick lowered me to them, taking two strops with me. The vessel was extremely unstable when I landed onboard so decided to prepare and send both the survivors to the aircraft together. When I reached out for the hook to send them up to the aircraft, I felt the boat was about to turn over, which made me realise this was a three on the hook situation.

Literally just as the three of us left the boat, it capsized. I feel quite sure that if I had sent them up on their own and it had capsized with just me onboard, I would have been able to dive clear. I do not have the same confidence that we would have all been able to clear the boat if it had happened while all three of us were onboard, as there were a lot of snagging hazards in the bow of the boat.

In the November, Nick Horst had another casualty in the water with a broken femur. Due to the swell at the time and the pain the casualty was in, he was unable to recover him to a boat prior to preparing him for winching.

Nick therefore opted to recover the casualty from the water, with the aid of four other people in the water with him all wearing buoyancy aids, they managed to float and secure him onto our aircraft stretcher. I was the winch-op and, on Nick's instructions, had to winch Nick and the stretcher just clear of the water while he completed securing the harness that would hold the casualty in the stretcher before full recovery to the aircraft.

It may be a strange coincidence but I believe Nick has had the majority of these immobilisation in the water tasks. They are never straightforward for the winchman; he has to try to control the casualty's pain as well as providing them with reassurance and the confidence to be strapped into a stretcher while in the water, in this case achieving that quickly before the cold water took its toll.

Also in the November, we had to recover three climbers from one of the spines leading from the mainland of the Isle of Wight to the Needles. This should have been a straightforward job but proved quite difficult. The crew was: Captain Simon Hornsby, co-pilot Richard Norris, I was the winch-op and Don Sowden the winchman.

The situation was quite unusual from the beginning and we had been pre-warned that we may be required; however, the climbers were very experienced and well equipped. They had set off on a planned but tricky climb that they expected to complete before it got dark.

As the light faded they realised they were at a dangerous point on the cliff, right on the spine, making it unsafe to continue in the fading light. It was a clear night with no wind; they had good protective clothing and were quite prepared to stay where they were until first light, before continuing with the climb. They also had radios and informed the Coastguard of their predicament, saying that they intended securing themselves to the cliff and would sit it out until the morning.

I could quite understand that decision: an experienced team would prepare themselves for those situations just as they would on a major climb spread over a few days. Nevertheless, this would be a difficult call for the Coastguard who knew how precarious that part of the cliff was. Not only were they on the spine of a very sheer cliff, that cliff and its spine are no longer stable with regular landslides and bits of the spine dropping away.

After many discussions between the climbers and the Coastguard, they agreed to recovery from their present predicament and 'R-IJ' was tasked to recover them.

On scene, it was obvious that it would not be straightforward. There was little wind and the aircraft required too much power for a safe hover.

The position of the casualties required us to hover facing the spine and, as the spine to the left of the aircraft was considerably higher than the one the casualties were on, it meant the left hand seat pilot would have to fly the aircraft as Simon (the captain) would have no visual references to the right. It also meant having to carry out a high winch above the rescue point.

Fortunately, we had two captains in the crew so Richard was able to take over from the left hand seat without any problems; nevertheless, we would have to hover about 90ft above the spine and about 350ft above the cliff bottom.

For various reasons it is quite common for the winchman to have to leave the aircraft at heights greater than that which we normally chose to put him out of the door (approx 40') but on those occasions, as a winchman you do feel very vulnerable, especially when the aircraft is pulling almost maximum power and the job is at night. Don had to opt for carrying out double lifts remaining on the wire and picking up one casualty at a time, so had to face leaving the aircraft from that height three times to recover them all.

The winching had to be precise to position Don to an exact spot; the climbers could not risk moving and there were no firm footholds for Don when alongside them, hence the reason he would not be able to leave the wire. Anyway, all three were winched to the aircraft safely.

The Coastguards had made the right decision insisting that they came off, when we went back later to look at the spot in daylight, it was a very small area with boulders ready to break away, including the one we reckon they had used to secure themselves.

Another problem arose this year which would inadvertently continue to cause problems over the next couple of years; this was the introduction of the European Working Time Directive, which restricted our working hours to a maximum of two thousand hours a year. The 2000 hour total included 50% of our overnight stand-by time. This directive took quite a while for the SAR flights and the company to come to terms with. The problems this rule would cause to the SAR flights would be far-reaching, not only in making it happen, but also in understanding the complexities of that requirement.

It soon became clear that it was not just a mathematical problem of a straight two thousand hours but that it was a rolling requirement and my records showed that all the crewman at Lee exceeded this four or five times a year by three to four hundred hours. The same would clearly apply to the pilots.

As this was law with a fixed implementation date, it created havoc trying to get everyone's hours down, at an incredible cost to the Company. I was quite convinced after spending a few weeks studying the problem and juggling with the aircrewman's roster, that the only way it could possibly be achieved would be by getting the base hours well below the two thousand hour level and increasing the crewing levels by one pilot and one crewman.

The Company tried to solve the problem by sharing an additional pilot and aircrewman between units. I fully understood that attempt as we are a commercial company and must run as cost effectively as possible. However, it soon became obvious, even to management that the shared extra crew would not solve the problem and eventually the flight's operating crewing levels did increase with an extra pilot and aircrewman on each of the twenty-four hour units. Even that would prove tight with crewmembers still bouncing along the two thousand hour limit, requiring relief crews at short notice.

This problem with the duty hours coincided with Chris Bond returning to Lee after his time on the North Sea trial, which was further extended for Chris as, on completion of that trial, he had been required to help set up a SAR contract at Den Helder in Holland. The new requirement for an extra aircrewman at Lee led to the decision for Terry (who was originally asked to stay on until Chris Bond's return) to remain for at least another year.

We were all pleased about that. Terry was still one of the fittest aircrewmen in the company and still on top of the job in every way. He was the first aircrewman on a dedicated SAR Flight in the UK to remain in the role full time past sixty. I only hope I will be the second with Mick Rowsell not far behind me. Terry was now approaching sixty-one and breaking new ground carrying out the job at that age and not showing any signs of the job being a problem to him.

A few people who did not know Terry were making waves about his age, but those that worked with him were more than happy and would soon say if we thought differently. Someone starting to slip behind in competency affects the whole crew, hence our annual practical assessments in several different aspects of our role covering both aviation and medical skills. I also knew that if Terry had any doubts himself he would stop.

However, the company had decided that there had to be a limit and started preparations to relieve Terry. They wanted to try training an ab-initio aircrewman, initially as a winchman only. I was not too happy about that, as it would dilute the way we carry out this role, which worked so well having everyone dual trained; nevertheless, it was clear we would have to look to the future and this was probably the best way to bring someone in to the role.

I was asked to assess the suitability of the person they wished to train up. Simon O'Mahony, who was a senior operations officer based at Norwich. Simon had been with the company for some years and was thought very highly of. He had been trying to get into this role for several years.

Simon had quite a lot of aviation experience with his operations role and had already trained as an aircrewman and carried out commercial load lifting duties on an ad-hoc basis. This was a requirement that came up occasionally and the company had a few people trained to carry out this role as a secondary duty.

I still had my doubts as to this being the way forward so when Simon joined us for the assessment, I was not going to make anything easy for him. I would be fair but would also make sure he was up to it. Simon had a very comprehensive few days with us; he was so keen that I could not help but warm to him. He took everything we threw at him with such enthusiasm, even all the wet winching in freezing cold seas which was quite alien to him, but nothing was going to stop him. I even had him picking me out of the water with the odd struggle thrown in but he coped well.

It was apparent that he was the right character for the role and all of us involved in his assessment, including Terry, were happy to recommend he proceed.

The plan was for him to carry out a winchman's course at the Royal Air Force Search and Rescue school at RAF Valley. He was one of the first (if not the first) UK civilians to be trained in this role by the RAF. He would then gain further training with the Coastguard SAR flight at Stornoway where he would also fly with the crews, observing the role.

Eventually Simon would join us for further training before being qualified to operate as a fifth member of the crew working alongside the duty winchman. He still had to pass the medical courses prior to qualifying in order to fly independently as a winchman. The whole process would take the best part of a year and would involve a considerable amount of self-study. It was also likely to take another few years to get him online as a winch operator.

Graham Sorge retired at the end of the year, something I was very sorry about as I found it very easy to work alongside him; he would be the last of the original pilots to leave. I had been hoping that Graham would stay on a little longer but his normal retirement date had coincided with family reasons for moving back to the Aberdeen area, which of course meant that he and Mona would be returning to live in Scotland so were leaving the area as well.

Richard Norris was appointed to take over as the Chief Pilot, which was nice to see. Richard had been trained by Bristow and had jumped through all the training hoops required to achieve his SAR Command, including two tours at Lee as a co-pilot. He had proved his ability to lead in Kosovo and now onto being the Chief Pilot at Lee. I felt the appointment was very much deserved and I would have no problems working with him as the Chief Pilot.

Graham's position as a SAR pilot was initially filled by Captain John Bell, a North Sea Commander previously working on a contract in Holland. John was not qualified as a SAR Captain, so joined the unit in the role of co-pilot and would be trained over the next year or two for command in the SAR role. John would be transferred from Den Helder moving to the area with his partner Julie.

Another Captain already qualified in the SAR role, Neill Stephenson, was appointed to Lee to be Graham's replacement as a SAR Captain, but he did not join until a few months after Graham left because he was waiting to be relieved from the Stornoway SAR flight. When Neill arrived, John remained at Lee as the extra pilot to complete the new compliment required by the duty hours directive.

Neill's transition to becoming a pilot was quite unusual. Neill is a New Zealander who, while serving in the New Zealand Army operating in Malaya, had his first experience operating with helicopters while carrying out exercises in the Malaysian jungle where helicopters were used to move the troops around.

Neill soon noticed that, while he was living in uncomfortable conditions in the jungle (with all the hardships that entailed) the aircrew when flying into the clearings, which had been prepared for them by the troops on the ground, always arrived refreshed and wearing smart, clean clothing. The aircraft operated from and returned to a comfortable operating base. Neill felt quite envious of them, thinking that was the life for him and from then on made every effort to transfer to aircrew!

Unfortunately, he was never able to achieve his wishes in New Zealand, either in the forces or as a civilian when he left the army. Having seen an advert for pilots required in the UK forces, he felt that if he came over to Britain then applied he would stand a better chance than applying from New Zealand. Neill had an uncle with a farm in Scotland, and in the search of the career he wanted, moved over to the UK to work on his uncle's farm.

As soon as he was settled in Scotland, he started applying to the forces to join as a helicopter pilot. The Royal Navy accepted Neill for training after he had passed all the necessary interviews and aptitude tests. On completion of officer training at Dartmouth he qualified as a Sea King pilot in the anti submarine role then went on to Search and Rescue based at Prestwick in Scotland.

On leaving the Navy, he joined Bristow Helicopters to train as a SAR pilot on the Coastguard SAR flight at Stornoway. After a few years in Stornoway, he transferred to Lee-on-Solent, moving down with his wife Jacqueline and children. Neill has no regrets about that decision taken while living in quite miserable conditions in the middle of a jungle in Malaya and I cannot help but admire the length he went to in achieving his goal.

In May of 2005, 'R-IJ' was tasked to the report of a man fallen overboard from the yacht 'Grandee' eighteen miles SSE of St Albans Head. The yacht was taking part in a cross channel race. They had managed to recover the man from a very rough sea but, having concerns' about the condition of the casualty, the skipper of the yacht asked for advice from the Coastguard. They in turn took advice from the on-call doctor who, being concerned about possible hypothermia and secondary drowning, recommended helicopter evacuation. The conditions were atrocious and the tasking was at night. The crew was: Captain John Rooney, co-pilot Simon Hornsby, I was the winch-op and Terry Short was the winchman.

As soon as we were airborne I knew it was going to be a difficult task in strong winds, rough seas, heavy rain and at night. The Coastguards had reported that the cruise liner 'Aurora' was on scene; they were hoping that having a large vessel like that on scene would provide protection for us by acting as a windbreak, allowing us to carry out the rescue in the lee of the cruise liner.

We had managed to use this technique before in a few isolated cases when the seas were a bit calmer than that night and the winds not as strong. The ideal situation to take advantage of the possibility of using the lee of a large vessel is when the seas are still rough but the winds abating.

This was not the case this night; the winds were so strong that we would have to be very close to the liner to gain any advantage. That would put us into disturbed air from the liner itself, making it even more unpredictable.

Because of my doubts about using this technique in these conditions, I was quite sure we would have to attempt the rescue well clear of the 'Aurora'. In view of that I requested that the Coastguard also launch a lifeboat, so Swanage lifeboat was asked to proceed to the area. At least it would be en-route should anything go wrong.

On scene, my prediction was right; it was extremely dangerous trying to position in the lee of the liner. The movement from the yacht when stationary in those conditions was impossible to read and the turbulence from the wind buffeting off the liner was very unpredictable. There was absolutely no way we would have been able to get Terry onboard. The only chance was to get the yacht underway into wind (providing a bit of stability) but it would still be extremely difficult with the mast all over the place and the yacht heaving and cork-screwing in the rough seas, possibly achievable in daylight but not at night.

Terry was prepared to go down and I know exactly how he would be feeling. I also knew he would attempt the impossible. This was going to have to be my call and I simply knew that Terry risked serious injury if we went ahead. We have all been in this position and if it is to save life, the risk will often be taken, unless it is impossible. This was close to that situation.

We decided that if we could get the hi-line onboard, we would continue. After attempts to get the hi-line onboard failed, I started to feel even more concerned for Terry. I even thought that swapping roles may help as I thought Terry to be just about the best winch-op I have known and felt that if anyone could achieve getting the line and then a winchman onboard, he could.

Anyway, between John Rooney and myself, we decided to gain more information on the casualty to see if the risk was really worth taking. In these conditions, the risk would not only be to Terry or the aircraft, but to the casualty as well. Trying to recover a casualty, possibly in a stretcher, from a vessel moving like that would be fraught with danger.

The yacht reported that the casualty was now able to sit up and was in a warm environment. He had been able to drink some tea and was aware of his surroundings. He had clearly been through an awful ordeal, having been thrown into seas like that and was extremely lucky that the crew had been able to locate and recover him to the yacht. I have been to many 'man overboard' incidents in rough seas over the years where the casualty was not recovered alive. He must have been suffering extreme shock but it sounded as though he was now managing to gain control of his situation.

This information put a completely different light on the incident and, after asking a few more questions, we decided that the casualty's condition no longer justified the risk. The lifeboat was en-route, although I expected it would be too dangerous for the lifeboat to affect a transfer either, but at least they could escort the 'Grande' to calmer waters before carrying out the transfer. If the lifeboat considered it safe to transfer the casualty, it would be possible for us to recover the casualty from them.

'R-IJ' was tasked to refuel then return to cover the lifeboat if they decided to attempt a transfer. On arrival back at base, we were informed that the lifeboat would not be attempting a transfer in these conditions. That decision had been taken for exactly the same reasons as ours; they would have had to put a lifeboatman and the casualty at risk if they attempted the transfer. However, that was something I am sure they would have attempted if the condition of the casualty had been worse.

This was one of the very few times that I have had to say 'no' to a tasking and something I hate to do; it is not in the nature of the job we do. Although having said that, there have been occasions that the winchman has been put at risk only to find the casualty has very little wrong with them.

For example, if a crewmember had lost a finger in an accident then clearly it would be nice to get him to hospital as quick as possible and if the conditions are favourable for a safe transfer that decision would normally be taken. Take the same situation on a stormy night, and knowing the vessel will reach port in the morning it would be unlikely the risk would justify that recovery.

Situations like that are less common now as the Coastguards do screen these medical rescue situations, even taking advice from on-call doctors who are trained in making these decisions.

This was the case that night. At the time of the initial call, I am sure the right decision was taken, it was just that by the time we arrived on scene, the casualty's condition had improved, allowing us as a crew to balance that against the risk. All the right decisions were made but it is still a difficult one to call for lots of reasons; there will always be doubts and 'what ifs'.

Television crews joined us again in May to cover our activities for the rest of the summer. This time it was the BBC for a programme called 'Seaside Rescue'. The brief was to cover coastal rescues on the South

Coast during the summer of 2005, also shadowing lifeguards operating in Cornwall and the crew of the Weymouth lifeboat in Dorset.

They put cameras in the cockpit to monitor the pilots and a fixed camera in the cabin. The winchmen were asked to wear a camera on their helmets and they used the cameras already fixed on the winch and the infrared. One camera operator flew on all our training and operational trips. This was more intrusive than the previous filming and something the flight had mixed feelings about, we just hoped that we got a team that would blend into the unit like the previous times.

In June, Mick Rowsell was scrambled to the 'Queen Elizabeth II' to carry out a medical transfer of a passenger who had been taken ill. This was during the Trafalgar celebrations in Portsmouth when all the passengers were waiting to watch the mammoth firework display at the end of the event. Earlier that day the liner had been involved in the Queen's revue of the ships in the Solent.

The transfer coincided with a cloudburst that turned the deck into an ice rink. Mick had a slightly heavy landing and slipped on the deck, smashing into a bollard, quite unusual for anything to go wrong on a huge deck like that.

Anyway, Mick shrugged it off, got on with the job and carried on for the rest of the shift. Nick Horst who was the winch-op that day asked Mick if he was all right, Nick had seen how hard Mick had fallen, but he assured Nick that he was okay. It was not until the next morning when his joints and muscles tightened up that Mick had to admit that all was not well. The whole of the side of his leg and most of his back was one huge bruise just about the worst I had seen.

As it turned out, Mick had not broken anything. The injury was superficial and he was back to normal within a week with the bruises remaining a little longer; nevertheless, this highlighted yet again the type of guys we had on the unit. An injury had to be serious before they would declare it, which goes as far back to Nick completing that rescue years ago before declaring his broken leg.

I am not saying that it is right to ignore these knocks, as clearly an ignored injury may prevent the winchman from carrying out the next job properly. However, that is the nature of the aircrewman and probably the same spirit that helps them perform the job as well as they do. We all clearly take knocks in this job but we are also quite good at assessing the damage. If we went to a doctor every time we took a knock, the doctor would normally advise rest, when often that was not required.

Later that year we were tasked to the report of an injured crewmember from the fishing vessel 'Zulu 525' ten miles south of Shoreham. The crew was: Captain Neill Stephenson, co-pilot John Rooney, I was the winch-op and Don Sowden was the winchman.

En-route 'R-IJ' was informed that the casualty's injuries were severe and that Shoreham lifeboat was also proceeding to assist if required. Don was winched to the vessel as soon as we arrived on scene, but we could see that it would be difficult to move the casualty to a suitable winching position. However, the initial task in hand was to stabilise and prepare the casualty for transfer.

The casualty had taken a severe knock from a fishing block, which fractured his scapula and several ribs and was suffering from extreme pain. This was Don's first problem as the only pain relief available was Entonox and the casualty was showing signs of a pneumothorax, which is one of the medical problems for which Entonox cannot be administered because of its nitrous oxide content. Trying to manoeuvre a casualty in extreme pain and screaming at the slightest touch is extremely difficult.

Don, with the help of the fishing boat's crewmembers, managed to transfer the casualty from a very awkward position to the stretcher, having to do everything a step at a time. However, Don was not relishing the next move, which was to manoeuvre the casualty to a winching position.

By the time Don had the casualty packaged in the stretcher, the Shoreham lifeboat had arrived on scene and was able to position itself alongside the 'Zulu 525' very close to the casualty's position, allowing Don with the aid of the lifeboatmen to transfer the casualty to the lifeboat. This allowed for a much easier transfer to the aircraft. The casualty was taken to the Brighton hospital-landing site where we were met by an ambulance. The paramedic was able to administer a painkiller intravenously prior to transfer between aircraft and ambulance.

This job would highlight our latest campaign; our drive to increase our additional medical skills, having chipped away over the years and making headways, thanks to Don's drive on this front. There were a few more skills we felt would be beneficial to our role and administering a strong painkiller, intravenously was one of them. We were qualified to cannulate and could administer drugs in the resuscitation situations; nevertheless, we were facing brick walls regarding carrying and administering pain killing drugs like Nubain and morphine.

Fortunately, the RAF aircrewmen were in the process of addressing this problem with their crews and I knew that would help speed up our objectives, as it did with them when we first started extending our skills. The paramedics on ambulances could administer Nubain and some were already trained to administer morphine. The casualty today was in such extreme pain that even the morphine administered by the paramedic was ineffective.

The TV crew settled in well, managing to integrate with the flight – very skilfully I thought, taking things easy until we got used to having them around, helped considerably by arriving every morning with cakes! We did not go hungry while they were here.

They did their job as they were required to do and we got used to cameras being pushed in our faces during jobs, but they would drop everything at any stage if we felt they were getting in the way, even to the point of being used to assist on a few of the jobs. Another advantage, as with the previous times of having a TV crew with us, was the feedback from our jobs, highlighting the conclusions after the incidents.

Later in the year Simon O'Mahony arrived, having completed his course with the RAF and further comprehensive training at Stornoway, before joining us to continue that training. He would do another couple of months training on the unit, before being signed up to join us as a fifth member of the crew, working alongside the duty winchman until completion of his 'Advanced Training Life Support' course in March when he would join the team as a qualified winchman.

My first assessment of Simon was spot on; he had done extremely well with the RAF at Valley, had worn the flight out at Stornoway with his enthusiasm and was doing the same down here. He was continually on the go, sucking in as much information as he could in preparation for his new role. Apart from that, which no one can knock, he was like a breath of fresh air and I was sure he would fit in perfectly well.

In the meantime, Simon would also be house hunting and making all the necessary arrangements required to move his family from Norwich. He had no doubts about this being the right move for him, although news announced shortly after his arrival would make him wonder if he had in fact made the right decision.

In the December, we had the news that would be like a cloud over the unit for months. Our company announced that we were no longer the preferred bidder for the renewal of the MCA contract; all four-Coastguard units would be affected by the contract, which was likely to be won by a Canadian owned company called CHC Scotia. When I joined Bristow Helicopters it was the largest civilian helicopter company in the world, but had now lost that position to CHC Scotia who had gone on to be the favourite in the fight for this contract.

The contract being bid for in 2005 was an MCA interim contract prior to a major contract due to be phased in from 2012, often talked about as 'harmonisation', an initiative to bring the entire helicopter Search and Rescue around the United Kingdom under one umbrella.

The project was already well underway and a fifteen strong team had been put together with representatives from the Ministry of Defence (MoD) Department for Transport (DfT) and the Maritime and Coastguard Agency (MCA). Harmonisation as I understood it was a joint MoD/DfT and MCA project with the team referred to as the SAR-H team overseeing all aspects of putting this ambitious project together.

The objective was to achieve this through private finance, providing all of the United Kingdom's SAR coverage operating as one joint military and civilian service, with the aircraft positioned in the most suitable places to meet the requirements of the tender, based on set parameters, for response times and requirements to reach extremities of each unit's area of cover.

The intention is to equip all these units with the most suitable aircraft for the role and with the best equipment available. Training standards and procedures will be common throughout the fleet and controlled by a centralized body.

The idea had been mooted for years but now it was almost certainly going to happen. The project is huge and will be for twenty to thirty years. Large helicopter companies had set up consortiums with other commercial organisations, bringing together the experience and capabilities required to meet all aspects of this contract, including purchase and implementation of all the new aircraft, training of crews and the logistics the project will require.

At crew level we knew this latest contract (commencing 2007/08) was the interim contract that would take us up to harmonisation and I guess we all thought the contract would continue with the present aircraft, until a suitable replacement for the 'S61' was decided on for harmonisation. My personal feelings were that this was the safest of all our contract renewals, how wrong was I!

A few days after being informed we were no longer the preferred bidder; the MCA announced that the contract had gone to 'CHC Scotia'. I cannot say it was not a shock as we had been operating here for 18 years.

The new company had bid with two new aircraft types, both equipped with state of the art equipment. The aircraft selected for the northern units (Stornoway and Sumburgh), would be the 'Sikorsky S-92' often suggested as the modern replacement for the 'S61'. The 'S-92' was the aircraft some of us had thought would be the eventual successor for the 'S61' but certainly not this soon.

The southern units (Lee and Portland) would get the medium-sized helicopter the 'Augusta Bell 139' (soon to become the 'Augusta Westland 139'). This was an immediate blow as the majority of us, if not all, felt the aircraft may be too small and was not proven in the role of SAR.

We had thought that choosing a suitable replacement for the 'S61' was still under review and that any replacement would have been proven in the role, or at the very least subjected to trials and evaluated in the role. At the time of this announcement, the 'AW 139' was a new helicopter type that had not even had its SAR system fitted, let alone trialled. The 'S92' that the northern bases would be getting, looked to be the right choice but was still not proven, with some question marks on its suitability.

We knew the 'S61' was an old girl, but she would take some beating as a SAR platform and we felt sure could have continued until the right aircraft had been chosen for harmonisation. We were promised an upgrade to see us through until then; this included a new auto-hover system and other improvements that we, the crews, had been pushing for, including the next generation of FLIR camera and an improved intercom and radio fit. Of course, none of this would happen having lost the contract and it was at least 18 months before CHC took over with the new aircraft.

I can only guess that many other reasons had gone into this decision way above my level so had no choice but to live with it. The other thing of obvious concern at the time was who was going to crew these aircraft as gaining the skills for this role would not happen overnight. Maintaining the current contract would be extremely difficult as crewmembers would have to move on as jobs became available; all this at the time made the future look extremely bleak.

The day after the MCA made the announcement; 'R-IJ' was scrambled to the report of a capsized fishing vessel, eleven miles south of Beachy Head. The crew was: Captain John Rooney, co-pilot Paul Mattinson, Alf Kitwood was the winch-op and I was the winchman.

En-route the Coastguards informed us that the merchant ship the 'Toledo Carrier' had sight of the fishing vessel and that a man was on the hull. On scene, we could see it was quite a large capsized fishing vessel with one man standing on the bottom of the hull, well clear of the water.

Alf lowered me to the upturned hull and, while preparing the casualty for winching, I was trying to gain further information as to how many people were onboard etc. The survivor was a little confused as to how long he had been on the hull and how many people had got out of the boat. He had seen one man in the water drifting away from the boat. That in itself must have been a tremendous shock to him, let alone remaining on the hull of a boat that might sink at anytime.

We quickly had him onboard the aircraft and covered him with blankets. Further questioning revealed that there had been four crewmembers onboard and he thought one may still be inside as he had heard knocking from underneath. Other vessels were arriving on scene including the warship HMS Severn and four lifeboats; they would carry out a surface search for any possible survivors while we took the young man to Eastbourne hospital.

While returning to the scene a lifeboatman who had been placed on the hull of the capsized vessel could hear tapping noises from inside the hull. 'R-IJ' was re-tasked to return to Portsmouth to pick up a team of Royal Naval divers. We picked up a team of five divers plus all their equipment and flew them to HMS Severn, which was by then on scene at the incident.

On completion of the transfer, we joined the search for survivors until required to refuel at Shoreham. While there, the lifeboats reported that two bodies had been recovered from the sea and a third may have been seen to disappear below the surface. 'R-IJ' was then told to hold at Shoreham to await the outcome of the divers' search of the fishing vessel.

The Navy team carried out three dives inside the vessel; in clear conditions but still quite hazardous, as the vessel was getting lower in the water all the time. They were confident that no one was inside as they had identified the noise that had been heard to be gear banging against the ship's side. 'R-IJ' returned to the scene to pick up the diving team and return them to Portsmouth.

The vessel was a Zebrugge-registered, family owned Belgian fishing vessel the 'Noordster' Z122. It would appear that the nets had snagged on an obstruction on the seabed at approximately five o'clock the previous evening. The vessel must have capsized immediately as there had been no time to make an emergency call. The 19-year-old man rescued was the nephew of the owner and had been on the hull for over 16 hours with the majority of that time being in the dark on a freezing cold night.

This tragic incident only fueled our feelings at the time, as the helicopter task could not have been carried out in the same way by the 'AW 139' as the space inside the cabin was too small. I am fully aware that this would not have made any difference to the outcome of this particular incident. However, it highlighted the advantages of the larger aircraft, in this case being able to pick up a full team of divers and all their equipment.

I am also sure that there would be other ways round this problem if we had less space – perhaps fewer divers and less equipment (that would compromise the diving team, as five divers should be the minimum requirement in conducting a safe dive). The only flight routinely carrying a trained SAR diver was the Culdrose flight in Cornwall; too far in this case.

The counter arguments for the 'AW 139' were that it is faster and more powerful and that it was unlikely we would have to worry about single engine capability in light winds (by that I mean the 'AW 139' will remain in the hover if one engine fails even in nil wind conditions). It would be equipped with the very latest avionics and equipment designed for Search and Rescue. I could counter many of these arguments but could also accept that it would be suitable for a large number of our incidents, as many involve the recovery of only a few people. However, I would not like to be on the job when it was not big enough…

The majority of crews who have flown the 'S61N' or 'Sea King' in the Search and Rescue environment would find it difficult to downsize. Other crews that had never carried out Search and Rescue in a larger aircraft would probably accept the 'AW 139' as a good SAR aircraft. I gave my views on the smaller aircraft types long before this decision was made based on my experience of the 'Aerospatiale 365N' against the 'S61'. The 'AW 139' is slightly bigger than the aircraft I was using in that comparison and more powerful, but I would still need considerable convincing to accept this decision as being right.

At the time of the announcement, our disappointment was considerable. I hope that is understandable as we felt we were under threat of losing our jobs and had genuine concerns about the aircraft selected.

Bristow Helicopters, like us, had no choice but to accept the decision and made every effort, as they were contractually required to do, to keep the contract running until the satisfactory transition took place.

Rumours ran rife over the next few months with talk of TUPE transfer rules applying, which supposedly meant our jobs were safe, although at the time, no one really knew what TUPE and its implications meant; something to do with European legislation protecting employees in situations like ours. We had absolutely no choice at that stage, but to carry on as professionally as we could. Obviously, for me, it was not quite as bad as I was coming to the end of my career anyway; nevertheless, it was very sad to see this happening.

It seemed impossible that a company would be able to change operator and aircraft type in the SAR role with the same crews, it would be very difficult to be operating a 'S61' one day then move on to an 'AW 139' the next. Many weeks of aircraft type training would be required, followed by experience on type, especially for the pilots and engineers and at the time we could not see how this would be achieved

We had to put the worry of this behind us and get on with things. Another job carried out that month was to the report of a man over the cliff at Fairlight Cove four miles east of Hastings. It was a night tasking and the crew was: Captain John Rooney, co-pilot Clark Broad (who was a SAR captain normally based in Aberdeen), Alf Kitwood was the winch-op and I was the winchman.

We were airborne at the time, returning from a previous tasking, so required a refuel back at Lee before proceeding. On scene, the casualty was spotted first on the infrared camera then by our spotlights. He was in quite a precarious position with a cliff rescue man and a paramedic supporting him, having reached him by ropes from the cliff top. This would require a precise winch to the spot as I would have to attach myself to the cliff team's rope when released from the hook.

When alongside the casualty, the predicament he was in was clear. It was taking all the cliff man and the paramedic's strength to stop him sliding down the loose screed. The casualty's head was firmly stuck in a ditch and any attempt to move him would risk him sliding the rest of the way. His position made it virtually impossible to get him into a stretcher, possibly achievable in daylight with a lot more ropes but too risky at night.

I therefore had to opt for placing two strops in the hypothermic lift; the aircraft would require a precise winch from quite a height as we eased the casualty's head out of the ditch. Incredibly, the casualty was still conscious; the main pain he was suffering was the pressure of his own body weight on his head. We could not feel any breaks and he still had feeling in his extremities.

I would have liked to have taken all the precautions, using a spinal board and have secured him into a stretcher, as I am sure the paramedic would also have liked to have done, but we agreed the only way was to winch him as I suggested.

The lift went as planned and we soon had him in the cab. He admitted that he had been trying to take his life and was now apologetic for the trouble he had caused. I can only hope that his problem was one that he would get over; going through what he had been through that night may well put his problem into perspective. For us, it was special to recover a cliff jumper who was still alive.

Terry's retirement do was fast approaching and it would be tied in with the Christmas party attended by lifeboatmen, Coastguards and of course, Terry's close friends and family. We all wanted to give him a good send off.

I had been practicing an after-dinner speech about Terry for weeks. It was extremely important to me that I gave the speech, not only as the Chief Crewman, but also as Terry's friend for over 35 years and he had been an influence on my life (as I hope I had on his at times). However, I did have a problem, as I was terrified of after dinner speaking; I fully appreciate this fear is irrational but can honestly say that I would rather be winched out of the door of an aircraft in a storm force ten!

The problem I have goes back to the dyslexic problem I have in reading. I find it very difficult to read aloud as the words I read swap places, so I have to learn everything almost parrot fashion and if giving a brief or instructing I have to make sure I know my subject inside out. If I lose track, I can find myself with awful problems. Even so, I would never forgive myself if I could not do this for Terry and his involvement in Search and Rescue could not be passed off with a short speech.

I prepared the speech well in advance and learnt it word for word. Richard Norris as the Chief Pilot had volunteered to deliver the speech, but I felt that would be a total cop out in my eyes. Richard understood my problem and agreed to familiarize himself with the speech, he would also keep a copy following it as I gave the speech and, if I messed up, he would take over. How awful is that, having to admit to something like that? However, I have been honest with my thoughts throughout this memoir.

Anyway, on the night it could not have gone better. Terry was dumbfounded; he had long known my problem in this situation and was not expecting me to be saying anything, which made it even more important to him. His grown up children, Mark and Tanya were in tears hearing all these things about their dad that he had never been able to tell them himself. He had many presentations that night from various groups and rescue services; we had pulled off a night he will always remember.

On Terry's last flight, a few days later, I had put him on shift with me and arranged for his son and daughter Mark and Tanya to be kitted out in survival equipment prior to being picked up by Hamble Rescue's lifeboat. The plan was that, at some stage during that flight, Hamble would call up and ask if Terry could have one last winch to the lifeboat so the crew could say their goodbyes. I was the winchman that day so we would have to swap round, even that I had planned, as I knew he would want to do both roles on that last flight.

Hugh Kirby from Meridian television came along to film Terry's last flight for the local news that night. We carried out a normal training flight, winching to vessels in the Solent. When Colin Olden, Hamble Rescue's coxswain called up, I asked him if we could carry out the exercise in front of the Solent Coastguards headquarters as this would tie in with Terry's final fly-past of the building and of course all pre-planned as Terry's family and friends were there on the slipway!

Terry did not have time to think it might be a set up, having to concentrate on changing into the winchman's gear. I lowered him to the lifeboat where Mark and Tanya were waiting, fully briefed, for Terry to recover them to the aircraft. We even timed the winching to take place as we passed his wife Hazel and friends on the slipway. He was well and truly caught out and virtually speechless other than to swear at me as he came in the door!

Hugh Kirby, who had flown with us both on several occasions for news reports, really captured everything as it was, not just the retirement of a long serving aircrewman, but as the end of the line for two friends who had worked together in an unusual job for more than 35 years. It was a news snippet, which could not have been portrayed any better.

When we landed, all the flight and many of the flight's wives were there for a small reception and a few more presentations. The most notable, being from Alf Kitwood, who presented Terry with a professionally-made Lolly Pop stick! Terry would not be using that as his local gym wanted him to go on to qualify as a gym instructor, probably the first to do that at his age.

I predicted then that we would see him back flying. He had already managed to remain flying four years after his normal retirement age and we still considered him one of the best aircrewmen.

Terry's Last Flight

Neill Stephenson, Mark Jackson, Mike Rowsell, John Spencer, John Rooney, Dave Gibbs, Nick Horst – Front middle – Dave Peel, Terry Short (Photo's Mick Rowsell)

**Don Sowden, Alf Kitwood, Dave Peel, Mick Rowsell, John Spencer,
Simon O'Mahony—Front Row: Chris Bond, Terry, Nick Horst**

2006

On the 31st January, 'R-IJ' was scrambled in the early hours of the morning to the report of a collision between two vessels thirty miles northwest of Guernsey. The crew was: Captain John Rooney, co-pilot Dave Gibbs, winch-op John Spencer and Alf Kitwood was the winchman. Simon O'Mahony had also joined the crew as part of his training process.

En-route it was established that the collision was between a bulk carrier the 'General Grot-Rowecki' and a chemical tanker 'Eke', the chemical tanker 'Eke' was taking on water and had been reported to be listing to the port side. The French Coastguards were coordinating the rescue from CROSS Jobourg and had requested our assistance through Portland Coastguard. An RAF helicopter, 'R-169' was also en-route from Chivenor and the Guernsey lifeboat launched.

On scene, the vessel was seen to be wallowing in a moderate to rough sea and listing quite heavily to port. Alf was lowered to the vessel with a hi-line, as this would speed up the evacuation. When he first arrived on deck, the crewmembers wanted to remain onboard and there was very little Alf could do about that as the vessel did not appear to be in imminent danger of sinking.

As Alf was coiling up the hi-line, in preparation for his return to the aircraft, the vessel suddenly listed further to port changing the situation completely, the list was enough to put the vessel at risk of capsizing. Obviously, this meant the crew needed evacuation immediately. Unfortunately, Alf's radio had failed as soon as he got onboard so he had to rely on the two Johns in the aircraft to read into the situation the urgency now required, which of course they did and Alf soon had the survivors heading to the aircraft two at a time.

The St Peter Port lifeboat from Guernsey had now arrived alongside and John Rooney recommended that they start taking off some of the crew, which they were able to do at the same time that 'R-IJ' was winching. The RAF helicopter had also arrived on scene but unfortunately there was not room for two helicopters to be winching at the same time. 'R-IJ' would take off as many people as they could then 'R-169' would recover any left.

'R-IJ' winched 12 casualties while the remainder transferred to the lifeboat. 'R-IJ' was then tasked to take the casualties they had onboard to Guernsey airport where they were to shut down to await further instructions. 'R-169' remained on scene while decisions were made regarding any attempts to salvage the chemical tanker. At this stage, the authorities would have been concerned about environmental damage caused by the chemical carrier's cargo.

It was later decided that it would be too dangerous to attempt salvage, as that would mean putting men back onboard a vessel that could capsize without any warning. Both aircraft were released from task and returned to their bases. The vessel stayed afloat overnight but eventually capsized and sank.

This was another incident quite likely saved by the weather; if it had been calm, it is possible that the vessel itself would have been saved as well as the crew. However, if it had been very rough the vessel may well have capsized before help had arrived. The sea being moderate to rough probably made the difference, allowing the vessel to stay afloat long enough for the crew to be recovered safely.

Simon O'Mahony came on line in March having completed his 'Advanced Training Life Support' course at Queen Alexander Hospital in Portsmouth. Simon was everything we could hope for, still full of enthusiasm and a pleasure to work with. He knew he still had a lot to learn but he would get all the help any of us could offer and, more importantly, he would seek that advice, discussing every job he did to see if there might have been any better way to achieve the outcome. Experience in actually doing the job will be the greatest help he could get from now on.

One of the tasks in March was to a man missing overboard from the yacht 'Past Times'. We were scrambled from home just before midnight and the crew was: Captain Richard Norris, co-pilot John Bell, I was the winch-op and Nick Horst the winchman. The weather conditions were quite bad with thirty-five knots of wind and rough seas.

En-route, the Coastguards informed us that the yacht's exact position was not known. The man overboard was the skipper of the yacht, leaving an inexperienced sailor onboard. The communication with him when he called the Coastguards was intermittent and the signal was not strong enough to gain a fix on his position. By the time we were airborne all communication with the yacht had been lost.

Carrying out the search would be difficult without an accurate datum to work from; all we could do was commence the search from an estimated position, looking for both the person in the water and the yacht. Swanage, Weymouth and Yarmouth lifeboats were launched and five other vessels had responded to the Coastguards mayday relay, all making their way to the area.

Approximately halfway through our initial search a flare was sighted and we broke off from the search pattern heading towards the sighting some miles away. The flare sighting was the missing yacht, sixteen miles southeast of Portland Bill and we could see the inexperienced sailor safe in the cockpit. Weymouth lifeboat was tasked to approach the yacht to assist and gain more information that may help the search for the man overboard. We then commenced a search pattern based on the yacht's position and its likely drift.

Shortly after commencing the search, I spotted the casualty, we had to use the aircraft's SAR system to relocate back to the position of the sighting. I was quite confident it was a man in the water I had seen and called Yarmouth lifeboat to our position. We quickly relocated the man and the lifeboat recovered the casualty who unfortunately had not survived. Weymouth lifeboat took the remaining inexperienced sailor from 'Past Times' back to Weymouth.

This was a very sad incident: I believe the man overboard (who was an experienced yacht skipper) was helping to reposition the yacht after its recent purchase by the inexperienced sailor who were both good friends.

In the April, the BBC crews returned for another series of 'Seaside Rescue'. They would remain with us for four to five months making a one-hour special, followed by nine thirty-minute episodes, mainly based on the previous format covering lifeguards in Cornwall, Weymouth lifeboat and ourselves.

Earlier in this year we had our first meeting with our company and the new company that would be taking over the MCA contract. The meeting was quite surreal with both groups and representatives from the Coastguards all in the same room talking about our futures. It was clear that the MCA and the incoming contract holders were keen to keep our expertise and that the TUPE agreement for transfer would apply. That meant that those who wished to transfer would be able to, and do so under their present terms and conditions.

This was all a little hard to believe at the time as we could not see how they could achieve that with all the training that would be required for the new aircraft types. We had all been working for Bristows for some years and they were a good company to work for, particularly before the pension fiasco (which many companies had gone through, including CHC Scotia who would be taking over and who had gone through a similar but not quite so radical process).

Many decisions needed to be made by the crews on the Coastguard units and many questions needed answering – such as whether we would transfer with the same seniority etc. I felt at the time that the majority of the Lee team would transfer, the job was just too good to walk away from and the fact that we no longer had a 'defined benefit' pension scheme would help to make the transfer decision easier for those who wanted to transfer.

It was a sad time and I could think back to the start when we had the best available equipment for Search and Rescue. Many upgrades had been fitted along the way including the double winch fit and keeping up to date with the various infrared cameras. We were also the first SAR helicopters to have a helicopter Integrated Health and Usage Monitoring System (IHUMS) fitted.

One of the most expensive changes was a retro-fit of EHSI's (Electronic Horizontal Situation Indicator) to the cockpit. This was extremely beneficial to the pilots and included radar with search overlays on glass screens directly in front of the pilots making our role a lot safer. The company had even won the Queens Award for Innovation to Search and Rescue for the upgrades. I felt most of these improvements (other than the double winch fit) had gone virtually unnoticed, as they were mainly technology upgrades and not that noticeable from the outside or to the internal fit.

The company gave its approval for me to continue beyond my sixtieth birthday, including remaining as the Senior Crewman, which I did for a few more months but felt it was really quite unfair. No-one was complaining but it was just that I felt it was not right; we had all these major changes ahead of us, which I may or may not be involved with. I had already stayed an extra two years in the role; if I had been required to become a contractor two years previously at my normal retirement age I would have been required to stand down then.

I thought long and hard about this, it was not an easy decision giving up a role that had offered so much job satisfaction, but I also had commitments at home with being a full time carer when off shift. I was feeling that I should not be as preoccupied with work; I was regularly taking my work home which was not fair on Margaret.

A change on the flight at this time could only be beneficial; it would allow some movement in secondary duties on the unit, make another training slot available and bring on the appointment of the next Chief Crewman.

This would be a long-needed change for the aircrewmen and, more importantly, give those in the new roles time to prepare for all the changes ahead with the new company and aircraft. I faced the situation and made the decision to stand down asking Richard to start the ball rolling. It would take a few months to put out the notifications of the position becoming available and to carry out the interviews.

On a personal level, I still felt more than capable of continuing. In fact, I even felt more capable then than I had two years earlier when I was expecting to retire. The extension then had completely revitalised me. I had felt it necessary to earn that extension and had increased my already quite active personal fitness training, making sure I kept on top of that on a daily basis and was really feeling the benefits.

I had also worked extra hard in keeping on top of the professional side of the job. I, like Terry Short and Mick Rowsell who was coming up close behind me, felt that we had moved into new territory. We felt this would become the norm in the future, as people are in general remaining fitter for longer, but was certainly not usual at the time.

New legislation would take effect later that year, which would see many more people continuing to work past various retirement dates. Nevertheless, anyone wishing to remain working in this sort of environment would clearly have to keep on top of his or her fitness and the professional side of the job, ability would always have to be proved – in our case with the many annual assessments.

On the 6th May, the crew was scrambled from home to the report of a passenger vessel the 'Calypso' with an engine fire onboard, twenty miles southwest of Beachy Head. The crew and passengers were reported to be at abandon ship stations. The crew was: Captain John Rooney, co-pilot Paul Mattinson, Alf Kitwood was the winch-op and Don Sowden was the winchman.

En-route 'R-IJ' was re-tasked to Tidemills at Newhaven to pick up two teams of fire fighters and their equipment; they would be winched to the vessel between refuels at Shoreham.

On completion of the lifts and while waiting for an MCA surveyor and paramedics, the aircraft had a Blade Integrity Monitor (BIM) warning light in the cockpit which required the aircraft to shut down. The main rotor blade spars are filled with a gas and if the gas pressure decreases it could indicate a crack in the blade. There are also visual checks on each blade that the engineers carry out after every flight. Both the internal warning and, the external warnings after shut down indicated a problem.

This was one of the very few times in eighteen years that I could recollect 'R-IJ' going unserviceable during a tasking. Fortunately, it was looking like the fire fighters we had taken out and the vessel's fire fighters had the fire under control. Hastings, Eastbourne, Shoreham and Newhaven's lifeboats were on scene, plus French lifeboats and helicopters and other merchant vessels who had responded to the mayday relay.

Once it was confirmed that everything was under control, the Coastguard tug 'Anglian Monarch' towed the 'Calypso' to Southampton where the Maritime and Coastguard Agency set up an emergency response centre to make arrangements for the vessel's 246 crew and 462 (mainly British) passengers. They were en-route from Tilbury to St Peter Port when the incident happened and none of the passengers or crew were injured.

On the 8th July, 'R-IJ' was tasked to the report of a person being recovered from the water after being hit by a boat's propeller. This incident had been going on for a while but we were on another tasking when it was first reported. The accident had happened close to a pontoon at Hythe in Southampton water. Paramedics and a 'BASICS' doctor were on scene.

(BASICS are a registered charity formed in 1977, made up of highly trained immediate care practitioners who are able to work alongside the rescue services at major incidents, including situations like this one today. They are able to provide analgesia if required and can even carry out certain surgical procedure that may be needed prior to extricating a casualty. They are all volunteers on call at short notice to attend serious incidents. Their skills and the equipment they have available have helped to save many lives since the beginning of this initiative).

When we returned from the previous task, this incident was still going on and it was becoming clear that the casualty would need helicopter evacuation, so we soon found ourselves on our way to the incident. The crew was: Captain Mark Jackson, co-pilot Dave Gibbs, winch-op Chris Bond and I was the winchman.

On scene, we could see the activity on the end of a pontoon but it was a nil wind situation, so we could not afford to simply run in and blast everyone with our downdraught. We decided that the safest approach would be to put me out at about 120ft to reduce the downdraught and lower me to a slipway a little way from the incident. A Coastguard vehicle picked me up, briefing me on the problem as we headed to the pontoon.

My first thought when I saw the casualty was virtually of despair. He was lying on the bathing platform of a speedboat, almost level with the water and was writhing in pain. His body covered the whole platform so the only access to him was from the cockpit of the boat. A lady paramedic and a 'BASICS doctor' had managed to stabilise the leg (which had been amputated by the propeller at the ankle) and were administering fluids and pain relief.

He also had considerable damage to the other leg. They had managed to stabilise him in the extremely confined space, while having to lean over from the cockpit to achieve what they had. The doctor and paramedics had undoubtedly saved the casualty's life but, if he was not transferred to hospital quickly, that would all be in vain.

Initially I felt the only way was to go into the water and try to slide our stretcher underneath him but that was not practical in this case. He was so badly injured that if we tried to roll him onto the stretcher supported in the water, he would be unaware what was happening and it would be impossible to assess the shock that would cause. We would also need many people in the water to have any chance of achieving it.

Someone spotted a dory offshore and as soon as I saw that, I knew we had a chance of achieving this rescue as the dory's hull was close to the water and approximately the same height as the platform. We caught the attention of someone on a ski-boat and sent him off to ask the dory to come to our assistance. I ran off to meet the boat as it came alongside the pontoon. The dory had several young lads onboard having a good day out and enjoying a few beers. It must have been quite a shock to them as I virtually commandeered their boat, getting them all out other than the coxswain, who I explained the problem to and he had no hesitation in agreeing to help. We had to manoeuvre the dory very carefully alongside the bathing platform on the stern of the speedboat.

Once alongside, I managed to jam the stretcher into a position where we could roll the casualty with one very careful movement onto it. The manoeuvre worked perfectly and, while I was preparing all the straps and harnesses, the doctor and paramedic were carrying on with their good work.

Nothing about this job was made easy; even now, we would have to move the dory and casualty to a safe winching position. The aircraft would have to winch us from a ridiculous height because of all the moored yachts and people in the area. The still wind conditions would force the downdraught directly onto the stretcher, which would induce a nasty spin as we were recovered to the aircraft. To counteract this we had to use a hi-line attached to the stretcher and controlled by people on the ground.

We moved the casualty in the dory to the winching position. I briefed the lads who I had taken out of the dory on handling the hi-line and had the BASICS doctor winched up to the aircraft while I was making the final preparations with the stretcher. He would be able to help with the casualty in the aircraft and would be invaluable in hospital giving the history of the incident and treatment so far. Finally, I was recovered to the aircraft with the casualty and, within a few minutes, we were landing at Lords Hill HLS for Southampton Hospital.

We later heard everything that had happened on this incident and it was quite harrowing. The man had been enjoying a day out with family and friends. He was a passenger on the back of a ski-boat and another group of friends including his sister were on the speedboat.

The two boats were close together and the group in the speedboat were passing some money to the ski-boat; I believe the ski-boat was going to head off to get some more fuel for the speedboat. Some of the money had fallen in the water and the notes were floating on the surface. The man had jumped into the water from the ski-boat to recover this money and when he had it, he decided to climb out of the water onto the bathing platform of the speedboat.

As he was climbing aboard the speedboat moved off and he felt himself dragged underneath with both of his legs going into the propeller. He screamed loud enough for them to know something awful had happened and the crew immediately stopped the engines.

The injured man managed to drag himself back onto the platform. His sister said she was in complete shock, he was asking her if he had lost his legs and looked so badly injured that she thought he was going to die. Her first memory after seeing her brother on the bathing platform of the speedboat was of a very efficient lady paramedic arriving on scene. The paramedic not only had the responsibility of the first response but also had a boat full of people in shock to deal with.

Somehow, they managed to get the vessel alongside the pontoon and the paramedic was joined by the BASICS doctor and other ambulance personnel. Between them, they managed to stabilise the casualty while also providing reassurance for all the others involved.

In hospital, the 40-year-old man had his leg amputated below the knee but, unfortunately, infection took hold and the surgeons had to amputate the leg above the knee. The hospital managed to save his other leg. He was extremely courageous and, in an interview for the TV programme explained that "life goes on", that he does not consider himself disabled and that it will make little difference to his life, he will carry on as normal. That same spirit is probably what got him through that first hour.

The BBC crew who had joined us in April had managed to fit in well, commencing as the previous year's crew, by arriving each morning with chocolate cakes, etc! It would not have been easy for them fitting in to this type of environment, in a job that they are required to be intrusive, but they managed it, gaining our confidence quite quickly, fitting in with our routines and dropping everything to help when requested.

Another unusual incident in the July was to the report of a boom injury on a yacht in the Solent during Cowes week. The crew was: Captain Mark Jackson, co-pilot Paul Mattinson, Nick Horst was the winch-op and I was the winchman.

The incident was just off the airfield so we were on scene in less than five minutes, very little time to assess the situation or for us to arrange the equipment that may be required for that particular incident.

Being Cowes week, there were hundreds of yachts racing in the Solent, making it very difficult to locate the yacht with the casualty onboard. In addition, information coming over the radio was reporting that two people were injured from two different yachts. We then had to find both yachts and try to prioritise which casualty would be the more urgent of the two. It was very difficult getting the information as everyone was trying to talk on the radio at the same time.

Eventually we managed to get one of the yachts to let off a flare; something we would have liked them to have done as soon as they saw us, but we could not get the message across with all the radio calls.

Gosport and Fareham Inshore Rescue Service had managed to locate the second yacht and had been able to get one of their crew onboard; he then recommended that the casualty was picked up by helicopter immediately.

When we arrived alongside, we could see the casualty lying in the port quarter of the cockpit, exactly where I would need to land when lowered to the yacht. This would cause a problem for us, as when winching to a yacht the pilot requires as many visual reference as possible – In this situation and in the majority of situations with yachts of this size, we need to winch to the port quarter. Moving to a position further forward risks the pilot running out of visual references.

My worry was the risk of actually landing on the casualty or indeed dropping the hi-line weights on him; however, Nick and Mark felt quite confident they could place me just forward of the casualty's position and that is what they did. I prepared the casualty for transfer using a spinal protector and cervical collar before being recovered to the aircraft with the casualty. Having the lifeboatman onboard made this process much easier as he was able to help me prepare the casualty for transfer and to control the hi-line during the winching phases.

The next decision was whether we should run with this casualty because recovering the next casualty as well would obviously take time to do. However, we also knew there could be a further delay at the landing site waiting for the ambulance. I managed to keep the casualty we had in the aircraft informed as to our predicament, so he was aware that another casualty also needed attention. He had made it clear that we should pick the other person up, although in reality, it was not that straightforward as both Nick and I would be required to achieve the second recovery and leaving someone who has just had a nasty head injury unattended would be unwise.

The lifeboat had managed to get a man on the second yacht and he was recommending transfer of this second casualty as a matter of urgency. I therefore decided to give a quick brief to the cameraman who was onboard with us for the next series of 'Seaside Rescue'. They had obviously watched, while filming, a lot of our patient care and in this case, I needed him to provide reassurance to the casualty and to catch Nick's attention if anything unusual was to happen. Apparently, he did this very well as the casualty later informed us in a thank you letter.

Nick lowered me to the second yacht. This time it was easier to get onto the yacht as I had a clear area to land on. The casualty was able to remember quite clearly, what had happened. He had taken a nasty knock on the head, but could feel all his extremities, just reporting a stiff neck. After a cervical collar was fitted, he felt confident he could make it to the cockpit, where I prepared him for transfer. Both casualties were flown to Lords Hill HLS for transfer to Southampton hospital.

Later that year we were informed how the transition to CHC Scotia would be conducted and it was confirmed that all of us could transfer if we so wished, under the same terms, conditions and seniority that we were on, at the date of transfer.

The plan was for the base transitions to take place over a one-year period, commencing on the 1st July 2007. CHC will move into Stornoway with a SAR equipped 'S61' with a trained transition crew to take over the Search and Rescue service for that region for a three-month period.

During those three-months, the existing Stornoway crews will train on the new aircraft, in their case the pilots' 'S92' type rating training will be carried out in America. For the aircrewmen the training will be split between further paramedic training at a facility set up for the RAF SAR aircrewmen, followed by SAR training on-type when the pilots returned from their type training in America. The decision for the engineers 'S92' training at the time was still being worked out.

On the 1st October 2007, the 'S92' will go on line as the Stornoway SAR aircraft. The transition crew on the 'S61' will then go to Sumburgh to complete the same process from 1st October to the 1st of January 2008 when they moved on to Lee-on-Solent, completing the process at Portland on the 1st July 2008.

At least we knew exactly how this process would work and for us at Lee it would not commence until January 2008, which at the time was nearly eighteen months away and two years after the original announcement. I was concerned that it would be difficult to keep things running smoothly until then and that people may start leaving. I thought the majority would stay at Lee but, even if people left from other bases, it would have a knock on effect as we couldn't just pluck qualified people out of the hat and I could envisage a lot of movement of crews between units.

This seemed a long time to have to keep a contract running after losing it. However, I could also see that some kind of transition like this was the only way to achieve it.

I could not imagine where I would end up in the decisions ahead. The way I felt at the time was that I would love to be a part of it. It would be great to finish my career on the new aircraft type but it was so far ahead I could not be sure if I would be given the chance.

My worries expressed about the size of the new aircraft destined for Lee still stood, I could not suddenly deny those thoughts, which were shared by the majority of the crews that would operate the new aircraft, particularly the crewmen. Even so, we were still looking forward to the challenge.

There would be many advantages and some of the new technology sounded incredible: if it was as good as stated it would help to make the role safer. To be part of finding the best way to make all that work would be quite something, as it was in the early days with 'R-IJ' when that was way ahead of anything else in the SAR world.

I stood down as Chief Crewman on the 1st of August. The interviews had taken place a few weeks earlier with Nick Horst selected to take over. Nick had been helping me for a few years and, as the other trainer, had always backed me up. This did not necessarily mean that he would take over but I was pleased that he was selected.

John Spencer moved into the SAR trainer's slot, Alf Kitwood took on the first aid trainer's role replacing Don Sowden who had earlier been selected as the company's medical standards aircrewman. Don would be controlling company policy on first aid and the medical side of things, which would require him checking the first aid procedures on all the units, continuing the good work that he had been progressing since we first formed the unit.

The changes would make a difference, because the new team would be in place to meet the challenges ahead when the new company took over, in particular the decisions that would be required regarding the new aircraft and the many new procedures requiring development around the aircraft's capabilities.

On the 22nd August, we were scrambled to search for the possibility of people in the water or wreckage ten miles south of the Nab Tower. The crew was: Captain John Rooney, co-pilot Richard Norris, I was the winch-op and Simon O'Mahony the winchman. A body wearing sailing equipment and an inflated lifejacket had been located earlier that day and all enquiries of anyone missing or boats missing had drawn a blank.

The Coastguards had scrambled 'R-IJ' as it was possible more people had been involved in the incident. The search pattern had been based on tide and conditions on the day in relation to where the body was found. Portland's aircraft 'R-WB' was also scrambled to assist in the search, allowing the two aircraft to take full advantage of the remaining daylight.

On completion of the initial search when nothing had been sighted, both aircraft were stood down. The Coastguards and Police would obviously continue their enquiries as to where this body had come from.

The following morning a worried lady, having heard about the body, called the Coastguard to report that her boyfriend was sailing with friends from Bembridge on the Isle of Wight and transiting to Dartmouth. They were not overdue yet but very late and she was worried. The body was later identified as her boyfriend.

This immediately sparked a massive search involving ourselves, Portland's aircraft, an RAF Nimrod, Yarmouth and Freshwater lifeboat, MoD vessels, warships and coastal search teams. We knew that we were looking for a 27ft single–mast, blue-hulled yacht called the 'Ouzo' that had sailed from Bembridge on the Sunday. Enquiries were still going on as to the exact time they had left. Our search that morning turned up nothing, which is quite unusual, as we would expect to find some flotsam from a vessel that had been involved in an accident even if it had sunk.

The search commenced all morning with a new crew taking over in the afternoon during a fuel requirement. The crew that relieved us was: Captain Neill Stephenson, co-pilot Richard Norris, winch-op Alf Kitwood and Mick Rowsell was the winchman.

On their second search, they located the two missing crewmembers' bodies, which were both recovered by Yarmouth lifeboat. With still no sign of the missing yacht it could only be assumed that something catastrophic had happened, like the yacht having been in collision with a larger vessel, or hitting a large object in the water and sinking before the crew had time to get any distress signal out.

The crew were friends working in the city of London and were heading to Devon to take part in the Dartmouth Royal Regatta. This was another tragic incident and, to date, the yacht has never been located, although several ferries and vessels have been examined for signs of a collision. A man has been arrested in connection with the incident, a watch officer from a cross channel ferry, but at the time of writing I do not know the outcome of that arrest.

The next quite awkward job was at the beginning of October, when we were scrambled to the yacht 'Sea Biscuit' south of The Needles. The yacht had reported that one of the crew; (a 35-year-old female) was unconscious but otherwise uninjured. The Coastguards had patched the radio call to a doctor who had recommended that a helicopter evacuation was required. 'R-IJ' was scrambled and Yarmouth lifeboat launched. The crew was: Captain Mark Jackson, co-pilot Dave Gibbs, winch-op Mick Rowsell and I was the winchman.

On scene, it was established that the 'Sea Biscuit' had engine problems and could not in the prevailing conditions make a heading into wind – it was blowing a force eight gale and there was a very rough sea. The casualty's condition sounded very worrying and we could see her on the floor in the open cockpit. She appeared to be jammed between a chart table and the starboard side of the cockpit. Knowing it would be a few hours before the yacht could make port we realised that we would have to attempt the rescue.

Yarmouth lifeboat was approaching, so we decided to see if they could get a man onboard to assess the possibility of transferring the casualty to the lifeboat, although we appreciated that was very unlikely – it would be difficult enough just getting a man onboard.

One of the lifeboat crew did manage to get onboard and reported that the situation was urgent as the lady was still unconscious and fitting; he also reported that a transfer of the casualty to the lifeboat would not be possible.

It would be virtually impossible to winch to the yacht on its present heading and, even if we could get the yacht to stop dead in the water, the movement would be too erratic. We therefore decided to try to get the yacht undertow by the lifeboat; it could then be turned into wind, making the yacht more stable. Having the lifeboatman onboard the yacht would make the task easier, especially for me, as he would be able to tend the hi-line, something we practice with them on a regular basis. The lifeboat was happy to do that and prepared their equipment to make it happen. I had now used this technique a few times since Peter Thomson had suggested it on a rescue years ago.

We were then able to watch, yet again, the magic produced by the lifeboat coxswain and his crew. The lifeboatman onboard the yacht had to position himself on the bows to receive and attach the tow, which in that sea, was quite an achievement. The coxswain then had to approach the yacht close enough to pass the tow without smashing into it – not easy in those conditions but he had already done it once to get his man onboard. Once the tow was established, the lifeboatman returned to the yacht's cockpit to tend the hi-line.

Mick and Mark picked the best moment to get me onboard, but I still hit the deck quite hard. I was prepared for that given the conditions, but there was fortunately no injury. One of the things that always amazed me was the number of times I had slammed into a deck and expected broken bones but just bounced up again uninjured.

The lady was jammed in the cockpit with a crewmember trying to protect her from the weather as, every time a wave hit her, she would start fitting. The crew assured me that she had not fallen or been injured in any way and there were no signs of injury. It would not have been possible to get her into a stretcher, as the space was too tight and the movement too severe.

(Photo Mick Rowell)

Preparing the casualty for transfer after the yacht was taken in tow by Yarmouth lifeboat

I had to try to get her out of the jammed position into a sitting position and then use the hypothermic lift to recover her to the aircraft which, fortunately, we were able to do with the help of the crew and lifeboatman. We could not position her in the best winching position (which would have been on the port quarter). This meant the helicopter crew had to wait for the right moment to pull us clear. It would induce quite a swing, which I was ready for, and the lifeboatman would control the swing as best he could with the hi-line. Once safely onboard the helicopter she was flown to Newport HLS on the Island.

After difficult winching like that, the crew look forward to getting their thoughts together and reflecting on what they had just done, then discussing the situation to see if any lessons could be learnt from the rescue.

However, this time a second job was brewing as we approached the hospital landing-site so we had to expedite the transfer and proceed straight to the next job. It sounded straightforward for us; it was to a woman trapped on a footpath with a broken ankle. Paramedics were with the casualty but unable to get an ambulance to her or her to an ambulance.

There was nevertheless some urgency as the woman (who I believe was in her late seventies) had been lying on the path for some while. We were in a quandary because 'R-IJ' did not have enough fuel to complete the job. We decided that we would locate the casualty and drop me off and then the aircraft could go to Bembridge on the Island to refuel, while I prepared the casualty for transfer.

When we arrived on scene, it was not as straightforward as we first thought. The casualty was in a bowl, surrounded by hills, and in the strong winds the disturbed air made it dangerous to land or even to get down low. This was not a major problem, but it would mean the winching and recovery of the paramedic and casualty would have to be from a much higher height than normal, in excess of 100ft.

I was lowered to the casualty with the stretcher and the aircraft went off for fuel. The injured lady was being looked after by paramedics but she had a nasty broken ankle, was in a lot of pain and having to endure lying on a wet muddy path, but she was still making every effort to keep cheerful.

We transferred her to our stretcher, which was awkward to achieve on the muddy path, while at the same time trying to avoid further damage to her leg. By the time we had the casualty ready for transfer the aircraft had returned from the refuel. We were recovered, along with the paramedic who had been looking after her on the ground. We had to use a hi-line to steady the stretcher to stop it spinning during the high winch.

Once we were all safely onboard the aircraft we returned to Newport to transfer the casualty to another waiting ambulance. We now had two jobs, which had both proved more difficult than we had expected, to debrief when we arrived back at base.

2007

With less than a year before our change to the new employer and the introduction of the new aircraft, the interim period (as I had expected) was proving an awkward time. There was quite a lot of uncertainty amongst the crews as to whether to stay with the company they knew, or to transfer and remain in the job that the majority of them enjoyed. For those who remained with Bristows it would mean uprooting completely, as there were no jobs for aircrew in the areas that the SAR flights operate from, but a few opportunities in SAR abroad were becoming available, which would entice some aircrew and engineers.

It was a difficult time. A few aircrewmen, pilots and engineers based on the northern flights had moved on and the company was working hard to replace them but found it very difficult. As mentioned before, it takes quite some time to get aircrew on line. Even if they have SAR experience, they would have to convert to the aircraft type then learn our procedures, not easy within the time scales of the contract. There had also been an unusual increase in sickness, which I could not help partly attributing to the uncertainty over our futures. I am possibly wrong about that but I have never seen so many requirements for sickness relief and there was certainly an air of despondency.

We seemed to be coping reasonably well at Lee-on-Solent with the majority of aircrew intending to stay on the unit; just a few were looking at other opportunities. However, the knock-on effect with the shortfalls on other units had affected Lee, as we had to supply aircrewmen and pilots to other units at short notice. This caused problems in rostering and duty hours, so causing problems on our own unit. All the moving of people around the country must have been costing the company a fortune.

When Terry retired the previous year, I had privately predicted that we would be short of crews and this indeed proved to be the case. I was sure that one of the ways of helping would be for the Company to ask Terry to return on an ad-hoc basis. I knew everyone agreed that it would be far safer using Terry as a relief aircrewman than a temporary replacement trying to learn how we operate for the few months remaining of the contract.

With this in mind, on Terry's retirement, I took it on myself to hang on to Terry's flying clothing and flying helmet, sealed it all in a large box and stowed it in the SAR store. Smiler Grinney (our standards aircrewman) had the same conviction and suggested that we bring forward and carry out Terry's annual assessments before he retired. This was obviously with Terry's approval as it meant extra checks for him, but would also mean we could get him back on line quickly if he was required.

Since retiring, Terry had completed his Gym instructors' course. He did not just pass it, he sailed through it and was employed at his local Gym, leaving little question as to his physical fitness.

We had also been suggesting that Terry would be the ideal person to have on the 'CHC Scotia' team as a member of the crew required to cover the units during the transition between CHC and Bristow. After a while, CHC did contact Terry offering him a place on their transition team, but this would have meant a year away from home. He was mulling that over when our difficulties started. Nick in his Chief Crewman role, kept pushing to get Terry back. Eventually the company accepted that Terry was the obvious solution and asked him if he would consider returning on an ad-hoc basis.

Terry jumped at that (as I knew he would) and joined us towards the end of 2006 for refresher training. He would also work a minimum of three shifts per month to keep his skills up and would carry out relief duties as required. The gym he was employed at wanted Terry to remain working for them and, agreed to keep him on a part time basis working their rosters around Terry's availability. Therefore, he had the best of both worlds – not bad for someone perceived to be too old nine months earlier.

His refresher training proved Terry to be the same confident professional aircrewman he was when he retired and no one at Lee would disagree with that, we all knew his capabilities.

The year had started quietly with no major incidents and the 'Seaside Rescue' team had joined us again for the summer months with a new set of camera people who had to settle in with our crews.

On the 20th of July, we had weather warnings reporting heavy rain in Southern England. The headlines in our papers were forecasting two months' rain expected over the course of just a few hours.

When the scramble went early that evening, I was expecting it to be to help in flood relief but I was wrong. The scramble was to a yacht calling a mayday in the Needles channel. The crew was: Captain Richard Norris, co-pilot Paul Mattinson, winch-op Mick Rowsell and I was the winchman.

Shortly after getting airborne, the Coastguards reported that the skipper of the yacht had collapsed and resuscitation was taking place by the crew; one of the crewmembers was a doctor. Yarmouth lifeboat had also launched to the yacht's assistance and was approaching the scene as we arrived. This would speed up my transfer to the yacht with our defibrillator, enabling me to be winched straight to the lifeboat from where I could be transferred to the yacht.

The casualty was right on the stern of the yacht in quite an awkward position with two crewmembers giving good CPR so I asked them to continue while I prepared the defibrillator. Unfortunately, the monitor was showing an unshockable rhythm. To have any chance at all we would need to continue the CPR and transport him to hospital as quickly as possible.

The safest way for the transfer would have been to put the casualty in a stretcher then transfer him to the lifeboat but to do this would have taken quite some time, especially as the casualty was virtually trapped on the transom, leaving very little space for the stretcher. The quickest way, although a little more difficult, would be to lift him by using two strops from his present position. Although this was awkward I felt it was achievable, but even this would take time to brief on the hi-line and preparing the casualty.

Knowing the experience of the crew, I felt that they might be able to carry out a straight winch to recover us from the transom without using the hi-line; this would save a little time. Richard and Mick carried out a quick dummy while I prepared the casualty for a hypothermic lift. The two crewmembers continued life support.

The crew decided they could proceed without the hi-line and Mick conned the aircraft overhead with Richard just managing to keep enough visual references to hold a good hover. Mick eased the casualty and myself clear from the after stays and the guardrail. Mick and I continued the CPR for the short trip to Southampton HLS where an ambulance crew met the aircraft.

It was with regret that the casualty did not survive the ordeal and we all went home that night feeling quite despondent. We had managed to recover the casualty to the aircraft in as short a time as possible but were very sad that we had not managed to get the result we would have liked. After a few hours at home on standby we were tasked again to the floods in Gloucestershire.

Gloucestershire Floods

At four-o'clock in the morning, the bleepers went off tasking us from home to assist in the awful floods taking place in Gloucestershire. An RAF Search and Rescue helicopter from Chivenor had been working throughout the night in quite awful conditions but the situation was deteriorating rapidly and it was now clear that more aircraft would be required.

We immediately hit problems en-route because it was not possible to stay in visual contact with the ground. We had to climb above the cloud base, forced up by the high ground between Lee-on-Solent and Gloucester. We knew that the cloud base on scene was between 200 and 300ft so could only hope that we would find a hole in the cloud at the other end. The back-up plan would be to let down on instruments at Gloucester airport when we arrived.

En-route we were tasked to recover two people from a canal boat at a position to the east of Gloucester, but that would not be possible if we could not let down below the cloud base. Our first attempt failed, as we were still not visual at our minimum descent height and not being sure of the obstructions below the aircraft, we had to abort the let down.

The next choice was to continue to Gloucester airport to let down and then proceed by map reading to the grid reference we had been given. However, it was soon clear that Gloucester air traffic was not available, which meant that the information we would require even to attempt a letdown had to be gleaned from the other rescue and police aircraft in the area. Another worrying factor was that no one could provide an accurate pressure reading for the airfield, information which would have allowed for a more accurate let down on the aircraft's instruments.

Being the winchman that day I could only help by finding maps and keeping a good look out. Mick was scouring the maps for obstructions, plotting positions of other aircraft etc. Richard and Paul tried to gather as much information as possible regarding the conditions on scene, working out the best approach profile for what would be a blind approach, re-studying the maps and re-affirming the positions of the other aircraft.

Once all the information was gathered we began a blind let down to the overhead position of the airfield again, in the hope that we would become visual prior to our decision height and, because of unavailability of an airfield pressure setting, we had to rely on our radio altimeter.

Fortunately, the let down was successful and, once visual with the airfield, we decided to land on and take a running-rotors refuel before proceeding to our first tasking.

There were two RAF SAR aircraft in the area and a police helicopter; our tasking instructions were coming from 'Kinloss Rescue', the rescue coordination centre in Scotland.

As there was no air traffic control available to us at the time, we had to keep our own clearances while flying around with a low cloud base and poor visibility, continuously updating our positions with the other helicopters over the radio.

We immediately knew that the task was not going to be straightforward. The scene was awful: flooded fields, houses, areas of complete devastation. A sight far worse than any flood situation I had ever seen; our hearts went out to the many thousands of people on the ground affected by this sudden and unprecedented sustained downpour.

Our next problem was that the map reading became a completely different ball game as the landscape had changed with many roads submerged, rivers that had become lakes and boundaries of fields marked on the maps that had disappeared. Even following a river or canal was difficult; in some areas, we could spot riverbanks by rows of trees etc but every so often, they would just disappear into large lakes. This made us realize what a tremendous job the Chivenor crews must have done as their initial response was at night.

We did however; pick up enough features to run straight into our first target – a lone canal boat now in the middle of a large lake with someone waving from a hatch. This was to be the start of a very hectic few hours. We located the canal boat earlier than we expected. The wind had dropped and, having just taken on fuel we were pulling too much power, so had to jettison fuel, to make the aircraft lighter before proceeding with the winching.

We lifted two people and their dog from the canal boat. It was questionable as to whether we should be recovering dogs in situations like this, but in all honesty I would have found it very difficult to have left them and owners will generally not leave without their pets. I could have deceived this couple, by promising to go back for the dog after I had recovered them to the helicopter and then not returned for the dog. However, my personality is not equipped to have done that. The other choice would be to try to appeal to the risks they may cause to rescuers later if I was forced to leave them behind with their dogs. At the time, I did not know that this problem would be something I would be facing for the rest of the morning.

Fortunately, the first dog I lifted was not too difficult and he allowed me to package him in a lifting bag so that I could safely control him as we were winched back to the aircraft. We landed in the nearest dry field where onlookers assured us they would look after the rescued people and then proceeded to a caravan park that had been completely cut off by the floods.

The sight on scene at the caravan park was terrible; the majority of caravans were waist deep in water, which was still rising. We relieved an RAF helicopter from this site while they returned for fuel; they were able to pass information to us regarding people still in the caravans.

The next two casualties were from a waterlogged caravan. Again, the couple had a dog that they were adamant they could not leave. I was soon to realize that the majority of casualties we would be tasked to recover would have pets, in fact that was probably the reason they were still there.

Those without pets had left before things got too bad; the ones that had stayed had remained because of their pets in the hope that the flooding would not get any worse. That may seem irrational to some people, but was quite logical really and, having been a dog owner myself, something I understood. These casualties would not have believed the situation would get as bad as it had and were willing, for their pets' sake, to take the risk that it would not.

The winching was quite awkward, not particularly for me as I just went where I was put, but Richard was pulling close to full power the majority of the time. We had to hover quite high to lessen the downdraught and to dodge power cables, trees etc. The recovery from the caravans, houses and roofs had to be extremely precise as it would have been even more precarious if I had dragged the casualties into the deeper water outside their raised porches or doorways.

When dropping the first two people from the caravan site onto dry land, they were expressing concern as to whether a lady who was well into her seventies and living on her own had been rescued. Unfortunately, it was difficult to find out exactly which caravan she was in, or indeed, whether she was still there, but I did know her name was Mrs Gilbert so I would obviously try to find out.

I was then lowered to assist the occupants from the next caravan who we could see were in a precarious position. This time I was met by two women and three dogs, one of them a lovely white Alsatian plus two smaller dogs. I was quite worried about lifting the Alsatian because it was too big for the bag I was using.

I decided to recover one of the women to the aircraft first so the dogs would have a friendly face to see when they arrived; particularly the Alsatian, as there was a serious risk that we would not be able to restrain him to stop him jumping out again from a height that would not be survivable. The other woman had to be recovered last as I would require her to help me prepare the remaining two dogs for lifting.

We virtually had to jam the Alsatian in the bag with just his head popping out; I had a firm grip of his collar and away we went; he calmed down while we were suspended on the end of the wire. When we arrived at the aircraft door, he managed to break out of the bag. Mick was able to leave me dangling at the door while he took the lead and moved him back to the lady that I had sent up initially. As soon as he saw her, he calmed down and sat by her side quietly.

The other two dogs I was able to put into the bag together and seal them in completely so they were not a problem. I was then able to recover the other woman, who again would not have left without her dogs, even though the situation with the flooding was getting worse.

I had time while preparing this woman for lifting to ask her about Mrs Gilbert. She was also very concerned about the elderly lady and was able to point out her caravan. We dropped these casualties off and returned to Mrs Gilbert's caravan.

As we approached the caravan, which was submerged a couple of feet, we could see a lady waving from her patio window. Mick was able to place me on a raised veranda close to a door at the side of the caravan, enabling me to wade through the water and gain entry to the caravan.

A lovely 77-year-old lady, who had clearly been through quite an ordeal, met me at the door. She had become convinced she would not get out and, in all honesty had put her own safety and discomfort to the back of her mind. She must have been freezing as she had been standing in a couple of feet of water for some time. All she was worried about was her 17-year-old Yorkshire terrier; she had managed to keep the terrier out of the water by placing her in the centre of her bed, which at the time was just out of the water.

Mrs Gilbert would have been happy to be left herself as long as she knew her dog was all right; it was clear that the beloved pet was her only concern. In this case (with the dog being so small) I was able to lift them both together, securing the dog in her coat and allowing her to retain control of her pet, which I knew would give her the confidence that I would look after both of them.

She was so relieved when she was safely in the helicopter; still not the slightest bit worried about herself but very relieved that her Yorkshire terrier was safe. We started a warming process, wrapping her in a special blanket and flew her back to Gloucester airport where an ambulance would meet us to check she was alright after her ordeal. I knew she would not let the terrier leave her side for long so was not at all surprised to see her interviewed on television that night with the Yorkshire terrier still in her arms.

We took on more fuel and headed the twenty miles back to the caravan park, as we knew at least one other couple was still on site. When we returned, I recovered two more casualties who were standing on the porch of their caravan holding on to their dog. The smallish dog went straight into the bag without any struggling, allowing me to lift the dog and one of the casualties at the same time.

Then it was onto a chalet where we could see someone waving. I was lowered to the flooded porch of this chalet, where I was met by a woman with two large, frightened dogs. Again, as expected, she would not leave without the dogs.

This winch was going to be more difficult. I would have to take the dogs up first, as I would need her to help me to put the dogs one at a time into the bag and hold them firm until I was lifted in the air. I had learnt by now that as soon as I was lifted with a dog, it could no longer get any purchase from the floor and would stay still until we reached the aircraft.

Having had the problem with the Alsatian when it reached the door I knew it could be worse with these dogs as they would not have anyone they recognized in the aircraft. We had a member of the film crew, Sarah, onboard from the BBC 'Seaside Rescue' team, so I was able to pre-warn the aircraft to ask Sarah to stop filming and be at the door on a dispatcher ready to control the dogs, allowing Mick to concentrate on the winching.

I made sure I had a firm grip of the dog's collar and, again with just the head poking out of the edge of the bag we headed towards the aircraft. As expected, the dog tried to break out of the bag on entering the door so I made sure Sarah had a firm grip of the lead before I let go. She took the first dog to the back of the aircraft and secured him while I was winched down to recover the next one. The same process was carried out with Sarah securing and calming the second dog while I recovered the lady. Once she was onboard, the dogs calmed down.

We dropped them off in the same field that we had used for the others where by now a reception team had congregated. Our next task was to the report of five young people stuck on a pub roof. Picking them off the roof was a novelty, no dogs this time and I was able to remain dry so we soon had them onboard and deposited on dry land.

We were then tasked to a house close to the caravan site that was now in the middle of what seemed like a lake. The lower floor of the house was flooded a couple of feet, even though it was a raised lower floor with quite a high porch, so I was heading back to the water. Mick lowered me directly to the high part of the porch from where I was able to wade inside. I was met by a man who had been collecting valuables, provisions etc. and moving them upstairs. The rest of the occupants were already upstairs, making themselves as comfortable as possible until help arrived.

There were four occupants plus four large dogs and (I believe a couple of cats) in this house. They assured me that they were fine in the dry upstairs, with enough provisions to see them through for a while. We had a discussion regarding their situation and decided that, as they felt secure for the time being, I would recover the two women to a safer place and arrange for the two men and their pets to be picked up later, possibly by ourselves or by boat. I knew small rescue craft would soon be heading towards the region from all over the country, provided by the RNLI, Fire & Rescue services and voluntary rescue services.

Just prior to preparing for the recovery of the women I had a radio call to expedite: we had been tasked to a more urgent situation, someone trapped in a flooded car under a bridge. The women, when aware of this situation, assured me that they would be fine staying in the house with their husbands. They felt safe upstairs and were quite happy knowing that help would come later.

I was recovered to the aircraft and we headed off to the position given, which was on the outskirts of Evesham some twenty-five miles away. When we arrived on scene, we could see the devastation and many trapped cars, but they all seemed to be empty. We noticed that a fire service rigid inflatable boat had arrived on scene, so we guessed they had carried out the rescue.

Eventually, the original informants managed to get the message through to 'Kinloss Rescue' that the casualty we had been tasked to was now safe and well. We then returned to Gloucester airport for more fuel and on arrival were informed that all the casualties at immediate risk had been accounted for and 'Rescue-IJ' was released from task.

The fire station at Gloucester had prepared a huge breakfast for us before our return to Lee-on-Solent and that was certainly welcome, although I have to say that, even after all the years I have been doing this job, I was so hyped up I could have easily gone on for many more hours.

Only a few weeks prior to this, the northern RAF units had carried out the same type of tasking during the Sheffield floods. I feel quite sure that any Search and Rescue crew in the country would have loved to be involved in helping out in a situation like that, whatever the risks; it incorporates everything that is good about the job and leaves the crews knowing that they have made a difference. I personally cannot think of anything better than that.

Caravan Park with the water still rising (Photo Mick Rowsell)

Recovery of five casualties from the roof of local public house
(Photo Mick Rowsell)

Mrs Gilbert after being recovered to the aircraft (Photo Mick Rowsell)

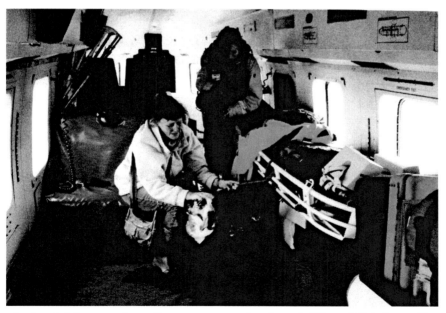

Lady with her two dogs after recovery to the aircraft (Photo Mick Rowsell)

2007 Continued

Less than a week after the Gloucestershire floods, we were scrambled to another unusual job that was to prove very challenging. The crew was: Captain Mark Jackson, co-pilot Dave Gibbs, winch-op John Spencer and I was the winchman.

The task was to a woman with a suspected dislocated hip having taken a fall on a coastal path on the Isle of Wight. I thought this would be a straightforward extraction, probably required because the ambulance could not get close to the casualty.

Once airborne it became clear that the exact position of the casualty was not known; the casualty's friend had passed the information on a mobile phone. She could explain where they had set off from but they were now in a forest and she was not sure how far in.

On scene, we followed the path as best we could until it disappeared into the forest. It was unlikely we would see anything, but were continuing to search while discussing the options open to us when John spotted a bit of pink clothing through a small hole in the forest's canopy. We circuited the same area a few times before John saw it again and was able to see enough to determine that what he saw was likely to be the casualty.

It was about half a mile into the woods and the entrance some distance from any vehicular access. The shortest route was from the coast through the undergrowth so our initial thought was to winch me to the beach so that I could make access from there.

We were at the time receiving information that the woman was in her seventies and was also experiencing chest pains; this information was adding some urgency to the task.

It was a very hot day with no wind and, having just left base with our normal fuel load, we would have to jettison fuel before attempting to winch. A couple of minutes were spent jettisoning fuel out to sea before running in to the position we had selected for lowering me to the beach. As we approached, it was clear that this would be quite difficult as the cliff leading to the forest was steeper than we thought.

While looking for another entry point we heard over the radio that the nearest help was still a long way from the casualty and that her condition was getting worse. We therefore decided to see if there was any way we could winch directly through the tree canopy.

John conned the aircraft back to the spot in question, but it was obvious it would be very awkward. We could not get close to the space John would have to winch me through as we were pulling close to full power and the downdraught simply closed the hole in the trees. In addition, as we were pulling so much power, Mark needed height to provide a flyaway if required. We quickly found the optimum height to achieve this would be 180/200ft.

The main problem was that the hover would have to be perfect; over a very small gap in the canopy, which Mark had not even seen! He would be relying totally on John's con, plus height and power information from Dave. It would not be easy even with Mark's many years of experience, as he would have to be accurate within a few feet.

This was a similar situation to a job I had done years ago, requiring recovery of a casualty and winchman through a tree canopy at night. On that occasion, the aircraft was close to a cliff top, which allowed the pilot more hover references to gauge my con against. In this incident, Mark would be looking to the distance for his references, which would make it even more demanding.

We discussed all the options again, in particular, whether we could wait until someone else got to the casualty to assess the situation on the ground, but again we were informed that help was some way away. Therefore, suspecting the casualty was having a coronary event on top of her possible injuries, we decided the sooner we could get someone to her the better chance she would have and all agreed to give it a go. John would winch me close to the gap in the treetops. If he then felt he could not get me through, he would abort the attempt and recover me to the aircraft.

All I could do was put my faith in the crew's ability, rather relieved I was not the winch-op. John would be feeling his heart in his throat as he worked hard on keeping a calm con while he lowered me to the small gap. We all wished we could have carried this out from a lower height which would have made it much easier, but that simply was not possible.

As I entered the tree canopy, I could not see where I was going and had to separate branches in order to clear my descent through the trees. This was rather disturbing but it was not long before I did actually see the casualty – I was coming down right on top of her! Guessing that John would probably have lost sight of me by now, I was able to talk direct on the radio about when I wanted him to stop or continue winching and to let him know when I was on the ground.

The woman was sat on the floor having fallen down a small ridge. After a few questions, I felt confident that she was not having a coronary event but she was very worried and clearly unable to move after her fall. I put her on oxygen while trying to assess the best way out of this situation.

The casualty's friend, who had done so well keeping the authorities informed, was clearly relieved to see help arrive; she was the first to admit that it was probably not a good idea to have tried to walk the path. To be fair, the path had clearly deteriorated the further they had gone along it, until they reached the point when it was difficult to tell whether it would be better to continue or go back.

Shortly after I arrived, two Coastguards came crashing through the undergrowth. They had entered the forest from the coastal side and had made their way to the incident by the noise and occasional glimpses of the helicopter. It was with some relief for me, as help would be required to get the woman into a stretcher. One of the Coastguards was an A&E nurse, which was lovely as she was able to comfort the casualty while I assessed the best way out of there.

Having the local knowledge from the Coastguards helped considerably, as they knew the best way out of the forest. Unfortunately, they could not recommend trying to carry the stretcher out. It would be approximately half a mile on a very rickety path, which because of all the rain was now a very muddy and slippery path; hence, the reason the lady had fallen in the first place.

With that information and seeing the state of the path in this location, I knew we would have great difficulty manoeuvring a stretcher just a few yards let alone half a mile. I would therefore have to look at the possibility of winching her back out through the trees.

After discussing this possibility with the John, Mark and Dave, we decided that they would see how they got on lowering the stretcher to me and re-assess after that. They would initially lower an extended 200ft weighted hi-line. If that was snagged, the weak link would break, preventing any further problems to the aircraft. Once we had the hi-line, the Coastguards and I would be able to control the stretcher through the gap in the canopy while John winched out. That worked well, although John again lost sight of the stretcher as it disappeared through the tops of the trees.

Another walker had arrived at our position while the helicopter was lowering the stretcher, so I was able to utilize him. Between the four of us, we managed to move the casualty as gently as possible into the stretcher and strapped her in ready for transfer.

Again, after discussion with the crew, we decided that the aircraft would remain at 200ft, I would attach the hi-line to the stretcher by the weak link and the Coastguards would guide us as we were winched through the canopy. Because there was no wind that day and the downdraught was being directed to the stretcher, I knew a spin would build up as I approached the aircraft, so it was important that the Coastguards kept tension on the hi-line at all times to prevent that spin.

The transfer went well with John controlling the winching as he guided us through the branches. It was nerve racking for him, as he would lose sight of us occasionally. Every time that happened he stopped winching until either he saw me again or reacted to me telling him over the radio to winch in.

Mark and Dave were also on tenterhooks, conscious of having to keep a very accurate hover and height while John eased us out of the canopy. They both mentioned afterwards the relief they felt when John reported that we were clear of the trees. I could feel the spin trying to build up as the downdraught hit the stretcher but that was checked by the hi-line being controlled by the Coastguards on the ground. Once at the doorway John released the high line to minimize the time the aircraft would be in a compromising high power hover situation.

The casualty was taken to the Island's hospital-landing site to be met by a waiting ambulance. Her companion was looked after by the Coastguards and escorted out of the woods. What had started out as straightforward job turned into an extremely challenging one, particularly for Mark and John.

Only a few days after this incident we were scrambled to another unusual and very tragic incident. The initial call was to a man in difficulty at Lepe Beach. The casualty had been recovered from the water and was being treated by rescuers and Coastguards, evacuation would be required. The crew was: Captain Simon Hornsby, co-pilot Paul Mattinson, winch-op Nick Horst and I was the winchman.

En-route it became apparent that the casualty was being resuscitated and that a baby was also in distress and being looked after by family. Paramedics were proceeding by foot, because they could not get their ambulance to the position of the casualty.

When we arrived on scene the beach was too packed to attempt a winch or landing so we landed in a field just to the north of the incident. Two paramedics were working on the casualty when Nick and I arrived, they continued with the CPR and other procedures in the fight to reverse the situation with the casualty. I was able to check that the baby was not in any immediate danger and safely in the arms of her mother.

Once the paramedics had done everything they could at the scene of the incident, we decided the quickest way to transfer him to hospital would be to winch directly from the beach. As usual at the height of summer, we were faced with no wind, high temperatures and a crowded beach, all factors requiring a high hover. There would still be considerable downdraught so Coastguards and Police set about clearing the immediate area.

Nick returned to the aircraft with the baby, the baby's mother and a paramedic to look after them. I transferred the casualty to our stretcher while the team working on him continued with the CPR, which I was able to continue while being winched to the aircraft. Only a few minutes later we were able to transfer the casualty to a waiting ambulance at Southampton landing site. Unfortunately, even with all the efforts of people on the beach, lifeguards, Coastguards, paramedics and ourselves the resuscitation was not successful.

Shortly after returning to Lee-on-Solent, the tragic story of the incident was unfolding. The man was a 43-year-old playing in the sea with his granddaughter, daughter and her friend. They were on a sand bar close to the shore when the tide rapidly started to cover the sand. The family then got into difficulty, caught out by the speed of the tide. The man had kept his granddaughter above the water as he struggled back to the beach even though part of the time his own head was below the water.

People on the beach saw the predicament and went to help. When the rescuers had the baby safe the grandfather insisted they helped his daughter and her friend, which they did, but when they went back for him he was floating on the surface unconscious. Solent Rescue lifeguards were soon on scene, so CPR commenced as soon as he had been brought ashore by his rescuers.

It was a very tragic incident; the man's main aim was to see his family safe at the cost of his own life. This was another night, when I would be going home with tremendous sadness in my heart and would find myself dwelling on that incident for some time. It was the third incident in as many weeks that left me feeling extremely sad and upset that we could not have had a successful outcome.

In the past few weeks, I had been involved in situations that represent the tragic side of our job. Two days prior to the Gloucestershire floods, I had been scrambled with: Captain Richard Norris, co-pilot Dave Gibbs and Nick Horst as the winchman. The task was to a rigid inflatable that witnesses had watched hit a ledge just off Bembridge on the Isle of Wight. The rigid inflatable had no occupants, yet it was obvious that there had been people onboard.

Shortly after arriving on scene, we located one person (a young man) floating on the surface. A lifeboat pulled him from the water and immediately commenced CPR. We recovered him to the aircraft, continuing the resuscitation as we flew the casualty to St Mary's hospital on the Island. Once the casualty was transferred to paramedics at the landing-site, we returned to the search area in case anyone else was involved.

It was soon apparent that a young lady had been on the boat with the young man and a thorough search was carried out involving several lifeboats, a Royal Naval vessel (plus its rigid inflatable boats) and ourselves. Our search continued for nine hours in total, but nothing was found.

The next day, only a few hours prior to the Gloucestershire floods tasking, we had the recovery of the cardiac arrest incident on the yacht, which was an awkward job, again without the satisfaction of successful resuscitation. Then the incident with the grandfather on the beach.

Jobs such as these which have a tragic side always leave the crews feeling down. Fortunately, as I have mentioned before, these types of jobs are in the minority, the majority of our jobs having successful outcomes.

The Gloucestershire situation was just that. Although it was very upsetting for all those caught up in the floods, our task was to remove people from a dangerous situation and take them to safety. All those people were fit and well when recovered to the aircraft and then taken to a place of safety, still fit and well.

Then there was the successful lift of the lady in the woods and a few days after that, a diver and his buddy flown from a dive boat to a compression chamber, in time to save any long-term damage. Other successful jobs were carried out by other crews in that busy three week period – we have to dwell on these successful jobs to help get over the sad ones.

Part 9

Transition to CHC Helicopter Corporation

2008

The move to our new company had come round fast and proved a very sad time for us all. As I expected, the majority of us went across to CHC. This was not an affront to Bristows as they had been a good company to work for but the most important thing for many of us was to stay doing the job we do.

A few will be remaining with Bristows for various reasons. Paul Mattinson went to Norwich to gain his command as a Captain. Chris Bond remained with Bristows to assist with the bid for the major SAR harmonisation contract in 2012. Dave Thomson accepted a senior position with Bristow's overseas working in Malaya, a position he could not turn down. Daryl Edwards & Mike Townend took floating contracts with Bristows; they had been at Lee since day one in 1988. It was a shame to see the break up a team that had gelled so well together and which helped to form the extremely successful unit we had at Lee-on-Solent.

The change of companies took place at midnight on the 3rd January. A few minutes prior to handing over to the transition team, the aircraft was scrambled for the final incident, which was a medical transfer from the Isle of Wight. Chris Bond was the winchman for that task, which for Chris could not have been timed better, helping him come to terms with moving on to his new, very important role for Bristows. He had carried out the very first job when we started at Lee in May 1988, so it was special for him to carry out the very last job on that long running contract.

The rest of us joined the new company on the 4th of January at the brand new building on the other side of the airfield. The building was purpose built for a SAR unit with a huge hanger; it had been commissioned and built for the MCA to house whoever serviced the SAR helicopter contract on their behalf.

We had moved from operating out of a pre-war building that had also been provided by the MCA and was a building that in many ways complemented the role we had, especially with the 'S61'.

The majority of us had spent twenty years operating from the old SAR unit and had held many functions there. Family days, sports days, barbecues, charity functions, arguments, plenty of laughter, hundreds of challenges that helped to keep us amused over the years, from riding unicycles to land sail boarding, windows had been broken while practicing our golf strokes, thousands of games of volley ball had been played while waiting for scrambles.

Six of the eight crewmen had even worked on the Naval SAR flight prior to Bristows, so for the likes of me, it was my third base move and fourth aircraft type all on the one airfield, so obviously there are many memories.

The new building is much more sterile, filled with lecture rooms and offices. I hoped at the time that it would not prove to be so big that it would break up the unity we had been used to, there is now so much space the crews may start disappearing to their various rooms. Time will have to be the judge of that.

The next problem we faced was a delay on the arrival of the new aircraft, initially the delay was for one month. This was not too much of a problem, as it gave us time to carry out the many ground school requirements. The pilots went to Italy to do their ground school, simulator drills and some flying. We started our ground school utilising the new facilities here at Lee. Other drills like fire-fighting, underwater escape and dinghy drills were carried out at Aberdeen.

The delay for the first aircraft stretched a further few weeks and proved to be a very frustrating time. This was not CHC's fault they had been let down for various reasons, certification problems, production line delays etc. This meant that the deadline to complete our operational training was extremely tight.

A further unanticipated change was announced in the first few days and that was that the crewmen would have to split into two groups, four of us as winch-ops and four as winchmen. This was to allow the winch-ops to concentrate on the operational side of the aircraft and the winchmen to start their paramedic training. Under the new contract, the winchmen would have to be fully credited under the national paramedic requirements and a paramedic carried within each duty crew. The training required considerable extra work over several months with quite lot of time away from the unit.

The decision to split the roles was not welcome at Lee as we all wanted to remain dual trained. We had many reasons for that, let alone the flexibility it allowed but, I could see that to get us on line in time for April it was the only way. It was also clear that Mick Rowsell, Don Sowden and I were coming up for retirement so the company would not get any return of service for the considerable cost of all the additional medical courses.

This meant, understandably, that Nick Horst, John Spencer, Alf Kitwood and Simon O'Mahony would fill the winchman role and went the following Monday to commence the first of the paramedic training modules on a course run by the RAF.

The RAF, as mentioned earlier had been proactive on this front and had already started the training package for their winchmen, knowing legislation would force the requirement for full accreditation at some time in the future.

Terry Short had initially been told that he would not be allowed to transfer because he was working as a contractor for Bristows and did not come under the TUPE deal. That decision changed at the last minute due to some legal requirement, which permitted him to be transferred as a contractor under the terms he had been on with Bristows. We were all pleased with that and Nick, as Senior Crewman, had been pushing that Terry came across; he would be invaluable at the setup stage.

The new company soon recognized Terry's value and due to all the extra training required, they asked Terry to be a trainer again along with myself. I had hoped to stand down as a trainer. I felt my situation at home would cause problems with all the extra work that would be required and I thought the younger crews should shape their own future. However, as mentioned it turned out they had enough on their plates with all the extra medical training.

Therefore, having the chance of doing the job with Terry again made me rethink; between us, we had a lot to offer and the rest of the lads were in agreement with the decision. Margaret understood it was something I would want to do and, fortunately, my mother was happy to increase the time she would spend staying with Margaret for the extra hours I would be at work.

Brian Johnson, CHC's Chief Crewman Standards and Chris Hughes (Spike) the CHC trainer for the new aircraft, trained myself and Terry, then Terry and I trained the rest with Brian and Spike's help when required.

It proved a very hectic and busy period. The aircraft did not arrive until late February but by continuously flying the aircraft when it did arrive, running rotors crew changes etc., we managed to meet all our training targets, which allowed two crews to commence the contract on time while the remainder finished their training.

This really was some achievement, initially thought impossible and only achieved by the hard work of everyone, involving the spirit shown, yet again, that has been with us from the first day we started at Lee and one I feel CHC was lucky to have inherited.

We all found it difficult coming to terms with this new aircraft. It was being championed as the future of SAR on the south coast and is an impressive looking aircraft brimming with state of the art technology. The advanced equipment includes: a glass cockpit; Westcam FLIR and camera system; Euronav electronic mapping system; Night sun search light; Skyshout loud hailer system; twin hoist; satellite phone; satellite tracking; aircraft avoidance system and four-axis auto hover.

We were also to have a SAR auto hover system with full SAR modes, but not fitted at the time as certification had not been completed, but when fitted will give us an all weather capability as we had in the 'S61'.

Unfortunately, the cabin space is less than the 'Whirlwind', the aircraft I had started flying in, and even back then we considered that too small. The aircraft has other issues such as hovering with a nose up attitude making the winching a little awkward. Adding to our frustrations, we had a lot of teething problems and, being a new aircraft type, the problem solving was not as slick as we were used to, so this proved a very difficult time for the engineers.

The main problem for the crewmen is space in the cabin, which is only 2.26m by 2.1m and 1.37m tall and fixtures that have to be accommodated within that space are four seats and the FLIR station.

The majority of our SAR and medical equipment is loaded into the tail, which is accessible from the cabin; the remaining space in the cabin is required to pull the equipment out of the tail when required. The stretcher in particular takes the full length of the cabin when removing it from the tail. More importantly, the free space we have in the cabin is required to manoeuvre the winchman and stretcher into the aircraft when being recovered on the end of the winch wire.

Working only on one casualty gets very difficult as the cabin being only 1.37m high means everything has to be done stooped over or crawling around on our knees. Dealing with multi casualties is virtually impossible, particularly if they require to be lying down. The decision makers appeared to have overlooked the fact that we pick up the majority of our casualties while on the move or in the hover, requiring a lot of manoeuvring room by the door.

We rarely have the option of stabilising a casualty before winching them onboard. Working on an injured casualty once recovered to the aircraft requires a build up of kit that could include defibrillator, aspirator, monitoring equipment, first aid bags, oxygen, entonox, drugs and fluids, the majority of which has to be accessible from the tail, and this soon takes up all the available space in the cabin.

Landing on to load a stabilised casualty is rare, so we are unable to have a built in stretcher area surrounded by medical and monitoring equipment like, for example, a road ambulance or air ambulance helicopter. That sort of thing requires careful loading from people stood on the ground outside the aircraft not normally available to us.

I have always been honest with my feelings and guess I do wear my heart on my sleeve so found it difficult to enthuse about the aircraft in the same way as I did when I started on the 'S61'. It may well be fast, have a lot of power and a wonderful pilot's aircraft but I would require an awful lot of persuading to accept that it is suitable for the role we do.

I did however, accept that this was the aircraft chosen and that there will have been reasons for that decision that I am not privy too. I did of course endeavour to get the very best out of the aircraft and worked hard on procedures and ways to work round these problems. The pilots have their own issues to work round and they fully understand our problems so we were all working hard to find the way forward.

That aside, the SAR equipment provided was brilliant and we had all the backing required when we wished to trial new equipment. No expense had been spared on training equipment, especially on the first-aid side, even to the point that each base has its own computer controlled training dummy that is able to simulate many of the problems we deal with. The additional equipment provided will go a long way towards us keeping on top of the perishable skills that are soon diluted when not used on a regular basis.

We came on line officially with the new aircraft on the 4th April 2008, taking over at Portland. This was not as originally planned, we should have started here at Lee, but the decision was changed because it was felt that, as Portland was a 12-hour unit from 0900–2100 it would give us more time to get used to the aircraft before being tasked at night.

The transition crew, who had been covering for us at Lee in our old aircraft on lease from Bristows, remained at Lee, to cover the 24-hour shifts, our crew's went to Portland with the new aircraft to cover the daylight 12 hour shifts, while the Portland crew's carried out their period of training.

It all made sense but proved awkward for me as being at Portland made looking after Margaret very difficult. Nick got round that by leaving me at Lee to continue with the training, I only went to Portland when my shifts could not be covered, which Nick kept to a minimum.

The jobs at Portland were much the same as at Lee and the diving season was well underway so, it was not surprising that our early jobs were to diving incidents plus quite a few cliff and coastal jobs.

A couple of standard type jobs I had at Portland are worth mentioning, as they highlighted a strange phenomenon that has been happening over recent years and that is the abuse suffered by emergency service personnel as they go about their jobs, including stones being thrown at fire engines and ambulances: it appears completely mindless and in my opinion a worrying aspect of our society today.

Fortunately, it is not something I have experienced too often, but had an insight to how nasty people can be on two jobs carried out on consecutive days. The first of these calls was to a beach close to Abbotsbury in Dorset. It was to an angler who had fallen and broken his leg on the foreshore. Paramedics had located him, but they were unable to get the casualty to the ambulance because of a steep pebble bank. We were tasked to recover him to the aircraft for onward transfer to hospital.

Spike Hughes, was the winchman and he had packaged the casualty ready for winching before clearing the area prior to our approach. Fifty metres along the beach another couple of men were fishing and had continued fishing as though nothing had happened.

Spike had to ask them to move as our downdraught would cause them problems but they refused to move. Spike said "I cannot order you to move but if you stay there you, or certainly your equipment, will be blown into the sea," they simply replied that if that happened they would sue us. Obviously, we would not have continued with the rescue until the Coastguards arrived on scene, as we could not risk further injury to people, but before they arrived, the anglers must have had a touch of conscience and did move.

The next day we were tasked to recover a man who had fallen on the cliffs at Portland (again with a broken leg). This meant lowering Spike to a position just down-wind of the casualty; he then climbed down to prepare the casualty for transfer. At the top of the cliffs, a crowd had gathered to watch what was going on. Unfortunately, they had gathered in the area we would need to hover when winching the casualty.

Spike could not ask them to move as he was on a lower ledge so we had to get as close as we could and gesture for them to move, which some of them did but a few would not. This meant we had to take it very careful, hoping that when they saw the downdraught coming towards them they would move. One lady walking a dog was knocked off her feet because she was not going to move for anyone and another man ran in front of us trying to take photographs. We should not have allowed that to happen but it was very difficult under the circumstances to spot the two that would not move.

A Coastguard arrived on scene shortly after this and had a word with them. The abuse he got was disturbing and the man who had been taking photographs said, "I live on the Island and no one can tell me to move." How are we supposed to deal with situations like that?

These incidents were a complete U-turn from when I started in this job, back then everyone wanted to help or otherwise kept well clear. The anglers in the first incident were refusing to move even though it was a fellow angler requiring assistance.

At the time we were at Portland it was coming up to four years since Michael, our grandson finished his treatment for Leukaemia and his latest tests were all fine. He had just finished in the sixth form and was waiting for his 'A' level results.

It was almost as though the episode never happened. He had also been filling his time over the previous few years carrying out many sensible activities outside of school such as the Duke of Edinburgh's award scheme, lifesaving classes, helping on the coaching side with local sporting groups, teaching Spanish to younger groups and raising money for cancer groups with the help of his sixth form classmates.

He was also preparing for a trip to Uganda to help at a respite centre for orphaned children and had secured a position as a helper at an outward bound centre in Ireland, which ran a summer camp for children with cancer. This was a place he went to when he was ill and thoroughly enjoyed, so was extremely pleased to be able to return as a helper. Both these trips would be during his gap year before going to university.

All this good work with Michael and seeing Jessica doing so well made Margaret extremely proud. Her insistence that all would be fine for Michael, I expect, has been the mainstay of her own continuing improvements. She lights up when the grandchildren come round and that spark rubs off on all of us. We had all come a long way since the gloom of 1997 followed by the scare with Michael.

Back on the flight, we came to the end of our three months at Portland and returned to Lee-on-Solent to take our patch back. It was nice to get back to some form of normality, it really had been a mad six months, coming to terms with a new company, training on the new aircraft, then operating from another unit and area.

The lads going the full paramedic route had been working extremely hard to fast track through their various modules as well as covering duties at Portland. Clearly, having the skills already gained on our 'Advance Life Support' courses, and subsequent years of experience and refresher courses, had helped to make the new requirements easier. However, they had to cover a lot more theory involving many hours with their heads in books followed by additional exams and modules.

I felt quite envious of them, having always been happier as a winchman, but I had to accept that I was extremely fortunate to be where I was; I already had an extra four years service after the date I was originally required to retire. I would still get some winchman duties having been cleared for both roles with Don Sowden, so was able to continue as winchman as well as winch-op until all the paramedic courses had been completed and the nominated winchmen had the accreditation required, which at the time was planned for July 2009.

We also hoped that once the winchmen on all the units had qualified they would eventually be able to continue training on the winch-op side to get back to the way we operated previously. Only time will tell; as the two disciplines get further apart it will become more difficult to keep both of the skills current. The biggest worry is if the future winch-ops do not come from the winchman side, how will the winch op skills be learnt? It takes a considerable time to gain the skills required and those skills require plenty of hands on practice, again, decisions for the future and ones that will be solved.

Many problems had been highlighted over the first twelve months, particularly for CHC who had to bring on line four different operating bases with two different aircraft types. The organisation requirements to achieve this were mind blowing and they had to provide SAR at each of those bases while the training took place. It was quite an achievement by anyone's standards.

Return to Lee-on-Solent

We finally returned to Lee on the 4th July 2008 and it felt every bit as good as I had hoped. The building had been host to engineering courses for the 'AW139', all our operational training, housing the transition team and numerous meetings regarding the way forward. It really had been a hive of activity for the previous six months, so we welcomed being able to settle down and start to mould the base that will see the flight into the future.

Two new winchmen joined us, both ex RAF with all the qualifications required for the future MCA 'SAR' contract requirements. They had spent the previous year on the transition team operating around the four bases and had been involved in training and setting up the medical requirements.

Neil Harrison, 'Gucci'. His nickname from the RAF also transferred with him. Neil is also a qualified instructor and the company appointed him as the SAR medical standards aircrewman, with the brief of coordinating the training program for the winchmen on all four bases, ensuring the winchmen complete the required modules and qualifications by the target date. He also had to deal with the implications involved in that requirement, of which there were many.

I could see straight away that it would take a great deal of his time, but to keep current in his main role as a SAR winchman he trained with us on the 'AW139' and became a floater between ourselves and Portland, filling in as and when he can.

Neil joined us with a wealth of experience in the role and one of the first aircrewmen to be trained in the RAF to the new medical standards. To add to that he is an 'Air Force Cross' holder and holder of a 'Billy Deacon Memorial Trophy'.

Mario Testa, 'Mazza' Mario joined us as a full time member of the unit and, like Neil, is a registered paramedic and qualified instructor. Mario completed his 'AW139' training at Portland prior to our return to Lee. He will take the role of medical standards for the two southern bases, with a brief to standardise equipment and procedures. We are limited by space on the AW139 as to what equipment we can carry, unlike the northern bases who have the 'S92' which has considerably more room in the cabin. Mario was tasked to evaluate and prioritize the equipment carried in the 'AW 139'.

Mario like Neil is extremely professional with a wealth of knowledge, particularly on the medical side; he keeps extremely fit, another exercise fanatic who also cycles daily from his home on the Isle of Wight. He like Neil is an 'Air Force Cross' holder and has also been awarded the 'Queens Commendation for Bravery'.

We are very fortunate to have both of them attached to the unit; our good luck regarding the standard of crews was set to continue.

A new co-pilot Martin Taal, joined to take over from Paul Mattinson. He is a Dutch pilot who had been working for CHC in Den Helder on the 'AW 139' and joined Lee with over five hundred hours experience on the aircraft. He completed his training as a SAR co-pilot shortly after we came on line with the new aircraft. Martin became a full time member of the team and later moved his family over from Holland.

Another captain and winch operator joined shortly after our return to Lee. They joined us as leave reliefs between Lee-on-Solent and Portland. The captain is Giles Duncan, ex Royal Navy SAR pilot and for the previous year had been the Chief Pilot for the transition team, covering the SAR at the four MCA bases with the 'S61', while each unit trained on their new aircraft.

Ian Copley joined as the relief winch operator between the two bases but based at Portland. Ian is an ex Royal Navy SAR Diver who had also spent a few years on loan with the RAF. On leaving the forces, he worked for Bristows as the leave relief on the 'S61' SAR fleet. Having the experience of the Navy, RAF and civilian Search and Rescue, it was not surprising that he was head hunted by CHC as the Chief Aircrewman of the transition team. Ian is also trained on the 'S92' so will also fill in on the northern bases as required.

Both Giles and Ian had a very difficult job holding everything together during the transition period with many problems to work round. We all knew Ian very well from his Bristow days so knew that he will fit in well and Giles had been working from Lee for the previous six months in the 'S61' and it was also clear he will become a valuable member of the units, both here and at Portland.

Finally, Tony Oliver also joined us, also ex Royal Navy and from the transition team as the winchman floater between all four units. Tony would have his work cut out for the next couple of years having to mix travelling between four units and operating two aircraft types; while at the same time completing his paramedic course.

I decided to remain in the role a little longer and felt fortunate to have the opportunity to do so. The job has been a lot easier for me since standing down as Chief Aircrewman giving me more time to cope with the situation at home.

Nick Horst was coping well in the hot seat (as I knew he would), I feel he has had quite a hard time of it since taking over, particularly with the recent company change, new aircraft type and paramedic modules. He has been doing a brilliant job, his main attribute is his calming nature that has helped to defuse the frustrations that have been brewing during this awkward period and he clearly enjoys the job, but it does come at a price: his hair is getting greyer by the day!

The engineering team has faced the largest changes at Lee with only the Chief Engineer Simon Gent, Mike McCutcheon and Dave Savage coming across from Bristows. Six new engineers joined: Craig Chaplin (Charlie), Ricky Groves, Adrian Parish, Mark Dolan, Freddy Sorensen and Glen Stansfield. They really had their work cut out having to get to grips with a new aircraft type made worse by all the teething problems we had been experiencing.

It will take many years to build the knowledge base the team had on the 'S61'; nevertheless, as always on SAR flights, everyone gives 100% so all stops were pulled to get on top of problems as quick as possible.

Pre take-off checks (Photo Capt. John Bell (CG Flt))

Augusta Westland 139

**Checking winchman's gear prior to winching
(Photo Mike O'Brien)**

Winching Out (Photo Mike O'Brien)

Winching with Calshot Lifeboat (Photo Mike O'Brien)

Winching with Swanage Lifeboat (Photo RNLI/P Elleray)

Cliff Training to the base of the Needles Isle of Wight

(Photo Ned Dawson-Oceania Media Group)

(Photo Ned Dawson-Oceania Media Group)

Mario being winched to 'Earthrace' in the Solent

(Photo Ned Dawson-Oceania Media Group)

Although we have been very busy with the many changes on the work side, it proved to be one of the quietest years that I can recollect. The jobs since returning to Lee from Portland had, in general, been standard problems faced in the summer: diving incidents; injured yachtsmen; missing vessels; a few cliff jobs and people stranded by the tide, the majority handled without too much difficulty.

Terry Short had one awkward cliff job at night, while crewed with: Captain Simon Hornsby, co-pilot Mark Jackson and the winchman Nick Horst. They had been scrambled to people stuck at the base of the cliffs close to the Needles on the Isle of Wight; the tide was rising in rough seas putting them in a very dangerous situation.

Yarmouth lifeboat had attempted to get them off and in doing so, had managed to get one of the lifeboat crew on to the ledge with the two casualties. The worsening weather and breaking waves made it impossible for the lifeboat to approach the rocks for a second time, which meant leaving the lifeboatman stranded with the two casualties, having to do that must have been very difficult for the lifeboat crew.

When 'Rescue 104' arrived on scene, the 26-knot wind was in the wrong direction to allow a straightforward recovery; a downwind hover in those winds at night was out of the question. Terry thought they might be able to achieve it from the left hand side, providing the rotor blades had enough clearance from the cliff face above the casualty.

We had a procedure for left hand cliffs but the procedure required more clearance from the cliff face than proved available that night. So the crew had to assess the situation very carefully, as to the best way to achieve the rescue.

Terry's plan was to lower Nick far enough below the aircraft so that he would be able to see him from the door on the left hand side of the aircraft (the winch being on the right). Once Nick was positioned, Terry would move across to the left hand door, he could take the winch controller with him, but would not be able to control the wire with his hand to prevent it rubbing against the step or catching on the sponson.

Because Terry would not be able to control the wire manually, it was important that a swing did not build up. Preventing a swing from happening would require a steady, calm con and as smooth as possible control of the aircraft from Mark who was the left hand seat pilot that night; Terry would only use the winch switch for final adjustments.

They knew the height they would have to be to see Nick hanging below the aircraft, so carried out a dummy run to check the feasibility and that Mark had enough references and able to cope with the turbulence.

The dummy was successful, Nick was happy to give it a go and they achieved the procedure three separate times, each time the video showed Nick going through breaking waves, which were snatching at the casualties on the ledge.

They had achieved the rescue using a procedure that we could not make standard because of its inherent danger; we really should have full control of the winch wire. However, it was a method we often discussed and Terry had now used successfully. It was the only chance for these trapped people and one Nick as winchman was willing to put his trust in Terry, Mark and Simon to achieve.

Another slightly unusual job was during a scramble to pick up two divers who had missed their stops due to an emergency. They required recovery from the dive boat 'Mac Dee' and flown to Horsea HLS, for transfer to a decompression chamber. En-route another dive boat, the 'Channel Diver', 10 miles south of the first dive boat reported one of their divers had returned to the surface having missed his stops.

The Coastguards took advice from dive doctors ashore and we were tasked to pick up all three, the quicker they could be treated the better the chance for a full recovery.

Fortunately, we were able to pick up all three divers without too much delay. John Spencer was the winchman and he had his work cut out looking after all three in the very cramped space.

Towards the end of the summer as the nights started to close in, we had to concentrate on training at night and it was becoming apparent that all was not well with the aircraft. As mentioned, we had known from day one that we did not have all the aids required to make it an all weather aircraft, in particular the SAR auto-hover system, which will also incorporate search patterns and the ability, when the pilot loses visual references, for the winch-op to control the aircraft (horizontal movements) from the back. This equipment is essential to an all weather SAR helicopter, especially when working low level or picking survivors from the water, life rafts or very small craft at night.

The system should have been fitted when we commenced training with the aircraft, but problems in getting certification meant it was delayed, the latest information suggesting it being available in March 2009; therefore, we were facing the prospect of spending the winter months without this essential equipment.

The company accepted our concerns and after consultation with the MCA, it was agreed we could only offer a reduced service. The main shortfalls were the inability to carry out searches at night, in certain weather conditions, or recoveries from the sea, life rafts and small craft in poor light or darkness.

Initially we felt we could achieve many of our requirements with the standard autopilot and hover facilities, at least we could winch to the majority of vessels at night and had managed to find ways of carrying out searches, providing the weather was within our newly defined safe minima.

However as we became more familiar with the aircraft other problems materialised, such as the lights not being powerful enough, very little or no redundancy when lights failed and equipment not working as it was meant to. We had highlighted All these deficiencies and a matrix of problems and safety case was being produced. Eventually it was accepted that too many problems were presenting themselves for us to continue operating safely at night.

The company agreed this was unacceptable and made the very brave decision to withdraw the aircraft from SAR after the hours of darkness. I felt that was the right decision, as I was sure that risks would eventually be taken. It would have been extremely difficult if we located a vessel in distress and had to watch a worsening situation develop while unable to do anything about it. If we had attempted a rescue in the situations mentioned without the aids required and anything went wrong, we, the crews, would be at fault and culpable.

Having said that, there will always be times when the boundaries are pushed, as with the job just mentioned with Terry and Nick. That was well thought out and risk assessed by a very experienced crew who accepted if things went wrong they would have questions to answer.

The consequences of the decision to pull the aircraft from operating after the hours of darkness was far reaching: the company was contracted to provide 24-hour cover for the area which at night covered from Hastings in East Sussex to Start Point in Devon, plus the extremely busy shipping lanes in the Channel south of those points.

This meant bringing back a SAR 'S61' to cover the nights and all the problems associated with that; sourcing one that was SAR capable was difficult and the majority of our crews were now out of date for the 'S61'. Fortunately, a few of the crews who had been on the transition team were available, some having to be pulled from other contracts and a few were hired on contract. The contractual requirements were met, but at tremendous cost to the company.

Everyone worked extremely hard to get one of the aircraft back flying at night. Teams of engineers and specialists from Augusta in Italy and engineers from various bases abroad and the UK were brought in to work on the aircraft. The plan was to fit an Enhanced Ground Proximity Warning System, an additional searchlight and other modifications that we hoped would make things safer until the proper SAR system was certified and fitted.

While this work was going on, the 'S61' on loan from Ireland had to return to Ireland, requiring the standby 'S92' from Sumburgh to cover for a few days. This obviously created more crewing problems, as it was another aircraft type.

All this kafuffle was also very embarrassing for the crews, as it was mentioned in some circles that we should have got on without the aids required. I only wish those who thought that had experienced our many worrying incidents while trying to achieve our training requirements, let alone on jobs. I am surprised we went on as long as we did.

The crews were desperate to get back to full 24-hour coverage, that is our job and we were acutely aware that the area was entitled to a service better than we were achieving at that time.

In a little under six weeks all the hard work paid off and the first aircraft to complete the modifications was trialled, risk assessed and we were back night flying. The same team of engineers remained to modify the next aircraft for Portland and the spare aircraft would follow that. All stops were pulled to get us back on line day and night.

Shortly after the modifications we had a tasking just after midnight on the 12th December '09, to carry out a medical transfer from Jersey to Lords Hill HLS in Southampton, the crew was: Captain John Rooney, co-pilot Martin Taal, I was the winch-op and Don Sowden the winchman.

We had just cleared the south of the Isle of Wight heading into the channel en-route to Jersey, when we were recalled back to the Solent on the report of a small sea-angling vessel sinking mid Solent. We were being tasked to locate the vessel; other lifeboat crews had been called in case the vessel sank, as even with all the latest modifications, we still did not have the SAR auto-hover system so were not cleared to winch from the water at night. However if the casualty was still on the vessel we felt we may have enough hover references to take him off the vessel.

I was able to talk to the casualty on the radio confirming he was the only one onboard. He had just dropped his clients off at Portsmouth and was returning to the Island when he had hit a buoy. His boat was taking on water fast and he reported that it was sinking. I was also able to confirm that he had flares onboard and asked him to fire one as soon as he heard or saw us approaching.

This had all happened so fast that no sooner had I finished talking to the casualty when he saw our lights in the distance and had fired off the flare. Don, who had been preparing the back of the aircraft for the medical transfer, had to suddenly switch role and prepare himself for a possible winch to a deck. Knowing we could not winch from the water he had not prepared for a wet winch and was just about ready when we approached the vessel.

John then reported that the casualty was stood on the bow of the sinking vessel and that it was about to disappear below the surface. We had a very quick decision to make, it was the middle of winter, the casualty had adequate protection from the weather, but not for survival in the water and there was no sign of any boats approaching. The coastguards confirmed the lifeboats were still launching.

We quickly assessed the situation, taking in all the things in our favour: it was a clear night; all our lights including the new one just fitted were working; the horizon was quite clear with the lights from the shore and so we all agreed to give it a go. This was exactly the sort of situation we had been dreading, thankful that the latest batch of SAR enhancements had been completed but still without the SAR auto-hover system which would make this sort of job much easier.

Don quickly prepared, as best he could, for a water recovery and was soon ready and, seeing the guy's predicament, keen to get on with it. While I was trawling Don towards the survivor, the boat disappeared below the surface and the guy came swiftly towards him, almost as if he had been catapulted off the vessel. This took us by surprise, but Don soon had the strop on the survivor and I was winching him back to the aircraft, probably the fastest water recovery we had ever done at night, leaving us all amazed – it had gone so well.

We took the casualty to St Mary's HLS on the Isle of Wight and transferred him to a waiting ambulance, then returned to Lee for refuel prior to proceeding to Jersey for the medical transfer. We dried the cabin of the aircraft en-route and Don had to stay in his wet gear until that transfer was completed a few hours later.

Don and I reflected on this job as it was so much like a job we had done together over thirty years ago, when we had recovered a lone sailor early in the morning off Southsea. That time I was the winchman and the man was just about to disappear below the surface when we arrived, the man's rescue was down to a postman reporting something he felt was not right and the fact that we were stationed so close to the incident.

Towards the end of this year, Terry was informed that he would have to retire. This was a real shame because we all knew he was well capable of continuing, something that almost happened anyway because with all that was going on at Lee, HR had not picked up on Terry's age. The company, realising Terry was required on contract so often, asked if he would go full time again. He explained that he was more than willing but pointed out he would be 65 in a few months time. A few days later the company informed him that he would be required to retire at 65.

I have mentioned the respect we all had for Terry many times and it was hard to envisage the flight without him: he will be a hard act to follow.

Terry's numerical replacement was Dave Green (Paddy). Paddy was a winchman on the Stornoway SAR flight, another ex Navy chief aircrewman and a qualified Navy aircrewman trainer. He joined us in the New Year to begin his training as a winch-operator.

Paddy is also a recipient of the Lyle Bradbury Memorial Trophy which was awarded annually for the top commando aircrewman from all the courses in a twelve month period. Lyle was the friend of mine who lost his life due to an aircraft wire strike in Norway, mentioned earlier in the book. So it is especially nice to meet a recipient of this trophy, along with Neil Harrison who as already mentioned, is a recipient of the Billy Deacon SAR Memorial Trophy. Their names will live on at this unit for many years to come.

Terry had his first leaving do three years ago when he had to retire at 62; it was not long before he was asked to return, so here we are again. We could not let him leave without another send off which Nick and Richard arranged. This was a more personal leaving do, just with the flight and families to say goodbye to the best SAR aircrewman I have known. Of course, that is my opinion, but I guess most of the crews who have worked with him would agree.

The MCA Chief Coastguard Rod Johnson and the MCA Search and Rescue Operations Manager Jim McWilliams came along to present him with a commendation, in recognition of all the rescues carried out over the forty plus years and to thank Terry personally for his endeavor's and dedication to the role.

Shortly after Terry's retirement he was awarded the MBE for his work in Search and Rescue – an honour that was supported and celebrated by all the flight and I am sure all those who had ever worked with him.

2009/2010

In my view, 2009 like last year was another very quiet year, certainly for me, not having had any jobs that I would consider particularly difficult or unusual. We have had roughly the average number of callouts over the year but the more challenging ones have not happened when I have been on shift.

However, the year has been busy with many changes, such as training Terry's relief and extra crewmen and pilots between the two southern bases, plus all the crewmen have had to complete additional medical courses.

The winchmen have completed their paramedic registration training, all qualifying with exceptional results in minimum time while continuing full time in the role: quite an achievement. We are still pushing for all the back seat crew to be dual trained to give us the flexibility we had before, but that will mean the paramedic side being more specific to our primary role, which is search and rescue, not air ambulance. To achieve this will require a few changes in legislation but not completely out of the question.

Two new engineers have joined us to replace Freddy Sorensen who was offered a job back in Holland which he could not refuse, and Mark Dolan who transferred to Portland when a position became available closer to his home. Mick Wells joined us from working as a contractor for the company: he was one of the transition team engineers that helped set up the unit when we moved to CHC. Duncan Bathgate joined us straight from completion of his apprenticeship with CHC. Both are fitting in well with the unit: Duncan turns his hand to anything and Mick is one of the characters that help the flight keep its sense of humour

The aircraft has finally been fitted with the 'Phase Five' software upgrade which includes the SAR auto hover modification which makes life safer and, eventually, will help get us back to all weather capability. This modification will also give the winch-op the ability to control the aircraft from the back as we could in the 'S61'. The system required additional training for all the crews to become competent in its use and to build confidence in the latest aircraft modifications.

In February 2010 the government announced that the Soteria Consortium of CHC, Thales, Sikorsky and the Royal Bank of Scotland are the preferred bidder for the SAR harmonisation contract. As mentioned before, the new contract is planned to commence in 2012 and run for 25 years. This is a major contract covering Search and Rescue for the whole country. The contract is extremely important to the company and has been a major concern for all involved. Maybe, now the decision has been made, we can get back to some security within the role.

The good news for Lee on Solent is a larger aircraft will replace the 'AW 139' I am pleased about that as I have never been comfortable with the aircraft and really do feel it was not suitable for our role in UK SAR. I am sure the 'AW 139' will make its mark in SAR in other regions, certainly in mountain rescue or warmer climates where the power would be a major advantage and multi casualty situations unlikely. It would also be a brilliant air medical aircraft.

The aircraft selected to replace the 'AW139' is the 'Sikorsky 92A' (S92A), the same airframe that has been used at Sumburgh and Stornoway and is proving to be a very useful SAR aircraft. We can foresee that there may be problems with this aircraft in our role on the south coast, particularly in relation to downdraught and the size making it difficult to get into the smaller landing sites but these are problems the crews will learn to work round as they did with the 'S61's and the Seaking's. However, the space in the cabin will be wonderful, enabling the aircrewmen to carry out their main role much more effectively.

The new aircraft will be an update of the ones presently used at Stornoway and Sumburgh with many modifications recommended by the crews at both those bases.

It had been quite a while since I had a job that I felt was particularly challenging, by that I mean a task that would make a real difference to a casualty's situation and that required all our flying skills to achieve that tasking. In April 2010 I had two such jobs very close to each other, both proving to be quite awkward because of the sudden change of situation when we arrived on scene.

The first was on Easter Sunday when the yacht 'Blue Argent' ran aground on the Shingles bank, a notorious sand bank close to and occasionally proud of the surface at the western entrance to the Solent. The bank is particularly lethal when the tide is on the flood with south westerly winds and heavy seas. The rough seas as they meet the calmer waters of the Solent are stirred into very rough water by the shingle bank. Occasionally for various reasons boats are driven on to the bank, by the waves and the strong tides produced by the volume of sea being forced through the narrow gap between the Needles and Hurst Castle.

I have been involved with many rescues on the Shingles over the years including several fatalities. Vessels hitting the bank often get forced beam on to the sea and winds. Once snagged by the sands the sea can force the vessel onto its side and occasionally the waves washing over the trapped vessel can wash the casualties into the disturbed seas.

Shortly after taking over the afternoon shift we were scrambled to the report of the yacht 'Blue Argent' aground on the Shingles Bank, four persons onboard and the vessel taking on water. The crew was: Captain Mark Jackson, co-pilot Martin Taal, winchman Simon O'Mahony and I was the winch-op.

We were airborne and on scene within 15 minutes to find the 'Blue Argent' firmly on the bank, it still had the sails up and was in the classic broached position, being forced on its side and being swamped by the incoming waves. A rigid inflatable boat was trying to get alongside but unable to achieve this due to the bank itself and the heavy sea breaking over it.

The precarious situation that the casualties were in was obvious, but we could have made matters even worse as, at that stage, the yachts sails were still up and if our rotor-wash was to hit the sails it would cause further problems. The Yarmouth Lifeboat was approaching but it was clear the lifeboat would not be able to get close to the yacht. The lifeboat carries a small inflatable onboard called a 'Y boat' and we thought this small inflatable may be able to attempt the rescue. I asked if this was possible and they reported that they were already preparing to launch the 'Y boat'.

While the preparations for that were being made a huge wave nearly washed the casualties off the vessel, completely swamping the yacht and putting the hull under the surface with just the mast, sails and rigging above. All four crew were clinging to the rigging making it clear we had to attempt the rescue because the casualties were in immediate danger.

Simon was lowered to the trawl position but as we approached the casualties I had to lift Simon out of the water to clear one of the main mast stays which was lying just clear of the surface; this induced a swing that forced him towards the main mast. I was able to pay out enough cable to get him back in the water before striking the mast but this put him amongst all the loose rigging, mast and flapping sails. He tried swimming towards the survivors who were holding on to the forward stays, but the sea and tide were too great to allow any headway.

This left me in a quandary: do I cut the wire or attempt to weave him out of the situation using the aircraft? I could not just winch him clear as he was now thread under the main mast stays and rigging.

These situations happen very fast and, as the winch-op, I did not have time to explain to Mark what was happening. His only hover reference was the sea, which in situations like this is very difficult to read because the tide is whipping past the target we were winching to. Mark could not see that target, yet he knew it was not moving with the tide, which can be quite disorientating. I just had to hope he would follow my instructions implicitly – which he did and we managed to drag Simon while he was still in the water and weave him around the obstructions to a safe position.

While we backed off to reassess the situation Yarmouth's 'Y boat' managed to nip in and grab one of the survivors but was immediately forced away by the tide and waves. The crew of the 'Y boat' were still clinging to the casualty they had plucked from the yacht and we could see it would be awkward for them to pull him aboard the small craft in those seas.

At this stage, the remaining survivors were trying to hold on to each other and parts of rigging still proud of the water. We took the decision to attempt another approach which was successful, recovering the second casualty, a lady, to the aircraft. The 'Y boat' nipped in and managed to grab the third casualty before being swept away again and we went back in to recover the last casualty who was the skipper of the yacht.

As Simon escorted the lady to the ambulance she remarked "hanging on to the rigging with the waves breaking over me was the most frightening experience of my life." Simon could not help himself replying, somewhat tongue in cheek, "it was for me as well."

In the debrief Simon said he had gained so much from the rescue, the most difficult he had experienced to date. This was a situation that can never be experienced in training: trying to put strops on survivors when they are wearing large buoyancy aids, being battered by the sea and trying to avoid being entangled with rigging and ropes, is not easy!

Rescues like this are a true test for a winchman and one that I am sure will leave Simon feeling real achievement and pride that he was able to cope with the situation. He'd had one real scare when he ended up amongst all the rigging but continued a second and third time to complete a successful rescue. Those moments, for me, especially when in the winchman role, are the ones that remain uppermost in my mind.

This would equally have been very difficult for the guys in the 'Y boat' who themselves had taken risks getting to the yacht and could easily have been swamped and thrown into the sea themselves, another perfect example of the helicopter and lifeboats working together.

Only a few days later we had a scramble to the report of a person over the cliff at Newhaven. The casualty was reported to be clinging on with one arm and the other suspected of being broken. The crew was: Capt, Neil Stephenson, co-pilot, Simon Hoare who is our TRE training captain and was standing in for the shift, Mario Testa was the winchman and I was the winch-op.

En-route we were informed over the radio that a coastguard cliff team was on scene with the fire service and ambulance, so we were half expecting the situation to be resolved by the time we arrived. As we approached the scene we could sense from all the radio calls that all was not well.

The Coastguard had lowered a cliff team member to the casualty but, because of the casualty's precarious position, his broken arm and, the fact he was clinging on with the other arm, the rescue man was unable to secure a line to him properly, ending up supporting the casualty manually, which he was unable to do for long.

Just as we arrived we were asked to expedite because the cliff rescue man could not hold on much longer, so like the last job we were put on the spot without time to fully assess the situation. The casualty was half way down the cliff which was covered in a heavy metal netting type retainer which had been secured to help prevent further erosion of the cliff. It was this netting that the casualty had managed to grab to stop his slide. The cliff rescuer was secured by a rope from the top of the cliff and holding on to the casualty.

We felt quite confident that we would be able to reach the man but unfortunately there was another man a policeman also stuck on the cliff and in the worst position for our downdraught. He had tried to reach the casualty, which probably looked possible from the bottom of the cliff, but because of the loose screed it proved not to be. Eventually he realized he could not go any further, finding himself unable to move in any direction. Fortunately for us he had the sense to wedge himself in and was holding on as best he could.

Because of the imminent danger to the original casualty we decided to proceed, but we would have to be higher than we would have liked to prevent our downdraught from blowing the other casualty off the cliff. Another problem was the casualty was effectively what we call a cliff hanger, the fact that he is being held or holding on to the cliff, meant a strop cannot be placed over his head then secured by the becket.

Mario would have to use an open strop so that he could feed the strop through any gaps between the casualty and the cliff face before securing the lose end back on the hook, then he would have to secure the two ends with his hand acting as the becket, at the same time knowing the casualty had a broken arm and other injuries. This meant we would not be able to recover them to the aircraft; we would have to leave them on the end of the wire and locate them to the top of the cliff by manoeuvring the aircraft.

By now it was getting dark and quite precarious for Mario who not only had to ignore the casualty's injuries as, in this situation, saving his life was the priority and he could not risk trying to secure himself to the rope because this may have disturbed the cliff rescue man's grip on the casualty. So Mario had to secure the casualty while remaining on the end of the wire and we had to maintain a good enough position to keep him there.

Mario, as mentioned previously, is a big chap and very strong. Once he had fitted the strop, he made the casualty very secure by a physical grip as well as the open ended strop, not an easy job for Mario but the type he thrives on.

Once he had handed the casualty to the ambulance we had to return for the policeman, again having to use the open ended strop because he was now a cliff hanger, then repeat the procedure once more for the cliff rescue man.

As Mario was positioning the strop the policeman admitted that "attempting this was not one of my better ideas." Perhaps it wasn't but it was one we could understand as so many times we have seen similar situations, especially with policemen who I guess feel an obligation to help in dire situations and it is amazing the risks they will take. Just like the lifeboatmen in the 'Y boat' on the last job, for example.

Michael our grandson has put his terrible scare with the leukaemia behind him and still doing very well. He is in his second year at York University aiming for a degree in nursing. He hopes to specialise in paediatric oncology in respect of the care and help given to him by a dedicated team at Southampton General and St Marys hospital in Portsmouth, during his long treatment which has led to his full recovery.

I have now commenced my final year feeling very fortunate that I have had the opportunity to remain until 65. I have been through many stages in this career from being very unsure of myself to being overconfident. I have been caught out on jobs that have brought me up with a jolt, I have experienced some quite traumatic times; have occasionally faced situations that have made me question, "What am I doing here?" – I have felt real despair after jobs with unsuccessful outcomes and felt euphoria after the many successful rescues.

One thing I am sure off is that I am one of those lucky people who have enjoyed the job they do to the full. Having had the fun times of early SAR to the perhaps more serious and controlled environment that is necessary today and for that, I consider myself extremely lucky and privileged to have been given the opportunity.

There have been changes to the role I do not like but I can accept that changes are necessary. Resistance to change is also healthy as it forces debate, questions get asked, wheels get re-invented and, occasionally even the wheel can be improved. At the end of the day, procedures do need reviewing as new equipment comes along. The role has certainly become more professional since I started, a requirement that has been essential, not only for health and safety but in keeping up with the sophistication of the helicopters and equipment used today.

As shown in the last two jobs the role will continue in safe hands and indeed, I question if I was as good as the new aircrewmen, even in my prime. The enthusiasm shown by them has helped me to stay on top of my game.

When I started this role there was considerable kudos to being a SAR diver and now to being a SAR paramedic. If I had one message to pass on to future SAR rear seat crews in UK SAR, it would be the real skills lie in being an 'aircrewman', whether as a winchman or winch-op. It is those skills alongside the skills of the pilots that keep everyone safe. Become a 'professional aircrewman' and everything else will become natural...

Flying in this role is a matter of continuous risk assessment and working around problems presented. How close can we get to the cliff..? What turbulence can we expect..? What obstructions to avoid on a deck..? How much is that deck moving..? How much windage on the winchman at the end of the wire..? How far will he swing when he loses that windage..? What is the best fly away if things go wrong..? Obstacles to avoid overland when forced down by weather..? Dealing with fog and icing conditions.

The list is endless and all discussed and dealt with by the crew as a team. Aircrew skills help solve these problems and that leads to good decision making, even when away from the aircraft, such as looking after a casualty in a precarious situation.

I have throughout this book referred to SAR aircrewmen because I have never met a woman qualified in the role, but it is not a male domain so feel sure that situation will be addressed in the near future, I believe it already has in Ireland. So look forward to hearing about the first woman aircrewman/person in UK SAR to backup Liz, our SAR pilot in Stornoway, and the other female pilots past and present on Military SAR flights.

In Search & Rescue, we are mainly going to the aid of fit young people presented with one emergency or another, be it through atrocious weather, damage to, or accidents on, vessels, incidents on cliffs, casualties cut off by the tide or lost at sea. They are situations that we are often able to make a difference, returning with very relieved survivors. You simply cannot measure the job satisfaction, felt by all the crews when returning with survivors, having removed them from a hostile situation that could have cost those survivors their life.

Finally, we are waiting for the details on SAR harmonisation the project that was so close to being implemented, but has now been suspended by the coalition because of the economic climate, with an urgent review promised. At the time of writing the end of January 2011 we had further reports of the possibility of even further delays due to a problem in the bidding process. I have no idea what the outcome of this will be nor will I speculate.

The military and civilian crews at all twelve Search & Rescue flights around the UK coast are again in limbo and quite honestly do not deserve all these uncertainties. I have throughout my time in SAR faced uncertainties and cut backs. Now just as it looked likely there was a long term future for the crews it has all been thrown into turmoil again.

Whatever happens UK Search & Rescue will commence a new phase, it will have to for many reasons. The top of the list is the fleet of aircraft that has done such a good job over the years and now needs replacing or at the very least, seriously upgrading. I will retire envious of not being part of the changes ahead, but have no hesitation in saying the future of 'UK SAR' will be successful, the crews will make sure of that.

Since the book has been with the publisher a couple of things have happened that I felt I would like to add just prior to publication.

With just two months before my final retirement, I have been informed that I may extend for a further year; I still enjoy my job so feel very lucky to be given this opportunity. I will be the first to continue after 65 and guess this opportunity will become normal eventually as new legislation on retirement ages are implemented. The extension is subject to a CAA medical and line checks and, providing they go well, will allow me to be one of just a few aircrewmen to complete 40 years in this role.

Secondly I was caught on the back foot when Nick Horst rang me on the 24th March to say he was popping round to drop something off, when he arrived he handed me a letter with the RNLI motif on the envelope. When I saw the motif I thought it was an award for Simon O'Mahony who I knew was being nominated for the 'Billy Deacon SAR Memorial Trophy', for his role in the rescue of occupants from the yacht 'Blue Argent' which was breaking up on the Shingles bank. This is a rescue that I have mentioned in detail a few pages back and I felt Simon deserved to be nominated. I was right in my assumption, however the letter said that I too was a recipient of the 'Billy Deacon SAR Memorial Trophy,' with Simon.

I was completely taken back; I had recorded in that rescue I had full admiration for Simon, and his action in this task highlighted my opinion of him. The emergency changed so quickly and he was put in a very dangerous situation, which we recovered from. Simon had no hesitation in further attempts that proved successful, but my part in recovering the situation after things went wrong, I would consider to be my role and only achievable by the Captain: Mark Jackson, interpreting my instructions so skilfully.

The 'Billy Deacon SAR Memorial Trophy' sponsored by Bristow Helicopters and Breitling UK is awarded to Winchmen/Winch Operators from the Coastguards, Royal Navy & Royal Air Force for meritorious service during helicopter operations from UK SAR bases.

The award committee is made up from very experienced aircrewman from the three services, independently chaired by the Operations Director of the Royal National Lifeboat Institution. The committee sits annually to consider nominations from which only one SAR incident is selected. For obvious reasons the award normally goes to the winchman on that incident. This year 2011 The 'Blue Argent' job was selected and unknown to me we had both been nominated.

I could not be more proud, what a way to end my career! - For many aircrewman especially those who knew Billy the award would be considered to be the one we would treasure the most. I was a good friend of Bill going back forty years; he is mentioned in the book many times including a chapter on the 'Green Lilly' incident and the ultimate sacrifice he made. So for me it is such an honour and to win it alongside Simon, who I consider to be from the same mould as Billy, is the icing on the cake.

We will receive the award from the Duke of Edinburgh at the Air League annual awards ceremony held at St James' Palace in June.

Good luck to all existing SAR crews and the crews of the future.

Glossary of Terms

No matter how hard I try some naval slang comes out in my writing, hence the list below, which also includes other abbreviations used.

'AW139'	Augusta Westland 139 Medium size Helicopter
'S61'	Sikorsky 61 Helicopter
'S92'	Sikorsky 92 Helicopter
AMC	Automatic Manoeuvring Control
CD	Clearance Diver (Royal Navy)
CPO	Chief Petty Officer
CPR	Coronary & Pulmonary Resuscitation
DfT	Department for Transport
Dunker	Helicopter Underwater Escape trainer
Fish Head	Royal Naval personnel serving in the General Service
Fleet Air Arm	Royal Naval (Aviation) Personnel
General Service	Royal Naval (Surface Fleet) Personnel
Hi-Line	Heaving in line
HLS	Helicopter Landing Site
Hypothermic/ Hydrostatic Lift	The use of two strops for recovery to the aircraft, one positioned under the arms the other round the knees.
MAIB	Marine Accident Investigation Branch
MCA	Maritime and Coastguard Agency
Mess	Military Accommodation
MOD	Ministry of Defence
Oppo	Good Friend
PO	Petty Officer
Run Ashore	Evening Out normally as a group
Safeguard	Used during exercises if a real emergency arises
SAR	Search and Rescue
Troop/Trooped	Put on a charge
Wafoo (Wafu)	Royal Naval personnel serving in Fleet Air Arm

THE AIRCREWMAN'S
ASSOCIATION

Aircrewmen and, more recently, women, their forebears, Rating Aircrew and Telegraphist Air Gunners, have served with distinction, many of whose service has been recognised with numerous decorations for gallantry and distinguished service. The first post-war Gazetted honour was awarded to CPOACMN Gilbert Charles Edward O'Nion, of HMS Triumph, when he was 'Mentioned In Dispatches' for his part in the successful rescue of a downed American Corsair pilot, Lt Wendell Munce USN, off the North Korean coast, on 19 July 1950. This was probably the last operational rescue by a flying boat, a Sea Otter, before the appearance of the helicopter.

Since then, the helicopter has enabled Search and Rescue to evolve into its modern form as a quick-response, flexible, wide-ranging, multi-functional international service for both military and civil purposes, effective over land and sea, by day and night, in both fine weather and foul and for 365 days of the year. Naval Aircrewmen are multi-tasked and operate in the Commando support role, Anti Submarine and Anti Shipping, counter terrorism and, of course, in both military and civilian Search and Rescue, 24 hours a day.

During this time, Branch Members have gone on to receive a number of decorations and awards both from the UK and overseas. In 2004, they took part in the one of the biggest rescue operation undertaken for many years in this country when they were airborne assisting local agencies during the Boscastle flood disaster. For these efforts in Cornwall, one Sea King crew received the Air Force Cross, a Queen's Gallantry Medal and 2 Queen's Commendations for Bravery in the Air. More recently, the crew of 2 Navy Sea Kings all received gallantry awards for their rescue of the entire 26 crew of the MSC Napoli which sunk off the Devon coast. Naval Aircrewmen have distinguished themselves in many conflicts around the world including Aden, Suez, the Falklands, Northern Ireland, Iraq (twice) the Balkans and, more recently, Afghanistan. Worldwide humanitarian missions are also part of their operational tasking.

The Aircrewman's Association was formed in 1977 when a group of ex-Crewmen decided that they missed the camaraderie and spirit of military flying and crewroom humour. A Committee was selected and the ACA was formed. It now numbers over 475 strong, drawn from all walks of life, from Wing Commanders to window cleaners and from Airbus pilots to policemen and meets every April for its Reunion and Social weekend. The Association has recently been recognised by the Royal British Legion and its Standard is paraded at the Royal Albert Hall at the RBL Festival of Remembrance. The following morning a contingent from the association marches with the annual parade of veterans at the Cenotaph in front of the Royal Family.

ABOUT THE AUTHOR

Dave Peel was born in Bolton, Lancashire, and at the age of 11 went to a naval boarding school (Royal Hospital School) in Suffolk. In 1961, at the age of 15, he joined the Royal Navy. A few years after joining he was fortunate enough to take a trip in a Search & Rescue (SAR) Helicopter, after which he had only one desire… to become a Search & Rescue Diver.

Since qualifying, he has been at the forefront of UK helicopter coordinated Search & Rescue, a career that has spanned almost forty years and has witnessed many changes since the early days.

Dave currently lives with his wife Margaret in Lee-on-the-Solent, Southern England. He has enjoyed his career to the full, and will take many enduring memories with him into retirement.

Lightning Source UK Ltd.
Milton Keynes UK
176214UK00001B/267/P